SB

INDIA'S RISE TO POWER

Also by Sandy Gordon

BUSINESSMEN AND POLITICS: Rising Nationalism and a
  Modernising Economy in Bombay 1918–1933
* INDIA'S STRATEGIC FUTURE: Regional State or Global Power?
  (*with Ross Babbage*)
THE SEARCH FOR SUBSTANCE: Australia–India Relations into
  the Nineties and Beyond

* *Also from the same publishers*

India's Rise to Power

in the Twentieth Century and Beyond

Sandy Gordon
Strategic and Defence Studies Centre
Australian National University
Canberra

First published in Great Britain 1995 by
MACMILLAN PRESS LTD
Houndmills, Basingstoke, Hampshire RG21 2XS
and London
Companies and representatives
throughout the world

A catalogue record for this book is available
from the British Library.

ISBN 0–333–63196–X

10   9   8   7   6   5   4   3   2
04   03   02   01   00   99   98   97   96   95

Printed in Great Britain by
Ipswich Book Co Ltd
Ipswich, Suffolk

03316815

First published in the United States of America 1995 by
Scholarly and Reference Division,
ST. MARTIN'S PRESS, INC.,
175 Fifth Avenue,
New York, N.Y. 10010

ISBN 0–312–12452–X

Library of Congress Cataloging-in-Publication Data
Gordon, A. D. D.
India's rise to power : in the twentieth century and beyond / Sandy
Gordon.
p. cm.
Includes bibliographical references and index.
ISBN 0–312–12452–X
. 1. India—Politics and government—20th century.
DS480.4.G67   1995
954.03'5—dc20
94–30738
CIP

In memory of my parents

CONTENTS

Acronyms and Abbreviations

AA	Anti-aircraft
AAGSP	All Assam Gana Sangram Parishad
AASU	All Assam Students Union
ACDA	Arms Control and Disarmament Agency
ADA	Aircraft Development Authority
ADB	Asian Development Bank
AEC	Atomic Energy Commission
AIADMK	All India Anna Dravida Munnetra Kasagham
AIDS	Auto immune deficiency syndrome
ALH	Advanced light helicopter
AMM	Anti-missile missile
ANURAG	Advanced Numerical Research and Analysis Group
APEC	Asia Pacific Economic Cooperation
APSOH	Advanced Panoramic Sonar Hull-Mounted
ARC	Aviation Research Centre
ASEAN	Association of South East Asian Nations
ASIC	Application specific integrated circuit
ASLV	Augmented Satellite Launch Vehicle
ASWAC	Airborne surveillance warning and control
ATV	Advanced Technology Vessel
ATVDO	Advanced Technology Vessel Development Organisation
AWAC	Airborne warning and control
BARC	Bhabha Atomic Research Centre
BE	Bharat Electronics Limited
BE	Budget estimate
BJP	Bharatiya Janata Party
BKU	Bharat Kisan Union (Indian Peasants Union)
BSF	Border Security Force
C^3I	Command, control, communications and intelligence
CAD/CAM	Computer assisted design/computer assisted manufacture

CENCOM	Central Command
CENTO	Central Treaty Organisation
CEP	Circular error probability
CFCs	Chlorofleuorocarbons
CIA	Central Intelligence Agency
CINCPAC	Commander-in-Chief Pacific
CIWS	Close-in weapons systems
COCOM	Coordinating Committee on Export Control
CPI	Consumer price index
CPI-M	Communist Party of India (Marxist)
CRPF	Central Reserve Police Force
CRS	Congress Research Service
CSIR	Council for Scientific and Industrial Research
CTOL	Conventional take-off and landing
CWC	Chemical Weapons Convention
D&D	Design and development
DAE	Department of Atomic Energy
DEAL	Defence Electronics & Applications Laboratory
DPSU	Defence Public Sector Undertakings
DRDL	Defence Research & Development Laboratory
DRDO	Defence Research and Development Organisation
DWT	Deadweight tonnage
EC/EEC	European Community
ECIL	Electronic Corporation of India Limited
EEZ	Exclusive economic zone
ELINT	Electronic intelligence
EPZ	Export processing zone
EW	Electronic warfare
FPA	Focal plane array
FSAPDS	Fin stabilised armour piercing discarding sabot
GaA	Gallium arsenide
GATT	General Agreement on Tariffs and Trade

GDP	Gross domestic product
GNP	Gross national product
GPS	Global positioning system
GSLV	Geo-Synchronous Launch Vehicle
HAL	Hindustan Aeronautics Limited
HDI	Human Development Index
HF	High frequency
HMS	Her Majesty's Ship
HYV	High yield variety
IAF	Indian Air Force
IC	Integrated circuit
ICBM	Intercontintental ballistic missile
IDSA	Institute for Defence Studies and Analysis
IGMDP	Integrated Guided Missile Development Program
IISS	International Institute for Strategic Studies, London
IIT	Indian Institute of Technology
IMF	International Monetary Fund
INSAT	Indian national satellite
IRBM	Intermediate-range ballistic missile
IRDP	Integrated Rural Development Program
IRS	Indian remote sensing satellite
ISI	Inter-Services Intelligence Directorate (of Pakistan)
ISRO	Indian Space Research Organisation
ITBP	Indo-Tibetan Border Police
JKLF	Jammu & Kasmir Liberation Front
JVP	Janata Vimukthi Peramuna (People's Liberation Front)
KGB	Komitet Gosudarstvennoy Bezopasnosti (USSR Committee for State Security)
LCA	Light Combat Aircraft
LCU	Landing craft, utility
LSM	Landing ship, medium
LST	Landing ship, tank

LTTE	Liberation Tigers of Tamil Eelam
MBT	Main battle tank
MEA	Ministry of External Affairs
MI	Military intelligence
MIDHANI	Mishra Datu Nigam Limited
MIMD	Multiple instruction multiple data
MIRV	Multiple independently targetable re-entry vehicle
MOD	Ministry of Defence
MOU	Memorandum of Understanding
MR	Maritime reconnaissance
MT	Million tonnes
MTCR	Missile Technology Control Regime
NAFTA	North American Free Trade Agreement
NAL	National Aeronautical Laboratory
NAM	Non-Aligned Movement
NASA	National Aeronautics & Space Administration
NEP	New Education Policy
NIC	Newly industrialised country
NPT	Nuclear Non-Proliferation Treaty
NRR	Net reproduction rate
NSCS	National Socialist Council of Nagaland
NWFP	North-West Frontier Province
OECD	Organisation for Economic Cooperation and Development
OIC	Organisation of Islamic Countries
ONGC	Oil and Natural Gas Commission
OPEC	Organisation of Petroleum Exporting Countries
PAC	Provincial Armed Constabulary
PACE	Processor for Aerodynamic Computations and Evaluation
PAF	Pakistan Air Force
PDC	Potential defence capacity
PLA	Peoples' Liberation Army
PM	Prime Minister

PNE	Peaceful nuclear explosion
POL	Petroleum, oils and lubricants
PPP	Pakistan People's Party
PREFRE	Power Reactor Fuel Reprocessing Plant
PSLV	Polar Satellite Launch Vehicle
PWG	People's War Group
PWR	Pressurised water-cooled reactor
R&D	Research and development
RAF	Rapid Action Force
RAMID	Re-organised Army Mountain Infantry Division
RAPID	Re-organised Army Plains Infantry Division
RAW	Research and Analysis Wing
RE	Revised estimate
RPV	Remotely piloted vehicle
RSS	Rashtriya Swayamsevak Sangh
RTUNE	Research & Training Unit of Navigational Electronics
S&T	Science and technology
SAARC	South Asian Association for Regional Cooperation
SAC	Scientific Advisory Committee
SAM	Surface-to-air missile
SEANWFZ	Southeast Asian Nuclear Weapons Free Zone
SEATO	South East Asian Treaty Organisation
SERC	Supercomputer Education and Research Centre
SIGINT	Signals intelligence
SIPRI	Stockholm International Peace Research Institute
SLAR	Side-looking airborne radars
SLCM	Submarine-Launched Cruise Missile
SLOC	Sea lines of communication
SLORC	State Law and Order Restoration Committee
SLV	Satellite Launch Vehicle
SROSS	Stretched Rohini Satellite Series
SSBN	Nuclear ballistic missile submarine

SSN	Nuclear powered, hunter-killer submarine
STP	Software technology park
TADA	Terrorism and Disruptive Activities Act
TISCO	Tata Iron and Steel Company
UK	United Kingdom
ULFA	United Liberation Front of Asom
UNESCO	United Nations Educational Scientific & Cultural Organisation
UNHCR	United Nations High Commission for Refugees
UP	Uttar Pradesh
US	United States
USA	United States of America
USSR	Union of Soviet Socialist Republics
VAT	Value added tax
VHF	Very high frequency
VLF	Very low frequency
VSTOL	Vertical/short take-off and landing
WPI	Wholesale price index

List of Figures, Tables and Maps

Figures

Tables

Maps

Preface

The fall of the Soviet Union and the ending of the Cold War came as a shock to an international system that had grown used to assessing a nation's power in terms of ships, tanks and nuclear warheads. In a less public way, commentators also assumed that India's rise as a regional power in the Indian Ocean was simply a manifestation of its gathering arsenal of sophisticated weapons. Thus even the Pentagon, with all the resources at its command, predicted a near certain and *imminent* rise to power for India in the Indian Ocean region.

As with the Soviet Union, it was a little noticed fact that the Indian polity was under stress, that India's traditional macroeconomic stability was being dangerously eroded, or that the somewhat grandiose blueprints of the Indian defence planners, such as the so-called Twenty Year Naval Development Plan of 1978, which planned for a fleet of hundreds of major vessels by the year 2000, were virtually impossible to implement, even in the most favourable economic circumstances.

The failure of the body of analysis predicting the imminent rise of India as a major power in the Indian Ocean has had the effect of making analysts point to China, rather than India, as the somewhat worrying emerging force in the Asia-Pacific region. India, in contrast, is now perceived to be burdened by political chaos, economic crisis and regional instability. Far from being a new power in the Indian Ocean region, it is perceived by some to be in danger of breaking up.

This sudden reversal in perceptions about India should teach the hapless commentator a number of lessons. The first is that the mix of chance, societal pressures, resource issues, reservoirs of national will, quality of leadership, geopolitics and geostrategy that are involved in the assessment of any nation's rise to power, but especially one as large, diverse and complex as India, is simply too volatile for us ever to approach in any way other than gingerly.

A second, related, point is that the study of the place of nations in the international system must in essence be an inter-disciplinary pursuit. The discipline of 'strategic studies' is only one of a number of tools that we require, the others lying in the realms of politics, history, sociology, anthropology and economics, to name but some. In short, we need to go well beyond any simple accounting of the raw apparel of military power.

But in our quest for deeper understanding, we should also avoid falling victim to the 'paradox of focus', according to which, the narrower and deeper our focus on an issue or subject and the more detailed our knowledge about it, the more complicated and inter-dependent with the 'seamless web' it apparently becomes. All good writing should be part of a dialogue towards greater understanding, and unless we are willing to chance our arm and to simplify sufficiently to draw at least some 'useful' conclusions, we are not true participants in that dialogue.

This work is written with the need to simplify and to expand beyond purely strategic issues in mind. As such, it is bound to prove unsatisfying both to academic purists engaged in the study of India and to those seeking the kind of quick and plain speaking direction for the conduct of policy that has become the perceived need of modern 'fast track' societies. For that I make no apology.

A third lesson that we need to keep in mind is that, in today's fast-moving world, the 'big book', which can often take years to write, edit and print, is increasingly taking on the character of a 'blunt instrument'. One has particular sympathy for those who were engaged in writing such books about the future of the Soviet Union in the years prior to its collapse. I have endeavoured to ensure that the data, information and analysis contained in this book are as current as possible. But especially in the context of a nation such as India, there is no accounting for the unexpected.

Over the years that I have worked on this project in Australia I have received help and kindness from a great many people. I would like to thank Professor Desmond Ball who, as Director of the Strategic and Defence Studies Centre at the Australian National University, gave me the opportunity to undertake the work and subsequently provided valuable advice along the way. Professor Paul Dibb, the current Director of the Centre, has been unfailingly helpful and sympathetic to my needs. He also has been free with his advice, despite his busy schedule. I would also like to thank Jena Hamilton, who provided first rate assistance with research and word processing, Keith Mitchell for his attention to detail in preparing the maps and charts and Robin Jeffrey, who read an early draft and provided highly valued comments. And I would like to thank Helen Hookey, Tina Lynam, Karen Smith, Elza Sullivan, Helen Wilson and my other colleagues at the Strategic and Defence Studies Centre. Additionally, I would like to thank the Hon. Kim Beazley, Coral Bell, Meredith Borthwick, Dipesh Chakrabarty, Brahma Chellaney, Graham Feakes, Ranajit Guha, Stuart Harris, Stephen Henningham, K.P. Kalirajan, Gary Klintworth, Krish Krishnan, Andrew Mack, John McGuire, Ken McPherson, Peter Reeves, Ric Shand, Ranbir Talwar, Stewart Woodman, Marika Vicziany and all my other colleagues in Australia who have lent advice and support for this enterprise over the years. The faults are, of course, my own.

In India I have received much help from a great many people over many years. Let me single out from amongst them Manoj Joshi, Air Commodore Jasjit Singh, Bharat Varma, Bishwant and Ashima Chaudhuri, Muni and Arvind Kaul, Ram Subramanian, General Bannerji and all the academic and general staff at IDSA, David Evans, Pera Wells, Bob Dagworthy, Michael Woods, and all my Indian friends at the Australian High Commission.

I would also like to thank the Department of Defence, whose financial support made this work possible.

And finally, I would like to thank my wife, Sue, for living with this enterprise over the years.

Map 1: India and the Indian Ocean region

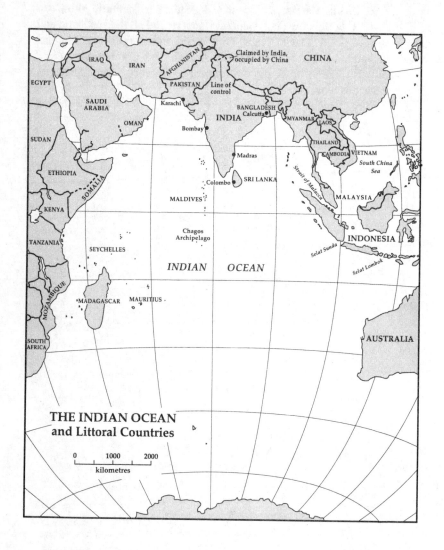

Introduction

Indians have always known that their nation has the potential to be a significant power in a way in which citizens of nations with smaller populations do not. Nehru himself, for all that he emphasised the benign nature of Indian power, was clear in his mind that India, with its vast resources and population, 'will always make a difference in the world ... Fate', he said, 'has marked us for big things.'[1]

But thirty years after Nehru's death those 'big things' have not eventuated. In military terms, India is not yet truly powerful beyond its immediate sphere of South Asia, and even its power in that venue is contested.[2] Nor has India yet obtained the kind of global influence through 'soft' power that might be expected of such a large country. In terms of economic performance, many other Asian nations, such as the other mega-population power, China, have been drawing away from India. Thus the more immediate questions about India's rise to power tend to relate to the nature of the restraint on its progress rather than to its potential.

Perhaps the most severe restraint of all is the very factor that makes India a candidate for big power status in the first place—its sheer size and associated diversity. While India is big, with a population approaching 900 million, it is a much more diverse nation in its ethnic, linguistic and religious constitution than China. China is 94% Han and predominantly Mandarin speaking. In China, religion has largely been subsumed by pragmatism in a way it has not in India. India has 15 major languages and literally hundreds of minor ones. It also has a major ethnic cleavage between the north and south, and many minor ones within those regions. Although 83% of its population is Hindu, there are 110 million Muslims living within its borders, not to mention members of smaller minority religions such as Sikhs, Christians, Jains and Parsis. And Hindu society is itself highly fragmented, both in terms of regional tradition and caste.

The South Asian region within which India is located is equally diverse. Pakistan comprises at least five major ethno-linguistic groups. The cement that binds these people is Islam, a fact that itself tends to place Pakistan in opposition to India. Sri Lanka has two major ethnic groups that are locked into a debilitating civil war. Bangladesh is more homogeneous, but it confronts serious developmental challenges. Millions of its citizens have been forced by economic circumstances and security factors to migrate to India. These transmigrations have upset the ethnic and religious balance in India's north-eastern region and damaged relations between the two nations. Like Pakistan, Bangladesh increasingly perceives itself to be an Islamic

1

nation juxtaposed to Hindu India.

These are not easy circumstances within which India is required to carve out an Indian Ocean role, let alone a global one. By virtue of its domestic and regional circumstances, India is restrained in the development of effective and committed policies in a way that China is perhaps not. It is a nation in which the polity is under severe stress, as caste confronts caste, religion opposes religion, regions seek autonomy from the central government and the countryside strives to assert its rights against dominant urban and industrial interests—all within the ambit of a rambling and, some would maintain, deteriorating democratic framework.[3]

Furthermore, to a far greater degree than China, India carries its large population as a burden to its further development rather than as an asset. Although India has invested large amounts in 'big science' and in tertiary education, its record in the social sector—literacy, nutrition, health, housing, employment and family planning—has not been as good as China's, to the point where it now has to apply significant new resources to these areas if it is to make up lost ground. In terms of its pressing need to reform its economy, it therefore faces a dilemma. On the one hand, it needs to spend massively on infrastructure in order to accommodate the economic growth likely to be stimulated by the process of economic liberalisation, but on the other, it is required to perform far better in the social sector if it is to achieve balanced growth with equity, and thus ensure stability. At the same time, it is required to keep a tight rein on the fiscal deficit in order to ensure that politically damaging inflation is kept to a minimum.

But India also has certain advantages over China. It is much more closely engaged in the kind of democratic politics that appear to be demanded as populations become richer, better educated and more sophisticated. It will not have to cross the 'Rubicon' of democratisation that China might one day have to cross. It is, on the whole, more versed in the rules of capitalism: the first stock exchange was opened in Bombay over a century ago. Its agriculture is probably still capable of much greater productive expansion than China's agriculture.[4] As Buzan has noted, it is located in a region—the Indian Ocean—that 'is distinguished by the fact that it is occupied entirely by relatively weak states.'[5] It therefore stands exposed as the only nation with potential large power status within its region, whereas China is but one of four large powers striving for influence in the northern Pacific.

This more exposed role for India was, however, severely restrained during the Cold War. The perspective on Indian power was distorted by the way in which the tensions generated by the Cold War were superimposed over the pre-existing structures of South Asia and the Indian Ocean. The Cold War enabled Pakistan to garner far more influence and military capability than it would otherwise have possessed. The presence of large extra-regional navies in the Indian Ocean also overshadowed India's navy, which would otherwise have been the preeminent Indian Ocean navy.

The ending of the Cold War is thus likely to benefit India more than Pakistan. While both lost the support of their superpower patrons, India is the larger power with the more substantial economy and greater capability to maintain its defence-industrial base without substantial outside assistance. In the words of Stephen Cohen, India stands out because it is one of the few nations with a potential for 'balanced' power.[6] Moreover, with the diminution of the regional role of the superpowers, India—as the only Indian Ocean power with potential strategic reach—stands to gain.

Yet contrary to perceptions widely held in the 1980s, India's rise to power is a longer term proposition rather than an imminent event.[7] As well as potentially assisting India, the end of the Cold War has triggered other events that potentially limit its regional role. Southeast and Southwest Asian nations are seeking to obtain new military capabilities to deal with the uncertain post-Cold War environment. India still fears that a revitalised China, itself freed from the restraints imposed by the Cold War, might eventually seek a more pronounced role in the Indian Ocean. Moreover, notwithstanding the optimism generated by the process of economic liberalisation in South Asia, the region still confronts significant political, social and economic problems. These on-going difficulties will for a considerable period tend to constrain India's role in the wider Indian Ocean region, at least as it might be expressed in purely military terms.

Another important issue that India will need to deal with before it can emerge as a more prominent power relates to the direction of higher—or grand—strategy. The uncertainty associated with India's domestic political and regional South Asian circumstances has caused a commensurate lack of direction in higher strategy, which has tended to exhibit periods of 'chaotic policy'.[8] The 'opacity' of India's strategic planning to which this lack of higher direction has given rise is exacerbated by the obsessive secrecy with which the Indian security apparatus has surrounded itself (perhaps understandable in a country that has fought four wars in its short independent history).

This lacuna in the area of higher strategic planning has implications for our assessment of the extent and nature of Indian power in years to come. Indeed, one of the more important of the additional determinants of a nation's rise to power that we need to consider is the perception that it has of its place in the world and of what constitutes its security, and the organisational capacities inherent in its society and culture that enable it to achieve that vision, or cause it to fail, as the case may be. These factors may be loosely summed up by the general term 'strategic culture'.

India's strategic culture has aptly been described as absorptive, defensive and inward-looking rather than aggressive, directed and expansionist.[9] In addressing this intangible and difficult area of strategic culture, however, we should also consider a society's capacity to alter its strategic thinking and organisational capacities in response to the challenges it faces. For while the well-springs of a nation's strategic culture are clearly important, it would be a mistake in the case of modern states to underestimate the power of the 'dialogue' that is constantly being conducted between the strategic cultures exercised within a nation and the present day circumstances in which it finds itself. Furthermore, given widespread media coverage and intelligence access, lessons are now learned not just as a result of a nation's own national experience, but also through the wider global experience.   Perspectives that govern a nation's strategic outlook *are* capable of change, and that surprisingly suddenly.

This capacity for change has certainly been evident in India. According to a number of writers, modern-day India is characterised not so much by the force of tradition—although that is still undeniably present, for example in the way caste impacts on politics—but more by the presence of change itself, particularly as it is introduced by 'bourgeois revolution'.[10] We can also observe instances in which India did change direction as a result of its own experience or through observation of wider global trends.

For example, as we will explore in greater detail below, the Gandhi-Nehru paradigm for viewing power, which tended to emphasise moral values in the conduct of foreign relations, was suddenly cast aside as a result of the *débâcle* suffered by a complacent India at the time of the 1962 Sino-Indian border war.   India has also sought to learn from wars around the globe such as the Falklands campaign of 1982, which precipitated a strong interest in the defence of India's island territories, and the 1991 Gulf War, which alerted India to the weakness inherent in its Soviet-derived doctrines and weapons.   The importance of so-called 'soft' power and global economic power has also been sheeted home to India by the fall of the Soviet Union and the successes of Germany and Japan. This lesson has been translated into a powerful new thrust into the process of economic liberalisation.

Yet it is important at this point to distinguish between patterns of strategic thinking and patterns of social intercourse that dictate attitudes and capabilities as they relate to the actual implementation of strategies. Even though strategic doctrine as it has been expressed officially may have changed to meet rapidly shifting circumstances, the actual way such doctrine is filtered through society may still tend to reflect more deep-seated perspectives and organisational patterns.

For example, it is sometimes said of Indians that they have a propensity to avoid decisions until the very last moment, until they are forced upon them.[11] According to Ved Mehta, Indians 'allow confusion, delay, and neglect to run their course in the hope that one day a compromise would emerge.'[12] Although fatalism may have a role to play in this tendency to avoid decisive action, it would be an error to ascribe too large a role to fatalism. The Indian tendency to favour synthesis also seems to play an important part in this desire to avoid decisive action. Rather than asserting a hard doctrinal orthodoxy, Indians have been inclined to make intellectual and emotional space for a range of views on how society should be organised. This process of compromise and reconciliation of opposing views and doctrines has proved an essential component of the art of living in a crowded and highly diverse environment such as India's. While it has created a society that is in many ways highly tolerant, it has not produced one noted for its ability to shape events according to its wishes.

These synthesizing and compromising elements within Indian society are well recognised. At a somewhat more controversial and less certain level, we can interpret the desire to avoid hard decisions as constituting a politically sophisticated attempt to 'hedge', to 'play both ends against the middle' and to 'see which way the wind is blowing' before making any decision.

At one level, therefore, the general propensity to avoid decisive action may be seen as presenting a facade of a non-combative and essentially *status quo* nation to the outside world, one that would prefer to learn to live with contradiction and diversity rather than to act decisively to shape events according to its wishes. At another level, however, it should not be forgotten that seeming lack of preparedness for forthright action can be used as a means of awaiting and seizing the exact time for fortuitous action, just as Mrs Gandhi did in 1971, when she bided her time until Pakistan attacked in the west and thus managed to win widespread international support for what was essentially a campaign of destabilisation of the state of Pakistan as it then existed.

This general attitude to decision making can be used in part to explain certain of India's key strategic responses. The relationship with the superpowers, for example, was very much one of maintaining options, of seeking to maintain at least some kind of relationship with the United States, even during those times when there was a decided pro-Moscow 'tilt'. It also involved 'playing both ends against the middle', at times with considerable success. By this means, for example, India was able to obtain access to the Soviet front-line MiG-29 fighter when no other non-communist power was able to do so.

The other area in which this type of hedging behaviour becomes patently obvious is India's position on nuclear weapons and ballistic missiles. While there was a genuine moral dimension associated with India's decision not to pursue vigorously the nuclear option after its so-called peaceful nuclear explosion of 1974, the Indian policy on nuclear weapons also involves a substantial element of indecision. According to one observer, India's strategy of ambiguity is 'cheap, safe and very Indian in that it takes no decisions that do not have to be taken'.[13]

The question we need to ask ourselves, however, is whether this lack of concerted action represents a failure of national will or whether it involves a skilful manipulation of events to achieve the advantage of ambiguity. Probably what originated in the realms of morality and indecision has now been incorporated into the realm of strategy; that is, flexibility through maintaining options, which is now seen as the keynote of India's nuclear policy of ambiguity, has emerged as a viable policy in itself, not least because it dovetails so neatly with the basic Indian predilection for avoiding hard decisions.

In purely *realpolitik* terms, however, there is little doubt that India would have been better off today had it 'gone nuclear' after 1974. As a nuclear power it would not only have enhanced its position in the 'hierarchy of nations' but also avoided the international penalties it must now confront in order to assume its place as a nuclear power. Like China, it would have been inducted into the 'nuclear club'. It would have been sitting in judgement on other aspiring nuclear nations rather than risking pariah status.

Another feature of what might be called 'traditional' attitudes to security planning is the obsessive secrecy with which the key decision makers in security policy development circles surround themselves.[14] As already noted, such policies are in part derived from India's difficult security circumstances. Sunanda K. Datta-Ray, however, also attributes the phenomenon to the fact that the elite that dominates the decision-making process in India is drawn from such a small catchment area, by which he presumably means the Brahmin-dominated bureaucracy and the other narrow elites that surround them in New Delhi.[15]

The hierarchical nature of caste naturally leads to a propensity towards compartmentalisation and exclusivity. This tendency has both costs and benefits. On the positive side, it has assisted India to contain knowledge of its nuclear activities extraordinarily well for a large, heterogeneous and democratic nation. This containment has been assisted by the tight controlling structure within the Department of Atomic Energy (DAE) and the PM's office, a situation that developed in the days of Nehru and Homi Bhabha (the first head of the atomic energy program in India) and that has not changed since. Additionally, India has relied on a highly compartmentalized organisational structure in the nuclear industry as a whole, with different operatives carrying out functions on a 'need to know' basis, rather than being informed in their actions by the wider strategies of the program.[16] In the Department of Space, policies and strategies have been protected by the existence of a tight-knit group in the top echelons, drawn largely from the ranks of South Indian Brahmins.

But as well as helping to maintain secrecy and cohesion at the micro-level, this 'clubbish' tendency toward compartmentalisation also has a decided 'down side'. Most importantly, on the wider national scale, it undermines seriously coordination and planning.[17] The former Cabinet Secretary and Principal Secretary to the Prime Minister, B.G. Deshmukh, has written of his frustrated attempts to introduce a coordinating mechanism between the external arm of intelligence, the Research and Analysis Wing (of the Cabinet Office, or RAW) and the internal arm, the Intelligence Bureau (IB). While such a mechanism would have been considered basic in most nations, in the Indian context, mutual suspicion and competition prevented it from being developed.[18] Similarly, the efforts of V.P. Singh while he was prime minister to institute a proper system of strategic planning by establishing a national security planning body were thwarted by rivalry and suspicion on the part of all the major players.

The problems that occur in the direction of higher strategy due to inadequate national coordination are illustrated by the decision of the Home Ministry to push Bangladeshi border crossers back into Bangladesh under 'operation pushback'. This was done without any coordination with the Ministry of External Affairs (MEA), which at the time had been trying to improve bilateral relations, including by handing back the Tin Bigha enclave. The MEA policy was undercut and any benefits that might have been gained were lost.[19]

The net result of this combination of successes in tight-knit units and seeming inability to coordinate the work of larger structures in the wider national interest is a security framework in which there are pockets of brilliance, but in which over-all effectiveness is vitiated by lack of coordination. Thus India has performed well in the manufacture of super-computers and software, but has not yet been able to translate these successes into an effective system of command, control, communication and intelligence (C^3I). Indeed, the three services have not yet been able to agree on a shared *modus operandi* involving joint facilities and commands—which is an essential feature of any functioning system of C^3I.

Excessive secrecy can also result in lack of critical examination of programs and unrealistic expectations. Thus India's efforts to produce a state-of-the-art fighter aircraft are probably unrealistic and premature. It is only recently that the parliament has started to give such projects the level of scrutiny that their size and complexity warrants.

But even these important shortcomings in the areas of planning and coordination should not necessarily be considered immutable. While India's propensity to accommodate alternative views has subverted the notion of a 'national will', it has also produced a society with a great variety of skills and an eclectic attitude to change. Moreover, South Asia as a region has been subject to massive change over the last four decades. With the collapse of the Soviet Union, the ending of the Cold War, and especially the liberalisation and globalisation of South Asian economies, the pace of change is speeding up. Some groups prosper, others lose out and social relationships come under increasing pressure. In this new world, the attitude of the bureaucrat—and here we include the military bureaucrat as well—will have to change also in response to the relentless push of the markets and of the need for greater efficiency.

Rajiv Gandhi initially attempted to harness this thrust for a more accountable and efficient India. His approach was, however, somewhat naive: he even tried to computerise the selection of candidates within the Congress Party! General Sundarji, who was Army Chief of Staff between 1986 and 1988, was before his time in attempting to change the culture of the military to bring about greater efficiencies. He largely failed in his endeavours because resistances built into the system were too strong and because the resources were not available to do the things he wanted to do. His successors, however, persist. The incumbent Chief, General Joshi, says he now wants an army 'that emphasises learning from the past'. By that he does not mean reference to Kautilya or the *Mahabharata*, but rather to the lessons of the abortive Sri Lankan campaign and the Gulf War.[20] Increasingly, the grand failures of men like Rajiv Gandhi are likely to give way to modest successes as India finds more culturally appropriate ways to develop its strategic and organisational cultures. But the process is likely to be a slow one of accretion rather than one of sudden change that could catapult India onto the world stage as a thrusting new power. It will, moreover, be set back by the constant tug-of-war between the power projection capabilities of the Indian forces and their growing role in maintaining the Indian state power.

If excessive secrecy, lack of planning and a tendency to hedge and vacillate constituted the backdrop against which India has conducted its strategy, how have the paradigms through which India has viewed its strategic circumstances shifted since independence?

The Gandhi-Nehru approach, according to which it was believed that India should engage itself globally primarily as a moral actor, is still brought out from time to time by specific interests, largely for domestic political purposes. But as a paradigm which is driving strategy it is virtually dead—killed off by the cold douche of realism of the 1962 border war with China. In its place we find a range of competing ideas that seem to rise or fall at different times according to circumstances. Important amongst them is what I have called elsewhere 'the weak-strong' paradigm.[21]

The 'weak' side of this equation involves the notion that India is at once vulnerable to internal and external threats, which feed off and reinforce each other. This symbiotic relationship between external and internal threats has certainly been evident in South Asia, especially in the relationship between India and Pakistan.

Informing the 'strong' side of the equation is a view of power that has emerged following the retreat from the idealism inherent in the Gandhian paradigm. According to this view, far from having worked, accommodation of regional and international rivals has only exacerbated India's problems, which are themselves explained increasingly in terms of malign outside influences, whether it be the influx of Bangladeshis into the north-east or assistance to Sikh and Kashmiri separatists from across the border in Pakistan.

Although this 'weak-strong' characterisation of the Indian state was first developed and popularised by the government of Mrs Gandhi, in recent years the emerging Hindu Right has tended to appropriate such views. The adverse developments within India and the way in which they interact with tensions elsewhere in South Asia have been used by the Right-leaning Bharatiya Janata Party (BJP) and the shadowy grass-roots organisation that supports it, the Rashtriya Swayamsevak Sangh (RSS), to foster and strengthen the view that India is weak and threatened. But at the same time, the BJP and RSS have attempted to project their foreign policy as being in the 'strength respects strength', or realist, tradition. They have also sought to reconcile such views with their own version of Hinduism. According to them, the Nehru-Gandhi emphasis on the moral and spiritual aspects of Hinduism is an aberration and its rejection represents a return to a 'Hindu' norm, which they believe was accurately expressed in the words of an earlier RSS leader: 'It is significant that all Hindu gods are armed'.[22]

This tendency to seek out the more forthright side of Hinduism is not confined solely to the ranks of those on the Hindu Right, but is a more general phenomenon, especially amongst the rapidly growing middle class. According to Girilal Jain, the time has come to give more balance to Hinduism by leavening the Bhakti (non-violent) tradition with the Kshatriya (warrior and ruler caste) tradition.[23] Just as the *Arthasastra* has for many years been scanned for what it has to say about the development of Indian statecraft, the *Mahabharata* is now being explored for what it has to say about the 'essence of the Indian military mind'.[24]

Yet at the very time that this new, more forthright, version of Hinduism and Indian nationalism is emerging, so too is a more internationalist perspective on power. The collapse of the Soviet Union, the 1991 Gulf War and the economic crisis in India have caused a shift in perception in favour of a multi-dimensional definition of power, one that accommodates more than simply military power, but also includes economic power and other forms of influence such as 'soft' power. This 'internationalist' perspective is driving important decisions to liberalise the trading regime, to foster closer relations with western nations, especially the United States, and to act jointly as a peace keeper in the Indian Ocean region, for example in Somalia. This more outward dimension brings with it a paradigm shift of a quite fundamental nature, which in turn underlines the growing flexibility of Indian foreign and security policies.

Important differences are now emerging between those who espouse this internationalist perspective on power and advocates of the more forthright interpretation of nationalism espoused by some elements within the Hindu Right. To date, these tensions have tended to be manifest in policy as it relates to the international trading regime and economic liberalisation rather than in security policy.

India's dilemma in dealing with these differences has been intensified by the way international trading regimes have been developing in recent years. Having lost its favoured trading relationship with the East bloc and its ability to play the two cold warring blocs off against each other, India must now decide where its best interests lie. It confronts this decision at a time when the international trading environment is more difficult than at almost any period in the post-war years. Increasingly, India appears to be squeezed by emerging trading blocs such as the EEC, the North American Free Trade Association (NAFTA) and the nascent Asia-Pacific Economic Co-operation forum (APEC). A resolution of these differences has been complicated by the fact that the new administration in the United States is experiencing difficulty in finding ways to incorporate India into what are often inchoate policies. At the same time, India's half-hearted attempts to resurrect the old 'Third Worldism' upon which it used to rely have met with little success.[25]

Yet the process of economic liberalisation potentially offers India a ready solution to these dilemmas. Given its size, a liberalising India is likely to generate its own momentum and itself be courted by different global trading interests—provided, of course, that the process of liberalisation can remain on track.

Liberalisation and entry into world markets also potentially offer India access to a wider range of state-of-the-art technologies than it ever enjoyed under the old, autarkic, economic order. Already new technologies are filtering into India along with new investment, albeit at a slower rate than New Delhi would like. New economic interests in the liberalisation process have been nurtured, even at the same time as some of the larger industrial houses that benefited from the old 'licence raj' are squealing under the pressure of more open trading regimes.

These developments have the potential over time to alter radically the Indian defence industrial base and to strengthen the economy that supports it. Indeed, as we shall see, there is evidence to suggest that one of the factors driving economic liberalisation forward has been the diminishing relative capability of Indian technology and the stagnation of the economy under autarky. In circumstances in which China's economy has been growing at perhaps two to three times the rate of India's, the possibility arises that India will simply be left behind by China and other East Asian powers. This issue is certainly not lost on the current Indian leadership.[26]

Another issue that confronts the Indian defence establishment at a critical period in the relationship with Pakistan is the loss of access to cheap arms and spare parts provided by the former Soviet Union. The question is, will this loss of Soviet support act as a retardant to India's emergence as a power, or will it, combined with the better management that may emerge with time as a result of economic liberalisation, provide a stimulus to Indian defence production? Furthermore, to what extent will loss of Soviet support in conventional weapons tend to distort the Indian force structure in favour of areas in which Indian industry *can* perform relatively well, such as ballistic missiles and nuclear weapons?

The process of economic liberalisation also raises other serious issues about the nature of the Indian polity and prospects for stability. We have noted that, to a far greater degree than China, India carries its large population as a burden because of its poor performance in the social sector. In that context, it is necessary to explore the relationship between the rapidly growing population and access to land, jobs, education and health on the one hand, and the chronic instability that appears increasingly to be a feature of Indian political life on the other. It is also necessary to assess how the process of economic liberalisation is likely to impact on the availability of resources in the social sector, and how any dislocation that might eventuate from it is likely to impact on political stability. Will India experience an uneven, bumpy growth path, punctuated by bouts of instability, such as has been the general experience of some of the large Latin American nations such as Brazil? Or will it be able to emulate the smaller 'Tigers' of East Asia, which have managed to achieve stability through the process of rapid growth itself?

To complicate matters further, it appears increasingly evident that instability in India is not an isolated phenomenon, but is closely related to the wider problem of instability in South Asia as a region. Increasingly, domestic political problems seem to 'wash back and forward' across permeable borders within South Asia like so much political flotsam and jetsam, contributing to tension between nations along the way. How serious a problem this process of interactive instability is likely to become, and how it is likely to be affected by economic liberalisation throughout the region, will be important determinants of India's future as a regional Indian Ocean and global power. An India that continues to be tied down by its domestic difficulties and the problems of its South Asian neighbourhood is unlikely to emerge quickly as an important actor on the wider international stage.

On the other hand, it may well prove to be the case that the equation *trouble at home-ineffective abroad* is an over-simplification that masks more than it reveals. It is important—indeed crucial—to our assessment to know what is going on behind this mask of regional instability. For example, might not India's current adverse circumstances, including its problems with Pakistan and loss of Soviet cheap weapons and spare parts, actually provide a stimulus to its own defence-industrial capabilities and strengthen its determination to achieve the self-sufficiency it has so long craved? And what of India's nuclear weapons program, which derives its being from within the South Asian regional setting, but ultimately has implications that extend well beyond that region? Furthermore, might not Pakistan, which has been India's principal regional protagonist and which has provided the most significant strategic restraint upon it, succumb to the war of attrition with the much larger power and assess that the attempt to maintain a rough strategic parity with India is not worth the extremely high economic and social costs that it entails?

Thus we need always be mindful of developments that are occurring behind the veil of regional instability that is drawn across India's rise to power. If that veil were ever to be drawn back, the world might witness the quite sudden advent of India onto the wider Indian Ocean stage as a significant pan-regional player. That is not to say that India will quickly overcome the organisational and internal political difficulties alluded to above; it is to make the point, rather, that as far as India's Indian Ocean region is concerned, its power potential is very high when viewed in comparative terms. In this sense, it would be quite wrong to set India against the powers of the northern Pacific and to judge its power potential according to those standards.

*

This book comprises three parts. In the first part we examine the raw basis of Indian power: that is, the evolving defence industrial base, the scientific, technological and economic capabilities that support it and the way these factors are translated into military capability. The key issues examined here are the ability of the rapidly changing Indian economy to support continuing growth of military capability and the degree of match between Indian scientific, technological and industrial capabilities and the requirements of a modern defence-industrial base.

While competency in the establishment of a defence industrial base is a necessary component of the power equation it is not sufficient. A defence industrial base must also be built on a stable polity and a balanced process of development. Part Two therefore deals with the societal base that is so important a factor in creating a nation's sustainable power projection capability and defining what sort of power it is likely to be. Crucial questions examined in this part are the relationship between resource issues and political instability, the nature of the interaction between local-level instability and national and international instability, and the way in which instability itself impacts on civil-military relations, military capabilities, human rights, the quality of democracy and the 'vicious circle' of instability, economic decline and further unrest.

In the third part we examine the geo-political and geo-strategic contexts within which India must operate. Issues addressed include the implications of the ending of the Cold War on regional politics, the effect on India of the loss of Soviet support and the way in which shifting large-power relationships have altered the nature of the complicated quintet played between India, Pakistan, the former Soviet Union, China and the United States. India's changing role as an Indian Ocean power is explored in light of the halting improvement in relations with the United States. We assess India's role in the Gulf, Southwest Asia and the newly emerged states of Central Asia in light of important domestic changes according to which India is seeking progressively to define itself as a 'Hindu' nation rather than a secular one. We examine India's strategy of broadening its economic and strategic interests to cover the Asian nations to its east. And, in the context of all these shifting circumstances, we describe the new ways in which India is seeking to project itself on the global stage.

Endnotes

1   Quoted in Baldev Raj Nayar, 'A World Role: The Dialectics of Purpose and Power' in John W. Mellor (ed.), *India: A Rising Middle Power*, Westview Press, Boulder, Colorado, 1979, p. 123.

2   For an account of the limitations of Indian power in the South Asian region see Mohammed Ayoob, 'India as Regional Hegemon: External Opportunities and Internal Constraints', *International Journal*, Vol. XLVI, No. 3, Summer 1991.

3   For a view that the Indian political system is in a state of systemic decay see for example, Atul Kohli, *Democracy and Discontent: India's Growing Crisis of Governability*, Cambridge University Press, Cambridge, 1991.

4   See The Roots of Instability, Part 2, below.

5   Barry Buzan, '*A Sea of Troubles? Sources of Dispute in the New Ocean Regime*', Adelphi Papers, No. 143, International Institute for Strategic Studies, London, 1978, p. 30.

6   Stephen Cohen, 'India's Role in the New Global Order', *The United States and India in the Post-Soviet World: Proceedings of the Third Indo-US Strategic Symposium*, National Defense University, Washington DC, 1993, p. 57.

7   For one such view of India's growing power see US Government, Department of Defense, *Soviet Military Power: Prospects for Change 1989*, US Government Printing Office, Washington DC, 1989, pp. 123-4.

8   See M.V. Bratersky and S.I. Lunyov, 'India at the End of the Century: Transformation into an Asian Regional Power', *Asian*

Survey, Vol. XXX, No. 10, October 1990, p. 928.

9　See George K. Tanham, *Indian Strategic Thought: An Interpretive Essay*, Rand Corporation, Santa Monica, California, 1992, for an excellent discussion of India strategic culture. W. Howard Wriggins explores the influence of Kautilyan thought on Indian strategic thinking in 'South Asian Regional Politics: Asymmetrical Balance or One-State Dominance?, in Howard Wriggins (ed.), *Dynamics of Regional Politics: Four Systems on the Indian Ocean Rim*, Columbia University Press, New York, 1992, p. 108.　An unpublished PhD thesis by Bruce Vaughn ('India Ascendent: An Interpretation of India's Aspirations to Great Power Status', Australian National University, 1994) also contains a useful and extensive discussion of the roots of Indian strategic culture. In a book that only became available just before this manuscript was submitted, Chris Smith also explores the roots of defence policy-making in India. See *India's Ad Hoc Arsenal: Direction or Drift in Defence Policy?*, SIPRI (through Oxford University Press), Oxford, 1994.

10　See for example Robert W. Stern, *Changing India: Bourgeois revolution on the subcontinent*, Cambridge University Press, Cambridge, 1993, p. 1. See also the writers referred to in footnote 2, Chapter 2, Part II, below, who are all engaged in interpreting change in India.

11　See for example Robert A. Scalapino, 'National Political Institutions and Leadership in Asia', *The Washington Quarterly*, Autumn 1992, p. 157.

12　Ved Mehta, 'The Mosque and the Temple: The Rise of Fundamentalism', *Foreign Affairs*, Vol. 72, No. 2, p. 18.

13　Manoj Joshi, 'Strategic Conundrums: The West and India's Middle Path', *Times of India*, 24 August 1993.

14　See Peter Lyon, 'South Asia and the geostrategics of the 1990s', *Contemporary South Asia*, Vol. 1, No. 1, 1992, p. 25.

15　'Security obsession', *Economic Times*, 20 July 1993.

16　For an account of the way in which the 1974 detonation was kept secret through compartmentalisation see Ashok Raina, *Inside RAW: The Story of India's Secret Service*, Vikas Publishing House, New Delhi, 1981, p. 77.

17　There are, however, many informal channels of communication, such as the one developed between the three service chiefs during the 1971 war with Pakistan.

18   B.G. Deshmukh, 'Intelligence Agencies: Coordination a must', *Hindustan Times*, 26 April 1993.

19   Manash Ghosh, 'Spirit of Bengal', *The Statesman*, 8 April 1993.

20   Interview with General Joshi, *India Today*, 15 July 1993, p. 78.

21   See the author, 'Domestic Foundations of India's Security Policy', in R. Babbage and S. Gordon (eds), *India's Strategic Future: Regional State or Global Power?*, The Macmillan Press, London, 1992, pp. 11-16.   The expression was originally used by Lloyd and Suzanne Rudolph to describe the Indian state more generally.

22   Golwalkar, quoted in K.R. Mulkani, *The RSS Story*, Impex India, New Delhi, 1980, p. 42.

23   Girilal Jain, 'Idiom of Public Debate: Combining Bhakti with Power', *Times of India*, 30 November 1992.

24   See for example, Lt. Col. G.D. Bakshi, *Mahabharata: A Military Analysis*, Lancer International, New Delhi, 1990. The quotation used here is taken from the foreword by G.N. Pant, keeper of the National Museum, p. xix.

25   The failure of India's efforts to resurrect the G-15 forum in the latter part of 1993 is a case in point.

26   It was, for example, an important factor in dictating reform of the Indian bureaucracy.   See Shefali Bhimal, 'Reluctant Reformers', *India Today*, 15 September 1993, p. 82.

Part 1

The Means to Power

1 Indian Science and Technology and the Defence Industries

Autarky in Indian security thinking

Economic exploitation was at the heart of India's colonial experience. To counter colonial rule, the Indian nationalists therefore evolved a doctrine of economic nationalism known as *swadeshi*, which translated roughly means 'home grown'. Eventually *swadeshi* was transformed into post-colonial policies of autarky in the management of the economy, science and technology and the defence industries.

But the freedom struggle produced more complex attitudes than simple economic nationalism. Generations of Indians during the long years of struggle for independence had become convinced that what the British had taken from India was literally its 'golden past', a past that matched and surpassed that of Europe in its wealth and mastery of technology, the sciences and the arts.[1] Modern day Indian commentators assert that the view that Hinduism is an 'unscientific' religion is a myth concocted by the West and emphasise instead the great discoveries in science of pre-colonial India.[2] There is a satisfying symmetry in the claim of the former head of India's missile program, Abdul Kalam, that Britain should return the rockets of Tippu Sultan because they are 'the last evidence of Indian technological superiority'.[3]

Paradoxically, it was also the view of nationalist commentators that Britain was able to conquer India in the first place because Indians had lacked technological capability. Historians such as K.M. Panikkar, who is frequently quoted approvingly by modern-day commentators and whose work is standard reference in defence colleges in India, argued that India was especially vulnerable because of its lack of a technically competent navy, which was in part seen as a manifestation of the loss of India's ancient sea-going skills and the destruction of the Indian shipbuilding industry by the British. Such arguments are today used to justify India's rapid naval build-up.[4] Rajiv Gandhi referred to a similar link between technological inferiority and subjugation in justifying the launch of the *Agni* intermediate range ballistic missile.[5] Thus technological and economic independence became synonymous in Indian thinking with political independence. India, it was thought, could not be truly independent unless it could also achieve a strong measure of independence in these aspects of national life as well. Because of this strong desire for 'true independence', the Congress party and Nehru from the beginning set out to do two things: to regain the lost edge in technology and in economic management at all possible speed and to do so through India's own, independent, means.

This desire for true independence was parallelled by a belief in the role of the state as the main agent of change and in the socialist model for economic management. But although Indian socialism involved a degree of nationalisation, including of enterprises that were later to become important suppliers of defence items such as Hindustan Aeronautics Limited (HAL), by and large significant enterprises such as Tata Iron and Steel Company (TISCO) remained in the private sector, a fact that is proving helpful now that the government has begun to lower its profile in the economy.

Rather than entering into wholesale acquisition, the state asserted its position at the 'commanding heights' of the economy through a series of five year plans, which allocated new investment both in the public and private sectors. By 1982, the state controlled 76% of paid up capital in the so-called organised sector.[6]   By then only two of the top ten firms and nineteen of the top fifty were privately owned.[7]   Nor was public sector growth checked as a result of Rajiv Gandhi's economic reforms of the mid-1980s.   Between 1980-81 and 1988-89, employment in the public sector rose by nearly 20%, while employment in the private organised sector stagnated.[8]   Besides a plethora of bureaucratic organisations at the central and state levels, on the eve of the 1991 economic reforms there were a staggering 319 public enterprises.[9]   The rate of return on capital within these enterprises averaged only 1.5% throughout the 1980s.[10]   Over 70% of employment in the organised sector of the economy was in the bureaucracy or state enterprises.[11]

The poor productivity of government enterprises was exacerbated by the fact that the government adopted a policy of purchasing and propping up so-called 'sick', or financially troubled industries.   By 1988 these owed $2.7 billion.[12]   Furthermore, a comprehensive set of subsidies was brought into being in response to the need of governments to cultivate 'vote banks', especially in the countryside.[13]

Under the planning process as it evolved, both foreign and domestic investment were severely restricted and were channelled through a set of labyrinthine regulations that became known as the 'licence raj'. Domestically, these restrictions gave rise to an excessive degree of control over the economy by a few large firms, such that by the end of the 1980s only four firms controlled over half the sales in the nine key sectors of the economy.[14] India also had the highest sets of tariffs in the developing world, at an average of about 125%.[15] These high tariffs contributed to a marked decline in India's share of world trade, from about 2.5% at independence to about 0.4% today.[16] Foreign investment was also severely restricted, especially by means of restrictions on repatriation of capital and profits, with foreign equity until recently being pegged at 40% of paid-up capital. These restrictions are reflected in the very low level of foreign investment in India on the eve of the economic reforms, as evidenced by Table 1.1, below. Indeed, in the course of the 1980s India received less than 2% of the amount of foreign investment received by China.[17]

Table 1.1: Cumulative foreign investment in India, 1981-1990 (in millions of rupees, with $ millions equivalent at the March 1992 exchange rate in parentheses).

Country	Amount	Adjusted
USA	2883	(99)
Germany	2098	(72)
Japan	1024	(35)
UK	812	(28)
Italy	530	(18)
France	352	(12)
Total (all nations)	11457	(395)

Source: Briefing Papers, Indian Investment Centre, Singapore, August 1990.

Because of restrictions placed on foreign investment, there have been a large number of technical collaborations and tie-ups as a means by which foreign firms might gain access to the Indian market. Of the 6,163 tie-ups approved between 1981 and 1988, 81% were 'technological', with only 19% involving equity capital.[18] More than 75% of electronic items, 60% of transport machinery and 35% of drugs in production were a result of these agreements rather than indigenous development.[19]

This large number of technology transfer agreements did not, however, result in India developing technology at the leading edge. On the contrary, in the absence of the incentive of equity and the protection of foreign management, foreign firms proved most reluctant to pass on their leading edge technology.[20] India in consequence failed to acquire the kind of technology acquired by the leading newly industrialised countries (NICs) through foreign investment. This failure contributed further to lack of competitiveness on international markets.[21]

If technology was poorly served by the autarkic economic model, the model for science that evolved in the post-colonial environment was equally unhelpful. Ironically in view of the thrust for 'true independence', many of the institutions of the newly independent nation were shaped by the very colonial model that the Indian nationalists strove to overthrow. The education system and the entire structure of science and technology (S&T) were, for example, derived from the British model. The Indian Council for Scientific and Industrial Research (CSIR), the preeminent scientific body in India, was a direct clone of the British Department of Science and Industrial Research.[22]   When Nehru decided India needed a defence science organisation, he called upon his British friend, Lord Professor P.M.S. Blackett, to advise India how to do it.[23]   As we shall see, this highly centralised model was far more suited to a developed nation such as Britain than to an emerging nation such as India. Indian science became obsessed with big laboratories engaging in fundamental research and in 'big science' in general. It emerged as poorly attuned to meeting the practical needs in industry, health and agriculture of a developing nation. It did, however, lay down an important base for subsequent work in the electronics, space and nuclear programs, areas that would come to figure prominently in India's new defence technologies in the 1980s and 1990s.

While one would have expected the logic of the anti-colonial struggle to have translated immediately into a desire for a strong, independent capacity in the defence industries, this did not initially occur. One reason was that it was considered impractical for India to develop and produce anything more than small arms and to maintain the basic ordnance industries built up during the Second World War. Also, Gandhian notions of morality and nationalist views on the role of the army in the maintenance of colonial rule characterised the military and the means of servicing it as 'both British and burdensome'.[24]   In the trade-off between the pressing needs of development and the requirements of a local defence industry, the latter definitely came second. As Gandhi remarked:

> Today they [the military] must plough the land, dig wells, clean latrines and do every other constructive work that they can, and thus turn the people's hatred of them into love.[25]

Given the prevalence of such views, it is not surprising that in the period up to the 1962 war with China, defence expenditure never rose above 2% of GNP.[26]   In these circumstances, defence production remained at the fairly basic level achieved in the Second World War. Although the Defence

Science Organisation had been started with the assistance of Lord Blackett in 1948, it consisted of only 150 scientists and a few laboratories.[27]

The complacency that had allowed for this level of defence expenditure was rudely dispelled by several events that occurred in quick succession after independence. A pre-cursor of what was to come was provided by the accession of Pakistan to CENTO in 1954 and the subsequent decision by the US to provide Islamabad with 'up to' $2 billion worth of arms.[28] It was following that decision that Nehru and his defence minister, Krishna Menon, decided to develop fully an indigenous arms industry and research and development (R&D) capacity and to establish the Defence Research and Development Organisation (DRDO), which was founded in 1958. Then came the Sino-Indian border war of 1962 and the second war with Pakistan over Kashmir of 1965.

Although the West was willing to supply arms freely after the 1962 war, during the war itself, when India considered that its back was to the wall, it found that the West sought to exact conditions on the supply of arms relating to its sensitive position with Pakistan.[29] At the time of the 1965 war, in which Pakistan opened hostilities, India found that the West froze the supply of weapons and spare parts to both sides.[30]

The perceived failure of the West to provide for India's needs during these crises tended to reinforce notions of autarky that were already prevalent in Indian thinking. The failure struck a chord with what India already knew of its history: India had been left weak and vulnerable to foreign invasion in the first place because of its failure to maintain its own technology. Independence had done nothing to remove this vulnerability. 'True' independence could only come about through the maximum degree of self-sufficiency attainable in the defence industries. Those industries, however, necessitated a degree of technological capability that was largely outside India's reach at the time, except in the case of basic ordnance. What evolved was a peculiar pattern of dependency on licensed manufacture—largely acquired from the Soviet Union, but also substantially from the West—that went under the guise of self-sufficiency. These government owned defence industries suffered from many of the inefficiencies that characterised the public sector in general.

In a sense, what actually evolved was a kind of 'Clayton's' autarky, an autarky underwritten by substantial concessional Soviet support. It took the collapse of the Soviet Union in 1991 to expose this situation for what it actually was. But as we shall see, at least some benefits have been derived from the years of autarky. Although autarky contributed to a distortion of the education effort in favour of the tertiary sector at the expense of basic literacy, it was also an important factor in the creation of the space, nuclear and missile programs and some of the successful work in fundamental research and electronics—programs that in future could provide the framework for India's emergence as a major Indian Ocean power. It also assisted in laying the foundations for heavy industry and engineering in India, industries that now leave India well-placed in some aspects of weapons production.

Science and technology doctrine and practice

The notion that the key to independence lay in technological self-sufficiency meant that, from the first, science and technology were accorded a very high status in the development of India. Nehru referred to scientific institutions as the 'temples of modern India'.[31] Such attitudes have given rise to the view that there is no area of science and technology in which India cannot and should not participate. Occasionally this approach has resulted in extreme positions on technological 'leap-frogging', such as the proposition that India should develop its own space plane or rail gun.[32] At a less whimsical level, it resulted in an emphasis on 'big science'. This type of science was fostered at the expense of science practised at the grass-roots level, where it would have been more closely linked with the immediate, practical needs of the people. 'Big science' also tended to supplant the practical application of a science more keenly attuned to the type of industrial production in which India had a comparative advantage.

The first head of the Council for Scientific and Industrial Research (CSIR), Sir Shanti Sarup Bhatnagar, managed to convince Nehru of the need for a chain of national laboratories along British lines. These laboratories were created as '"science for science sake" [and] their relationship with ... industry was completely ignored'.[33] This strong emphasis on competition at the fore-front and on 'big science' led to an over-ambitious approach to the task of technology transfer and an underestimation of the costs involved.[34]

For a poor, developing country, India embarked on a substantial expansion of its science and technology base. At independence there were 30 universities and a 'handful' of research laboratories. There are now 160 universities and 1700 research laboratories, 900 funded by the government.[35] The student body in tertiary institutions 'exploded', rising from 150,000 in 1948 to 5 million by 1985.[36] It is a system that produces about 170,000 graduates in science and technology each year.[37] The total number of technically trained people in India is now estimated at between 2.2 to 3.8 million,[38] which is the third highest cohort in the world after the

US and Russia. Comparatively few of these people, however, are involved in R&D.[39]

Table 1.2: Rise in total expenditure on S&T as a percentage of GNP and private sector spending on S&T expressed as a percentage of public sector spending, 1950-1990.

Year	% GNP	% private
1951	0.02	0
1956	0.12	N/A
1959	0.23	N/A
1966	0.39	N/A
1971	0.47	8.4
1976	0.60	N/A
1981	0.66	14.9
1986	0.96	N/A
1987	N/A	11.1
1988	1.1	11.5
1990	0.89	12

Sources: V. Govindarajulu, 'India's S&T Capability', *Economic and Political Weekly*, 17-24 February 1990, Table 2, p. M-35, and Table 3, p. M-36; 'Tough times ahead for R & D labs', *The Hindu* (International Edition), 20 February 1993; Praful Bidwai, 'Missing the technology bus', *Times of India*, 19 August 1992.

It can be seen from the above table that overall expenditure on science and technology was until recently rising as a percentage of GNP, but that the fiscal restraint evident in recent years has caused the rise to level off. Within overall expenditure, the government sector incurs the lion's share. In fact there are only 25 private research units in the country that employ more than 100 researchers.[40] Within the sciences themselves, expenditure on engineering and technology is rising in relation to other elements.[41]

For all that India's expenditure on S&T has levelled off in recent years, it still constitutes a significant effort for a poor, developing nation. India now spends more as a percentage of GNP on S&T than any other developing nation with the exception of Korea and as much as some developed nations such as Canada and Australia.[42] It is, however, still behind the leading industrial nations such as Japan, the United States and Germany, which generally spend double in percentage terms and a great deal more in absolute terms.[43]

Because of Rajiv Gandhi's strong belief in technology as an engine of growth and panacea of many of India's ills, under his leadership a significant new commitment was made to S&T. The so-called New Education Policy (NEP), adopted in 1986, gave particular emphasis to S&T. Expenditure as a percentage of GNP was to rise from 1.1% to 2% in the course of the Seventh Five Year Plan (1985-90). Science was to become more applied and `mission' oriented. A Scientific Advisory Committee (SAC) was established with the purpose of integrating S&T better into the planning process and providing a 'perspective' plan for the role of S&T for the year 2001. The pre-eminent S&T institution, the CSIR, was reviewed and directed to recover 33% of expenditure from commercial sales by 1992-93 and 40% by 1999-2000. Recently that figure has been raised to 50%.[44]

Despite fears of dependence and the strong desire for autarky, necessity has dictated that foreign collaboration has played an important role in Indian S&T. The foreign role has been accomplished at two levels. First, there have been a large number of collaborative projects. Between 1981 and 1987 alone there were 5,294 international collaborative ventures, the majority with Britain, Germany, France and the United States and mostly in the areas of electronics, industrial machinery, mechanical engineering and chemicals. India receives $260 million per annum in support of these agreements.[45]

The most important nation in terms of transfer of technology in S&T has been the United States. Even when relations between the two nations were characterised by mutual suspicion because of India's relationship with the Soviet Union, there was a healthy level of scientific exchange between them. This was in part fostered by the large numbers of expatriate Indians working in American science and achieving significant successes there. For example, when the US National Science Foundation reported on Indian science in 1987, many key people involved in the report were leading scientists of Indian background. The tenor of the report was, on the whole, favourable.[46]

Germany also has a strong program of scientific cooperation with India. The program is covered by eight special agreements in areas ranging from nuclear energy, to space and aeronautical research and medicine.[47] Under these programs about 200 scientists travel each way each year to engage in 120 projects. Other programs of note include those with the United Kingdom and France. Figure 1.1, below, gives an insight into the percentage of foreign collaboration by sector and by country.

The second, and perhaps more important, way in which technology transfer has been accomplished is through the large numbers of Indian scientists who have trained or worked overseas. There are now 25,000 Indian scientists registered on the CSIR's register of Indian scientists trained

Figure 1.1: Percentage of foreign collaborations by country and by sector of collaboration between 1981 and 1987.

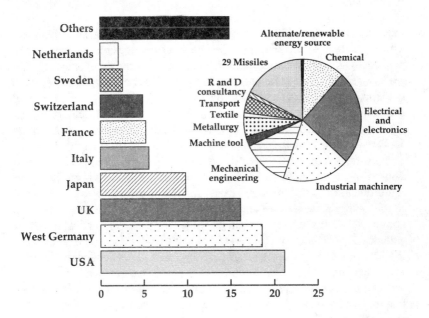

Source: Stephen Hill and Shantha Liyanage, 'The Status of Indian Science and Technology Capabilities', Briefing Paper prepared for the Australian S&T mission to India, July 1990, (courtesy of the Department of Industry Technology and Commerce), Figure 10, p. 31.

abroad,[48] and there would be many more who have worked overseas. The phenomenon of the so-called 'brain drain' is discussed in more detail below.

How good is Indian S&T?

For the purposes of the present work we need to assess how good Indian S&T is and how well it is integrated with those aspects of the economy that serve the defence industries. Within the available literature there seems to be general agreement on the broad strengths and weaknesses of Indian S&T. Almost all commentators, for example, agree that the basic fault of Indian science is its failure to relate closely to the practical needs of its clients in industry and the developmental needs of the people. The Rais Ahmed Committee (1989) noted that only about 2% of projects had any relevance to the country.[49] There is also 'a consistent opinion that Indian scientists are above average but that Indian research activity is below average ...'[50] There is a feeling that Indian science is duplicative rather than functioning at the 'leading edge'.

There is also general agreement about the causes of some of these weaknesses. Indian science is encapsulated in a rigid process of planning which has failed to accommodate the rapidly changing scientific scene. The philosophy guiding the allocation of funds tends towards the 'science-push' model rather than the 'technology pull' model. The corollary of this attitude is the excessive bureaucratisation of Indian S&T. In the CSIR, the ratio between working scientists and other employees is 1:4.5. Overall, in India's S&T institutes only 37% of the 268,000 staff are actually engaged in S&T.[51] There is a rigid system of hierarchy that tends to stifle creativity. It is noteworthy that Indian scientists often perform brilliantly once removed from the restrictions placed on them within India. In some institutions there is a problem of regionalism and caste-ism. Equipment is often outdated or simply unavailable, and this tends to lower productivity.[52] There has been a failure of liaison between the public and private sectors and a predatory attitude to R&D in the private sector, where only 0.7% of sales turnover is invested in R&D.[53] Then there is the view, such as was expressed recently in a damning article by Dhirendra Sharma, that Indian science has concentrated excessively on nuclear, military and space research and on 'big science' generally, at the expense of the needs of the Indian people.[54] There is a lack of public scrutiny of science, which can lead to over-blown claims that are rarely verified and a general air of unreality.

The quality of scientific education is also mixed. The best educational institutions, such as the Indian Institutes of Technology (IITs) at Bangalore, Bombay, New Delhi, Kanpur, Madras and Kharagpur, certain universities such as Delhi University (especially the faculty of Engineering), Jawaharlal Nehru University and Banares Hindu University are very good. Students of biotechnology and computing sciences at Bangalore IIT are, for example, 'head hunted' by US firms before even graduating. The standard of entry to these institutions is in some cases higher than leading overseas institutions. But at the lower end of the scale the system is not nearly so adequate. The SAC noted that the state of universities had 'significantly deteriorated, with a proliferation of colleges with inferior faculties ...'[55]

There is a similar spread of quality within the research institutes. The strongest of these includes the Bhabha Atomic Research Centre (BARC), the Tata Institute for Fundamental Research, the National Chemical Laboratory, the Indian Institute of Science, the Solid State Physics

Laboratory, New Delhi, the Centre for Cellular and Molecular Biology, Hyderabad, the Central Food Technological Research Institute and the National Physical Laboratory and the Industrial Toxicology Research Centre. But with over 1700 institutes scattered throughout the country, there is considerable scope for research positions to be treated as sinecures.

One of the results of the emphasis on quantity instead of quality is that, despite the significant level of spending on S&T and the fact that India has the third largest pool of technically trained people in the world, according to a World Bank assessment based on a UNESCO survey, comparatively few Indian scientists are actually engaged in the practice of S&T and R&D. The study also found that what was assessed to be India's poor performance was closely related to the 'human capital' investment within India, which as we shall see in the next part of this book, is very low. Those nations that performed well in terms of utilisation of their scientists had undertaken very substantial investment in human capital during those times when they were industrialising rapidly. Another interesting correlation occurs between the very high investment in R&D by the private sector in nations such as Korea and the lower private sector investment in nations such as India, which were less well represented in terms of practicing scientists.[56]

Within specific areas of research and development, there is a consensus that India is strong in the following fields: microelectronics and computer software development within the field of electronics; polymers, chemical synthesis of new ceramics, materials processing of special oxides and sulphides, powder metallurgy, interfacial structures and nuclear material and maraging steel (developed in collaboration with Krupp) within the materials sciences; biotechnology; and, at the level of fundamental research, in particular areas of chemistry, physics, and mathematics.

The NEP and subsequent government policy decisions seem to be framed in the context of a full realisation of the faults of Indian science. But how much progress has actually been made in correcting these faults since the NEP was formulated? Far from reaching the target of 2% of GNP, expenditure on S&T as a percentage of GNP has fallen slightly as budget cuts have eaten into the program. The efforts at cost recovery in the CSIR have exceeded expectations, however.[57] The CSIR is also making genuine efforts to emerge as a 'leaner' organisation. Efforts are underway to sideline the large numbers of non-performing scientists who were recruited in the 1950s and 1960s. Limited efforts have been made to harness the skills of the cream of Indian science who are now working overseas. In the case of biotechnology, the Indian government has established a Standing Advisory Committee for North America which brings leading US scientists in the field back to India once a year for consultations. This committee has been judged a success and a similar committee may be established for the field of computer technology.[58] Bharat Electronics (BE) is also making an effort to harness the skills of potential 'brain drain' scientists before their departure overseas.[59]

Despite these efforts, the impression still remains that there has been no radical re-direction of Indian science away from 'big science' and towards the genuine needs of the people. It is telling that the CSIR's solution to the problem of its 'dead wood' is to move people assessed as falling within this category out to the rural areas, presumably on the basis that work in the rural and village sector is not as important as work for industry and 'big science'. It is also noteworthy that the report of the SAC devotes the first of its two volumes to a highly descriptive account of certain areas at the forefront of big science in which India might be expected to excel, such as parallel processing, photonics, lasers, advanced materials science and genetic research. Although relevant work in the social sector is emphasised in the 'perspective plan', nowhere in the volume is there contained what might be called a strategy for achieving a fundamental shift in Indian science in favour of relevant work in that sector.

The broad conclusion to be drawn from the above is that while Indian science might become more effective as a vehicle for industry and as a participant in fore-front research, it will not be transformed in the short-term into an effective vehicle the better to meet India's pressing development needs. By the same token, the maintenance of the thrust in 'big science', in industry-related science and in fundamental research clearly has implications for the nation's eventual emergence as an important strategic player in the Asia-Pacific region, because of the ways these aspects of science relate to the defence industries and the private sector economy which supports them. Equally, India's emphasis on tertiary education, particularly in the sciences and engineering, has left it possessing one of the largest and cheapest pools of technically trained manpower in the world. This has facilitated industries such as software engineering, but it has also contributed to a significant 'brain drain' of Indian talent.

The 'brain drain' and Indian science

By no means all of the ethnic Indians outside India may be said to constitute the 'brain drain'. Many, for example, are engaged in business. These people cannot be said to be part of a 'brain drain', in the sense that there is any number of highly skilled entrepreneurs to replace them at home. One estimate puts the number of scientists who have left India and presumably not returned at between 400,000 to 500,000.[60] A study by the New Delhi-based Centre for Planning Research and Action found that approximately 30% of these are in the US, 23% in West Asia and 11% in Europe, and that by the year 2000 the number of skilled Indians abroad would reach 540,000. The study further found that about 20% of the present cohort are highly skilled scientists, 32% of whom are engineers.[61] Of these, perhaps only one in ten would return to India on a permanent basis.[62]

The issue of whether the brain drain is a positive or negative phenomenon as far as India is concerned is complex. In some respects it is clearly a negative. For example, in the computer software business 8,000 programmers enter the US on contracts each year.[63] These departures have contributed to an impending shortfall in computer engineers, estimated by the Department of Electronics to amount to 80,000 in the next five years. Yet the IITs are graduating only 15,000 per year. Some claim that as many as the top 25-30% of graduates of the prestigious IITs are 'creamed off'; others put the figure somewhat lower, at about 5% to 10%.[64] A 1989 study of the IIT at Madras revealed that 75% of computer technology students had applied for work overseas.[65]   Because of these departures of recent graduates, salaries of computer professionals are rising, a factor that will eventually blunt India's competitive edge.[66] But even in the case of those who depart permanently, the result is not always completely negative. Some are now devoting their energies to persuading their host companies overseas to set up joint ventures in India. This will prove a considerable benefit for the Indian industry.[67]

There are also a number of examples of people who have been successful overseas returning to contribute to the 'new India'. One such is 'Sam' Pitroda, who ran a highly successful electronics digital switching company in the United States and returned under Rajiv Gandhi to help sort out India's chaotic telephone system.[68]   Another is Mathukumalli Vidyasagar, who returned from a professorship in Canada to head India's new Centre for Artificial Intelligence and Robotics at Bangalore (which is engaged in defence-related work).[69]   Other examples may be found in the former Head of DRDO, Dr Arunachalam, a metallurgist who worked in Britain, and the former Head of India's missile program, and Dr Abdul Kalam, who learned his skills in the US, including at NASA's Langley Research Centre and at Wallop's Island Flight Centre in Virginia.[70] In fact, of India's pre-eminent R&D and S&T institutions, the Heads of most have actually worked overseas.

Another advantage is derived from the fact that Indians in the West have assumed highly prominent positions in a variety of walks of life, including the sciences. These people help forge strong people-to-people links that in turn have a range of benefits for India. This is particularly true of the relationship with the United States.

But do such intangible factors together with the small number of returnees outweigh the losses imposed on India through the departure of its brightest and best? One very common argument is that they clearly do because India has sufficient talent easily to replace those who depart.[71] While this argument might be sustainable in theory, especially given the large number of science graduates in India, in practice it is seriously flawed. As we have seen, the structure of Indian tertiary education is such that there are a few institutions producing graduates as good as any in the world, while a vast number are trained who are probably well below the standard in developed countries and who never, in any case, become involved in R&D. Those who emigrate, therefore, tend to be drawn from what is really a very small pool of excellence that India can ill-afford to lose. In the end it is not so much the presence of a vast pool of talent that is at issue, but rather, the lack of institutional infrastructure to train it. There is another side to this issue also. The IITs and similar institutions consume, comparatively, a lavish portion of the Indian educational resource. If 30%, or even 5%, of graduates from such institutions depart, that constitutes a devastating loss on investment for a poor, developing country.

Indian science and defence research and development

The degree of match between Indian science and technology and the defence R&D effort needs to be assessed at several levels. At one level, there is the issue of capability in the process skills; that is, the degree of competence of Indian industry in actually translating the ideas and skills manifest on the R&D side into hardware such as missiles, radars and aircraft. At another level, there is the issue of how well matched are the strengths of the broader Indian S&T establishment with the needs of forefront research and development in defence. This latter type of match will tend to involve a broad cross-section of those engaged in generic areas within Indian S&T/R&D rather than with the capabilities of individual R&D units as they apply to individual types of weapon. In this chapter, the latter is our chief concern. The former will be dealt with in a subsequent chapter on the defence industries.

To a significant degree there is an 'automatic' quality to the interface between science and technology in India and the needs of the defence industries. This is because so much S&T actually occurs in the military sector or in those areas that support it closely, such as the nuclear and space programs. Of government spending on S&T/R&D (which itself constitutes 83% of the total), 26.7% is spent directly by the DRDO and, if expenditures on space and the nuclear industry are included, the total comes to a massive 61%.[72] In fact, if we review India's access to 'critical technologies' for modern defence industries, we find that most reside in the public sector in the defence-related industries. We also see that the Indian effort in the public sector is reasonably closely aligned with the requirements of fore-front defence technology, at least in its aims, if not in its actual capabilities.

Critical technologies and defence

The Pentagon's critical technologies plan was intended as a means of identifying those technologies that are likely to be at the fore-front of defence production. Although the list, previously updated annually, was recently abandoned in favour of a stronger emphasis on space and a more goal-oriented approach, it will be useful to examine its contents in relation to India's capabilities.[73] Within the 1990 list, which was the last one compiled, those technologies under the broad head 'electronics' commanded 14 or 15 (depending on definition) of the 20 listed technologies. The others related to jet engine design, the materials sciences and biotechnology.[74] For economic performance more generally, the US Department of Commerce has listed 12 key emerging technologies. Of these 12, seven are unambiguously related to electronics and computers, while a further two cross boundaries between electronics and other disciplines.[75] The new Pentagon list of critical technologies is much more closely focused on military capabilities (what they refer to as goals) rather than on technical processes to attain them, and is consequently less detailed, containing 11 rather than 20 key areas. These are: **information technology** (computers, software, communications, sensors, electronic materials and devices, and environmental effects); **materials technology** (structural materials); **energy technology** (storage, propulsion/conversion); and **human performance technology** (design, man/system interface).[76] Another key technology plan has been developed by the aerospace industry in the US. In that list also considerable weight has been given to electronics; indeed, seven of the 10 key technologies relate in some way to that field. However, there is also an emphasis on propulsion and composite materials.[77]

The importance of electronics to modern defence systems such as the *Patriot* and *Tomahawk* missiles and stealth fighter as they were used in the Gulf War of 1991 thus cannot be over-stated. It is well summed up by an Indian analyst: 'Whatever be the manner of application of these sophisticated systems, the life-blood of all of these technologies is essentially supplied by micro-electronics'.[78]   The other three areas that emerge as important are propulsion, the materials sciences and the organisational sciences. Areas such as space are broadly encapsulated in one or other of these areas.

In terms of India's own thrust in S&T/R&D, there is a strong match between the critical technologies favoured by the Pentagon and those emphasised by the Indian government, notwithstanding the decision to make S&T more relevant to the day-to-day needs of the people. The SAC, for example, gives heavy emphasis to frontier research in advanced materials, photonics, genetic research, lasers, parallel computing, instrumentation and robotics and manufacturing automation.[79]   The work of the SAC was intended to provide funding direction in the formulation of the Eighth Five Year Plan. The authors of the SAC report state that they see 'no real conflict in planning for a quantum leap in industrial growth and at the same time making all out efforts in solving the pressing problems of our society.'[80]

The following survey describes the thrust of Indian S&T and R&D in some of the foundation areas that might one day allow India to advance into the full production of sophisticated weapons systems. For purposes of analysis, these areas have been reduced to four: **electronics** (including hardware development, software development, computation and those aspects of the material sciences relevant to micro-electronics), **space**, the **nuclear sciences** and the **material sciences** (as they relate to structural materials as distinct from conductivity). The discussion of some of the Pentagon's list of key technologies that are more clearly related to specific projects, such as propulsion technology, will be conducted when individual projects are examined in the following chapter.

Electronics, Software development and computation

According to the World Bank, India's strengths in the electronics sector rest on its large pool of trained manpower, which gives it labour costs in the sector only one-tenth of those in the West, its large market for consumer electronics, and its relatively large industrial base and managerial cohort. However, these benefits are to some extent offset by workplace rigidities in the unskilled and semi-skilled workforce, isolation from world markets, supply uncertainties, lack of infrastructure and bureaucratic interference.[81]

The strengths within the sector are particularly pronounced in the software sub-sector, where knowledge of English is a particular advantage. Costs for software development in India are therefore 25-30% less than they are in developed nations. The government has, moreover, treated the sector liberally, allowing for unlimited importation of hardware for software exporting firms. A recent World Bank survey rated India as the best choice both for on-site and off-shore software development, ahead of competitors such as Israel and China.[82]

Indian software exports have been rising steadily, as indicated by the figure below. During the 1992 calendar year exports grew by a further 74% and the overall growth in the sector was 60%.[83] The targeted export value for 1992-93 is $250 million.[84]

Figure 1.2: Domestic and export sales of Indian software, 1988-89 to 1991-92, in crore of rupees.

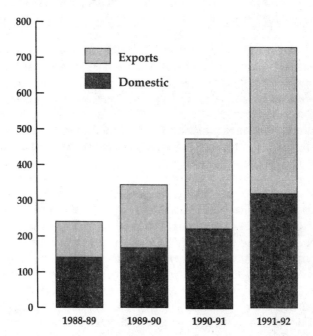

Source: 'Higher overseas sales for India software', *Times of India*, 4 June 1992.

This capability has developed through collaborations with firms such as Texas Instruments, ANZ Bank of Australia, IBM, Hewlett Packard, Motorola, Pacific Intelidota, to name only a few. These firms initially operated out of computer software technology parks (STPs) such as the ones at Bangalore and Pune and export processing zones (EPZs) like those in Bombay and Madras. The STPs have not, on the whole, proved a success,

their infrastructure development being excessively hampered by bureaucratic delay.   The government has now allowed companies to establish what virtually amount to private EPZs.[85]   Some, such as Texas Instruments, communicate with the parent company by satellite link, but the system is struggling to prove cost-effective because it is too expensive for smaller firms.[86]   In order to try to address this issue and to stem the flight of Indian programmers to the West, in 1989 the government established its own direct link for use by smaller firms.[87]

A significant factor in the success of the industry has been the fact that many of the personnel in the leading companies have received training or experience overseas.[88]   Perhaps 10-20% of Indian computer labour is employed overseas on contract at any one time.   These people provide constant feedback for the industry and develop new technical and managerial skills which help to maintain the industry's international competitiveness.[89]   As we have already noted in our discussion of the 'brain drain', however, these departures are now placing strain on the pool of well-trained professionals and India is in danger of losing some of its competitive edge.   Another problem is the high level of software pirating in India.[90] This has strained the trading relationship with the United States.   Because the US 'Super 301' trading penalties are so severe, India recently strengthened its anti-pirating legislation.

India has embarked on a major program in parallel architecture.   Parallel computers are, however, limited in their applicability to defence applications that require specific capabilities rather than repetitive tasks because of the difficulty in preparing software.   Normally, super-computers such as the ETA, Cray and NEC's SX2 are used to solve these types of complex problems.   Although the experts remain divided on the issue of whether parallel computers can be adapted through innovative software to engage in some of the tasks normally reserved for 'traditional' supercomputers, India's abilities in applications may eventually help alleviate this problem.[91]   Indeed, parallel architecture has featured on the more specific of the various Pentagon accounts of critical technologies.[92]

India has two super computers acquired from the US, a Cray and an IBM 3090.   The IBM provides workstations for CAD/CAM, located at the National Aeronautical Laboratory (NAL) for design work on the Light Combat Aircraft project (LCA).[93]   The Cray is used at the Monsoon Research Centre in New Delhi.   India is, however, denied access to the Cray for military purposes: Cray has posted its own people at the Monsoon Research Centre where the computer is located.[94]   India was denied a second Cray, which was to have been located at the Supercomputer

Education and Research Centre (SERC), Bangalore, because of Washington's non-proliferation concerns.

Washington's reluctance to provide further access to super computers caused the SAC to recommended that the government set up an independent establishment to build a parallel computer facility and design associated software.[95] The Centre for Development of Advanced Computing (CDAC) was charged with this responsibility in 1988. By 1990 the Centre had reportedly already designed a machine capable of operating at over 100 Mflops. Hardware development for a 64 node machine had been completed and major projects had been undertaken, including for the NAL in the area of fluid dynamics.[96] The work for the NAL was undertaken by a machine known as PACE (for Processor for Aerodynamic Computations and Evaluation), built by Electronic Corporation of India Ltd (ECIL). The machine, now known as Flosolver-Mk-3, is able to perform calculations in eight seconds that take the Cray-XMP supercomputer 3.25 seconds. But the Indian machine costs $96,000, compared with $25 million for the Cray. It would seem that it was this machine that formed the basis of subsequent work by the super-secret Advanced Numerical Research and Analysis Group (ANURAG) of the DRDO.[97] This machine, the PACE-128, is based on the hypercube architecture developed at the California Institute of Technology and marketed by Intel. ANURAG also developed the mission computer that will be used in the LCA, apparently with French assistance.[98] It is working on a supercomputer known as ANUCO, which will enable each processor to have over 1.3 Mflops of 'floating point' performance. This type of machine could have SIGINT applications.[99] The most successful machine commercially is CDAC's PARAM, built around the i860 chip, with 256 nodes. Four of these machines have been sold abroad. One is to be located at SERC along with a Flosolver machine, to replace the Cray that India was denied because of non-proliferation concerns. CDAC is now seeking to build a machine in the teraflops range (capable of trillions of operations per second).[100] The Bhabha Atomic Research Centre is now fully linked in with the CDAC program to produce parallel computers that are the fastest in India. It has now produced its own 16 node machine, variously known as ANUPAM and BPPS, reportedly four times faster that the IBM 6000/560 system. The machine has multicomputer, message passing multiple instruction multiple date (MIMD) architecture.[101]

Of other leading edge technologies associated with microelectronics, DRDO is involved in research into silicone MBE, reduced vapour phase epitaxy and electron beam lithography. As a result of this work India should eventually be able to produce sub-micron feature sizes.[102] The Solid

State Physics Laboratory, another DRDO institution tied to the defence industries, has reportedly performed impressively in the development of GaAs devices and wafer/device fabrication.[103]   The only Indian work on the synthesis of metalorganic compounds (group IV alkyls), is being undertaken at the Defence Science Centre, New Delhi.[104]   India also produces optical fibres through two joint-ventures in the public sector, but has not yet developed all the technologies that go along with the process, which are currently industrial secrets.

The picture in the commercial sector of computer hardware manufacturing and electronics generally, however, has not been such a happy one. Despite persistently high rates of growth in the region of 30% annually (compared with about 20% annual growth in the ASEANs and 'Tigers' from the 1970s on),[105] the industry, and especially sectors such as computer hardware manufacturing, is highly protected, inward-looking and relies heavily on imported components and semi-knocked-down kits.[106] It is also fragmented, containing 620 units employing 26,000 people. Prices are generally over three times international levels.[107]   In consequence, despite the high level of growth, the industry has yet to achieve import-export neutrality,[108] Between 1990-91 and 1991-92, the level of exports of hardware actually fell by 12.6%.[109] The profile of the electronics industry as a whole is heavily oriented towards consumer electronics (34%), communications and broadcasting (17%), electronic components (17%) and instrumentation (15%). Although computer manufacturing constitutes only 8%, its relative share is growing.[110]

India's current capability in the production of integrated circuits is modest.   Simple ICs have been manufactured for some time.   The government-owned Semiconductor Complex in Chandigar manufactured 8 bit micron and 3 micron products about one generation behind the US in collaboration with AMI and Rockwell, but in 1989 the complex burnt down.[111] A 'state of the art' six inch wafer fabrication plant is being built on the site.[112] Bharat Electronics has also manufactured ICs of a simple nature for some time, and ICs are assembled near Madras. So far, however, growth has been very slow, with consumers preferring the imported product. Economies of scale have been difficult to achieve, and it is estimated that indigenously-made ICs cost twice the amount of imported ones.[113] But many of these restraints could soon be removed. With the rapid expansion of electronics in India, demand for ICs is estimated to rise to Rs10 billion by 1995 and Rs20 billion by the turn of the century.[114] A number of other collaborations are in train that should lift India's profile in the semi-conductor market. These joint venturers include Motorola and Matra, which will work on developing micron and sub-micron products.

One area in which India is likely to have a very bright future is the major growth area in ICs, custom designed integrated circuits such as application specific integrated circuits (ASICS) and linear ICs. In this field, India's large pool of cheap, trained manpower is likely to serve it well. Already ASICS are being designed in Bangalore for American production and plans are now afoot for indigenous production.[115]

Nuclear technology

From their inception, the nuclear sciences in India were removed from the purview of the universities and placed under the tight control of the state. Through the control of Homi Bhabha and the close personal interest of Nehru, the atomic energy establishment grew up in a closely held and highly secretive environment. Under the arrangements worked out for the pre-eminent body controlling the nuclear sciences, the Atomic Energy Commission (AEC), Bhabha, its head, was accountable only to Nehru.[116] Today the structure laid down by Bhabha and Nehru remains virtually intact, with the Prime Minister communicating directly with a few senior people in the DAE and AEC and with a minimum level of public accountability exercised in the industry.[117]

The edifice created by the thrust into 'big science' and atomic energy is on the surface impressive. India's program for the development of nuclear power is currently one of the two most ambitious in the world (the other being Japan). By the year 2000 India hopes to generate 7,000 MWe through nuclear power, a target recently lowered from 10,000 MWe because of poor performance and scarcity of finances. India's Department of Atomic Energy currently employees 31,000 people, not including Nuclear Power Corporation staff. Of these, 21,000 are trained nuclear scientists and technical staff. India currently operates nine commercial power plants now generating 1,720 megawatts. A further seven are being built and 10 are in the planning stage.[118] The four older plants, Tarapur 1 and 2 and Rajasthan 1 and 2, were supplied by the West and operate under international safeguards. The others are unsafeguarded. India also has two plants reprocessing spent fuel and plutonium as a by-product, both located near Bombay. A third, which will have a capacity to reprocess 150 tonnes of spent fuel a year, is to be opened shortly near Madras. India is developing fast breeder technology intended ultimately to breed U-233 from thorium, which it has in abundance. Its first fast breeder is scheduled to start operating in 2005 with a core-load of 2000 kg of plutonium. It currently operates five research reactors and an experimental 40mw sodium-cooled fast breeder facility, none of which is subject to international safeguards, and one of which, Cirus, may be subject to bilateral safeguards.[119]

Initially, India was required to import heavy water for its unsafeguarded reactors from Norway and the Soviet Union (and possibly also China) through a West German middle-man. These imports were made in breach of the NPT.[120] It now produces all of its requirements for heavy water, however. The Nuclear Fuel Corporation at Hyderabad is now in a position to manufacture and supply all of the fuel requirements from indigenous supplies of Uranium.   India is one of only two nations capable of manufacturing and exporting zircaloy tubes (in the form of zirconcum metal derived from India's zircon sand).[121]

With all the extent and depth of the nuclear program, however, it is capable of supplying only just over 2% of India's electricity needs.[122] The program has been subject to a number of breakdowns and under-capacity performances within its plants and is now 'seriously behind schedule'.[123] Recently, accusations of widespread environmental pollution and cover-ups at the Rajasthan 1 and 2 plants have made international headlines. These allegations remain unsubstantiated. First hand evidence of an independent observer available to this writer supports the view that, contrary to some claims, there was no river water pollution as at the end of 1991. Nevertheless, the controversy surrounding the plants indicates a rapidly increasing level of concern on the part of environmentalists within India about the program.[124] Should this level of concern continue to rise, or should there be a serious nuclear accident or even a 'near miss' in India, the growth of the program could be seriously affected. Taken together, such problems mean that India has little chance of meeting its decade's end target of 7,000 MWe of generated power. A more realistic figure might be in the region of 3,000 MWe.[125] A summary of India's commercial nuclear program is given in Table 1.3, below.

Despite these problems, the important point to note for our purposes is that India, unlike Pakistan, has reached the stage where it is virtually self-sufficient in almost all aspects of the nuclear sciences associated with both the generation of power and the creation of weapons grade fissile material. The Bhabha facility alone now trains 250 nuclear scientists annually, including some from Vietnam, Malaysia, the Philippines and Tanzania and, prospectively, Thailand also.[126] All stages of the nuclear fuel cycle have now been mastered. As we shall see when we come to examine the military applications of the civilian S&T programs, the fact of this self-sufficiency, combined with the heavy reliance on plutonium technology, places India in a strong position to develop a significant nuclear arsenal, should it so desire.

Table 1.3: Commercial nuclear reactors in India

Unit	Type	MWeN	CMOP	Unit	Type	MWeN	CMOP
In Commercial Operation 9 Units 1593 MWeN							
Kakrapar 1	HWR	202	1993	Rajasthan 1	HWR	90	1973
Kalpakkam 1	HWR	205	1984	Rajasthan 2	HWR	187	1981
Kalpakkam 2	HWR	205	1986	Tarapur 1	BWR	150	1969
Narora 1	HWR	202	1991	Tarapur 2	BWR	150	1969
Narora 2	HWR	202	1992				
Under Construction 7 Units 1910 MWeN							
Kaiga 1	HWR	202	1996	Rajasthan 4	HWR	202	1997
Kaiga 2	HWR	202	1997	Tarapur 3	HWR	450	0
Kakrapar 2	HWR	202	1994	Tarapur 4	HWR	450	0
Rajasthan 3	HWR	202	1997				
Firm Plans 10 Units 3508 MWeN							
Kaiga 3	HWR	202	0	Kudankulam 2	HWR	450	0
Kaiga 4	HWR	202	0	Rajasthan 5	HWR	450	0
Kaiga 5	HWR	202	0	Rajasthan 6	HWR	450	0
Kaiga 6	HWR	202	0	Rajasthan 7	HWR	450	0
Kudankulam 1	HWR	450	0	Rajasthan 8	HWR	450	0

Source: Nuclear Developments in the Asia and Pacific Region, M.J. McMillan and J.M. Silver, Australian Nuclear Science and Technology Organisation, July 1993, p. 34.

Space

The Indian space program is substantial. In 1990 it constituted 20% of total government spending on R&D, and in 1993 spending was raised by a massive 55% over the previous year. The space R&D budget is thus considerably larger than the nuclear program budget, which itself consumes 14% of total government R&D spending.[127] The space program is coordinated by a nodal Space Commission similar in function to the AEC, with the Department of Space constituting the executive (equivalent to the DAE). The key operational body is the Indian Space Research Organisation (ISRO), Bangalore. The agencies of the Department of Space cover all aspects of space activity, including development of an independent launch capability, remote sensing, communications and meteorological applications. While there is no formal nexus with the military program for the uses of space, in practice the nexus is extremely close, as we shall see.

India first launched a 35 Kg 'satellite' in 1980. This was, however, little more than a rocket monitoring device intended to monitor the performance of the Space Launch Vehicle, which was in turn almost identical to the US *Scout*, the plans of which had evidently been passed to the Indians.[128]

The Indian space program now involves the development of three families of satellites: the Indian remote sensing satellite (IRS), the Indian national satellite (INSAT—a communications and meteorological series built initially by Ford Aerospace), and the stretched Rohini satellite series (SROSS—a space science satellite, but also a tester for a launch vehicle that could eventually provide the basis for an ICBM).[129]

The IRS series of satellites are locally built but to date launched by Russia. The current series has resolution of up to 36.25 m. The second generation in the IRS series, designated for launch in the 1993-96 period, will have a better spatial resolution capability and will be indigenously launched using the Polar Satellite Launch Vehicle (PSLV).[130] It is believed that these satellites, along with the INSAT-ID weather satellite developed by Ford, will be used for photo-processing and weapons targeting by a joint Defence Electronics and Applications Laboratory (DEAL) National Remote Sensing Agency team. When completed, the project will reportedly increase India's capability for targeting cruise and ballistic missiles.[131]

The INSAT series is also scheduled to be indigenised for both production and launch in the 1990s.[132] The INSAT-II series was progressively delayed due to lack of funds because of the fall in the rupee in the 1980s and the consequent need to apply more of the budget to purchase the INSAT-I series. The latter was reportedly used for military communications purposes in the Sri Lankan intervention.[133] The first of the indigenously built INSAT-II series was launched in July 1992. It has an 18 C band, two S band transponders and a delta relay transponder. The series has been described by a foreign observer who specialises in Indian science as 'outstanding ... one of the most complex that people are using for general-purpose communications. It seems to work in every respect'.[134] A 2,500 kg geosynchronous communications satellite, the INSAT-III series, is to be launched later in the decade or early next century.

There will be three families of launchers: the Augmented Satellite Launch Vehicle (ASLV), the Polar Satellite Launch Vehicle (PSLV) and the Geo-Synchronous Launch Vehicle (GSLV). The ASLV is a derivative of the vehicle that made the 1980 launch, with two strap-on boosters. It is designed to launch 150 kg satellites into 400 km orbits. Its navigation system was developed with significant assistance from the West Germans, especially in the guidance system, which depends either on a Motorola M 68000, or a similar system indigenously built but based on it.[135] The first two attempted flights of the ASLV in 1987 and 1988 failed. The third attempt was successful in June 1992. On that occasion the ASLV launched a SROS-C satellite, primarily for ionosphere research.

The PSLV will contain six strap-on solid fuel rocket boosters similar to the two boosters used on the ASLV. The first and third stages use solid fuel and the second and fourth stages use liquid propellant, with the second stage being based on Ariane's *Viking*.[136] The vehicle was originally designed to launch a 1,000 kg remote sensing satellite into a 900 km polar, sun-synchronous orbit, but due to cost over-runs and delays the payload has been downgraded to about 850 Kg. The vehicle was tested unsuccessfully in 1993. Another test is scheduled within a year.

The GSLV will be a derivative of the PSLV. It will retain the PSLV core stage and *Vikas* liquid propellant second stage, but the two upper stages will be replaced by a single cryogenic powered stage.[137] It was originally intended to launch a 2 tonne satellite of the INSAT-II series into geo-synchronous orbit sometime after 1995.[138] The indigenisation of the cryogenic stage of the GSLV was apparently abandoned in favour of imported technology after a one tonne cryogenic engine test failed in 1990.[139] This transfer of technology has now been blocked as a result of pressure from the United States, however, and India is now to attempt to develop the technology itself. While some are confident that India can quickly overcome the problems associated with the technology, one well-informed observer believes that the cancellation of the cryogenic technology transfer will cause a 10 year delay in the GSLV.[140] Some have argued that, with the delays in the GSLV resulting from the crogenic ban, the six solid-fuelled boosters of the PSLV should be replaced by four liquid fuelled boosters, as in the GSLV, in order thereby to obtain a vehicle capable of launching a one tonne payload into geostationary orbit, with the combined functions of the larger INSAT-2 satellite hived off into several satellites in order to give the reduced weight.[141] As discussed in Chapter 4, below, such a vehicle could also provide the basis for an ICBM.

Structural material sciences

India is generally not yet strong in the material sciences.[142] The private sector has been singularly uninvolved in the development of materials, and most work is undertaken by defence-related government research institutes.

Polymer production in India is not very far advanced and is characterised by a general lack of expertise.[143] Although India produces Kevlar 49 at the NAL in small quantities, there is no substantial production. HAL was required to import sophisticated fibre technology for its Advanced Light Helicopter.[144] Nor is there any comprehensive program in the area of high performance composites, although again, NAL does have a program and has produced composite rudders for the MiG and *Dornier* aircraft.

In metals, India has set up several plants for the beneficiation of titanium, which it has in plentiful supply. Working with significant assistance from France (Crueset Loire and Perchiney-Ugine Kuhlman) and Germany (Krupp), Mishra Datu Nigam Ltd (MIDHANI), a public sector undertaking supplying mainly the defence industries and nuclear program, has facilities to melt, cast, forge, roll and draw titanium.[145] MIDHANI also supplies armaments-grade steel for the T-72 tank.[146] It produces maraging steel for the missile program, and perhaps also for the nuclear weapons program, and powder metallurgy products.[147] Although there is a large production base for aluminium and its alloys (Indian alumina is amongst the purest in the world), no facility yet exists for the production and processing of aircraft grade aluminium. DRML is working on nickel and titanium aluminids, which are used in the production of gas turbines, but industrial scale production of these materials is not yet possible.[148] TISCO has successfully developed low carbon steel structures, micro-alloyed with titanium, special corrosive-resistant steels for marine use and creep resistant steel.[149] Indian Rare Earths Ltd produces monozite, which India also has in good supply, for the production of rare earth concentrates. A new plant is being constructed that will bring total production to 8,000 TPY.

*

The foregoing discussion has demonstrated that, generally speaking, the Indian sciences are much stronger in their top practitioners than they are through the broad mass of science. To a significant degree the strengths of Indian science are located within the public sector undertakings and defence R&D establishments, rather than the mainstream of Indian industry. While the government claims that Indian science is changing direction away from 'big science' in order better to relate to the needs of industry and the people, in practice the share of 'big science' in the public purse has not been reduced. There continues to be a significant public thrust in areas such as the nuclear sciences, space, the leading edge of computation, electronics and some aspects of the materials sciences, particularly as they might be applicable to defence production. Indian science thus seems to be structured in order to meet many of the needs of emerging defence industries. At the same time, Indian science has not served Indian industry well, largely because it has tended to reside mainly in the public sector. An additional problem for India is that the inward-looking economy has not been able to attract state-of-the-art technologies to the country. As we shall see, these failures in turn impacted negatively on those industries producing conventional weapons.

Endnotes

1   For the role of the nationalist historians in illuminating this past in the context of the nationalist movement see Romila Thapar, *A History of India*, Vol.1 Penguin, Middlesex, UK, 1969, p. 17.

2   See K.R. Mulkani's description of the views of the founder of the RSS, *The RSS Story*, Impex India, New Delhi, 1980, pp. 69-70. Mulkani's view is that Hinduism is a 'scientific' religion in so far as it is a utilitarian one that allows the participant to choose his or her best path to spiritual peace without the intercession of dogma.

3   'Dr Kalam seeks return of Tippu's rockets', *The Statesman*, 2 December, 1991.

4   For an expression of these views see Admiral R. H. Tahiliani, 'Maritime strategy for the nineties', *Indian Defence Review*, July 1989, p. 21.

5   Quoted in Dilip Bobb and Amarnath K. Menon, 'Chariot of Fire', *India Today*, 15 June, 1979.

6   Lloyd I. Rudolph and Susanne Hoeber Rudolph, *In Pursuit of Lakshmi: the political economy of the Indian state*, University of Chicago Press, Chicago, 1987, p. 26, Table 4.

7   Rudolphs, *In Pursuit of Lakshmi*, p. 26.

8   Calculated from Table 1.6, p. 54, World Bank, *1991 Country Economic Memorandum on India*, May 1990, Vol. 1.

9   James Clad, 'Patience sorely tested', *Far Eastern Economic Review*, 24 January, 1991, p. 42.

10   India Country Survey in *The Economist*, 4 May 1991, p. 11.

11   World Bank, *1991 Country Economic Memorandum*, Table 1.6, p. 54.

12   'Freeing India's Economy', *The Economist*, 23 May 1992.

13   Government of India, Ministry of Finance (Economic Division), *Economic Survey 1990-91*, Government of India Press, New Delhi, 1991, Table 7.3, p. 102.

14   See M.S. Ardeshir (Ed.), *Eighth Plan Perspectives*, Lancer, New Delhi, 1991, p. 5.

15   'India Country Survey', *The Economist*, 4 May 1991, Table i, p. 9.

16   S.V.S. Raghavan, 'The Permit Raj Must Go', *India Today*, 15 June 1990, p. 101.

17   'The elephant awakes', *The Economist*, 23 May 1992, p. 21.

18   Non-attributable source.

19   Surendra J. Patel, 'Main Elements in Shaping Future Technology Policies for India', *Economic and Political Weekly*, Vol. XXIV, No. 9, March 1989, p. 463.

20   Ashok V. Desai, 'Technology Acquisition and Application: Interpreting the Indian Experience', in R.E.B. Lucas and G.F. Papanek, *The Indian Economy: Recent Developments and Future Prospects*, Boulder, Colorado, 1988, p. 167.

21   R.M. Sundrum, 'Growth and Income Distribution in India: Policy and Performance Since Independence', as cited in Debesh Bhattacharya, 'Growth and Distribution in India During the Last Four Decades', (paper provided for the *Standing Committee on Foreign Affairs, Defence and Trade of the Australian Senate's inquiry into Australia-India relations*, 11 July 1989, Commonwealth Government Printer, Canberra, 1989, p. 7).

22   See B. D. Kapur, *Building a Defence Technology Base*, Lancer International, New Delhi, 1990, pp. 26-27.

23   Kapur, *Building a Defence Technology Base*, p. 74.

24   Ron Matthews, *Defence Production in India*, ABC Publishing House, New Delhi, 1989, p. 49.

25   Matthews, *Defence Production in India*, p. 49.

26   Government of India, Ministry of Finance (Economic Division), *Economic Survey 1988-89*, Government of India Press, New Delhi, 1990, Table 1.1. p.1.

27   Kapur, *Building a Defence Technology Base*, pp. 74-6.

28   Matthews, *Defence Production in India*, p. 38.

29   Matthews, *Defence Production in India*, p. 53.

30   Amit Gupta, 'India's Mixed Performance', *Defense and Diplomacy*, Vol. 7, No. 5, May 1989, p. 44.

31   S.R. Valluri, 'Science Policy and National Goals' (Unsourced paper in the posession of the author). Valluri is the former director of the National Aeronautical Laboratory, Council for Scientific and Industrial Research.

32   See *Pacific Defence Reporter*, Vol. XVI, No. 11, May, 1990, p. 31, for the statement of Dr Abdul Kalam, Director, Defence Research and Development Laboratory, on the space plane. The rail gun is reportedly being researched at the Armament Research Development Establishment at Pune. See *Asia-Pacific Defence Reporter*, Vol. XVIII/XIX, No. 12/1, June-July 1992, p. 25.

33   Kapur, *Building a Defence Technology Base*, pp. 26-27.

34   Interview, senior foreign official involved in technology transfer in the defence industries, New Delhi, 1989.

35   Valluri, 'Science Policy and National Goals'.

36   Surendra J. Patel, 'Main Elements in Shaping Future Technology Policies for India', p. 463.

37   S.R. Valluri, 'Building on know-why-technology drives essential' (nunsourced paper in the possession of the author).

38   For the higher estimate see Stephen Hill and Shantha Liyanage, 'The Status of Indian Science and Technology Capabilities' (paper prepared for the Australian S&T mission to India, July 1990), p. 1. The lower estimate is given in a paper by the US National Science Foundation, *Indian Scientific Strengths: Selected Opportunities for Indo-US Cooperation*, Washington DC, 1987, p. 196.

39   US National Science Foundation, *Indian Scientific Strengths*, p. 200.

40   Hill and Liyanage, 'The Status of Indian Science', p. iii.

41   Govindarajulu, 'India's S&T Capability...', *Economic and Political Weekly*, Vol. XXV, Nos. 7/8, 1990, p. M-37, Table 7.

42   Patel, 'Main Elements', p. 463.

43   Govindarajulu, 'India's S&T Capability...', p. M-37.

44   Council for Science and Industrial Research, *Status Report on Science and Technology in India: 1988*, Government of India, Publications and Information Directorate, New Delhi, 1988, pp.1-25.

45   Hill and Liyanage, 'The Status of Indian Science', p. v.

46   US National Science Foundation, *Indian Scientific Strengths, passim.* The section on materials sciences was compiled by Professor P. Somasundaran of Colombia University; ceramics was covered by Professor Rishi Raj of Cornell; and microelectronics by Kash L. Mittal of IBM.

47   P. Englemann and C. Manthey, '15 Years of Bilateral Cooperation in Science and Technology between the FRG and the Republic of India', Forschungzentrum Julich Gmbh International Bureau, Köln, 1990, p. 48.

48   Council for Scientific and Industrial Research, *Status Report ... 1988*, p. 25.

49   Quoted in Govindarajulu, 'India's S&T Capability...', p. M-37.

50   US National Science Foundation, *Indian Scientific Strengths*, p. viii.

51   Council for Scientific and Industrial Research, *Status Report on Science and Technology in India: 1990*, Government of India, Publications and Information Directorate, New Delhi, 1990, pp. 3-4.

52   US National Science Foundation, *Indian Scientific Strengths*, p. viii.

53   Science Advisory Council to the Prime Minister, *Perspectives in Science and Technology*, Vol. 1, Vikas Publishing House, New Delhi, 1990, p. 39.

54   Dhirendra Sharma, 'India's Lopsided Science', *The Bulletin of the Atomic Scientists*, Vol. 47, No. 4, May 1991.

55   Science Advisory Council, *Perspectives in Science and Technology*, p. 15.

56   World Bank, as reported in the *Times of India*, 27 May 1992.

57   Interview with Mr Johri, Head, International Collaboration, CSIR, New Delhi, December 1991.

58   Interview, Johri.

31   BEL has established a laboratory for newly recruited scientists in which they are free to pursue their projects unencumbered by bureaucracy. The laboratory has developed some remarkable innovations. Interviews and site inspection by the author, BEL, Bangalore, December, 1991.

60   See Patel, 'Main Elements', p. 463 for the higher estimate. The lower estimate was provided to the author by the Centre for Planning

Research and Action, New Delhi.

61   Centre for Planning Research and Action.

62   These estimates were made by Dr A. Aatre, head of the Naval and
        Demographic Research Laboratory, Cochin, in response to a question
        at a conference on implications of the 'new technology' for the
        military, Canberra, November 1989.

63   Sunita Sohrabji, 'Is the spree over?', *India Today*, 15 January 1994,
        p. 193.

64   For the higher figure see James Clad, 'Paradise Abroad', *Far
        Eastern Economic Review*, 26 April 1990, p. 27. The lower figure
        was provided by Dr N. Srinivasanan, Managing Director,
        International Data Corporation (India), New Delhi, December, 1991.
        Dr Srinivasanan is engaged in developing an export strategy for the
        industry for the World Bank. The figure of 5% is confirmed by
        Salim Lakha, 'The BJP and Globalization of the Indian Economy',
        unpublished paper from the 'After Ayodhya' conference, Curtin
        University, Perth, July 1993, p. 2. For the 10% figure, see Dr Aatre,
        as in fn. 62 above. See also Saritha Rai, 'Software: People at a
        Premium', *India Today*, 15 May 1992, p. 137.

65   'Logging on to India's Potential', *India Today*, 30 June, 1991, p. 83.

66   Rai, 'Software: People at a Premium'.

67   'Logging on to India's potential', *passim*.

68   James Clad, 'Status symbol', *Far Eastern Economic Review*, 26
        April 1990, p. 26.

69   'Canadian Indian to Head Defence Unit', *Hindustan Times*, 8 May
        1989.

70   Gary Milhollin, 'India's missiles: with a little help from our
        friends', *The Bulletin of the Atomic Scientists*, Vol 45, No. 9,
        November 1989, p. 32.

71   Susumu Awanohara, 'In the melting pot', *Far Eastern Economic
        Review*, 26 April 1990, p. 32. See also 'Large skilled workforce in
        India', *Times of India*, 25 April 1992.

72   Centre for Science and Industrial Research, *Status Report ... 1990*, p.
        8 and Table 13, p. 100.

73   'Pentagon dumps "critical technologies" plan', *Current News
        Supplement*, US Department of Defence, Thursday, 23 April 1992, p.
        B 30; and 'New Science and Technology Role Focuses Research

Efforts on Key Areas', *Current News Supplement*, US Department of Defence, 1 May 1992, p. B 28.

74   US Government, Department of Defense, *The Department of Defense Critical Technologies Plan for the Committee on Armed Services*, United States Congress, Washington DC, 15 March 1989, revised 5 May 1989, p. ES-1.

75   US Government, Department of Commerce, *Emerging Technologies: A Survey of Technical and Economic Opportunities*, Washington DC, Spring 1990, p. vii.

49   'New Science and Technology Plan', *Current News Supplement*.

77   For an account of these technologies see Ravinderpal Singh, 'Trans-Century Technologies', *Strategic Analysis*, Vol. XIV, No. 4, July 1991, pp. 449-50.

78   Ravinderpal Singh, 'Trans-Century Technologies', p. 443.

79   See Science Advisory Council, *Perspectives in Science and Technology*, Volume 1, *passim*. The second volume is devoted to the so-called 'socio-economic areas of relevance'.

80   Science Advisory Council, *Perspectives in Science and Technology*, Vol. 1, p. 9.

81   As reported by Sundaram Shankaram, 'IBRD sets objectives for Indian electronics sector', *The Economic Times*, 28 August 1993.

82   Pranjal Sharma, 'Systems failure', *India Today*, 15 November 1992, p. 126.

83   Salim Lakha, 'The BJP and Globalization of the Indian Economy', p. 2.

84   'Electronics exports top Rs 1000 cr mark', *Times of India*, 27 June 1992.

85   Pranjal Sharma, 'Systems Failure'.

86   Lincoln Kaye, 'Problem program', *Far Eastern Economic Review*, 2 March 1989, p. 87.

87   'India, U.S. Plan Link to Develop Software', *Asian Wall Street Journal*, 8 March 1989.

88   The foregoing information was taken from a paper by Salim Lakha, 'India Aims for an "Electronics Revolution": Growth of Computer Software Industry', pp. 1-11.

89   Lakha, 'India Aims for an "Electronics Revolution" ' p. 15.

90   Lakha, 'India aims ...' p. 17.

91   Yogi Aggarwal, 'Supercomputer race: Indian efforts yield results', *Frontline*, 27 August 1993, pp. 79-80.

92   US Department of Defense, *Critical Technologies Plan*, p. ES-1.

93   'India-US defense relations thaw', *International Defense Review*, No 8, 1990, p. 831.

94   'Scientists denied access to US supercomputer', *Times of India*, 26 May 1992.

95   Science Advisory Council, *Perspectives in Science and Technology*, Vol. 1, pp. 298-300.

96   Government of India, Department of Electronics, *Annual Report 1989-90*, New Delhi, 1990, pp. 25-7.

97   'India developing supercomputers', *Times of India*, 1 October 1991.

98   'India developing supercomputers'.   However, elsewhere Manoj Joshi claims that it is an organisation known as ASIEO that has developed the mission computer for the LCA.   See Joshi, 'The Indigenous effort', *Frontline*, 13-16 April 1991, p. 55.   See also Hamish McDonald, 'Indian computing power', *Far Eastern Economic Review*, 17 December 1992, p. 74.

99   'Mission computer for LCA ready', *The Hindu*, 3 October 1991.

100   Aggarwal, 'Supercomputer race: Indian efforts yield results', *Frontline*, 27 August 1993, p. 80.

101   Aggarwal, 'Supercomputer race'; 'BARC develops supercomputer', *Times of India*, 28 August 1993.

72   Science Advisory Council, *Perspectives in Science and Technology*, Vol. 1, p. 75.

103   The list of activities is derived from Science Advisory Council, *Perspectives in Science and Technology*, Vol. 1, pp. 75-6; the assessment was provided by visiting foreign scientists.

104   Science Advisory Council, *Perspectives in Science and Technology*, p. 76.

105   The growth rate in the 6th five year plan was 25%; the projected rate for the 7th plan is 35%.   See Government of India, Department of Electronics, *Annual Report 1989-90*, p. 1.

106   See B. Bowonder and Sunil Mani, 'Government Policy and Industrial Development: Case of Indian Computer Manufacturing

Industry', *Economic and Political Weekly*, Vol.XXVI, No.8, 23 February, 1991; and Sudha Mahalingam, 'Computer Industry in India: Strategies for Late-Comer Entry', *Economic and Political Weekly*, Vol. XXIV, No. 42, 21 October, 1989.

107   'Computer units yet to be self-sufficient', *The Statesman*, 9 May 1992.

108   Government of India, Department of Electronics, *Annual Report 1989-90*, p. 3.

109   'Electronics exports top Rs 1000 cr mark', *Times of India*, 27 June 1992.

110   Department of Electronics *Annual Report 1989-90*, p. 8.

111   National Science Foundation, *Indian Scientific Strengths*, p. 144.

112   Department of Electronics *Annual Report 1989-90*, p. 52.

113   N.N. Sachitanand, 'Dilemma of the chip maker, *The Hindu*, 25 July, 1991.

114   Sachitanand, 'Dilemma of the chip maker'.

115   Sachitanand, 'Dilemma of the chip maker'.

116   Sharma, 'India's Lopsided Science', p. 33.

117   Sharma, 'India's Lopsided Science', p. 35.

118   'India may not get Russian N-reactor', *Times of India*, 23 April 1992; 'New Delhi begins operating another nuclear reactor', *Asian Defence Journal*, October 1992, p. 100; Australian Nuclear Science and Technology Organisation, 'Nuclear power and the Nuclear Fuel Cycle' (a quarterly review of overseas events), December 1993.

119   The above information is taken from Peter Galbraith, 'Nuclear Proliferation in South Asia: Containing the Threat', a staff report to the Committee on Foreign Relations of the US Senate, US Government Printing Office, Washington DC, 1988, p. 4; Indian Department of Atomic Energy *Annual Report 1989-90*, New Delhi, 1990, para 1.1; and SIPRI (1993) as in *Pakistan Times*, 'India's reprocessing program', E. Bokhari, 12 May 1993.

120   'Indian Defence', *The Australian*, 3 November, 1988; Leonard Spector, *The Undeclared Bomb: The Spread of Nuclear Weapons 1987-88*, Carnegie Endowment for International Peace, Ballinger, Cambridge, Massachusetts, 1988, pp. 102-5.

121   'India develops new N-expertise', *Statesman*, 27 March 1993.

122 Australian Nuclear Science and Technology Organisation, *Newsletter*, June 1991, p. 1.

123 See for example Gita Piramel, 'India reacts to troubled nuclear programme', *Financial Times* (London), 19 September 1990.

124 See for example '"Eyewitness", exposes lax safety at RAPS', *Times of India*, 11 September 1991; and 'Health Survey of Villages near RAPS', *Times of India*, 14 September 1991. However, water taken from the river at Rawatbhata by independent observers was analysed outside India and found to contain pollution levels that were within the normally accepted safe levels. (Account from the person who took the samples given to the author.)

125 Akhtar Ali, 'A Framework for Nuclear Agreement and Verification', in Stephen Cohen (Ed.), *Nuclear Proliferation in South Asia: The Prospects for Arms Control*, Westview, Boulder, Colorado, 1991, p. 275.

126 Brahma Chellaney, 'Regional Proliferation: Issues and Challenges', in Cohen (Ed.), *Nuclear Proliferation in South Asia*; p. 299 and fn. 3.

127 Council for Scientific and Industrial Research, *Status Report ... 1990*, Table 13, p. 100; Norliza Dali, 'India's Budget Boosts Space Programme Spending', *Asian Defence Journal*, No. 4, April, 1993, p. 87.

128 Gary Milhollin, 'India's Missiles—With a Little Help from Our Friends'.

129 Prasun Sengupta, 'India develops new satellites, launchers', *Aerospace*, September 1990, p. 54.

130 Council for Scientific and Industrial Research, *Status Report ... 1990*, p. 26.

131 See Prasun Sengupta, 'Indian satellites find military uses', *Aerospace*, April 1992, p. 7. See also Sengupta, 'India develops new satellites, launchers'.

132 Government of India, Department of Space, *Annual Report 1989-90*, New Delhi, p. 12.

133 Sengupta, 'Indian Satellites find military uses'.

134 Hamish McDonald, 'Price of self-reliance', *Far Eastern Economic Review*, 10 December 1992, p. 48.

135   Milhollin, 'India's Missiles ...', p. 32.

136   Milhollin appears confident about the *Scout*-SLV-3 relationship. See Milhollin, 'India's Missiles', p. 32. Leonard Spector is somewhat more circumspect concerning the theory of a close relationship between the two. See *The Undeclared Bomb*, pp. 38-9.

137   Tim Furniss, 'India aims for polar launcher', *Flight International*, 3-9 June 1992, p. 20.

138   Sengupta, 'India develops new satellites, launchers', p. 54.

139   Manoj Joshi, 'Fiasco was foreseeable', *Times of India*, 6 August 1993.

140   For the optimistic view see the comments of the Chairman of ISRO, Professor Rao, as reported in K. Raghunathan, 'Rocket Deal: ISRO chief still optimistic', *The Hindu* (International Edition), 31 July 1993. For the pessimistic view see R. Ramachandran, 'ISRO must now rethink on INSAT-3', *Economic Times*, 20 July 1993.

141   R. Ramachandran, 'ISRO must now rethink on INSAT-3'.

142   For the strengths see National Science Foundation, *Indian Scientific Strengths*, Vol. VIII.

143   Science Advisory Council, *Perspectives in Science and Technology*, Vol. 1, pp. 81-82.

144   Hormuz P. Mama and Ramon Lopez, 'India's Advanced Light Helicopter', *International Defense Review*, No. 9, 1989.

145   Science Advisory Council, *Perspectives in Science and Technology*, p. 76; US Congress, Office of Technology Assessment, *Global Arms Trade*, US Government Printing Office, Washington DC, 1991, p. 156.

146   See 'Industry builds up strength', *Jane's Defence Weekly*, 26 May 1990, p. 1042.

147   'Principal Indian Defence Manufacturers', *Defense and Foreign Affairs*, Vol. XVIII, No. 4, April 1990, p. 39.

148   Science Advisory Council, *Perspectives in Science and Technology*, p. 81.

149   Council for Scientific and Industrial Research, *Status Report 1990*, p 42.

2 Arming India

The industrial and resource base for India's defence industries

In the 1970s, Kennedy identified a number of industries in the civilian sector that he believed were key elements in sustaining an expansion in military capability. These were: iron and steel; non-ferrous metals; metal products; non-electrical machinery; shipbuilding and repairing; and transportation equipment.[1] Using 1984 data, on the basis of these industries Matthews proceeded to calculate a potential defence capacity (PDC) for India. He found that India rated strongly. The selected industries constituted 33.7% in terms of gross output and 40.4% in terms of value added. India was thus rated above Turkey and not far behind South Africa and Israel.[2]

Kennedy's list was, however, compiled in 1974. We noted earlier the importance placed upon electronics in the modern defence industries by the Pentagon. Indeed, electronics now comprises a major proportion of the value of any single weapons system. For example, it accounts for 60% of the cost of a P-3C *Orion*, 40% of a F/A-18 and 25% of a modern submarine.[3] Additionally, any complete assessment of India's capacity should also take account of its resource base in strategic and other minerals and in energy.

Despite its poverty and large population, India is, on the whole, a resource rich country. In this part we confine the discussion to mineral and energy resources: human, agricultural and environmental resources are discussed in the next part of the work. The first, and possibly most important resource is energy.

Energy

As we can see from Table 1.4 below, energy constitutes something of an 'Achilles' heel' in India's rise to power. India's most significant energy resource is its steaming coal, of which it has reserves of 192 billion tonnes (to a depth of 1200 metres). However, due to antiquated production methods, production is comparatively low, at 21.17 million tonnes in 1990-91.

Even so, coal constitutes 60% of India's commercial energy consumption and India ranks fifth in terms of global production.[4] According to one private government estimate, Coal India would need to shed a massive 250,000 positions in order to provide for efficient exploitation of the resource.[5] Given the political problems any government would confront should it seek to implement such economies, India is unlikely in the near term to be in a position to meet its major energy requirements from coal.

Table 1.4: Per capita recoverable energy reserves in India and selected countries.

Country	Coal (billion tonnes)	Oil (billion tonnes)	Gas (billion cu.m.)
CIS	20,066	30.30	142,860
USA	13,488	16.00	25,000
China	1,168	2.30	900
India	192	0.78	1,005

Source: C. Ratnam, Chairman, Oil India Ltd., 'Energy Perspectives in the 21st Century', *The Sunday Times of India*, 16 February 1992, p. 25, adjusted with some data from other sources.

India lacks substantial proven reserves of oil but is somewhat better placed in its natural gas reserves. Sixty percent of indigenous oil production occurs off-shore, most of it in the Bombay High and Bombay Off-Shore fields.[6] Recoverable reserves of oil were estimated at 758 million tonnes in 1990. Gas reserves were estimated at 686 billion cubic metres.[7] In 1990-91 India imported 48% of its crude oil requirement, a rapid increase from only about 20% in 1984-85.[8] This adverse situation was due to stagnating production, due in turn to over-exploitation of the Bombay High field and the consequent need to slow down production, failure to develop new fields in a timely manner due to excessive bureaucratic restrictions placed upon private and foreign enterprises, failure to exploit natural gas reserves, 15 million cubic metres of which are flared daily,[9] and political instability in Assam, which currently produces about one-sixth of India's oil. These factors together resulted in a decline in domestic production of some 3 million tonnes between 1990-91 and 1991-92.[10] Added to this, consumption has been rising at well above the growth rate of the economy. One reason is the rapid growth in private transport. The number of cars rose from 44,000 in 1970 to 212,000 in 1989 and the number of two and three wheelers from 117,000 to 1.8 million during the same period. Since private vehicles account for 60% of petrol consumption, the amount of petrol consumed has risen sharply, from 1.5 million tonnes in 1981 to 3.5 million tonnes in 1990.[11] Yet it has been the rapid pace of industrialisation, and particularly the rapid growth of the petro-chemical industry, that has created most of the new demand. Over the last three decades growth in demand for commercial energy has risen at 6-7% per annum, whereas over the same period economic growth has averaged only 3.5%.[12]

At the time of writing there are encouraging signs of new oil strikes in Bombay Off-Shore field, nearby to Bombay High at the Mukta and Panna fields, the Ravva structure in the Krishna-Godavari basin, and on-shore in Assam, Gujarat and Rajasthan. A new assessment of the geo-morphology of the Gangetic plain offers the possibility that the basin may contain vast oil reserves. There are also much better prospects for the utilisation of India's supplies of gas. An extensive system of gas pipelines is to be built linking the southern states and north-western states to the sources of supply at a cost of $1.5 billion. The Oil and Natural Gas Commission (ONGC) has been re-vamped into a limited public company. However, given the ONGC's current difficulties, the Commission will be lucky to meet its Eighth Plan target for production of 183 million tonnes. In the context of India's ambitious industrialisation schedule, the nation is likely to remain delicately placed in relation to oil and subject to sudden disruption of the current account should international prices again rise.

The poor performance in the power sector has also constituted a significant restraint on the pace of economic development. Heavy subsidisation of rural electricity in order to foster vote banks and meet developmental needs has led to growing inefficiencies and rapidly rising demand. Subsidies to the rural sector totalled Rs41 billion in 1990-91 and were a major factor in the high debts of state electricity boards.[13] The rural sector now constitutes 26% of the consumption of electricity produced by the state electricity boards, whereas consumption was only 17% in 1978-80.[14] The situation has been exacerbated by a poor record of capacity utilisation of 32.5%.[15] Since 29% of installed capacity is dependent on hydro (68.6% is thermal and 2.35% is nuclear),[16] power generation is to a significant degree dependent on the vicissitudes of the monsoon. Other losses of up to 25% occur in transmission. For all these reasons, despite a massive investment in the power sector there have been persistent shortfalls of up to 10% per annum.[17]

India's continuing rapid economic development will require substantial investment in power generation. The Eighth Plan document estimates that Plan public expenditure on the power sector will be close to 80,000 crore of rupees (about $26.7 billion), with a significant proportion accruing as foreign exchange.[18] The World Bank initially refused to lend to the power sector in order to force it to operate on a viable economic basis. However, the Bank recently decided to re-open lending to the sector.

In order to cope with rapidly rising demand in the context of scarce resources, the state electricity boards have since 1990 been privatising new capacity. Industry has sought to alleviate the situation by installing its own generating capacity. Since these units are usually diesel powered, this has added significantly to the oil import bill. Private power companies have also been permitted to generate electricity into the public grid. The government has allowed for 100% repatriation for foreign firms and some have recently started to invest, especially in Maharashtra. Proposals for new generating capacity totalling more than 5000 MW have been approved since the sector was freed up.

Minerals

In contrast to its energy reserves, India's reserves of most minerals are excellent. India currently possesses the third largest reserves of iron ore in the world after Brazil and Australia, with reserves of nearly 12 billion tonnes. It also has excellent reserves of manganese (150 million tonnes), bauxite (2.8 billion tonnes, of the highest grade in the world and the fifth largest in quantity), 'huge' deposits of barytes, 630 million tonnes of copper ore, 'vast' resources of Kaolin, plus good resources of tungsten and the refractory minerals kyanite and sillimanite.[19] Yet these mineral resources remain largely unexploited, with mining (including oil and gas) constituting less than 2% of GDP (1986 figure) and only 11.5% of industrial production in 1990.[20]

Iron and steel

As illustrated by Figure 1.3 below, India's production of iron and steel has risen substantially since independence. These data, however, do not provide the full picture. The Indian steel industry has been characterised by distorted pricing, under-utilisation of plant due mainly to a poor record of plant maintenance and gross under-capitalisation, unrealistic projections and a high price structure by international standards.[21] India is, moreover, severely deficient in good quality coking coal and this has had a negative impact on steel production in terms both of quality and quantity. Under the old policy of autarky it refused to import the necessary requirement. Inadequate performance in the power sector has also restricted the output of steel.

India's per capita steel consumption is thus far lower than China's and has risen more slowly. In 1950 China consumed 5 kilograms per head and India consumed 2 kilograms per head; by 1986 the figures had risen to 70 and 19 respectively.[22] Perhaps more importantly, Indian steel is significantly above the world price, especially if internal levies are included. Despite the depreciation of the rupee throughout the 1980s, the Indian product was becoming less competitive.[23] The net result of these ills is that prior to the the economic reforms India was a relative pygmy in terms of international steel production, as illustrated by Table 1.5 below.

Figure 1.3: Saleable Steel Production in India in million tonnes, 1951-1991, and anticipated demand and production to the year 2000.

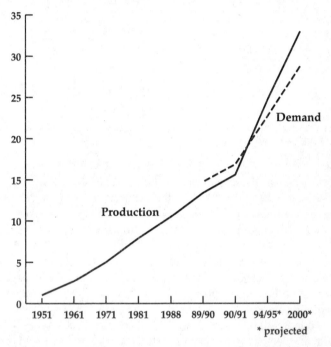

Sources: V.S. Arunachalam, 'Defence Technology and Development: The Indian Experience', in Desmond Ball and Helen Wilson (Eds), *New Technology: Implications for Regional and Australian Security*, p. 80; 'A New Sheen', *India Today*, 31 August 1990, figure on p. 125.
*   projected.

Failures in the industry, combined with a restrictive import regime, have squeezed downstream industries such as metalworking, in which India should have been highly competitive.[24]   Even in key defence projects requiring significant amounts of high grade steel, such as the Project 15 destroyer project, steel had to be imported.[25]

In recent years, the shortfall in supply led to the introduction of dual pricing (at a significantly higher price than the regulated market) and the growth of a secondary industry based mainly on non-blast furnace mini-

Table 1.5: Steel production in selected countries in 1987 (in million tonnes)

Country	Steel (mt)
USSR	161.9
EC	126.7
Japan	98.5
USA	80.9
China	55.0
Brazil	22.0
S.Korea	17.0
India	13.0

Source: J. Batliwala and R. Nath, 'Demand-Supply Scenarios in the Steel Industry in the Future', in *Metals in India's Development: The Vision of Jawaharlal Nehru*, Ministry of Mines and Steel, Government of India, New Delhi, 1989, Tables IV and VI, pp. 60-61.

plants, for which the capitalisation falls below the ceiling at which restrictions came into play. This small-scale sector now contains 160 plants and produces 5 million tonnes annually.[26]

As well as freeing up the small-scale sector, the government established 19 coking coal washeries and raised coking coal imports to 5.5 million tonnes.[27] It recently instituted an ambitious program of modernisation in the public sector, including modernisation of existing plant and construction of a new 3 million tonne plant at Visakhapatnam. These measures are expected to increase installed capacity by the end of the Eighth Plan to 27-30 mt; and to 37-40 mt by the year 2000. They should also bring India into the field of special high-technology steels and alloys and will produce exports of up to 4 million tonnes of steel by the year 2000.[28] The modernisation program includes a continuing program within the Steel Authority of India Ltd. (SAIL) to reduce the number of employees; but at the same time, the cost of each employee has been rising sharply due to inflation.[29]

In 1991, the government realised that such ambitious goals could not be met through the public sector alone. In a bold move, it decided to deregulate large-scale units as well as the smaller ones, thus allowing the private sector to enter the market. The liberalisation measures also involve a lowering of the tariff on pig iron from 45% to 25%. The tariff on coking coal has also been lowered. These measures should have a significant positive flow-on effect on the metal trades industries, engineering industries, mini-plants and throughout the economy generally. The quality of Indian steel is also apparently improving, and this will be beneficial to the defence industries. India can now, for example, reportedly produce steel of sufficiently good quality for use in warships, whereas to date it has had to import steel at significant costs in terms of foreign exchange.[30]

Non-ferrous metals

India is heavily dependent on imports for supply of the four main non-ferrous metals, aluminium, copper, lead and zinc. These imports cost India about $300 million each year. Aluminium production has suffered due to power shortages. In 1989 the pricing and distribution of aluminium was decontrolled.[31] Copper production was only 39,400 tonnes in 1984-85, but was scheduled to rise to 47,500 tonnes by 1989-90.[32]

Engineering

The engineering industries (which for statistical purposes include software engineering) are the fastest growing of India's industries. They also constitute one of the growth areas of India's exports, with the developed nations now providing a destination for one third of India's exports in engineering items.[33] The Eighth Plan calls for an annual export growth rate of 15% up to 1996-97, by which time exports will have grown to $3.5 billion at 1991-92 prices.[34] Throughout the 1980s there was a marked shift in focus from the production of capital goods to consumer goods, especially following the liberalisation measures adopted in 1985-86, which enabled producers to import capital goods that were much nearer the state-of-the-art.[35] However, performance in the heavy engineering sector (which is still dominated by large public sector organisations such as the Heavy Engineering Corporation) has been 'unsatisfactory', with significant under-utilisation. Until the public sector can be reformed, it is likely to constitute a significant drag on the performance of the sector as a whole.[36]

Transport and communications

The light transport sub-sector, especially light commercial vehicles and two wheelers, performed exceptionally well during the 1980s, largely because of a series of collaborations with leading Japanese and European firms and rapidly growing demand from the middle class. This performance tailed off during the early 1990s, due principally to the very high interest rates then prevailing. The car industry also recorded a significant achievement as a result of a collaboration with Suzuki. The Indian Suzuki plant (known as Maruti) is now the most efficient outside Japan.[37] The collaboration injected some much-needed competition into the near moribund industry, with a new indigenous design from Tatas and four collaborations with Toyota, Mitsubishi, Mazda and Nissan. However, at present the market is in danger of suffering a proliferation of new entrants and consequent inefficiencies.[38] The very poor state of Indian roads and the high pollution levels in many Indian cities are also likely to provide a barrier to the rapid increase in the use of private transport throughout the 1990s. India has decided to invest substantially in upgrading roads during the Eighth Plan period. Railways, which by developing country standards are comparatively extensive, are also scheduled for a substantial upgrade in the Eighth Plan period.

Indian telecommunications can fairly be described as abysmal. The sector constitutes a serious bottle-neck to business and industry. It is scheduled to receive substantial investment in the order of $8 billion at 1991-92 prices in the course of the Eighth Plan, but it remains to be seen how well such a large program can be implemented.[39]

In terms of heavy transport equipment, India currently meets all of its requirements for trucks, railway locomotives and rolling stock, although it could certainly do so more efficiently in the case of the rail-related industries (there is currently a political controversy raging over the government's decision to import locomotives from Switzerland).

The shipbuilding industry is contained wholly in the public sector and is highly inefficient. It has been estimated that, despite a government subsidy of 30%, it still costs twice the amount to construct a vessel in India as it does in an efficient overseas yard, and that 60% of the components are in any case imported.[40] One reason for this very poor performance is the chronic over-manning in Indian yards, with up to four welders performing a task it would take a single welder to accomplish overseas.[41] The industry has only been kept afloat by the captive market of the largely government-owned merchant fleet and through the defence build-up. While the yards owned by the Ministry of Defence are active in supplying the civil sector, the reverse is not the case. Even non-lethal craft such as supply vessels, tankers and landing transports are constructed by the military-owned yards.

The largest of the civil yards is Hindustan Shipyards at Visakhapatnam. The other major civil yard is Cochin Dockyard, which is actively seeking to be awarded the contract for the construction of the new 15,000 tonne aircraft carrier, largely on the basis of its record in the construction of large oil tankers of up to 86,000 DWT.[42] Hindustan Shipyards recently sought a government bail-out from its financial problems. The government, however, refused to supply the necessary funds. The yard will therefore have to implement drastic economies. If this is a harbinger of things to come, the Indian shipbuilding industry will either have to become more competitive or sink into decline. Since shipbuilding is labour intensive, it is an industry in which India should be able to compete if it can introduce greater efficiencies into the labour market and into the steel industry, (steel comprising by one reckoning 17% by value of a shipyard's inputs).[43]

India should also have a highly competitive shipping industry because of its large coastal trade and low labour costs. The industry grew rapidly until 1980 and then came to a sudden halt. It is constrained by excessive bureaucracy and poorly performing and congested ports.[44] Nevertheless, the industry comprises 364 ships with a tonnage of 5.5 million GRT. Over half the tonnage is government owned.

During the Seventh Plan period (1985-90), the government embarked on a large program of port modernisation to bring capacity up to 161 million tonnes. These programs focused particularly on Haldia, Madras, Visakhapatnam and Nhava Sheva ports.[45] In terms of recent performances within the industry, the investment has already started to pay off and there are now 11 major ports instead of the original four. However, the hard decisions to provide the land and infrastructure for substantial container ports in key centres such as Bombay have not been made. Consequently, India is likely to fall behind Sri Lanka, which has invested heavily in the port sector in an effort to become the 'Singapore' of South Asia. The poor state of India's ports will remain a significant micro-economic barrier to its rapid entry into world markets and increasingly, the needs of the military are likely to compete with those of the civil sector.

The development of a defence industrial base

The defence industries and associated research organisations in India are now, along with those of China, the largest in the developing world. Figure 1.4, below, illustrates the growing role of domestic procurement in India's overall defence expenditure. The exception to the upward trend occurred in the early 1980s, when expensive foreign purchases, such as the $3.3 billion *Mirage* 2000 deal, were considered necessary to counter Pakistan's acquisition of the F-16 and other weapons from the United States.

The industry is divided into the ordnance factories, which tend to produce the technologically simpler items and consumables, mainly for the army, and the Defence Public Sector Undertakings (DPSUs), which tend to be involved with the production of the more sophisticated weapons systems and platforms. There are thirty-eight ordnance factories and fifteen other establishments associated with ordnance, as well as eight DPSUs.[46] The

Figure 1.4: Value of arms production in India as a percentage of total defence expenditure, 1963-64 to 1988-89.

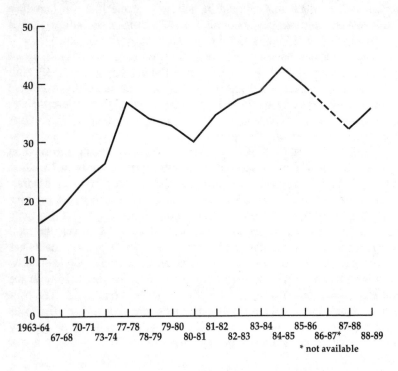

Sources: Matthews, *Defence Production in India*, Table 1, p. 43 and Table 4, p. 67; Military Yearbook 1990-91, p. 300; Defence Services Estimates.

value of goods produced in the ordnance factories in 1989-90 was Rs22,420 million and the DPSUs produced Rs25,220 million worth of goods, or a total for both sectors of about \$2.4 billion at the then prevailing exchange rate.[47]   The defence industries employ 277,000 people.[48]   The paid-up capital in the DPSUs alone now constitutes 20% of public sector investment, which itself commands the lion's share of the organised sector.[49] The heavy capitalisation of the DPSUs in relation to the ordnance factories means that productivity has been growing much more rapidly in the DPSUs than in the ordnance factories.[50] These enterprises together now produce a vast range of the requirements of the Indian armed forces.

Hindustan Aeronautics Limited (HAL) is the largest of the DPSUs and the most defence-oriented in terms of its production mix.[51]   HAL has produced over 2,400 aircraft of indigenous and imported design. These included the MiG-21, the MiG-27M, assembly of the Mig-29, the Anglo-French *Jaguar*, the *Gnat*, the *Ajeet* (a derivative of the *Gnat*), the abortive *Marut* fighter, the *Kiran* trainer and the *Allouette* III and *Lama* helicopters.

Because of the slow-down in demand due to defence cuts HAL is now planning to move to a position in which 50% of its production will be for the civil sector. The high loss rate of the Indian Air Force also precipitated a review of operations and quality control within HAL in the later 1980s, as a result of which greater efficiencies have been achieved and the loss rate reduced to a respectable level. HAL is now computer linked to British Aerospace's mainframe computers with a one second response time. The company is working extensively with BAe, using BAe design and management, and providing in return a wage rate of one-seventh that at BAe, especially in computer software design. It has re-capitalised, including with computer-controlled milling and electro-chemical machining. It is also endeavouring to reduce its inflated manpower structure with a program of reduction from 45,000 to 35,000 (current levels are at 40,000).[52]

In future, HAL will be producing the indigenously designed Advanced Light Helicopter (ALH) in a standard form as well as in ASW and anti-tank configurations. It is about to restart production of the *Jaguar* after the production line was shut down due to budget restraints. It will co-produce parts for the full inventory of MiGs with Migoyen, and is engaged in retrofitting the full range of MiG engines with western assistance. It will also upgrade between 80-100 of the MiG-21 inventory. It is building the prototypes of the Light Combat Aircraft and may eventually produce that aircraft should the project proceed.

The ordnance factory at Nasik is in the process of up-grading 500 of India's 800 T-55 tanks by up-gunning with a locally produced 105 mm gun and adding a locally produced fire control system, to be produced by Bharat Electronics Ltd. (BE). Four hundred of the locally built *Chieftain* tanks, known as the *Vijayanta*, are also being fully upgraded locally, including with indigenously built T-72 diesel engines, locally made composite armour, FSAPDS ammunition, a new semi-automatic loading system and computerised fire control. Eight hundred of the locally built Soviet T-72 MBTs are also being upgraded. The Bofors FH-77B 155 mm field gun is being produced locally under licence. The ordnance factories also produce an indigenously designed 7.62 mm self-loading rifle, known as the *Ishapore*. It is to be replaced shortly by a locally designed 5.56 mm weapon, which has been indigenously designed at great extra cost.[53]

India produces frigates, including the *Godaveri*-class, which is a locally produced enlarged version of the UK *Leander*-class (also produced locally under licence). Mazagon Docks in Bombay has now produced under licence two German type-209 1500 submarines and the hull has been launched of the *Delhi*-type destroyer, which is an enlarged version of the Soviet *Kashin*-class destroyer. It will contain a mix of indigenous and imported sensors and weapons systems. Smaller vessels such as corvettes are also produced.[54]

The scientific R&D sector has also expanded significantly since independence. The DRDO now contains 47 laboratories covering a wide range of disciplines and employs over 16,000 scientists. The DRDO and the DPSUs (which each have their own R&D units) have developed and produced an air defence artillery weapon, a multi-barrel rocket system, a wide range of communications and EW equipment, including new generation HF/VHF communication and frequency hopping and encryption facilities,[55] navigation, air-surveillance and side-looking airborne radars (SLAR), gun control and meteorological radars and sonars. Production of indigenously developed items is now worth Rs18,000 million ($0.6 billion).[56] Five missiles are currently under development and have been tested by the DRDO. The DRDO is developing a new main battle tank, the *Arjan*, the LCA and the ALH. It is also working on an AWAC with a phased array radar.

The strong emphasis on autarky led to a decision in the early 1980s to increase expenditure on R&D. Since then it has increased rapidly in absolute terms as defence expenditure has grown. Until recently it has also increased as a percentage of total defence spending. With the cuts in defence expenditure towards the end of the 1980s, however, R&D spending by DRDO in percentage terms dropped off. But the strain placed on imports of weapons and on access to spares by the loss of the Soviet source meant that, by 1992-93, spending again increased sharply, as illustrated by Figure 1.5 below.

The data in Figure 1.5, however, relate only to spending by the DRDO and thus tend to understate the overall spending on R&D. They do not account for a rapidly increasing level of expenditure on R&D within the DPSUs. Unlike the case of the DRDO, this expenditure does not appear to have levelled off in the lean years between 1989 and 1992. For example, HAL increased its expenditure on R&D from Rs22.8 crore in 1985-86 to Rs98.2 crore in 1990-91, a level that brought its R&D to almost one-fifth of the cost of the work undertaken by the DRDO.[57] In 1990-91, BE incurred R&D expenditure of Rs33 crore.[58] It seems likely, therefore, that the

Figure 1.5: R&D expenditure (not including in the DPSUs) as a percentage of total defence spending and in crores of rupees, 1982-83 to 1991-92.

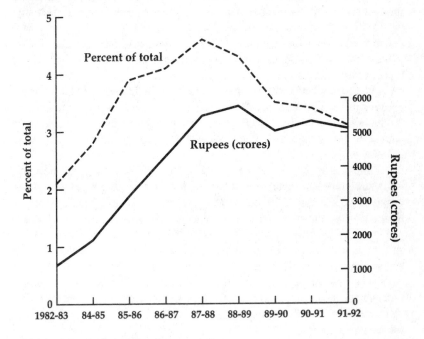

Sources: Thomas, *Indian Security Policy*, p. 185; Defence Services Estimates; and *Asia-Pacific Defence Reporter*, June-July 1993, p. 20 for 1992-93 percentage figure.

expenditure on R&D of the eight DPSUs would bring the total level of military related R&D expenditure to a much higher level than has hitherto been credited.

The second reason R&D is seriously understated is that the figures fail to account for the trade-offs and potential trade-offs provided to the military by the space and nuclear programs. The difficulty in attributing these expenditures, or even a portion of them, to the military, however, is that their effect remains in part contingent on India's actually developing nuclear weapons capable of being delivered by ballistic missiles. It seems highly likely, on the other hand, that the space program will eventually bring considerable benefits in the form of enhanced C^3I capabilities. The military implications of this type of R&D will be discussed in more detail below.

For the present we simply note that there is an effect within these expenditure heads that remains un-accounted for in the official figures, and that it is potentially a significant one.

Organisationally, the defence production units are an arm of the Ministry of Defence, with their own sub-ministry, the Department of Defence Production. Similarly, the defence R&D organisation is also a sub-ministry, the Defence Research and Development Department. The Head of that department is the Chief Defence Scientist, who is also the scientific adviser to the Ministry of Defence. There is also a separate Department of Defence Finance within the Ministry of Defence.

It has been asserted that there is no 'military-industrial complex' in India because there is no large-scale involvement of the private sector in defence production. Indeed, fear of the emergence of such a complex is said to be one of the reasons why the government resisted involvement of private industry in the first place.[59]

While it may be true in the technical sense that there is no military-industrial complex, there is certainly such a body in the sense of a large group of people each with a common interest in sustaining the position of their sector within the economy and the bureaucracy. In fact, the military and the associated bureaucracies now constitute one of the largest single sectors in the organised, or formal, labour sector. The military sector accounts for almost 7% of employment in the organised sector, there being over 1.6 million people involved in the armed forces and associated bureaucracies and productive units. If the paramilitary forces are included, there are over 2.3 million people involved, or 10% of the organised sector of the labour force.[60]

Not only is there now a large body of people employed in the defence sector but, at the upper echelons, they form a very tight network based primarily on the military connection. The Indian system entails the separation of serving officers from the primary nodes of decision making within the civil sector, which is a cause of considerable bitterness within the officer class. But the nexus between the officer corps and the defence research, development and production units is a much closer one. This close relationship comes about in part because of the practice of employing ex-military officers extensively in the defence industries and bureaucracies on a 'revolving-door' basis. For example, in 1990 the Chairmen of HAL and BE were both retired military officers. Of the eight DPSUs, military officers (either serving or retired) are listed with rank in 24% of positions in the senior executive. The situation is now such that retiring officers of ability know that they can have an on-going career in one of the defence organisations, especially if they have developed close links with that organisation during their service careers, as is often the case. It is also the practice of the DRDO to circulate serving officers through the ranks of the organisation in order to ensure that the work undertaken is of a practical nature.[61]   Indeed, Abraham goes so far as to argue that the scientific participants in much of India's publicly funded S&T programs have also now been inducted into the military-industrial complex and exist within it as an 'enclave'.[62]

The role of foreign collaboration and purchase

While autarky has been the stated objective of defence production in India, in practice, foreign collaboration—mainly through licensing and foreign purchase rather than co-production—has played a key role in the provision of weapons systems. The relationship between foreign supply by type of weapon and foreign purchase by type of weapon is illustrated by the four pi graphs shown in Appendix 1.

A number of features stand out from these graphs. As would be expected, India has generally been most heavily involved in straight imports in relation to very high technology items such as tactical missiles. Another feature that stands out is that the Soviet Union tended to sell completed systems to India, whereas Western nations were more frequently involved in licensed production, suggesting that Western technology has been more favoured over Soviet technology, but that Soviet weapons have filled an important need due to their low initial cost and serviceability.

The decision to go down the path of licensed production was made as early as 1973.[63] But even equipment supposedly manufactured in India under licence is often not truly indigenous in the sense that the majority of parts are sourced overseas, as admitted in 1988 by the then Defence Secretary, T.N. Seshan.[64] Moreover, the indiginisation program has not successfully provided for India's needs, as reflected in the fact that between 1985 and 1989, India was a significant importer of weapons, having imported according to one account $17.35 billion worth in that period, surpassing even Iraq by over $5 billion.[65]

In fact, almost 70% of the major weapons in the airforce and between 75% and 80% of those in the navy are of Soviet origin or Soviet compatible. Non-Soviet major foreign purchases include the Anglo-French *Jaguar* strike aircraft, the British *Leander* class frigates, aircraft carriers, *Harrier* VSTOL aircraft, the *Sea King* ASW helicopter, the French *Allouette* helicopter and the Bofors field howitzer.

Overall, despite the heavy reliance on the former Soviet Union, India's acquisition policy may be described as eclectic. Some commentators argue that this eclecticism was the result of India's desire to achieve greater balance between the power blocs and to retain its capability of independent manoeuvre.[66] On another level, however, it may be a reflection of the fact that India's main concessional supplier, the Soviet Union, was not always willing or able to supply all of its needs for high technology items. The decision to acquire the *Mirage* 2000, probably in response to the acquisition of the F-16 by Pakistan, falls into this category. At the time the decision was made to acquire the aircraft, the Soviet MiG-29, which subsequently came to provide the backbone of India's front-line fighter force, was not available to India. It was only once the *Mirage* had been acquired that Moscow decided to provide the MiG-29— the first time the aircraft had been provided to a non-communist country.[67] The way the MiG-29 deal was struck also illustrates the way in which India has tended to play one side off against the other between the superpower blocs in order to get a better deal.[68] As Thakur and Thayer claim, while diversification was of self-evident direct benefit, it had the additional indirect advantage of exerting pressure on the USSR to improve the terms of its offer.[69]

The effects of diversification in terms of efficiency were not, however, entirely positive. In the case of the navy, one retired admiral has described the mix of vessels as 'an admiral's nightmare'.[70] Moreover, the actual mode of selection and purchasing is described by senior military officials as 'bureaucratic, cumbersome and costly'.[71] The loss of the Soviet *Petya* class corvette, INS *Andaman*, in August 1990, is in part attributable to the breakdown in maintenance schedules because of the fact that schedules were different between Soviet and non-Soviet vessels. Nor was the width of the steel in the hull suitable for the corrosive Indian Ocean conditions.[72] Similarly, the airforce has suffered from a plethora of MiG-23 varieties.[73]

The mix between overseas purchase and indigenous manufacture has also served India poorly. The Indian Auditor General commented adversely on the fact that the *Mirage* 2000, which had cost $3.3 billion to acquire in the first place, was left without weapons for a period of *two years* while such weapons were produced locally.[74] India's fleet has also been left vulnerable to missile attack because of the absence of AMM and CIWS defences while these are developed locally.[75] The hull of the first *New Delhi* class destroyer has been incomplete for two years while the development of indigenous equipment is awaited. In a sense, India has adopted the reverse policy of Pakistan, which has chosen to acquire cheap, out-dated platforms on an-off-the shelf basis, while purchasing the latest in weapons and defences such as the *Phalanx* CIWS and the *Exocet* and

Harpoon anti-ship missiles.

The need to quarantine the Soviet-acquired fleet vessels from those acquired in the West also greatly complicated the management of the navy and detracted from efficiency. Until recently, basing, repairs and refitting of Soviet-origin vessels had to be conducted at Visakhapatnam on the east coast, while Western-origin vessels were based on the west coast. More importantly, the division between East and West was reflected in a doctrinal separation in terms of training needs, a separation that ultimately had a highly detrimental effect on the cohesion of the armed forces. These problems have perhaps been most seriously manifest in the navy, where accusations of bias between Western and Eastern trained officers fed into a debilitating row over promotions.[76]

Yet despite the disadvantages associated with India's close association with the Soviet Union for weapons transfers, it cannot be denied that to a significant degree the nation owes its position as a leading Indian Ocean military power to access to Soviet weapons at bargain-basement prices over a period of almost three decades. It therefore behoves us to look at the Soviet relationship in more detail.

The Soviet role

We have seen how the two wars of the 1960s played a key role in India's decision both to arm itself and to build up an indigenous weapons production capability. India's first reaction was to go to the West to accomplish these goals. This decision was dictated both on ideological grounds and because India felt at the time that Western weapons had an edge in capability over Soviet weapons, which were then an unknown quantity. After both wars, but particularly after the 1965 war with Pakistan, the West refused to provide the level of sophisticated weapons that India considered it needed. This refusal was particularly irksome in light of the fact that the US had already provided weapons such as the F-104 *Starfighter* to Pakistan. In its dealings with New Delhi, moreover, Moscow proved much more willing to support licensed production and technology transfer than the West.[77] The importance of the two wars in the early part of the 1960s in turning India towards the Soviet Union as the source of its supply of weapons is illustrated by Figure 1.6, below.

The first of the major acquisitions by India of Soviet weapons was the MiG-21, acquired in the aftermath of the Sino-Indian war. As we have seen, this contract involved licensed production of the aircraft. From this time on, it made sense for India to continue to work with the MiG line of aircraft from the technological point of view, whatever the political situation might dictate. Soviet aircraft technology was acquired in an incremental way, with each model building on a number of key features and even actual components of previous models. Western aircraft, in contrast, tended to be designed much more from the clean blueprint.[78] The incremental approach was particularly suited to a developing country such as India.

Figure 1.6: India's major arms suppliers, 1951-1985 (five year average percentages)

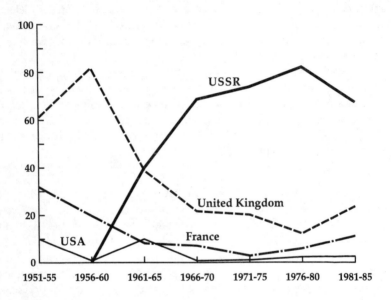

Source: Ramesh Thakur and Carlyle A. Thayer, *Soviet Relations with India and Vietnam 1945-1992*, Oxford University Press, New Delhi, 1993, p. 92.

The next major purchases from the Soviet Union were not made until the early 1980s. Apparently concerned at India's trend towards diversification of its sources, Moscow made New Delhi an 'unexpectedly good' offer in order to woo back the Indian custom.[79] By the time the deal was finalised in 1984 it involved: India selling parts for the MiG-21 to the entire Warsaw Pact region, manufacture of the MiG-23, assembly of the MiG-29, a pipeline proposal for manufacture under licence of the MiG-31, supply of advanced versions of the *Kilo*-class deisel-electric attack submarine, *Nanuchka* guided missile corvettes and *Kashin* class guided missile destroyers, and the transfer of technology for the composite armour for the T-72 tank, which was already manufactured in India under licence. The entire deal was worth an estimated $20 billion (imputed value) and constitutes the largest single arms transfer ever.[80] It is difficult to calculate the exact terms of these transfers, however, since they occurred as a number of separate agreements, each with its own terms and conditions. For example, a $1.6 billion agreement was signed in 1980 at 2.5% interest over 17 years.[81] Other deals were struck with the equivalent of a 42% grant element; and the terms of the MiG-27 deal meant that it was acquired at one-quarter the unit cost of the equivalent *Mirage* 2000.[82] Not only were the terms themselves highly favourable, but India was also permitted to pay for the weapons in rupees. This facility proved irresistible in the aftermath of the second oil crisis (1979-80), when India was hard-pressed for foreign exchange. The net result has been a heavy reliance on Soviet sourcing overall, as indicated in Table 1.6, below.

Table 1.6: Percentage Soviet origin of some major systems in the Indian armed forces

Item	number	% Soviet
MBTs	3250	48
Towed arty	2165	34
SP arty	100	38
AD missiles	691	96
Subs	14	85
Destroyers	5	100
Frigates	23	35
Aircraft carriers	2	0
FGA aircraft	422	60
AD Fighters	275	85
Transport	143	70
MR aircraft	22	59
ASW helicopters	75	23
Fleet air arm	24	0

Sources: Derived from Ravinderpal Singh, 'Indo-Soviet Military Cooperation', *Strategic Analysis*, December 1990, pp. 1082-3 and *The Military Balance*.

The arms relationship with the Soviet Union was not a complete bed of roses for India, however. As we note in detail below, India suffered considerably in the relationship from an artificially high rouble in relation to the rupee, a situation that worsened throughout the course of the 1980s.

Throughout that decade India had run up an enormous rouble debt of the order of $11 billion, 70% of which was military.[83] Although India stood to gain because of the very long repayment periods and low interest rates, these benefits were offset by the fact that the exchange had been fixed too high at the time of purchase and that the rate became even more unfair after the rouble went into 'free fall' in the early 1990s.

However, given the fact that the rupee had itself deteriorated by 62% against the US dollar even before the sharp devaluation of 1991, India's circumstances would have been far worse had the defence deals been struck with hard currency nations.[84]

What did become a problem was that the Soviet Union's growing hunger for hard currency forced it to insist on hard currency payments for the spare parts and refitting sales that it accrued annually from India.[85] Worse, with the 'implosion' of the Soviet Union in 1991, supply of spares for most of the Soviet weapons simply dried up. India found itself on a 'labyrinthine' search for spares from the estimated 3,500 suppliers scattered around the former Soviet Union, a task previously coordinated from a central Soviet ministry.[86] The problem was exacerbated by the fact that the Soviet Union had traditionally kept its 'client' states on a short rein in supply of spare parts because it had not forgotten its unhappy experience with Egypt.[87]

The most immediate impact was on India's anti-aircraft defences, both missiles and AA guns.[88] We can see from Table 1.6, above, that 96% of India's air defence missiles are of Soviet origin. The lack of spares for these missiles left India highly vulnerable at a time of rising tension with Pakistan. In any case, the radars of the older SAMS and the AA guns were presumed to have been compromised as a result of their use in Lebanon in 1982 and the Gulf in 1991. Other problems occurred in the navy and airforce. The *Kashin* destroyers and all other Soviet origin gas turbine powered vessels were periodically sent to the Soviet Union for engine refits.[89] This was no longer possible. Some of India's MiG-29s were grounded for considerable periods in 1992-93 because of lack of radar components.[90] The massive T-55 tank upgrade was also jeopardised. India has had to address some of the more critical shortages by actually buying more of the weapons systems in question in order to cannibalise them.[91] What spares were available were costly, and by October 1993 India had spent about $300 million on spares alone.[92]

Such was the degree of Indian dependency on Soviet purchasing of defence equipment and the commitment of the Indian bureaucratic elite to the Soviet relationship, that rather than seeing the reality of the situation in which it was placed, India at first attempted to persist with the relationship in its old form in order to salvage as much of the old arrangements as it could.

In mid-1991 an Indian team opened talks with the Soviet Union aimed at resolving the problem of supply of spares. The Indian side also sought an expanded role for joint production in the DPSUs in order to export, and thus alleviate their chronic under-utilisation. Moscow, however, continued to demand hard currency payments and the talks came to nothing.[93] Further talks with Russia in March 1992 supposedly established a mechanism for coordinating the supply of spare parts, but on a hard currency basis.[94]

There were additional problems with the Soviet relationship. New Delhi was not convinced that Soviet equipment was a match for the best that the West had to offer. The comparatively poor performance of Soviet equipment in the Lebanon and in the 1991 Gulf war strengthened these doubts.[95] Reports that the *Charlie*-1 nuclear-powered submarine suffered serious leaks of radioactive material remain unsubstantiated.[96] What is more probable is that Indian technicians were denied access to the propulsion technology on the vessel. Soviet equipment, moreover, has generally proved to be poorly adapted for a tropical environment. Often the Indian purchaser was forced to buy a 'pig in a poke', since the Soviets were reluctant to reveal the full capabilities of a system before purchase.[97]

With time, India also came to realise that the Soviet relationship did not provide for all its needs. Although India reportedly allowed up to 500 Soviet technicians to gather SIGINT at Ludhiana and Bhatinda in Punjab, during the 1987 crisis over 'Operation Brasstacks' the Soviet Union had reportedly refused to make satellite imagery of Pakistani troop movements available to India.[98] India was, moreover, concerned at Soviet criticism of its refusal to agree to the five-power nuclear proposal mooted by Pakistan in 1990.

More important still, India's end goal was autonomy in defence production, or as near to it as it could get. Such autonomy required more than just licensed production. It increasingly involved access to 'dual use' technologies in computation, electronics, the materials sciences, space and the nuclear sciences. During the 1980s, India turned to the West for these technologies, and in particular to the United States.

At the sharper end of the technology spectrum, India initially benefited from Russia's new thirst for hard currency. While the West in the past played a significant role in the development of India's space program, the Missile Technology Control Regime (MTCR) was tightened by Western signatories in the aftermath of the Gulf war and India could no longer expect such support, especially in view of the increasing evidence of the strong linkages emerging between the space and missile programs. Prior to the collapse of the former Soviet Union, Moscow also adhered to the principles of the MTCR, even though it was not a signatory party. The deteriorating economic circumstances in which Russia found itself, however, persuaded Moscow to provide for a purchase price of $250 million, cryogenic booster engine technology for India's Geo-Synchronous Space Launch Vehicle (GSLV), a space vehicle that could eventually form the basis for an ICBM, or so Washington claimed.

Although senior US officials now admit that the cryogenic technology is not an appropriate one for modern-day ICBMs and would be most unlikely to be used for this purpose, the US cracked down on the deal under the provisions of the MTCR. One point of particular concern to the US was that the transfer not only involved the engines themselves, but also the technology: under the deal, 25 Glavkosmos scientists were to be located in India to transfer the technology.[99] The US consequently embargoed any dealing with either Glavkosmos or ISRO for a period of two years.[100] The threat of loss of lucrative US contracts was eventually sufficient to persuade Moscow to cancel the deal. According to one report, however, at least some of the cryogenic technology had already been transferred at the time of the ban, and India seems intent on developing its own cryogenic engine, perhaps with clandestine Russian support.[101]

Prior to Moscow's withdrawal from the cryogenic deal, the defence relationship between Russia and India had been showing signs of recovering. Whatever doubts New Delhi may have had about Russian capabilities and reliability seemed to have been dispelled by the resolution of the dispute over India's rouble debt and a decision taken in February 1992 to lock into a further $830 million in Russian credit at 5% interest for defence purchases. Under this deal India was to buy 36 MiG-29 aircraft for an amount of $466 million, the SA 11B surface-to-air missile and badly-needed spare parts.[102] Moscow has, however, experienced some difficulty in forcing its defence units to supply the items at contracted prices. This problem, together with the cryogenic back-down, has caused New Delhi to look more to the West, Israel and the more sophisticated Asian countries such as Singapore for sophisticated weapons and dual use technologies.[103]

Dual use technologies and weapons sales: the US and Western role

Foreign collaboration is crucial to India if it is to attain its ambition to design and manufacture complete weapons systems. As we have seen, due to its autarkic nature the Indian economy has generally performed poorly in terms of its ability to provide for dual use technologies. This poor performance means that dual use technologies have had to be imported with military purposes specifically in mind.

The most important nation in terms of the import of sophisticated dual use technologies was the United States. While the US exported weapons to Pakistan in large quantities, it realised by the early 1980s that what India really wanted from it was not so much the weapons themselves, but the transfer of the underlying technologies. Washington was thus willing to play a dual game in South Asia; its aim thereby was to move beyond the 'zero-sum game' in its relations with India and Pakistan. While it needed Pakistan because of its front line status *vis à vis* the Soviet Union, it recognised that India was the power of the future not only in South Asia, but throughout the Indian Ocean. A major restraint on the transfer of sophisticated technology to India, however, was Washington's fear, probably well-founded in view of the omnipresent role of the KGB, that these technologies would be 'transferred' to the Soviet Union.

Notwithstanding these concerns, in 1984 National Security Directive No 147 instructing US agencies to seek better relations with India was signed by President Reagan against the will of the Pentagon.[104] Following the promulgation of this directive, in November 1984 the US and India signed a Memorandum of Understanding (MOU) on technology transfer. The document was designed, among other things, to protect US technology from transfer to the Soviet Union. Even after it was signed, however, the Pentagon opposed the transfer of sophisticated items because it felt they would not be properly protected. It was only after the US Defence Secretary, Casper Weinburger, went to India in 1986 that the log-jam was completely broken. By that year the value of items transferred under the MOU had risen to $371 million, and by 1988 it stood at $870 million per annum ($685 million of which covered 'controlled' goods).[105] Between the time Directive 147 was signed in 1984 and 1989, the number of high technology transfers approved by the US rose five-fold.[106] Equipment thus transferred included the IBM 3090 computer for design work on the LCA and associated work-stations, a Cray computer, design verification work on the LCA, a gyro ring guidance system, also for use in the LCA, assistance from NASA for ISRO in the interpretation of data from the Indian remote sensing satellite, and regular exchanges of information between ISRO and NASA.[107] One estimate is that 80% of the equipment now used by ISRO is based on NASA technology.[108] Cryogenic rocket engines were at one stage on offer to the Indians from General Dynamics.[109] Overall, the US has been particularly prominent in the sale of computer related equipment and integrated circuits.[110]

The relationship with the US is important not just in terms of transfer of dual use items, however. It is also emerging as a means by which India is obtaining technology and sub-components more directly relating to its arms industry. These include sophisticated propulsion units such as the F-404 engine, 11 of which have been sold for use in prototypes of the LCA; power units for the new *Delhi* class destroyer (a deal subsequently cancelled due to lack of funds); and reportedly (but still not confirmed), state of the art munitions guidance technology such as laser-guided copperhead anti-tank ammunition technology.[111] The shopping list also probably extends to 'underwater technology'.[112] As early as 1990 India had sought Doppler radar technology from the US and is likely to have been provided with it.[113] In 1991, the US reportedly agreed to the transfer of $400 of superseded equipment relating to electronic warfare (this amount, however, included payment for the IBM 3090 for LCA design mentioned above). Other items in the package reportedly included 'passive intelligence' EW equipment to replace Soviet designed equipment that had shown itself to be 'compromised' in the Gulf War. An Indian defence analyst believes that India's DRDO will use the equipment acquired from the US in order further to develop its own capabilities.[114] The package may also include sophisticated artillery control radars such as the AN-TPQ-36 and the AN-TPQ-37 (already possessed by Pakistan).[115] India is also contemplating joint software development with the Pentagon for non-lethal military operations.[116]

Despite the transfer of important dual-use items listed above, the United States persists in its resistance to the transfer of some of the more sophisticated force multipliers that India would like to obtain from it. As Raju Thomas points out, the US is still wary of transferring highly sophisticated technologies to a developing country such as India.[117] Items apparently requested at various times but denied include aerial re-fuelling technology for India's *Jaguars* and *Harpoon* missiles. Nevertheless, the relationship is an evolving one, and the ending of the Cold War has at least opened up the prospect that more sophisticated technologies will eventually be provided. Recent reports indicate continuing collaboration on the LCA in certain 'specialised areas'.[118]

Germany has also reportedly been involved in India's plans to upgrade its C^3 capability.[119] Germany provided invaluable assistance to India's missile program, including in what Gary Milhollin describes as three indispensable technologies: guidance, rocket testing and the use of composite materials.[120] The new relationship with Israel, which India recognised in 1991, will likely prove invaluable to India. India could obtain from Israel some of the technologies so far denied it by the US, such as night vision technology, aerial refuelling technology, RPV technology that may ultimately have implications for the development of an Indian cruise missile, ASWAC related technology, EW technology and aircraft upgrading technology, especially for the MiG-29B and assistance with the LCA. The RPV-related technology could prove especially significant. Apparently discussions to date include ground control and real-time imagery processing systems and digital data link technologies.[121] India has also acquired from Israel 'mothballing' and associated mobilisation technologies, which will be important methods of cutting costs and reducing the tail to teeth ratio.[122] It is reported from time to time that Israel clandestinely assisted China in missile guidance technology. If such reports are true, similar assistance might also be offered to India.

The role of the private sector in defence production

Despite early offers from firms such as Tatas to participate in the defence industries, private enterprise has traditionally played only a minor role in defence production. Only an estimated 3% of production in 1989 was undertaken by the private sector.[123] The reasons for the government having shied away from substantial private sector involvement relate to the initial incapacity of the sector to provide the necessary technologies on an economic basis due to lack of economies of scale, continuing doubts within the military and the defence bureaucracy concerning the ability of the sector to provide items within the very high tolerances demanded by warfare, the high profile generally of the government in the economy and government concerns about the emergence of a military-industrial complex.[124]

Nevertheless, by the mid-1980s it was generally recognised that the time had come for a more substantial role for the private sector in defence production. A number of senior politicians and bureaucrats began to express such views, including Defence Minister Pant (1987), Defence Secretary Seshan (1988), Air Chief Marshal Mehra (1990) and Minister of State for Defence Ramanna (1990).[125] In part this shift in perception was the result of the new philosophy underlying the economic reforms initiated by Rajiv Gandhi in 1985-86, and in part it was brought about by the lack of performance by the public sector as it tried to enter the field of fully indigenous manufacture of sophisticated weapons systems for the first time.

In order to give substance to the new policy, in 1984 it was decided not to import vehicles under 10 tonnes weight.[126] In 1985 an apex body was established consisting of representatives of the defence industries, the government and the private sector, to meet annually and coordinate requirements from the private sector.[127]   The organisation conducted a review of items of a non-lethal nature that it felt could be supplied by the private sector and came up with a list of 800.[128]

These measures, however, have not on the whole resulted in the private sector playing a significantly greater role in the defence industries to date, except in some specific areas such as ballistic missiles. Neither the vehicle import nor the development defrayment scheme were fully implemented. In the three years up to 1988-89, overall payments to the private sector for defence production actually diminished, from Rs2.77 billion to Rs1.65 billion.[129]   The fact is, the public sector and the military appear to have closed ranks to protect their positions. As shown by Table 1.7, below, the percentage share of the private sector remained flat throughout the 1980s.[130]

Table 1.7: Value of orders for defence production filled by private industry, in crore of rupees and as a percentage of the total defence budget, 1982-83 to 1989-90.

Year	value (cr, rs.)	percentage
1982-83	78.46	1.45
1983-84	142.15	2.45
1984-85	149.72	2.24
1985-86	224.53	2.81
1986-87	227.41	2.17
1987-88	245.73	2.05
1988-89	134.00	1.00
1989-90*	170.50	1.18

Sources: 'Arms and the Businessman', *Business India*, 25 June-8 July 1990, p. 87; Submission of the Confederation of Engineering Industry on 'Indian Engineering Industry Participation in Defence Production', made to the Government of India in 1990, p. 1.   * Data extend to December 1989 only.

The private sector has counter-attacked, arguing that it has been kept out of defence production by long trials for products and excessively rigid quality controls.[131]   The delays in the implementation of the official policy prompted the Confederation of Engineering Industry to petition the V.P. Singh government in 1990. The engineers argued that the private sector had the capacity to participate successfully—as it already did in the space program and nuclear programs—and that it was common practice in the UK and US for the private sector to control the lion's share of defence production. The Confederation also suggested a comprehensive action plan designed to integrate the civilian sector better with the military sector.[132]

State-of-the art weapons systems production

India's desire for autarky in the defence industries was always going to have to be tested on the anvil of the design and production of fully fledged weapons systems of a sophisticated nature, such as main battle tanks, fighter aircraft and ballistic missiles. These items are the high cost ones at the cutting-edge of military capability. Any power that aspires to the status of a major regional actor will eventually have to grapple with the production of such items. Yet as India has discovered, there is a quantum leap involved between the production of a field gun, or even a frigate, to the production of a modern fighter or a sophisticated ballistic or tactical missile.

In terms of production of fighter aircraft, the state-of-the-art has now become so complex and the associated technologies, such as the computer sciences, material sciences and propulsion technologies, so difficult to master that not even a nation like Japan has yet fully mastered them.[133] Most European countries except France and Sweden (whose aircraft are in any case largely derivative) have abandoned the field in favour of joint production of the Eurofighter, and even that now has problems in achieving production runs. Israel, a more sophisticated nation technologically than India and one with a strong incentive to perform in the area because of its potential international isolation, has abandoned efforts to produce its own fighter.

Of course, not all modern weapons systems are as difficult to produce as a fighter. The following survey assesses India's progress in production of more sophisticated weapons systems.

The Light Combat Aircraft

The idea of designing and building a fighter from the ground up was always an ambitious one for India. The notion first emerged in the early 1970s, following the excellent performance of the tiny *Gnat* in the 1971 war with Pakistan.[134] The idea was 'sold' to Mrs Gandhi in the early 1980s by aircraft design technocrats who were 'restless' following the closing down of the indigenous design program in the wake of the failure of the *Marut* project. Originally, the idea was to build a light, and hence cheap and simple, aircraft within India's technical means. The IAF, however, wanted a state-of-the-art, multi-role aircraft. The tonnage grew from 6 tonnes to the current 10-12 tonnes. (Senior Indian officials still insist, however, that the aircraft will weigh 8.5 tonnes.)[135] The LCA is now intended to be a light, advanced, single-engined, air superiority aircraft with a secondary ground attack role.[136] Prototype development of the planned 200 aircraft program is estimated to cost $2 billion, with eventual fly-away costs of $20 million per aircraft.

The LCA project has many critics within India. It is asserted in some circles that S.R. Vallouri, former Director of the NAL, was replaced in 1985 because he was critical of the project.[137] The airforce top brass reportedly would prefer an off-the-shelf purchase such as the SU-37 or the MiG-35, rather than having to wait till after 2005 for an aircraft that will by that time be somewhat outmoded.[138] The Auditor General has been critical of the excessive delays associated with the project. The design and development (D&D) phase was scheduled to have been completed by 1982, but it was only in 1983 that the program was sanctioned by the government. The sanctioned cost for the D&D phase was Rs5.6 billion over 10 years.[139] According to some reports, expenditure has already amounted to Rs15 billion, yet the design was well short of completion.[140] The project has also been criticised in the parliament because of the over-dependence on the United States for the supply of the engine for the aircraft. According to one member of the Indian upper house of parliament, the US would 'hold you to ransom and will not give you a single engine more' should the indigenous GTX engine project fail.[141] Increasingly, the LCA is being seen in India as a 'white elephant' that only continues because 'the Arunachalams of India refuse to learn, and their successive political masters do not have the gumption to insist on even a minimum accountability.'[142]

One of the most common criticisms of the project is that it is not truly indigenous. Wags quip that 'the only thing Indian about it will be the coconut cracked on the nose of the prototype'.   The position with collaboration is as follows:

- **Project definition**: Dessault (France) and Messerschmitt-Boelkow-Blohm (Germany);
- **Engine**: prototype, GE F-404-F 213 turbofan (US); production, GTX-35 Vs (Indian, with Dowty Smiths, GE and SNECMA (US and France);
- **Flight control system**: fly-by-wire, cockpit display, ring laser gyroscope; Allied Signal Aerospace (US);
- **Radar**: an improved Doppler 'look-down' PS-05 (Ericcson-Ferranti);
- **Mission computer**: India;
- **Composite materials technology—airframe**: Northrop (US);
- **Fuel system**; Intertechnique (France);

- **Oxygen system**: Intertechnique (France);
- **Airframe**: Dessault (France); Northrop (USA);
- **Short range missile**: Matra Magic (France);
- **Medium range missile**: Astra (India);
- **Cannon**: Russia;
- **CAD/CAM facility**: IBM (US);
- **Wind tunnel testing**: preliminary, NAL Bangalore; final US.[143]

The project has also come under strong criticism on organisational grounds. In 1984, the Aircraft Development Authority (ADA) was formed to provide management, which had previously been in the hands of HAL. The concept of the ADA was itself a sound one. There were over 50 organisations involved in the project, most of them from the public sector.[144] Coordination of such a large number of authorities, especially in the Indian bureaucratic context, was a daunting task. Besides, the model of a project coordination authority is one that has worked reasonably well in the case of the Integrated Guided Missile Development Program (IGMDP).

But in 1985, two key members of the ADA resigned: Vallouri, and leader of the ADA design team, Raj Mahindra. The ADA was consequently thrown into disarray and was not really operational as an organisation until 1986. One observer suggests that these early resignations arose from bureaucratic pressures on the ADA to 'rush the gate' by dispensing with preliminary technology acquisition. A number of analysts advising the US government were also of the view that India needed further technology acquisition before it could embark on the project. The fact that it only paid India to indigenise 40% of the components of the Mig-21 and that the *Jaguar* cost twice the imported amount to build suggest that India was not ready for the project.

The tension within the ADA over the issue of technology acquisition suggests that the ADA was driven by external bureaucrats and lacked sufficient authority to implement its decisions.[145] There followed a series of vacillations in design and choice of collaborator, fuelled by competition between competing companies and countries, especially France, the US and USSR. The test flight of the prototype was delayed from 1990 to 1995. Costs escalated substantially. In the words of one observer, 'The LCA ... [was] beginning to follow the same lines as earlier Indian aeronautics projects—chaotic, subject to flux, cost overruns and time delays.'[146] It is now believed that the project has been downgraded to the production of two prototypes, to be completed by 1997.[147]

Nevertheless, there are still those in the Indian system who defend the

LCA. They tend to see the project as a learning exercise as much as a means of attaining a cheap state-of-the-art fighter. According to this argument, the Indian aircraft building capacity has been damaged by the 'stop-start' approach of the government to funding. The design team that worked on the *Marut* was lost, and a new team must now be developed for the LCA.[148] As Arunachalam put it, 'we shot down more aircraft on the drawing boards than in the sky'. He argues that, because the project is as much about technology acquisition and development as it is about production of an aircraft, it should be expected that it will take many years to 'mature'. In his words, one needs 'staying power'.[149] Others argue that the LCA will not be as expensive as the figures currently suggest, since much of HAL is now under-utilised.[150] Arunachalum also defends the project by arguing that to a significant degree the delays are now due to the restraint imposed by the lack of foreign exchange and that, were it not for this restraint, the project would now be progressing well. Others associated with the project blame bureaucratic delays rather than faults with the project.[151] Project Director, Kota Harinarayan, insists that the GTX engine will be used in the third prototype. He claims that the first prototype will be ready in 1995, the second 9 months later, and the third about 6-9 months after that.[152]

While it is true that almost every assembly and sub-assembly requires foreign components and assistance, this is to be expected in what is essentially a learning project. The important question over the longer-term is whether the project will result in the transfer of technologies that can eventually be used effectively in the defence industries as a whole. Moreover, even if the project has been downgraded at this stage to a 'technology demonstrator', it is debatable what this actually means. If the drawing down of the project is, as Arunachalam claims, due to financial problems rather than technical ones, then should India's balance of payments position improve, it is possible that the project may one day be resumed.

The main battle tank (Arjun)

The MBT project, as it is known, has also had its share of difficulties. The project commenced in 1974. It was intended to design and build a state-of-the-art tank with a 120 mm rifled gun, computer-controlled, integrated fire control system comprising a laser range finder, ballistic computer, thermal imager for night sight with composite armour of indigenous design known as *Kanchan* (developed originally for the Indian version of the T-72), a speed of 70 km per hour (which matches the M-1), a power-to-weight ratio of 27 HP/tonne (the actual is 24 HP/tonne) and hydropneumatic suspension.[153] In other words, the tank is intended to be truly state-of-the-art. To date about $280 million has been spent. The criticisms of the MBT project broadly parallel those of the LCA. Imported components comprise 55% of current pre-production models. The project is nearly four years behind schedule. The indigenously built engine has never materialised, and engines (the 1400 hp MTU MB 873 Ka 501 turbocharged, water-cooled) will now be imported from Germany and subsequently built under licence. The tracks and fire control system are also German based. The primary sight is Dutch and the suspension is based on US technology.

Because the tank was to be all things to all people, it 'weighed in' initially at 60 tonnes, well above the 50 tonne weight that can be carried by India's military bridging systems. The tank was also initially too wide for transportation on the bogies in use on India's rail system. The gas suspension leaked. The engine overheated because of the excessive weight of the vehicle, and acceleration was poor for the same reason. Traditional ammunition was found to be accurate only during static firing and the FSAPDS ammunition did not work at all. The tracks were subject to excessive shedding. In these circumstances, the army naturally resisted bureaucratic pressure to place orders for the tank.[154]

According to Arunachalam, it is only some 'subtle' design problems that now remain. The government is rushing the tank into production and the new army Chief of Staff, General B.C. Joshi, has accepted the vehicle. Sceptics assert that the acceptance is premature and that the tank is under-gunned and under-powered. The army is reportedly looking at purchase of the Russian T-80 as a an interim measure. However, other evidence bears Arunachalam out and the major design problems of the tank appear to have been overcome.[155]

The missile program

Like the LCA program, the Integrated Guided Missile Development Program (IGMP) is a substantial undertaking for a developing country. Indeed, by any standards the program—which involves the simultaneous development of five missiles—is large. Launched in 1983, the program now comprises sixty-four contributing organisations. These are coordinated by an umbrella organisation, the Defence Research and Development Laboratory, Hyderabad (DRDL), under the direction of Abdul Kalam (Kalam took over from Arunachalum as Head of the DRDO in 1992, but maintains his position in charge of the missile program). He is an outspoken and highly nationalistic Muslim who is totally dedicated to the program and is its main driving force. The main organ of production is Bharat Dynamics, a DPSU located nearby to the DRDL in Hyderabad. The DRDL coordinates a budget that has so far totalled Rs7.88 billion.[156] Another important contributing organisation is the Research and Training Unit of Navigational Electronics (RTUNE), which undertakes work associated with navigational software development.

The extent of the program and status of its constituents are as follows:

PRITHVI: *Prithvi* is a single stage, liquid fuelled (fuming nitric acid oxidiser and 50/50 xylidiene triethylamine fuel), road-mobile, surface-to-surface missile first tested in 1988. *Prithvi* reportedly has the highest warhead weight to overall weight of any missile in its class. Although *Prithvi* has been described as similar to the Soviet *Scud*, of all the IGMP projects it has the highest indigenous content. However, according to one report its liquid-fuelled engine had its origins in a Soviet 'technology demonstration project called Devil', which was based on the SAM-3.[157] Other reports describe it as a derivative of one of the stages of the ASLV.[158] The strap-down inertial guidance system incorporates a twin microprocessor based computer with interrupt-driven, real-time software. The missile has a reported accuracy of one percent plus, which translates into a circular error probability (CEP) of less than 250-300 metres over a maximum range of 250 Km for a half tonne payload (range is reduced to 150 Km with a warhead of 1 tonne). According to senior DRDO officials, the accuracy of the weapon is 'excellent' and 'exceeds expectations'.[159] It is capable of being manoeuvred up to 15 degrees in flight. It will reportedly carry five conventional payloads, including cluster munitions warheads and possibly a fuel air explosive warhead (the ERDL has already developed this technology for use in mine-clearing missiles). The army's 11th Corps has already reportedly taken delivery of some of the missiles.[160]

Prithvi has come under some criticism, including from within the army, because of its use of highly unstable liquid propellent, which will complicate its use on the battlefield. The project has also been criticised because, with its strap-down targeting, it will not be accurate enough to be cost-effective if used with a single, conventional warhead. Indeed, critics assert that it will be a costly method of 'excavating a large hole in the ground' when used against military targets.[161] It is likely that liquid fuels have been chosen because of the low cost and the capability they provide for in-flight manoeuvring. Each missile would cost an estimated $700,000, which is well below the cost of a western equivalent. This suggests a substantial production run of between 100 and 200.[162]

AGNI: *Agni* is an intermediate range ballistic missile that was first tested in 1989. It consists of two stages, the first solid-fuelled and based on the first stage of the ASLV, the second liquid-fuelled and based on *Prithvi*.[163] At the time of launch it was reported to have a range of 2500 kms with a payload of one tonne.[164]   It was also reportedly described by Dr Arunachalam as 'embarrassingly accurate' on its first launch.[165] Neither of these claims was likely correct at the time. However, it is likely that over time the range has been increased, particularly by use of the ASLV's booster system, and also the accuracy improved. One report describes the range of *Agni*-II (which was not boosted) at 2500 km with a payload of one tonne.[166] Reports at the time of the successful test of *Agni* in February 1994 claimed that terminal guidance had been tested. If true, this would have represented a significant breakthrough for India. Other reports suggest, however, that terminal guidance would be difficult for India to achieve at this stage.[167]   The fact that the first stage of *Agni* is based closely on the first stage of the ASLV, which is in turn based on the US *Scout*, illustrates the close nexus between the space and military programs, and via the space program, the military program and overseas assistance.

There is also an interesting cross-reference between a number of the high technology programs and the US relationship. We have seen that the US supplied an advanced ring laser gyroscope for guidance of the LCA. This is a solid state device and, according to Gary Milhollin, there is no reason why it should not be adapted for use on a variety of Indian missiles, including *Agni*, thus improving considerably their accuracy.[168]   Milhollin speculates that the closed-loop guidance system used in *Agni* is a product of a joint German-Indian project utilising the Motorola M 68,000 chip processor.[169] German government authorities deny this claim.[170]   The composite heat shield for the re-entry vehicle is manufactured in India from material imported from Germany. Two US firms have been charged with supplying materials to enable India to build a hot isostatic press, used for the manufacture of heat shield materials for re-entry.[171]

Indian authorities have asserted repeatedly that *Agni* is only a cheap 'technology demonstrator' and that plans exist for only five launches.[172] The fact of its being a demonstrator, they assert, is indicated by its utilising both solid and liquid fuel technology, a configuration that has been criticised as irrational if one is seeking a true IRBM capability.[173]   The claim that *Agni* is a demonstrator may be true, but not in the sense that Indian officials mean. Rather than being a 'technology demonstrator', it would be more accurate to depict *Agni* as a cheap (in that it is comprised of the ASLV and *Prithvi*) 'test bed' vehicle, with the primary purpose of testing re-entry vehicles and guidance systems.[174]

In other words, *Agni* as it is now configured is unlikely ever to be put into production. But nor need it be. India's nuclear posture, as well as being one of ambiguity, is still to an extent unresolved. Until the missile program has progressed to a point where all the pre-production problems have been resolved, or until the position on nuclear weapons is firmed up, there is little point in declaring *Agni* to be other than a technology demonstrator or even intending it to be so. In that sense, the attitude is very much one of 'wait and see'. When the time comes, India would be able to use the PSLV or its equivalent as the primary vehicle, or else develop an entirely solid-fuelled IRBM; but meanwhile *Agni* would have been used as a quick and cheap means to solve the difficult problems of re-entry and guidance while the PSLV, or some other vehicle, is under development.

Indian officials also claim that *Agni* is intended for use with conventional warheads, an assertion that seems to contradict the claim that it is a demonstrator. The probability that India is developing a terminal guidance capability for *Agni* means that, should it ever become a nuclear power, India would likely progress to the development of MIRVs. Officials support their claim that *Agni* is intended to be used with conventional warheads by reference to a US paper on the doctrine of 'discriminating deterrence', which concluded in 1988 that missiles had now achieved accuracies of up to CEPs of 80 m, which means that they could be used effectively with conventional warheads. It was this perception that motivated the *Agni* program, so they claim.[175] Such a position, however, does not accord with the timing of the development of *Agni*, which, as we have seen, was first launched in 1989 and was under development well before then.

AKASH: *Akash* is a surface-to-air missile of 25 km range with RAM rocket propulsion (supposedly adapted from a SAM 6) that is claimed to be manoeuvrable, hardened against counter-measures, controlled initially by a locally built 3-D phased array radar and then by a built-in active seeker for terminal homing. According to Kalam it has *Patriot*-like features.[176] *Akash* was first tested in 1990 and was scheduled for introduction into the armed forces in 1993 after a nine-test program. However, more work was apparently required on the phased array radar, which will reportedly be capable of tracking eight targets simultaneously.[177] Some of the problems with the radar may have been solved in 1992 with the assistance of the British firm Marconi.[178]

TRISHUL: *Trishul* is a short range SAM that was successfully tested in 1991. The missile uses radar line-of-sight guidance and a 'gathering system'. It reportedly has difficult-to-jam guidance based on microwave frequencies. It has high manoeuvrability and is powered by a two stage solid propellent system, with a highly powerful HTBP-type propellent similar to the one used in the *Patriot*. It is constructed of maraging steel to withstand the related stress. It also has sea skimming capabilities, and this, combined with its high degree of manoeuvrability, will give it the navy's first anti-missile-missile capability.[179]

NAG: *Nag* is intended as a state-of-the-art 'fire-and-forget' anti-tank missile. It has a radio-command-to-line-of-site guidance system with a thermal sight, carbon dioxide range finder, imaging infrared seeker head and millimetric wave seeker system. Joshi asserts that these highly sophisticated technologies were developed in country, with the focal plane array (FPA) sensor being developed by the Solid State Physics Laboratory and the Semiconductor Complex and the W-band millimetric wave seeker being developed by CEERI, Pilani, IIT Kharakhpur, Osmania University, and the three DRDO laboratories. *Nag* has been 'tested' (it is not clear whether the full guidance system was part of the test, however) and is expected to go into production between 1993 and 1994.[180] Again, cross references become crucial; for Joshi asserts that the guidance system for *Nag* can be used in the 'super accurate' warheads of *Agni* and *Prithvi*.[181]

As well as these programs that fall within the IGMDP, there are two missile programs that are additional. One is the *Astra* air-to-air missile program to provide a weapon for the proposed LCA. The other is a long-range (45 km) multi-barrel artillery rocket to be known as *Pinacha* that would fire rockets in 'ripple' mode, saturate a 2 square kilometre area and have a modern 3-D radar. It will replace the old 'Stalin Organ' type, formerly obtained from the Soviet Union. *Pinacha* was tested successfully in single rocket mode in 1990.[182]

There has also been a good deal of speculation concerning India's capacity to manufacture a cruise missile. Much of this speculation centres on a program to build an RPV.[183] At this stage, India may have some difficulty in developing terrain following guidance systems, although this could perhaps be accomplished with the assistance of Israel (see above). According to some, guidance could be achieved through the Global Positioning System (GPS), which relies on communication with a satellite. The current US GPS system is not directly amenable to military use because settings are slightly off coordinate precisely to avoid such use. However, TV guidance for the final stage of the flight might be utilised to give a high degree of accuracy (1-5 m are regularly achieved with precision guided munitions).[184] A cruise missile capability would become more viable with the launch of the second series of the IRS towards the mid-1990s.

Finally, it should be noted that there is considerable potential for synergism between the space and missile programs. According to Gary Milhollen, *Agni* itself is a close derivation of India's first space launch rocket, the SLV-3, which is in turn a derivation of the US *Scout*.[185] India's second space launch vehicle, the ASLV, is essentially a version of the SLV with the addition of two strap-on booster motors. Thus, presumably, the range of *Agni* could be quickly increased should the need arise. However, should India one day assess that it requires an ICBM, the PSLV would fit this role best of all. The payload of the PSLV using solid-fuelled boosters would be between 600-1000 kg, sufficient for a nuclear weapon. Should liquid fuelled boosters be substituted for the current solid-fuelled boosters, it could be raised to 1200 kg. The re-entry technologies and guidance technologies currently being tested on *Agni* could be used in the PSLV without too much difficulty.

As we have seen, India is rapidly gaining in other technologies relevant to its missile and nuclear programs. These include computation and software development, in which it has considerable aptitude and even a measure of brilliance, and the materials sciences, in which it has recently made some advances. Sophisticated guidance systems and manoeuvrability capabilities currently under development with international assistance for a number of tactical Indian missiles could potentially assist with ballistic missile re-entry vehicle guidance and even a MIRV capability. Multiple conventional warhead technologies under development for *Prithvi* could also possibly facilitate the development of MIRVs. Thus many of these technologies under development within India are likely to 'come together' within the next decade, at which point India's capabilities could start to develop rapidly.

Nuclear propulsion

The nuclear propulsion program is one of India's most secret. Its primary purpose is to develop a mini-reactor capable of powering a submarine (SSN). Several years ago there appeared to be consensus within the senior ranks of the navy that nuclear propulsion is a highly efficient way to power major naval surface vessels as well as submarines.[186]

Such views gave rise to speculation that the principal purpose behind the acquisition of the Soviet *Charlie* class SSN (re-named INS *Chakra*) was not so much to add the vessel to the Indian inventory, but rather as a means of supporting India's indigenous program to build an SSN.[187] In fact, the 1989-90 Annual Report of the Ministry of Defence categorised the *Chakra* acquisition as a useful 'experiment' in case India were to decide to 'go in for' nuclear propulsion.[188]

The project was initially conducted under the auspices of BARC. Work reportedly commenced in 1976 under the code name Plutonium Recycling Project. Up until 1984, however, very little progress had apparently been made. It was supposedly as a 'tacit admission' of this failure that the decision was made to lease an SSN from the Soviet Union. Apparently as a face saving device it was also decided to continue the indigenous program. But, as we shall see, another interpretation can be placed upon this decision.[189]

In 1984, after considerable criticism from the navy concerning lack of progress, primary carriage of the project was removed from BARC and given to a new team. The project was re-titled Advanced Technology Vessels Development Organisation (ATV) and placed under the control of the DRDO. The new project was more closely linked with the navy and was headed by a vice-admiral.

One observer, Manoj Joshi, argues that, from the first, the acquisition of Soviet *Kilo* class submarines, the leasing of the Soviet *Charlie* class submarine and the ATV project were linked as part of a package negotiated at the time the *Kilo* deal was struck. According to Joshi, the original plan was for India to acquire the *Kilo* plus one or more Soviet nuclear powered submarines, pending the development of its own nuclear powered submarine, and that it was given the working plans of both the *Kilo* and the *Charlie* to this end.

Joshi claims that with the collapse of the Soviet Union the original concept of relying on Soviet SSNs until an indigenous one could be built was no longer viable. He says, however, that the ATV program is progressing well, especially now that India has its own unsafeguarded source of enriched uranium. According to Joshi, once the problem of designing a miniature reactor has been overcome, the reactor would then be linked to the hull, which would be based on the *Charlie* hull (i.e. a double hull construction) but would be more modern and sophisticated. Joshi believes that at this stage the intention would be to have a launch sometime in the period before 2005, and to equip the vessel with a submarine-launched cruise missile (SLCM). In line with this view, New Delhi's offer to sell a miniature reactor to Iran in 1991 is seen as a signal to the world that India had overcome the problems associated with the production of mini-reactors.[190]

While not denying the use of a Soviet design as the basis for the hull, senior defence officials in New Delhi maintain that it was not the *Charlie* plans that were transferred, but the plans of another vessel. If this is indeed the case, it would likely be a more sophisticated vessel than the *Charlie* that is involved.[191]   The apparent decision to move German equipment associated with the production of the single-hulled Type-209 1500 from Mazagon Docks to Visakhapatnam would tend to support the view that the plan is for a more sophisticated and modern vessel with a single hull design. Western observers based in New Delhi assess that the progress on the reactor for the ATV has not been as great as the Joshi article suggests. If this view is correct, it would likely set back the launch of any vessel to after the 2005 date suggested by Joshi.[192]

Nuclear weapons

There have been a number of near admissions on the part of senior politicians and officials of the existence of the Indian nuclear weapons program. The most important of these was made by Rajiv Gandhi in 1985 in an interview, when he said that 'if we [India] decided to become a nuclear [weapons] power, it would take a few weeks or a few months'.[193]   Other senior officials who have commented in this way on India's capability are former Army Chief of Staff Sundarji, who is quoted as saying that 'There may be the odd person [in Pakistan] who has kidded himself into believing that they have nuclear weapons and we don't have ... The sooner they wake up to reality the better.'[194]   Former Defence Minister Pant has made similar, if slightly more elliptical references.[195]   Even the Head of the Department of Atomic Energy admitted as far back as 1988 that India's commercial program would entail the compilation of a stockpile of thousands of kilograms of unsafeguarded potentially fissionable material.[196]

The CIA Director, Robert Gates, told the US Senate in January 1992 that both India and Pakistan had all the necessary components to produce nuclear weapons at short notice, but so far had not done so because of safety reasons.[197]   Yet shortly after Gates made this statement, the US State Department was forced under close questioning virtually to admit that at least Pakistan did have a nuclear bomb.[198]   In a 1992 interview, the CIA's Director of the Non-Proliferation Centre, Gordon Oehler, was reported as saying that India could assemble 25 nuclear weapons 'in a matter of days.'[199] And indeed, given the likelihood that Pakistan now has at least several nuclear weapons—or at least would be little more than 'a screwdriver's turn away' from having them—it would be most surprising if India had not positioned itself to be able to follow suit within a *very* short time indeed.

In a sense, it is merely 'academic' whether India actually has or has not usable nuclear weapons. Two other points are more important in terms of a longer term analysis. One is India's capacity to produce fissionable material—for it is on this capacity that the size of the arsenal that India may eventually develop will depend—and the other is the degree of miniaturisation that Indian scientists would be able to achieve in the production of any nuclear weapons, for it is on this capacity that long-range delivery via ballistic missiles will depend.

Albright, Berkhout and Walker estimated in a 1993 SIPRI publication that India would have had sufficient weapons grade plutonium already separated to produce 58 nuclear weapons by the end of 1991, using a 5 kg per weapon breakdown (elsewhere Albright and Hibbs use a 6 kg per weapon rate). On the same basis they estimated a production of 425 kg of fissionable material by the end of 1995, potentially enough for 85 weapons. These calculations are based on a decision to use only spent fuel from the smaller Cirus and Dhruva research reactors, but not on the basis of use of fuel from the larger unsafeguarded commercial reactors such as MAPS I and II and the new reactors that are rapidly coming on stream. They are of the view that fuel from these large commercial reactors, reprocessed at the Kalpakkam facility near Madras (to come on stream in 1994) will be used for the core for India's breeder program, which would preclude its use in nuclear weapons.[200]

The Cirus reactor operates under bilateral (although not international) safeguards, however. Notwithstanding these safeguards, India used fuel from Cirus for its 1974 test. It is possible that spent fuel from the unsafeguarded commercial reactors has been substituted for the Cirus fuel for inventory purposes on an on-going basis, and that the Cirus fuel has been consequently available for manufacture of weapons-grade plutonium. Should India have chosen to honour the intent of the Canadian safeguards placed upon Cirus fuel, however, SIPRI calculates that it would have had only enough fissile material for 20 weapons in 1991.[201]

India has two enrichment facilities, one small one located in BARC and a larger one called the Rare Materials Plant at Ratanhalli, near Mysore. Albright, Berkhout and Walker estimate that these facilities might together produce 8 kg of weapons grade uranium per year.[202] It is likely that at least some of this material may be being used for mini-reactor fuel for the SSN program, however.

India has reportedly imported or obtained many of the ingredients and components that comprise nuclear weapons, including beryllium and tritium. There is also speculation surrounding India's capacity to mount a thermo-nuclear (hydrogen) explosion. The fact that India has monitored fall-out from China's atmospheric thermo-nuclear explosions and that it has fusion and enrichment programs also lends credence to the view that it is at least maintaining the option to produce thermo-nuclear weapons.[203]

The key point about India's unsafeguarded nuclear program is not so much the amount of unsafeguarded plutonium that might have been separated to date, but the significant capacity within the Indian program rapidly to increase the annual amount separated throughout the 1990s. Although conscious of the uncertainties surrounding the program, Albright, Berkhout and Walker estimate that PREFRE alone could separate between 500 and 1500 kg of *reactor grade* plutonium in the remainder of the 1990s, while Kalpakkam could be processing 150 tonnes per year by 1995, to give about 525 kg of plutonium per year, or 2625 kg by the end of the century, for a total of about 3000 kg using the lower rate for PREFRE or 4000 kg using the higher estimate.[204]

While it is unlikely that the commercial program would be diverted into the production of fissionable material (to do so would mean a serious diminution in the generation of electricity), such a diversion is certainly theoretically possible should India find itself in some kind of nuclear arms competition with a larger nuclear power such as China. If such a diversion of production were to take place, then the amount of weapons grade material that could be produced through the commercial reactors would be roughly one-tenth the amount of reactor grade material that could be produced. However, with so many new reactors scheduled to come on stream, the theoretical limitation might still be imposed by the reprocessing facilities rather than the availability of spent fuel for re-processing. In any case, such an approach would mean that India would have a significant annual capacity to produce fissionable material.

Although analysts are divided concerning India's capacity to miniaturise nuclear devices in order to make them deliverable by missile, it would be logical that New Delhi has in place a comprehensive program towards this end. Given the depth of the nuclear sciences in India and its capabilities in ordnance, it is also reasonable to suppose that it is fairly well advanced. India would hardly have invested the massive amount of time, money and effort that it has in its ballistic missile program, and at considerable political cost in terms of its relationships with the US and other Western nations, unless it had a parallel program intended to develop nuclear weapons for its missiles.

The Indian official position that its missiles are intended to be conventionally armed is not tenable. Leaving aside the technical issue of whether the degree of accuracy of India's missiles would be sufficient to justify their use as conventionally armed weapons, India currently has clear air superiority over both Pakistan and China and does not require conventionally armed missiles for tactical purposes, except perhaps for highly specialised tasks such as knocking out key military installations, a task that would seem to be better suited to precision guided weapons than less accurate conventionally armed ballistic missiles.

Nor would India necessarily need to conduct a new nuclear test in order to emerge as a fully-fledged nuclear power. India's skills in computers and software could enable it to 'bench test' or 'cold test' any nuclear device in the same manner as Israel did in order to build up its substantial arsenal. As already noted, BARC has now undertaken its own program in parallel computing to skirt around possible boycott of access to international computation facilities because of the NPT. Although parallel computers are not as well suited to weapons design as fully-fledged super computers, to an extent the problems associated with them can be avoided by skilful software design. Albright and Hibbs maintain that data obtained from the 1974 test could also have been used to miniaturised the design, making it easier to deploy on attack aircraft and perhaps on missiles.[205] Additionally, there is some evidence to suggest that India has developed a Prompt Burst Reactor that could assist it in weapons design.[206]

Command, control, communication and intelligence (C³I), electronics and electronic warfare (EW).

One of the most significant problems India faces in developing a modern system of C³I is the lack of organisational integration within the armed forces themselves. The fact that the political system has tended to divide the military to reduce its power and to keep it at arm's length from the decision-making process has precluded the development of an adequate system of integrated command. There is no commander-in-chief in a position of authority over the whole of the armed services. Each force, rather, operates as an independent command, linked only through the Ministry of Defence. In the last major war fought by India in 1971, it was only the close personal relationship between the heads of the three forces that enabled the armed forces to perform with credit.[207] Since then, the process of adjustment towards a greater degree of integration within the armed forces has continued to be a painful one.

For example, a recent decision was made to transfer part of the helicopter force from the airforce to the army in line with integrationist trends being adopted world-wide. However, resistance from within the IAF has so far prevented transfer of all but light observation and utility helicopters. The key attack helicopters that should be integral to the army's

force structure have not been transferred.[208] Neither has tactical air power
so far been integrated into the force structure of the army. Rather, the two
forces tend to 'take each other for granted', with the IAF preferring to
concentrate its efforts on knocking out the Pakistan air force rather than in
lending tactical air support to the ground forces.[209] Nor is the maritime
strike force properly integrated with the navy. The land based force, which
currently consists of only 8 *Jaguars* and some antique *Canberra* bombers, is
controlled by the IAF rather than by a unified command or the navy
itself.[210] An additional problem with the introduction of a modern system
of C^3I relates to the educational standards of the forces as a whole.

Whether the prospect of the development of a modern system of C^3I will
act as a stimulus for the development of a more integrated approach to
military command and the placing of additional resources into personnel
development remains to be seen. Some remain sceptical and assert that 'we
[Indians] are attaching a jet engine to a bullock cart'.[211] However, at least
in terms of the development of hardware, there is already a momentum in
place.

To an extent, this momentum was given impetus by the fact that the
Soviet Union refused to provide satellite intelligence to India about
Pakistani troop movements at the time of operation Brasstacks, the multi-
divisional Indian exercise that brought India and Pakistan close to war in
1987. The dangers posed by the lack of satellite surveillance in the difficult
strategic environment of South Asia were also illustrated when RAW
reportedly misinformed the Indian government about Pakistani troop
movements in the context of the deteriorating circumstances between India
and Pakistan that occurred over Kashmir in early 1990. According to some
interpretations, it was only provision of satellite intelligence by the US and
USSR that prevented a dangerous escalation into war.[212] The *de facto*
nuclearisation of South Asia has given greater urgency to the problem of
initiating effective systems of C^3I in both India and Pakistan.

The army's communications system has now been modernised and
computerised.[213] The new INSAT-II series of communications satellites,
the first of which was launched in July 1992, should give India the means
greatly to improve its military communications. Imagery, however, is still a
problem. One report states that a computerised system capable of
identifying military targets from the current IRS-1 A/B and INSAT weather
satellites is in the final stages of development by the Defence and
Electronics Applications Laboratory (DEAL—a part of the DRDO).[214]
Elsewhere, however, the current resolution of the IRS is estimated at about
36 metres, which is not considered sufficient for military purposes. Yet

another account claims that the current IRS satellite can be used to gain strategic information but not tactical information, and is being used for strategic purposes over the Tibet plateau, with tactical data being obtained from MiG-25R reconnaissance aircraft.[215] (India has now agreed to stop these over-flights as part of its September 1993 border agreement with China.) The next generation of the IRS—to be launched indigenously between 1993-95—will, however, have considerably better resolution, such that it will be suitable for military purposes. After that, it will take some time to integrate all the systems into a fully-fledged real time system of C^3I, especially given the overall lack of coordination between the forces evident to date.

Since 1986 India has also been attempting to develop an ASWAC (airborne surveillance warning and control) capability. The project was initiated because it was believed at the time that Pakistan was to acquire the US E-2C *Hawkeye*. The work is being undertaken at the Bangalore Aircraft and Systems Testing Establishment in association with the DRDO, HAL and Bharat Electronics. The rotodome was designed and built by Deutsch Aerospace. To date, a BAeHS-748 has flown with a test rotodome in November 1990 and, reportedly, a second aircraft is being fitted out with a conformal active phased array radar, under development at the Electronics and Radar Development Establishment at Hyderabad.[216] When it was learned Pakistan was no longer to acquire the *Hawkeye*, and in light of tight defence budgets and of difficulties in developing software, the project was either slowed down or shelved. However, recent progress with phased array radar in relation to the guided missile program, particularly the *Akash*, suggests that it may have been re-activated. *Jane's Radars and Electronic Warfare Systems 1992-93* reports that the completed system is scheduled to be tested shortly.[217]

According to Ball, India possesses SIGINT-ELINT gathering capabilities that have been in place since colonial days. SIGINT interception and analysis is conducted by the Electronic Technical Section within RAW, while airborne SIGINT operations are conducted by the Aviation Research Centre (ARC) of RAW from Charbatia base just outside Cuttack in Orissa, and Saharanpur in Uttar Pradesh. These operations are targeted primarily at Pakistan and China, but Ball claims there is no reason why they could not also be employed against India's other eastern neighbours.[218] Other SIGINT is collected by Military Intelligence (MI). According to Joshi, the Signals Intelligence Directorate of the MI collects 40% of India's SIGINT collections, mainly targeted on Pakistan.[219] Joshi maintains that there is a serious lack of coordination and integration amongst the various collection organisations and that India's considerable capacity in parallel computation (see above) has not yet been harnessed for SIGINT purposes.[220]

Unlike India's front line fighters, Pakistan's F-16s contain EW suites. This lack of airborne EW capabilities on the part of India will be exacerbated with the acquisition by China of the *Sukhoi*-27 and the possible acquisition of the MiG-31. These aircraft are equipped with an extreme standoff capability that India does not yet possess. Until it can equip its aircraft with active homing air-to-air missiles such as the MICA R-72, it will be dependent on EW to conduct stand-off wide band jamming over tactical areas. It will further require anti-radiation missiles and missile early warning systems.[221] These important lacunae in India's EW capabilities have caused a concerted push in EW.

India's abilities in the area of electronics have generally been helpful in the development of sensing capabilities. India has developed an indigenous omni-directional transmission scanning type sonar, known as the Advanced Panoramic Sonar Hull-Mounted (APSOH) sonar. The latest (1991) version has been fitted into the *Godaveri* class frigate, and this version is evidently to be used on the *Delhi* class destroyer project (Project 15).[222] Other sonar systems either in place or under development include a cylindrical transducer array (in production), a hull-mounted variable depth sonar (under trial—also destined for Project 15 vessels), an airborne sonobuoy receiver processing unit (prototyped), a passive, omni-directional sonobuoy system (in production) and an active-passive homing torpedo.[223] A towed array sonar was under development in 1990. Its current status is unclear.

India is also developing or has developed a range of radars. The most extensive system is a multi-sensor, multi-radar air defence networking system based on the indigenous *Indra* low-level radar, to be centrally linked through sophisticated computer systems via satellite, fibre optics and micro-wave links by 1995, to be developed with the assistance of Thomson-CSF by Bharat Electronics. Many of the *Indra* components of the system are already in place.[224] This system is to be integrated with the data transfer system already developed for the army. The main work for this project is being undertaken at the Defence Electronic Research Laboratory (DRDL) in Hyderabad. Tracking radars and navigation radars for Project 15 (the *Delhi* class destroyer) and Project 16 (the enlarged *Godaveri* frigate) projects will also be indigenously built. The trackers for Project 15 are reportedly Oerlikon-Contraves TMX/Ka dual frequency tracking radars fitted with a TV camera and downlink to the *Trishul* missile (also indigenously built). Project 16 will reportedly have RAWL-02 L-band long-range surveillance radars, RAWS-03 S-band medium range target designation radars and a *Rashmi* X-band navigation and surface search radar. All will be developed by Bharat Electronics from former Signaal radars. Project 16 will also have indigenously developed ESM, infra-red search and track and IFF sensors, all supplied by Bharat Electronics.[225]

Naval shipbuilding

Shipbuilding has generally been one of the more successful of the defence industries in India. India is now able to produce relatively large and sophisticated warships and single-hulled submarines. One of the strengths of the Indian program is the ability to integrate various systems. It is reported that on some vessels India has integrated equipment from as many as eight nations. Moreover, as much as 60-70% of foreign-based equipment is now made in India.[226] Generally, the Indian shipbuilders appear to have performed well in the production of the hulls and fittings of frigates and the Project 15 destroyer. Foreign naval personnel who have inspected *Godaveri* class vessels have been impressed.[227] The indigenous shipbuilders have not been so successful, however, with more complex tasks such as production of submarine hulls and propulsion units. Hindustan Aeronautics was to have produced the GE LM2500-30 gas turbine engine for the Project 15 destroyer. However, a Russian unit will now be used because there were production problems and cost over-runs associated with the LM2500-30. Nor did Mazagon Docks perform well in the production of the Type-209 Class 1500 SSK. Reportedly, not one of the high pressure welds was satisfactory. The initial hull had to be scrapped, and the vessel cost considerably more than an import would have.[228] Yet the cost over-run, variously estimated at between 50% and 20%, should be seen in the context of the devaluation of the rupee in relation to the mark in the course of the contract period.[229] And for all these difficulties, it would appear that India has now obtained both the necessary equipment and skills to construct a single-hulled submarine.

India has three military shipbuilding yards: Mazagon Docks, Bombay; Goa Shipyard Ltd. (which is a subsidiary of Mazagon Docks); and Garden Reach Shipbuilders and Engineers, Calcutta. Almost 70% of the production of Mazagon Docks is for civilian use, including oil rigs for the Oil and Natural Gas Commission.[230] Mazagon docks is nevertheless the largest of the domestic producer of warships, including the indigenous *Godaveri* Class frigate, the Project 15 destroyer (the hull of the first of which was launched in 1991), the license-built Type-209 submarine (built under license from the German firm GDW), the *Khukri* class corvette and a missile boat. The 6500 tonne destroyer will be the largest naval vessel ever built in India. To date two hulls have been completed. The first vessel is scheduled for commissioning in 1995. As well as the EW equipment outlined above, it will be fitted with the *Akash* SAM and the *Trishul* point-defence missile, which will also provide the navy's first AMM capability. In addition, the vessel will be fitted with the Russian SS-N-22 anti-ship missile and two ALH helicopters. Goa Shipbuilders Ltd. produced the licensed *Leander* class frigates and the Soviet *Tarantul* class missile boat, but is noted mainly for ship repairs. It also obtains 30% of its work from the civil sector. Two-thirds of the output of the Garden Reach yards is for the civil sector, mostly cranes, pumps and other machinery.[231] It is noted for construction of supply vessels and transport craft, such as the very large *Magyar* class of vessel.

*

Although India has laid down a strong base for its defence industries in its strategies of industrial and resource development, it has not acquired the technological capability to enable it to perform well in state-of-the-art weapons design and production. This failure partly reflects the autarkic economic and scientific policies described earlier, and it partly reflects the stage India is at in its development. Because of this failure, India has had to rely more heavily on imported technology than it would have liked. Far from having undermined policies of autarky and self-sufficiency, the crisis generated by the collapse of the Soviet Union appears to have reinforced the view that India should persist in the development of its indigenous defence industries. Indeed, the loss of the 'easy option' of cheap Soviet arms appears actually to have strengthened India's determination to gain maximum autonomy. In the next chapter we examine the economic base that underwrites this considerable effort in the defence industries with a view to determining how much support there is likely to be for a continuing thrust into indigenous production and how cuts to defence caused by the economic crisis have affected the capacity of the armed forces.

Endnotes

1   Ron Matthews, *Defence Production in India*, p. 83. Matthews cites G. Kennedy, *The Military in the Third World*, Duckworths, London, 1974.

2   Matthews, *Defence Production in India*, p. 84.

3   Paul Dibb, *Review of Australia's Defence Capabilities*, Australian Government Publishing Service, Canberra, 1986, p. 111, fn. 9.

4   Government of India, *India: Yearbook 1991*, Department of Information and Broadcasting, New Delhi, 1992, p. 580

5   Private source, New Delhi, December 1993.

6   Verbatim transcript of a presentation by Admiral Nayyar to the US Global Strategy Council Forum, Wednesday September 27, 1989, p. 29.

7   *India: Yearbook 1991*, pp. 585-586.

8   *India Today*, 15 November 1990, p. 11; World Bank, *India: 1991 Country Economic Memorandum*, Vol. I, Figure 1.3, p. 14.

9   *India Today*, 15 November 1990, p. 11.

10   World Bank, *India: 1991 Country Economic Memorandum*, Volume 1, pp. 13-14.

11   'Petrol: The Coming Crunch', *India Today*, 15 June 1990, graphs, p. 91.

12   The Indian Institute of Public Opinion, *Monthly Commentary*, Vol. XXX, No. 2, September 1988, 'Blue Supplement', p. III.

13   World Bank, *India: 1991 Country Economic Memorandum*, Vol. II, p. ii.

14   Arun Ghosh, 'Eighth Plan: Challenges and Opportunities—IV', *Economic and Political Weekly*, 23 February 1991, p. 409; Government of India, *Economic Survey 1990-91*, p. 57.

15   Ghosh, 'Eighth Plan—IV', p. 407.

16   Ghosh, 'Eighth Plan—IV', p. 407.

17   Government of India, *Economic Survey 1990-91*, p. 58.

18   Planning Commission, Government of India, *Eighth Five Year Plan 1992-97*, Controller of Publications, New Delhi, 1992, Table 3.18, p. 60.

19   *India: Yearbook 1991*, pp. 639-643.

20   The percentage of GDP figure is at 1986 (Source: *The Asia and Pacific Review 1988* (9th ed.), World of Information Press, Essex, UK, 1987, p. 92.)   For the percentage of manufacturing see Government of India, *Economic Survey 1990-91*, Table 1.32, p. S 38.

21   Sen, Goel and Sengupta, 'Growth of the Indian Steel Industry', in *Metals in India's Development: The Vision of Jawaharlal Nehru*, Ministry of Mines and Steel, Government of India, New Delhi, 1989, Tables 3 and 4, pp. 46-47 and p. 56.

22   Sen, Goel and Sengupta, 'Growth of the Indian Steel Industry', p. 43. To an extent per capita consumption is a distorted measure of the success of industrialisation, both on statistical grounds (see p. 44 of the above article) and on the grounds that higher technologies no longer consume as much steel as they used to.   However, it does have value in the indicative sense.

23   Arvind Pande, 'International Competitiveness and the Indian Steel Industry', *Metals in India's Development*, Table 1, p. 27.   Net of levies, Indian prices are competitive internationally.   See Table 1A p. 28.

24   Sen, Goel and Sengupta, 'Growth of the India Steel Industry', p. 45.

25   Manoj Joshi, 'The indigenous effort', *Frontline*, 13-26 April 1991, p. 50.

26   Sen, Goel and Sengupta, 'Growth of the Indian Steel Industry', p. 53; 'Going gets good for mini steel plants', *The Times of India*, 6 June 1992.

27   *India: Yearbook 1991*, p. 580.

28   R. Venkatanarayanan, 'Iron and Steel—Planning for the Next Decade' in *Metals in India's Development*, p. 10.

29   Steel Authority of India, *19th Annual Report 1990-91*, p. 29.

30   *Xinhua*, as in *Defense News*, Friday 19 June 1992, p. 16.

31   *Seventh Five Year Plan*, Vol. 2 pp. 179-80; D.S. Sethi, 'Non-Ferrous Metals—The Indian Scenario', in *Metals and India's Development*, p. 81; 'Aluminium, cement decontrolled', *Hindustan Times*, 1 March 1989.

32   *Seventh Five Year Plan*, Vol.2 pp. 179-80.

33   *Newsweek* (India supplement), 7 May 1990 (no pagination).

34   Planning Commission, Government of India, *Eighth Five Year Plan 1992-97*, Controller of Publications, New Delhi, 1991, Volume 1, Table 3.31, p. 82.

35   *Seventh Five Year Plan*, Vol. 2, p. 181.

36   *Seventh Five Year Plan*, Vol. 2, p. 181.

37   For a detailed account of this collaboration, see Raja Venkataramani, *Japan Enters Indian Industry: The Maruti-Sazuki Joint Venture*, Radiant Publishers, New Delhi, 1990.

38   Venkataramani, *Japan Enters Indian Industry*, p. 207.

39   *Eighth Five Year Plan*, Vol.1, Table 3.18, p. 61.

40   T.R. Seshadri in the *Economic Times*, 26 July 1989.

41   Admiral R.H. Tahiliani, 'Maritime Strategy for the Nineties', *Indian Defence Review*, July 1989, p. 22.

42   'Cochin Shipyard may build aircraft carriers', *Times of India*, 4 March 1992.

43   Daniel Todd, 'Naval Shipbuilding: prerequisite for rising powers?', *International Defence Review*, No. 3, 1991, p. 229.

44   S.S. Banyal, 'Stagnation mars shipping industry', *Hindustan Times*, 15 January 1989.

45   S.S. Banyal, 'Stagnation mars shipping industry'.

46   There are, in fact, 39 ordnance factories. The existence of one is, however, secret.

47   Jayant Baranwal (Ed.), *Military Yearbook 1990-91*, Guide Publications, New Delhi, 1990, p. 300. Production in the ordnance factories rose to Rs 2651 crore in 1992-93; however, we have no comparable figure for the DPSUs.

48   Baranwal, *Military Yearbook 1990-91*, p. 303 and p. 309.

49   Raju Thomas, *Indian Security Policy*, Princeton, New Jersey, 1986, p. 207.

50   Matthews, *Defence Production in India*, p. 70.

51   Bharat Earth Movers Limited has a larger total turnover, but much of it is involved with non-production imports and exports.

52   Arthur Reed, 'Hindustan Aeronautics: A Force to be Reckoned With In The World Of High-Tech Aerospace', *British Aerospace Quarterly*, Summer 1992, pp. 3-7.

53   Rahul Bedi, 'Indian arms buys defy cash shortfall', *Jane's Defence Weekly*, 8 May 1993, p. 29.

54   Adapted from Matthews, *Defence Production in India*, pp. 76-78.

55   'Bharat Electronics—a growing force in India', *Defence*, Vol. XXI, No. 2, 1990, p. 150.

56   Baranwal (Ed.), *Military Yearbook 1990-91*, p. 325; and 'Unrestrained ambition', *Defense and Foreign Affairs*, Vol. XVIII, No. 4, April 1990, p. 33, interview with Dr Arunachalam.

57   Hindustan Aeronautics Limited, *Annual Report for 1990-91*, p. 11.

58   Bharat Electronics Limited, *37th Annual Report 1990-91*, p. 14.

59   Matthews, *Defence Production in India*, pp. 81-2.

60   The armed forces contain almost 1.3 million people and the paramilitary forces 700,000. There are 177,000 people in the defence productive units and 16,000 scientists in the DRDO. With support staff in the DRDO and MoD officials the total involvement would in fact be over 2.3 million. There are an estimated 23 million people in the organised sector, see Rudolph and Rudolph, *In Pursuit of Lakshmi*, p. 22.

61   Kapur, *Building a Defence Technology Base*, p. 49.

62   Itty Abraham, 'India's Scientific Enclave: Civilian Scientists and Military Technologies', *Armed Forces and Society*, Vol. 18, No. 2, 1992, p. 23.

63   'Industry builds up strength', *Jane's Defence Weekly*, Vol. 13, No. 21, 26 May 1990, p. 1038.

64   Interview, as reported in Gregory Copley, 'India: A New Great Power Arrives', *Defense and Foreign Affairs*, Vol. XVI, No. 12, December 1988, p. 18.

65   'Swords not ploughshares', *The Economist*, 23 March 1991, p. 52, material based on SIPRI. However, the SIPRI figures have been challenged by G. Balachandran in an article discussed in detail below.

66   Rosemary Foot, 'The Sino-Soviet Complex and South Asia', in Barry Buzan and Gower Rizvi, *South Asian Insecurity and the Great Powers*, St Martin's Press, New York, 1986, p. 200.

67   Although India had been negotiating on the *Mirage* from 1979 on, the deal was not finalised until 1982, after the Pakistanis had struck

their deal with the US on acquisition of the F-16 in 1981. The Mig-29 was ordered by India in 1984. See Ian Anthony, *The Arms Trade and Medium Powers: Case Studies of India and Pakistan 1947-1990*, Harvester Wheatsheaf, UK, 1992, Table A1.2, p. 190 and A1.5, p. 199, and p. 125.

68   Anthony, *The Arms Trade and Medium Powers*, p. 125.

69   Ramesh Thakur and Carlyle Thayer, *Soviet Relations with India and Vietnam*, Macmillan, UK, 1992, p. 95.

70   Ramesh Thakur, 'India as a Regional Seapower', *Asian Defence Journal*, No. 5, 1990, p. 16.

71   Rahul Bedi, 'Indian arms buys defy cash shortfall', *Jane's Defence Weekly*, 8 May 1993.

72   Financial restraints were also blamed for the lack of maintenance. See 'In choppy waters', *India Today*, 30 September 1990, p. 145.

73   'Heading for a crisis', *India Today*, 28 February 1989, p. 94.

74   *Vayu Aerospace Review*, III, 1990, p. 3. India was subsequently required to acquire the relevant weapons from Matra.

75   'In deep waters', *Sunday*, 18-24 November 1990, pp. 24-5.

76   See 'Succession Storm', *India Today*, 31 October 1990, pp. 48-55; and Robin Jeffrey, 'Political Admirals: A Neglected Aspect of the Growth of the Indian Navy', forthcoming.

77   Thakur and Thayer, *Soviet Relations with India and Vietnam*, pp. 92-4.

78   Romesh Thakur, 'India as a Regional Seapower', p. 14.

79   Thakur and Thayer, *Soviet Relations with India and Vietnam*, pp. 95-6.

80   Thakur and Thayer, *Soviet Relations with India and Vietnam*, pp. 96-97.

81   Sumitra Chisti, 'Indo-Soviet Economic Relations', in S. Kumar (Ed.), *Yearbook on India's Foreign Policy, 1987-88*, McGraw-Hill, New Delhi, 1988, p. 146.

82   R. Matthews, 'The Development of India's Defence-Industrial Base', *The Journal of Strategic Studies*, Vol. 12, No. 4, December 1898, p. 411.

83   On the trade position generally, see *The Statesman*, Editorial, 24 May 1990. See also Ravi Rikhye, 'Indian Defence Budget: Fact and

Fantasy', *Economic and Political Weekly*, 29 April 1989, p. 907. Rikhye claims that the rouble might be over-valued against the rupee by as much as 400%. See also 'Problems of Parity', *India Today*, 15 February 1992 and Julian Gearing, 'Russian connection revitalized', *Asia-Pacific Defence Reporter*, June-July 1993, p. 27.

84   Calculated from Government of India, *Economic Survey 1990-91*, Table 6.5, page S-76.

85   In 1990 Moscow warned New Delhi that it would accept rupees for only two more years. See Vijay Mahajan, 'Air Force Faces New Problems', *Times of India*, 29 November, 1990.

86   'South Asian Nations Scramble For Arms After Soviet Crackup', *The Washington Post*, 5 January 1992.

87   Hamish McDonald, 'Looking for Friends', *Far Eastern Economic Review*, 19 September 1991, p. 25.

88   'Indo-US defense relations thaw', *International Defence Review*, Vol. 8, 1990, p. 831;   Pravin Sawhney, '200 Soviet guns to be cannibalised', *Times of India*, 22 October 1991.

89   Yashwant Raj, 'India developing N-propulsion technology', *Times of India*, 25 October 1991.

90   Vivek Raghuvanshi, 'Russians ship arms to Asian powers', *Defense News*, October 11-17 1993, p. 11.

91   'India faces critical spares shortage of Soviet arms [sic]', *International Defence Review*, Vol. 12, 1991, p. 1308.

92   Vivek Raghuvanshi, 'Russians ship arms to Asian powers'.

93   'India, USSR talks fruitful', *Times of India*, 17 August 1991.

94   'Russia keen to sell N-sub to India', *Times of India*, 9 March 1992.

95   For the comparative performance in the 1982 war see Ravinderpal Singh, 'Indo-Soviet Military Cooperation: Experiences, Trends and Opportunities', *Strategic Analysis*, December 1990, p. 1087.

96   P.L. Lahkanpal, 'India's N-sub is defective: SIPRI', *Hindustan Times*, 29 May, 1989.

97   Manoj Joshi, 'Sea Power', *Frontline*, 20 December 1991, pp. 5-6.

98   I am indebted to Professor Desmond Ball for the reporting on the alleged Soviet SIGINT facilities. For the Soviet refusal to supply immagery see Amit Gupta, 'Fire in the Sky: The Indian Missile Program', *Defense and Diplomacy*, No. 10, 1990, p. 47.

99   Jyoti Malhotra, 'Russian scientists in ISRO', *Times of India*, 11 July 1992.

100 Andrew Lawler, 'Indian Deal With Russia Brings US Reproaches', *Defence News*, 11-17 May, 1992, p. 10.

101 See R. Jeffrey Smith, 'US, Russia Near Accord On Technology for India, *Washington Post*, 14 July 1993.

102 Anthony Spellman, 'Asians Attracted by Russian Deals', *Armed Forces Journal*, May 1993, p. 16.

103 D. Ravi Kanth, 'Defence purchases from Russia to be whittled down', *Economic Times*, 11 August 1993; Vivek Raghuvanshi, 'Indians Propose Joint Ventures', *Defense News*, 11-17 October 1993.

104 Mohammed Ayoob, *India and South East Asia: Indian Perceptions and Policies*, Routledge, London, 1990, p. 80.

105 C. Raju Mohan, 'India, America and the Gulf', *The Hindu*, 12 February 1991; Submission of G. Balachandran of 21 July 1992 to US Department of Commerce.

106 Presumably on a per annum basis.   See Statement of Howard Schaffer, Deputy Assistant Secretary of State, to the *Subcommittee on Asian and Pacific Affairs, Committee on Foreign Affairs*, US House of Representatives, March 1989, p. 542.

107 'Indo-US defence relations thaw', *International Defense Review*, No. 8, 1990. p. 831; Akhtar Ali, 'A Framework for Nuclear Agreement and Verification', in Stephen Cohen (Ed.), *Nuclear Proliferation in South Asia: The Prospects for Arms Control*, p. 296.   In 1992 all exchanges between US institutions and ISRO were banned following the transfer of rocket engine booster technology from Russia to ISRO.

108 Tim Furniss, 'India aims for polar launcher', *Flight International*, 3-9 June 1992, p. 20.

109 'Speak softly and carry a big stick', *Aerospace*, June 1992, p. 1.

110 Raju Thomas, 'US Transfers of "Dual Use" Technologies to India', *Asian Survey*, Vol. XXX, No. 9, September 1990, Table 3, p. 842.

111 Economist Intelligence Unit, Great Britain, *India, Nepal Country Report*, No. 2, London, 1989, p. 9; 'Pawar's US visit to cement defence ties', *Times of India*, 14 March 1992.

112 'Parwar US visit to boost defence ties', *Sunday Times of India*, 5

April 1991.

113   'US okays radar for Indian navy', *Hindustan Times*, 14 June 1990.

114   Pravin Sawhney, 'India to get US electronic warfare aids', *The Sunday Times*, 3 November 1991. Although this report was widely quoted in the defence media, it is difficult to see how such a substantial amount of money could be spent on passive EW equipment.

115   See 'South Asian Nations Scramble For Arms After the Soviet Crackup', *The Washington Post*, 5 January 1992; 'India to buy US guns', *Sunday Times of India*, 8 March 1992; Anon, 'India's Influence increasing: Pentagon', *The Hindustan Times*, 24 March 1990.

116   For the Pentagon possibilities I am thankful to Ravinderpal Singh of IDSA. For the British connection see 'India looks to Far East arms market', *Reuter Textline*, 2 December 1991.

117   Raju Thomas, 'US Transfers of "Dual Use" Technologies to India', pp. 843-44.

118   'The Jane's Interview', *Jane's Defence Weekly*, 6 November 1993, p. 56.

119   Gregory Copley, 'The Pragmatic Approach', *Defense and Foreign Affairs*, Vol. XVIII, No. 4, April 1990, p. 43.

120   Millhollin, 'India's Missiles—with a little help from our friends', *The Bulletin of the Atomic Scientists*, Vol. 45, No. 9, November 1989, p. 32.

121   Atul Aneja, 'Israel know-how for India?', *The Hindu*, 20 April 1993; Anon, 'Israelis negotiate US $1 bil deals in India', *Aerospace*, November 1992, p. 6.

122   Pravin Sawhney, 'Army equipment to be "mothballed"', *Times of India*, 7 March 1992.

123   Matthews, *Defence Production in India*, p. 87.

124   Matthews, *Defence Production in India*, pp. 51-2 and pp. 87-8; Thomas, *Indian Security Policy*, pp. 203-5; interview, Air Commodore Jasjit Singh (Ret'd), IDSA, New Delhi, 17 October, 1989.

125   Matthews, *Defence Production in India*, p. 89; interview as reported in Gregory Copley, 'India: A New Great Power Arrives', *Defense and Foreign Affairs*, Vol. XVI, No. 12, December 1988, p. 18; *Vayu*

Aerospace Review, No. III, 1990, p. 21; James Clad, 'Power amid poverty', *Far Eastern Economic Review*, 7 June 1990, p. 47.

126 Text of the petition of the Confederation of Engineering Industry to the Government of India, 1990. p. 6.

127 'Arms and the Businessman', *Business India*, 25 June-8 July 1990, p. 87.

128 *Defense and Foreign Affairs*, Vol. XVIII, No. 4, April 1990, p. 30.

129 Shekhar Gupta and Paranjoy Guha Thakurtha, 'Heading for a Crisis', *India Today*, 28 February 1989, pp. 96-97.

130 'Arms and the Businessman', p. 87, and Confederation of Engineering Industry petition, 1990, p. 1.

131 See 'Defence Tech must boost industry', *Times of India*, 9 February 1992.

132 Confederation of Engineering Industry petition, 1990, *passim*.

133 For the difficulties Japan is having in developing its FSX fighter see 'Japan's new Zero the FSX set to fly in 1995', *Australian*, 23 June 1992.

134 'India's last Chance Aircraft—The LCA!', *Vayu*, No. IV, 1990, p.17.

135 'India's Last Chance Aircraft', p. 17. The view that it will be 8.5 tonnes emerged in an interview with Dr Santhanam, Advisor, DRDO, and Dr Harinarayan of the LCA project, New Delhi, December 1991.

136 Hormuz P. Mama, 'India's light combat aircraft', *International Defense Review*, No. 9, 1989, p. 1198.

137 Interview, James Clad, New Delhi, December 1990.

138 See James Clad 'Technical knockout' *Far Eastern Economic Review*, 7 June 1990, p. 48; 'India evaluates new Soviet fighters—LCA may be axed', *Aerospace*, August 1991, p. 4.

139 Government of India (Commercial), *Report of the Comptroller and Auditor General of India*, Part VIII, HAL LTD, New Delhi, 1987.

140 Mama, 'India's light combat aircraft', p. 1199; Rahul Bedi, 'Collaboration invited for LCA programme', *Jane's Defence Weekly*, 29 January 1994, p.4.

141 Suresh Kalmadi, Starred Question in the Rajya Sabha, No 24, to be answered on 27 March 1990 (uncorrected—not for publication).

142 Dilip Mukerjee, 'LCA A White Elephant', *Times of India*, 21

January 1992.

143   Compiled from a large number of sources.

144   Ministry of Commerce, *Indian Trade Journal*, 8 February 1989, p. A 446-A-447, gives an extensive list of authorities that may import items duty free for the LCA.

145   Chris Smith, 'Indecision may clip LCA's wings', *Jane's Defence Weekly*, 12 August 1989, p. 251-2.

146   Smith, 'Indecision may clip LCA's wings', p. 253.

147   Hamish McDonald, 'India: Iron Rations', *Far Eastern Economic Review*, 2 September 1993, p. 22.

148   Air Commodore Jasjit Singh (Ret'd), director of IDSA, is one who recognises the value of the LCA from this perspective. Interview with the author, New Delhi, October 1990. At that time, however, Singh would have preferred to see an upgrade of the MiG-21 using US systems. See David Silverberg, 'India Pushes Indigenous Combat Aircraft Despite Delays', *Defense News*, 18 November 1991, p. 30.

149   Interview conducted by David Silverberg with Arunachalam, *Defense News*, 24 February 1992, p. 86.

150   Interview with Manoj Joshi, New Delhi, October 1990.

151   David Silverberg, 'India Pushes Indigenous Combat Aircraft', p. 30.

152   Interview, New Delhi, December 1991.

153   Sanjiv Prakash, 'Indian Defense: A Conscious Attempt at Pragmatism', *Defense and Foreign Affairs*, Vol. XVIII, No. 4, April 1990, p. 43 and various other sources.

154   See Pravin Sawhney, 'Arjun—a tank full of faults', *Times of India*, 27 March 1992.

155   See interview of David Silverberg with Arunachalam, *Defense News*, 24 February 1992, p. 86; Indian Express report, as in *Defense News*, 23 March 1993, p. 14; see also Kanwar Sandhu, 'MBT Arjun: On Course, Finally', *India Today*, 15 July 1993, pp. 67-8; Hamish McDonald, 'Iron Rations: Armed forces face lean times as money runs short', *Far Eastern Economic Review*, 2 September 1993, p. 22. For a more positive account of the rectification of the power loss problem see *Asia-Pacific Defence Reporter*, October-November 1993, p. 21.

156   This amount of 'sanctioned' expenditure is given by Manoj Joshi. See 'The Indigenous Effort', *Frontline*, 13-26 April 1991, p. 51.

157   Manoj Joshi, 'The indigenous Effort', *Frontline*, 13-26 April 1991, p. 51; Anon, 'Improved Prithvi missile launched', *International Defence Review*, No. 8, 1992, p. 784.

158   'Prithvi launched successfully', *Times of India*, 6 May 1992.

159   Interview with Dr Santhanam, Advisor, DRDO, New Delhi, December 1991 for the comments concerning Prithvi's accuracy. However, see Pravin Sawhney, 'Prithvi deployment unlikely by '93', *Times of India*, 7 May 1992, for the higher CEP of 300 m.

160   The foregoing description is taken from the following sources, *inter alia*: Hormuz P. Mama 'Progress on India's new tactical missiles', *International Defense Review*, No 7, 1989, pp. 963-4; Andrew Hull, 'The Role of Ballistic Missiles in Third World Defence Strategies', *Jane's Intelligence Review*, October 1991, p. 467; IDR Research Team, 'Weapons and equipment state; Are we getting our money's worth?', *Indian Defence Review*, July 1988, p. 145; K. Ravi, 'The Military Implications of India's Space Programme: Some Observations', *Defense Analysis*, Vol. 5, No. 3, 1989, p. 269; Joshi, 'The Indigenous Effore, *Frontline*, 13-16 April 1991, p. 51; Pravin Sawhney, 'Prithvi deployment unlikely by '93', *Times of India*, 7 May 1992; 'Prithvi launched successfully', *Times of India*, 5 May 1992; and 'India deploys new missile at border', *Asian Defence Journal*, No. 7, 1993, p. 81.

161   IDR Research Team, 'Weapons and equipment state', p. 145.

162   Hormuz Mama, 'Improved Prithvi missile launched', *International Defense Review*, No. 8, 1992.

163   Milhollin, 'India's missiles: with a little help from our friends', p. 32.

164   Dilip Bobb and Amarnath K. Menon, 'Chariot of Fire', *India Today*, 15 June 1989, p. 28.

165   Amit Gupta, 'Fire in the Sky', *Defense and Diplomacy*, October 1990, p. 44; see also an interview with Dr Arunachalam by Gregory Copley, 'Unrestrained Ambition', *Defense and Foreign Affairs*, Vol. XVIII, No. 4, April 1990, p. 32.

166   Pravin Sawhney, 'Agni-II failure no setback', *Times of India*, 1 June 1992.

167   For reports that terminal guidance was tested see *The Hindu* (International Edition), 'Missile programme crosses milestone', February 26 1994. But see also Tim McCarthy, 'India's Missile program: Part I', *Asian Defence Review*, September 1993, p. 17, for the view that the technology would be difficult for India to acquire.

168   Milhollin, 'India's missiles: with a little help from our friends', p. 32.

169   Milhollin, 'India's missiles', p. 34.

170   *Indian Express*, 10 July 1989.

171   'US firms accused of giving N-tech to India', *Times of India*, 31 July 1993.

172   See interviews with V.P. Singh (then Prime Minister) and Raja Ramanna (then Minister of State for Defence), *Defense and Foreign Affairs*, Vol. XVIII, No. 4, April 1990, p. 20 and p. 23.

173   This position was put to the author by Dr Santhanam, Advisor, DRDO, New Delhi, 1991.

174   Manoj Joshi, 'India's "Technology Demonstration" Strategy', draft paper delivered at the Research School of Pacific Studies, Australian National University, Canberra, November 1992, pp. 2-4.

175   Interview, Santhanam, 1991.

176   Kalam quoted in Edmond Dantes, 'Missiles in Gulf Buoy India's Development Drive', *Defense News*, 25 February 1991. See also *Asia-Pacific Defence Reporter*, May 1991, p. 22.

177   *The Hindu* (International Edition), Saturday 25 August 1990.

178   Anon, '"No clandestine deal with U.K. firm": Parwar', *The Hindu*, 18 August 1992.

179   'Trishul: Fulfilling triple battle roles', *Times of India*, 4 November 1991; Joshi, 'The Indigenous Effort', *Frontline*, 13-16 April 1991, p. 51.

180   *Asia-Pacific Defence Reporter*, May 1991, p. 22. See also 'Nag missile test successful', *Times of India*, 30 November 1990.

181   Joshi, 'The indigenous Effort', *Frontline*, 13-16 April 1991, pp. 51-3.

182   'Nag missile test successful', *Times of India*, 30 November 1990; Joshi, 'The Indigenous Effort'.

183   Matthews, 'India's Defence-Industrial Base', p. 423.

184 Joshi, 'The Indigenous Effort', box, pp. 52-3.

185 Gary Milhollin, 'India's missiles—with a little help from our friends', pp. 32-33.

186 See for example a speech by Admiral K.K. Nayyar (Ret'd) to the US Global Strategy Council Forum, 27 September 1989, Verbatim Transcript, p. 30, confirmed in an interview by the author with Admiral Nayyar, New Delhi, October 1990. A similar point was made by Commander Bhaskar of IDSA in an interview with the author, New Delhi, October 1990.

187 Written testimony of Robert A. Peck before the Subcommittee on Asian and Pacific Affairs, US House of Representatives, 18 February 1988, p. 23 (p. 13 of Peck's testimony).

188 Ministry of Defence, Government of India, *Annual Report 1989-90*, p. 18.

195 'In the dock', *The Illustrated Weekly of India*, 28 May 1989, p. 22.

196 Manoj Joshi, 'Undersea thrust', *Frontline*, 20 December 1991, pp. 9-10 and interviews, New Delhi, December 1991.

191 Interview, Dr Santhanam, Advisor, DRDO, New Delhi, December 1991.

192 Interview with Western officials, New Delhi.

193 Quoted in Spector, *The Undeclared Bomb: The Spread of Nuclear Weapons, 1987-88*, Carnegie Endowment for International Peace, Ballinger, Cambridge, Massachusetts, 1988, p. 85.

194 Quoted by Dilip Mukerjee in the *Times of India*, 7 January 1990. Mukerjee in turn quotes an interview with Sunderji in *India Today* which took place in August 1990.

195 Mukerjee, *Times of India*, 7 January 1990.

196 Brahma Chellaney, 'Regional Proliferation: Issues and Challenges' in Stephen P. Cohen, *Nuclear Proliferation in South Asia: The Prospects for Arms Control*, Westview, Boulder, Colorado, 1991, p. 299, in reference to an article by Steven R. Weissman in the *New York Times* of 17 May 1988.

197 As reported by Gautam Adhikari, 'India, Pak have N-arms parts', *Times of India*, 17 January 1992.

198 'US confirms Pak has N-device', *Times of India*, 16 January 1992.

199 Bill Gertz, 'India, Pakistan cited in spread of nuclear arms', *The*

Washington Times, 31 October 1992.

200   David Albright, Frans Berkhout and William Walker, *World Inventory of Plutonium and Highly Enriched Uranium 1992*, SIPRI, OUP, Oxford, 1993, pp. 160-61. For the calculation based on 6 kg see David Albright and Mark Hibbs, 'India's Silent Bomb', *Bulletin of the Atomic Scientists*, September 1992, (as in US Department of Defense *Supplement*, September 3 1992, p. B-16).

201   Albright, Berkhout and Walker, *World Inventory of Plutonium ...*', p. 161.

202   Albright, Berkhout and Walker, *World Inventory of Plutonium ...*', p. 162.

203   Albright and Zamora, 'India, Pakistan's nuclear weapons', *Bulletin of the Atomic Scientists*, Vol. 45, No. 5, June 1989, p. 26.

204   Albright, Berkhout and Walker, *World Inventory of Plutonium*, pp. 107-8.

205   Albright and Hibbs, 'India's Silent Bomb', p. B 17.

206   From discussion with a former senior scientist from Los Alamos, USA.

207   Major K.C. Praval, *Indian Army After Independence*, Lancer International, New Delhi, 1990, p. 319.

208   Pravin Sawhney, 'Army Aviation Corps yet to take off', *Times of India*, 27 May 1992.

209   Ravi Kikhye, *The War That Never Was*, Prism India Paperbacks, New Delhi 1989, p. 170.

210   IDR Research Team, 'Weapons and equipment state: Are we getting our money's worth?', p. 141.

211   IDR Research Team, 'Weapons and equipment state: Are we getting our money's worth?', p. 149.

212   Jeffrey T. Richelson, 'US Space Reconnaissance after the Cold War', Desmond Ball and Helen Wilson (Eds.), *Australia and Space*, Canberra Papers on Strategy and Defence, No. 94, Strategic and Defence Studies Centre, Research School of Pacific Studies, Australian National University, November 1992, p. 111.

213   *Asia-Pacific Defence Reporter*, June-July 1992, p. 25.

214   Prasun Sengupta, 'Indian satellites find military uses', *Aerospace*, April 1992, p. 7.

215 Prasun Sengupta, 'China Expands Air Forces', *Military Technology*, No. 8, 1992, p. 54.

216 Prasun Sengupta, 'China Expands Air Forces', p. 55.

217 'Phased array radar developed', *Statesman*, 2 March 1993; 'India's ASWAC spotted in the open', *Jane's Defence Weekly*, 14 August 1993, p. 7; Bernard Blake (Ed.), *Jane's Radars and Electronic Warfare Systems 1992-93*, Fourth Edition, Jane's Information Group, UK, 1992, p. 221.

218 Details are from Desmond Ball, *Signals Intelligence in the Post-Cold War Era, Developments in the Asia-Pacific Region*, Regional Strategic Studies Programme, Institute of Southeast Asian Studies, Singapore, 1993, pp. 73-5.

219 Manoj Joshi, 'Signal Wars: Indian capability in perspective', *Frontline*, 10 September 1993, p. 76.

220 Joshi, 'Signal wars', p. 78. Probably Indian parallel arrays are not yet large enough to fulfil the SILGINT role.

221 Prasun Sengupta, 'China Expands Air Forces', p. 54.

222 Jim Bussert, 'Sonars of the Indian Navy', *Jane's Intelligence Review*, November 1992, p. 511.

223 'Principal Indian Defense R&D Establishments', *Defense and Foreign Affairs*, Vol XVIII, No. 4, April 1990, p. 41.

224 *Asia-Pacific Defence Reporter*, July 1990, p. 28, report of a speech by Director of the Weapons System of the DRDL.

225 'India builds by numbers', *Jane's Defence Weekly*, 16 January 1993.

226 James C. Bussert, 'India's Navy Blends Eastern and Western Ships, Systems', *Signal*, Vol. 48, No. 4, December 1993, p. 41.

227 The INS *Godaveri* visited Sydney in 1988 and was inspected by Australian naval personnel. Private conversations with the author.

228 'Soviets offer Sierra SSN but Indians eye Oscar SSGNs', *Navy News and Undersea Technology*', 6 May 1991, p. 1, as in *Current News Supplement*, 21 May 1991, p. B 14. See also John Jordan, 'India: The Indian Navy—Major Expansion Ahead', *Jane's Intelligence Review*, Vol. 3, No. 7, July 1991, p. 297; 'First Indian-built submarine commissioned', *International Defence Review*, No. 4, 1992, p. 386.

229 Hormuz P. Mama, 'India's naval future: fewer ships, but better',

International Defense Review, No. 2, 1993, p. 162.

230   Matthews, 'The Development of India's Defence-Industrial Base, p. 414.

231   Matthews, 'The Development of India's Defence-Industrial Base', p. 414; see also Daniel Todd, 'Naval Shipbuilding', p. 233.

3 The Economy and Defence

Given the rapidly escalating cost of modern weapons systems, the capacity of economies to generate sufficient surpluses to sustain comprehensive programs of military modernisation has become a critical determinant of modern military power. An associated question is the degree of efficiency with which a defence establishment is able actually to utilise resources available to it. This latter issue becomes especially important in a period of fiscal stringency such as the one through which India is currently passing. These key aspects of the relationship between the economy and defence form the subject of the present chapter.

India's economic crisis

Before the mid-1970s, India's economy was encapsulated within the so-called 'Hindu' rate of economic growth of 3.5%.[1] Indian policy makers argued that, given the nation's large population of people living a marginal existence, it was required to trade off growth with equity. They also feared that more rapid growth would have to occur at the expense of India's cherished economic self-sufficiency.[2] The Tiananmen Square episode in China in 1989 seemed to lend weight to the official Indian view that there was a need to balance growth with equity to achieve stability. As recently as 1990, the proponents of command economics and a slower rate of growth seemed firmly entrenched. What went wrong?

Following the mid-1970s, the growth rate had risen to 4.5% and the underlying growth rate in the 1980s was 5.5%. Under the reforms implemented by Rajiv Gandhi in 1985-86, investment barriers were lifted, tariff controls were substituted for quantitative controls in trade, a VAT was introduced to simplify the complex system of indirect taxes, the foreign equity ceiling was raised to 49% and a number of other measures were introduced.[3]

Economists on the Left argued that the 1985-86 reforms led to an import blowout to fuel rising consumption by the new rich.[4] However, what the data suggest is that since the mid-1980s, India has been much better placed to cover its imports—in fact coverage went up from only 51.8% in 1985-86 to 93% in 1989-90.[5] The position is illustrated by the following figure.

Figure 1.7: Imports and exports between 1987-88 and 1990-91, in crore of rupees.

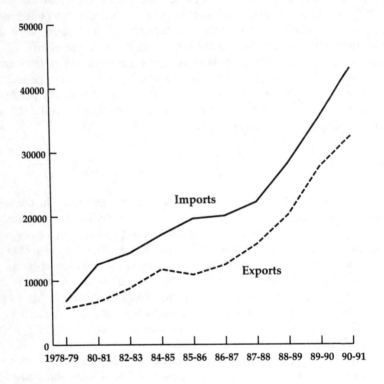

Source: Derived from *Economic Survey 1990-91*.

The reforms of 1985, however, failed to address the issue of rising recurrent expenditure and falling investment on the part of the government, as illustrated by Figure 1.8 below.

Within this rising pattern of non-productive expenditure, defence rose from 15.9% of central government spending in 1980-81 to a high point of 16.9% in 1987-88, but thereafter fell to 15% in 1989-90 (revised estimate).[6] Interest payments rose from 10% of central government outlays in 1980-81 to nearly 19% (budget estimate) in 1990-91. Subsidies rose from 8.5% in 1980-81 to 11.5% in 1989-90, but fell in the budget estimate for 1990-91 under the program of adjustment introduced at the behest of the IMF.[7]

Figure 1.8: Consumption, investment and government spending as a percentage of GNP, 1960-61 to 1989-90.

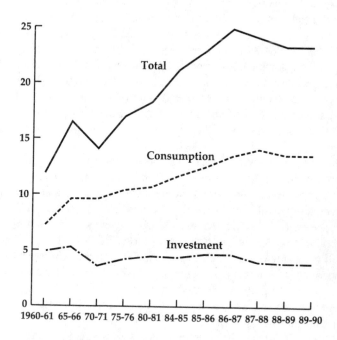

Source: Derived from B.B. Bhattacharya, *India's Economic Crises, Debt Burden and Stabilisation*, B.R. Publishing Corporation, New Delhi, 1992, Table 5.3, p. 104.

One of the reasons that interest payments rose to such an extent was that more and more of the government's borrowings were accruing at commercial rather than concessional rates, and more and more government investment was financed by borrowing rather than saving.[8] One consequence was that the debt servicing ratio rose from 9.4% in 1980-81 to 23.3% in 1987-88. Thereafter it declined to about 21%, at which point it has remained steady. While debt itself as a proportion of GDP continues to rise, since 1989 external commercial borrowings have remained virtually static in proportion to GDP because of the concessional finance provided by the IMF.[9]

The increase in non-productive government spending during the 1980s and the consequent sharp rise in the budget deficit was also an important factor in the rising level of inflation experienced in the latter years of the 1980s and early 1990s. Politically, India is extremely sensitive to inflation.

The sharp rise in prices that occurred in 1979 is considered an important factor in the downfall of the Janata government.[10] By 1990-91, inflation had increased to over 13%.[11]

Despite the reforms of the mid-1980s, throughout the latter part of the decade the percentage of trade in relation to GNP had actually been falling from 12.4% in 1984/85 to 11% in 1988/89.[12] The restrictive nature of the trading regime stemmed both from very high sets of tariffs (they averaged 125%, as compared with China's 90%), but more particularly from the extremely complex licensing regime imposed on imports, which had not been significantly modified under the reforms of the mid-1980s. The Indian economy was thus still one of the most closed in the world by the end of the 1980s.

While this low level of trade was not a problem in normal times, it allowed no flexibility in terms of India's increasing requirement for petroleum products to fuel its industrialisation. Given the small percentage of the economy involved in trade, there was little scope to cushion any rises in the price of oil within the overall trade balance. For example, the comparatively modest oil price rise that accompanied the 1990-91 crisis in the Gulf translated into a 21.9% increase in the import bill in rupee terms.[13] The extent of the emerging problem is discernible from the fact that in 1965 India's energy imports constituted only about 8% of the value of its merchandise exports, whereas by 1990 energy imports constituted nearly 25% of the value of exports.[14]

Additionally, India also lost remittances of some $205 million from Indians employed in Iraq and Kuwait as a result of the 1990-91 Gulf crisis; it lost an amount of $500 million owing to it from Iraq at the start of the crisis; and it lost about $112 million in trade with Iraq and Kuwait.[15] At the same time, trade with the old East bloc had suffered severely with the collapse of that system and the end of communism. Consequently, by mid-1991, foreign exchange reserves had fallen to only enough to cover two weeks' imports and India was forced to go cap-in-hand to the IMF.[16]

Economic liberalisation

India had borrowed $4 billion from the IMF in the early 1980s in response to the 1979-80 oil crisis. On that occasion the debt was repaid on schedule. On this latest occasion the crisis was far more serious. The borrowings were larger and the position from which the funds had to be paid back was more precarious because of the high public debt and debt servicing ratio. The necessity for fresh concessional finance and grants was much greater: in fact concessional finance will amount to $6.7 billion once fully disbursed.

Consequently, the Banks imposed a set of harsh conditions on India. The Government has moved to fulfil these conditions through a series of measures introduced in budgets since 1991-91. These measures now include:

- initially, devaluation of the rupee by about 30% against the US dollar, with the aim of achieving full convertibility;
- raising the ceiling of foreign ownership to 51% and higher in some instances, with partial repatriation of capital at market rates on a 60:40 basis (with 40% being at the government rate);
- removal of restrictive controls on the import of most items and lowering of the tariff. The import duty on capital goods was recently further reduced to 35% from 55%, with a special 25% rate on capital goods destined for priority sectors. The import weighted tariff is to be reduced to 25% in two to three years;
- abolition of the internal licensing system in all but 18 industries;
- preparation for sale in principle of up to 49% of the government's share in state enterprises;
- in 1993, the floating of the rupee on trade accounts;
- reduction of the excise duty;
- reform of the financial sector; and
- in 1994, a substantial reduction in the rate of company taxation.

These reforms constituted, in the words of *The Economist*, 'not a bonfire of controls, but still a healthy blaze.' *The Economist* felt that the government could have done better in four key areas of reform: the labour market, the financial system, agriculture and its own finances.[17] Moreover, while many of the reforms have taken place on paper, implementation has proved more difficult. For example, although the rupee is supposedly convertible on trade accounts, it is difficult in practice to buy foreign exchange because of the limited number of licensed dealers. Nor has the size of the public sector been significantly reduced.

Moreover, due to political restraints, the government's deficit reduction program has not been fully sustained. The government intended to cut the deficit from 8.5% of GDP to 6.5% in 1992-93 and 5.5% in the following year. In order to accomplish this task, it took the politically sensitive step of lowering the subsidy on fertilisers such that the cost of fertilisers rose by 30%. Food and export subsidies were also cut. In the 1992-93 budget a range of cuts were imposed on poverty alleviation schemes, rural water supply and electrification and education. These cuts were reversed in the 1993 budget, however, but with a re-alignment in favour of basic needs programs in education, health and welfare and away from poverty programs such as the now discredited Integrated Rural Development Program (IRDP). Given these restorations, in the latter part of 1993, money supply was rising rapidly and double-digit inflation was again a possibility. It remains to be seen whether this problem can be removed in the aftermath of the 1993 state elections. The problem of the central government's deficit is exacerbated by ill-discipline in the states. Since the state governments are nearer to the grass-roots, they have been tempted to maintain high subsidy regimes, especially in the power sector, and this could jeopardise the reform program itself if it is not rectified.[18]

In order to reduce inflation, the government tightened the money supply markedly, such that growth fell from an underlying rate of 5.5% to 2.5% in 1991-92. Real interest rates remain high at about 10% and inflation initially dropped to 6.5%.

The reforms have not so far released a flood of actual foreign investment into the country. However, approvals (as distinct from actual in-flows) now amount to over $4 billion. Part of the lag between approvals and in-flows is due to the continuing drag imposed by the Indian bureaucracy. But part also is due to the long-maturation periods of the investments in train, which fall heavily in major infrastructure projects and the chemical/petrochemical sector. Leading investors are the United States, with 43% of investment, Switzerland (13.5%), Japan, (8.5%) and the United Kingdom (6.4%).[19] Moreover, to a significant degree the lack of actual foreign investment response has been offset by a most impressive performance in domestic investment in the order of $10 billion over 1992-93, which represents a rise of 218% over the past two years. According to L.K. Jha, this investment surge would lead to a growth rate of 8-9%, if sustained.[20]

Foreign exchange holdings are currently high due to access to concessional finance, but also to an impressive export performance in the second half of 1993. Debt is currently estimated at $79 billion and expected to rise to $84 billion in 1994. This should remain sustainable at around 31% of GDP, before falling toward the end of the decade.[21] Although productivity is dragged down by the poor performance of the public sector, savings at about 25% of GDP are high. Savings are likely increasingly to be dominated by the private sector, and this should ensure greater productivity in future years.[22]

The IMF, World Bank, ADB and the US investment firm Merril Lynch all believe that, by the mid-1980s, growth will again resume at least at the level of the 1980s, with Merril Lynch holding the position that in the next two years it may go as high as 8%.[23]   A recent Australian government report predicts an average growth rate of 6.3% over the next decade.[24] These optimistic projections would appear to be well on the way to being realised, with growth for 1993-94 being 4% and anticipated growth for 1994-95 being 5%.

Overall the reforms have been conducted with some care and skill and prospects for the economy must be considered good, so long as political stability can be maintained and reform-minded governments remain in office—an issue we address in Part II, below.

The economic crisis and defence

Throughout the decade of the 1980s, Indian defence expenditure began to rise in real terms. Data from the US Arms Control and Disarmament Agency (ACDA) suggesting the pattern of expenditure between India, China, and Pakistan during the course of the 1980s are illustrated in Figure 1.9 below.

With hindsight, it is possible to see that at least some of the rapid rise in Indian defence spending was due to the need to pay for a series of purchases made early in the decade against the background of the steady fall in the value of the rupee, the costs of the intervention in Sri Lanka, and the rapid rise in the cost of military manpower. Nevertheless, a considerable portion of additional spending was 'un-accounted for' by these factors. As such, it caused concern amongst a number of India's neighbours.

In recent years, however, the squeeze on government spending resulting from the economic crisis triggered a series of substantial cuts in the defence budget. The balance of payments crisis also caused a severe blockage in the importation of those weapons systems and items that India could not produce locally. This latter problem was exacerbated by Moscow's decision to demand hard currency for defence exports.

Yet the extent of the cuts has tended to be exaggerated by commentators. The issue is clouded by the fact that the official statistic on defence spending are understated. It is also difficult to assess the effects of losses on currency exchange and inflation. Furthermore, the impact of the cuts on India's long-term security objectives needs to be assessed in light of the actual strategies employed in translating budget cuts into patterns of expenditure. It is these aspects of the cuts that we now turn to assess.

*

The statistics used by international commentators tend to be most seriously flawed in their assessment of the effect of exchange variations. For reasons of international comparison, total defence spending is frequently translated into US dollars without any consideration of the actual amount accrued in country.

In the case of India, the evidence suggests that foreign exchange still constitutes only a relatively minor proportion of total defence spending. While the translation of the total amount into dollars for comparative purposes does not matter so much within a particular year (although even here it tends to underestimate the defence effort of 'soft currency' nations such as India), it causes severe distortions in the calculation of rises and falls over time.[25]

Figure 1.9: Comparative defence expenditures and military force levels, China, India and Pakistan

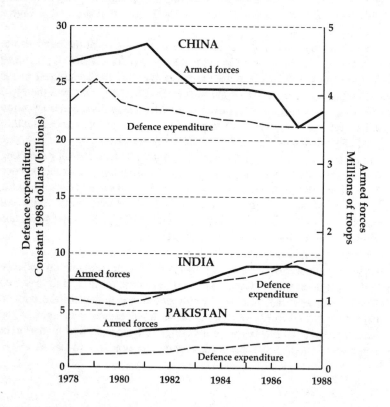

Source: US Congress, Office of Technology Assessment, *Global Arms Trade*, Government Accounting Office, Washington DC, 1991, Fig. 10-1, p. 153.

For example, we have calculated elsewhere that the imputed 'loss' on hard currency exchange due to the fall in the value of the rupee would be only 3.4% of total defence spending for the entire 1981-82 to 1990-91 period.[26] In addition to these hard currency losses, however, we must also factor in at least some losses in terms of the rupee-rouble exchange. For bilateral trade purposes the rupee deteriorated against the rouble from Rs9 to the rouble in 1978 to Rs36 by 1991, notwithstanding the fact that the rouble declined in value far more than the rupee.[27] This meant that for individual years in the 1980s India would have suffered at least some exchange loss on its rouble transactions. Such losses are, however, likely to be significantly reduced as a result of the setting of an exchange rate for settling of the balance of India's outstanding debt to the CIS at a rate considerably below Rs36 to the rouble.

Nevertheless, what the above figures suggest is that there has been a tendency amongst almost all commentators to discount Indian defence spending too heavily on account of exchange. The argument here is somewhat analogous to the one about purchasing power parity (PPP) in calculating the overall size of an economy. The important fact to note is that most Indian defence spending is still conducted in rupees. To translate it into US dollars at a time when the rupee is declining rapidly in value is to give a highly distorted picture.

While the burden of foreign exchange fluctuations on defence spending has been over-stated, it must be acknowledged that the burden of defence-related hard currency spending viewed in the context of the balance of payments crisis through which India has been passing is far more serious than its rupee effect within the defence budget would suggest. What we see here is that in 1990-91, the last year for which we have hard data (the CRS figure), the hard currency burden incurred by defence constituted some 14.8% of the nation's hard currency earnings, or 25% of the visible trade gap with hard currency countries.[28] This certainly constitutes a very significant burden.

One report asserted that, in the 1991-92 budget, the defence forces request for funding to cover $1 billion in hard currency was arbitrarily cut by the government to $0.6 billion, which only left $200,000 for new purchases after existing contracts had been serviced and POL products purchased.[29] The shortage of hard currency that resulted reportedly caused Hindustan Aeronautics Limited to cease production on the *Jaguar* assembly line in 1991. Vital equipment required by Bharat Electronics, but unavailable because of the shortage of foreign exchange, reportedly reduced the delivery of radars by 75% and delayed the Advanced Light Helicopter project.[30] Moreover, the fact that Russia will from now on require payment for defence items on a hard currency basis means that the hard currency component of defence spending borne by India will rise significantly.

Another factor that needs to be accounted for in examining Indian defence spending is that a considerable amount of spending is obscured in the official statistics, as indeed it is in countries like China and Pakistan. In fact, we have calculated elsewhere that if all items that would normally be regarded as part of a nation's defence effort were included in the defence budget, the total defence spending would be higher by about 20% of the defence budget as it is more usually presented by the government.[31]

Table 1.8: Defence expenditure not normally attributed to the defence head (in crore of rupees), 1991-92 (revised estimate).

Head	Department	Amount
Administration	Defence	235.93
Pensions	Defence	1840.00
Paramilitary*	Home Affairs	1008.00
Border roads	Surface Transport	172.29
Air traffic	Civil Aviation	#
Nuclear	Atomic Energy	#
Space	Space	#
Electronics+	Electronics	13.64

Source: Budget Papers 1992-93, revised estimates for 1991-92.
*   Includes Assam Rifles, Border Security Force and Indo-Tibetan Border Force.
\#   Indicates that an amount cannot be attributed within the overall departmental expenditure.
+   Includes National Radar Council Projects, Centre for Development of Advanced Computing, applied microwave research and Photonics Development Program, but does not include those items 'sold' to the DPSUs, the ordnance factories and armed forces (to avoid double counting).

In terms of the relationship between defence spending and GDP, when the additional expenditure is accounted for in the way described above, the position is shown in the Table 1.9, below.

Several observations are in order concerning this table. First, if we factor in additional costs not usually recorded as part of defence spending by the government, defence spending as a percentage of GDP is considerably higher than the official figures would suggest.[32]   It is, however, somewhat lower than the level suggested by commentators such as Rikhye, who placed it at its high point at 5% of GDP for 1988-89.[33] Secondly, on the basis of these figures, it would appear   that defence spending as a percentage of GDP has not fallen in recent years as much as the government asserts that it has.[34]

Table 1.9: Indian defence expenditure in current prices, GDP at current prices, defence expenditure inflated to include items not in the official statistics and defence expenditure as a percentage of GDP, 1981-82 to 1993-94 (crore of rupees).

Year	Defence (current)	GDP (current)	Defence (+ 20%)	% GDP
1981-82	4327	142876	5192	3.6
1982-83	5408	158851	6490	4.1
1983-84	5823	185991	6988	3.8
1984-85	6661	208577	7993	3.8
1985-86	7987	233476	9584	4.1
1986-87	10477	259055	12572	4.9
1987-88	11967	333200	14360	4.3
1988-89	13341	396200	16009	4.0
1989-90	(RE)14416	454000	17299	3.8
1990-91	(RE)15750	530900	18900	3.6
1991-92	(RE)16350	609500	19620	3.2
1992-93	(RE)17500	(E)700437	21133	3.0
1993-94	(BE)19180	(E)786941	23016	2.9

Sources: Government of India, *Defence Services Estimates* for respective years for defence spending; Institute for Defence Studies and Analysis, *Asian Strategic Review 1992-93*, IDSA, New Delhi, 1993, Table 2.7, pp 42-3 for GDP. GDP figures for 1992-93 and 1993-94 are based on rough estimates.
NOTE: The official figures for defence spending have been inflated by 20% for all years except 1991-92 and 1992-93, which are based on the actual expenditure projected or incurred including extra items, as in the Budget Papers for 1992-93.

However, the reason for the differing effect against GDP between the official and inflated figures (i.e. those inflated by 20% in the table above) relates mostly to the rise in the percentage of expenditure on the paramilitary and on defence pensions, items which have not been included in the official figures. Neither of these heads of expenditure enhances the power projection capabilities of the nation in relation to more distant regions.

In real terms, then, defence spending has been falling in recent years, although not as much as suggested by a direct translation of the rupee expenditure into hard currency. Table 1.10, below, provides a summary of the effect of exchange movements and inflation on defence spending. We can see that there was a plateau in real defence spending in 1989-90 and a decline thereafter. The percentage of spending commanded by hard currency transactions went up somewhat throughout the decade, but not to a significant degree. The burden of the foreign exchange loss relative to the movement in real spending, however, became more serious towards the end of the decade, more than cancelling out the rise in real spending in 1988-89, and in effect adding to the decline in real spending that occurred thereafter.

Table 1.10: Change in real defence spending, by percent, expenditure on hard currency exchange as a percentage of total defence spending, and 'loss' attributable to fall in value of the rupee over the previous year, expressed as a percentage of total current spending, 1981-82 to 1991-92.

Year	Total defence real growth (%)	Hard currency (% total defence)	Loss on foreign exchange (%tot)
1981-82	-	8.3	1.7
1982-83	19.2	10.1	0.7
1983-84	0.1	7.7	0.5
1984-85	7.4	6.5	0.9
1985-86	14.9	11.7	0.3
1986-87	24	12.2	0.5
1987-88	5.5	12.3	0.2
1988-89	3.7	11.6	1.2
1989-90	0.6	12.3	1.6
1990-91	(RE)-0.9	11.9	0.9
1991-92	(RE)*-5.0	N/A	N/A
1992-93	(BE)*-5.3	N/A	N/A

Sources: WPI increase: *Economic Survey 1990-91*, Table 5.1, p. S-61, (av. of weeks); defence spending, as in column 4, Table 2.9, above; arms imports, ACDA figures (with CRS for 1990-91), as in Balachandran, 'India's Defence Expenditure', in *Strategic Analysis*, September 1991, Table 3, p. 1053 (translated into the hard currency component at 40% and then as a percentage of current defence spending, from a translation to rupees at the current rates as in *Economic Survey 1990-91*, Table 6.5, p. 84). The ACDA figures for exchange have been chosen in preference to SIPRI or Balachandran as a more realistic compromise between the two and because they are expressed in current dollars. The figures are then expressed in rupees at current exchange rates.
*   Denotes rough estimates based on a WPI increase of about 12% for 1991-92 and 13% for 1992-93.

The effect of the cuts

Within total defence spending, the share between the three forces immediately before and during the period of stringency was as follows:

Table 1.11:   Division of resources between the three forces, with percentage share of total attributed defence spending in parentheses, 1985-86 to 1992-93, in crore of rupees at current prices.

Year	Army	Navy	Air force
1985-86	4871.9(63.0)	1000.23(12.9)	1859.58(24.1)
1986-87	6527.22(64.3)	1311.41(12.9)	2311.39(22.8)
1987-88	7284.58(62.9)	1537.54(13.3)	2764.92(23.9)
1988-89	8061.19(62.7)	1798.59(14.0)	3001.43(23.3)
1989-90	8588.84(62.1)	1929.28(13.9)	3310.14(23.9)
1990-91	(RE)9382.73(61.8)	2099.80(13.8)	3692.61(24.3)
1991-92	(RE)9637.80(61.1)	2127.06(13.5)	4015.80(25.4)
1992-93	(BE)10195.42(60.2)	2232.18(13.2)	4476.57(26.5)

Source: For capital spending to 1990-91, Joshi, Table 4.4 in Babbage and Gordon, *India's Strategic Future*, p. 80; other data are from Defence Services Estimates for various years and Budget Papers for 1992-93.
Note: Breakdown includes capital spending but does not include items such as ordnance factories, defence administration and R&D, which cannot be attributed. Pensions have also been excluded on the assumption that any changes would be experienced on an equal basis between services. The 1990-91 capital expenditure is a budget estimate. Percentages have been rounded and may not add up to 100%.

We can see from Table 1.11, above, that the rapid expansion of the defence budget in the mid and latter part of the 1980s apparently allowed greater latitude to expand the share of expenditure incurred by the navy. With the straitened circumstances suffered in defence budgeting from 1989-90, by which time the pace of real increase in spending had begun to level off, the percentage share on the navy was again slightly reduced. At the same time, the share of the air force has been increasing, probably in recognition of the ending of the life cycle of a large number of the aircraft inventory and the continuing high share of hard currency spending related to the air force. The trend in the fall in naval expenditure was confirmed in the budget estimate of 1993-94, in which the share of the navy fell to 11.4%.[35]

Although expenditure on the army was also somewhat reduced in percentage terms, this probably in part reflects the withdrawal from Sri Lanka in 1990.[36] Moreover, although the percentage fall in the army is larger than the one suffered by the navy, because of the far greater allocation to the army the fall was not as burdensome as the one suffered by the navy. In fact, in nominal terms, the army had a 5.8% increase between 1991-92, whereas the navy had an increase of only 4.9%. It is also noteworthy that while the navy did better than any other force in the budget estimate for 1991-92, by the time of the revised estimate its position had deteriorated sharply.

What these data tentatively suggest is that the navy is seen as a more 'expendable' force than the army and air force.[37] This view is supported by the fact that from 1990 on, tension between India and Pakistan over the issue of Kashmir rose to the point where it actually threatened war in early 1990. Had war occurred, the army and air force would have borne the brunt of the fighting.

An examination of the relationship between capital and non-capital expenditure will also be useful in providing an insight into the progress of modernisation. The Indian military environment is essentially one that is manpower rich, with large fixed placements of troops, rather than one that relies heavily on weapons, communications and mobility. Since the time when General Sundarji was Army Chief of Staff (1986-88), however, India has been attempting to modernise its forces by reducing reliance on manpower and increasing expenditure on mechanisation and weapons, particularly to provide greater mobility and more effective weapons for the army through the creation of what is known by the acronym RAPIDS (Re-organised Army Plains Infantry Divisions) and RAMIDS (Re-organised Army Mountain Infantry divisions). The concept of RAPIDS is to integrate armour, air defence, artillery, helicopter support and infantry into highly mobile, self-contained divisions. Since mobility and mechanisation were deemed to constitute a force multiplier, implicit in RAPIDS was a trade-off between men and machines.

By the time of the fall of the Rajiv Gandhi government in 1989, little progress had been made with either modernisation or RAPIDS. In part this failure was the result of resistance within the army. As one commentator put it: 'The Armoured corps lobby will find it hard to accept the cut-down in force levels'.[38] Moreover, cuts were made all the more difficult politically and logistically because of the increasing reliance by the government on the army to maintain the civil authority with the growing level of dissent against the central government in Kashmir, Punjab and Assam.

Efforts to achieve greater integration and rationalisation between the armed forces have also largely fallen on fallow ground. The efforts of the V.P. Singh government to establish a military planning body capable of standing above the competition and jealousies evident between the forces in order to plan for the future in a structured and rational way and to tailor the force structure according to the nature of the likely threat proved largely still-born. The body, known as the National Security Council, was largely ineffectual because it had no dedicated professional staff assigned to it.

As a stratagem to neutralise opposition to rationalisation within the armed forces, V.P. Singh appointed a committee, the Committee on Defence Expenditure (the Arun Singh Committee), to advise on rationalisation and modernisation.[39] The Singh Committee reported to the government early in 1991, but the report was not made public. Its recommendations are reasonably well-known, however. The basic thrust was that the services had to give priority to modernisation, and that this was to be financed by manpower ceilings (under the ambitious Army 2000 plan the army was to have been increased to 45 divisions) and even cuts. A schedule of funding was set out to cover modernisation and rationalisation over the following five years. Areas of inefficiency such as the ordnance factories, which are operating well under capacity because of the reduced demand from the services in the tight financial circumstances, were identified for cuts. The chiefs of staff were also to be made an integral part of the defence planning mechanism by being placed directly under the defence minister as an active part of the governmental machinery, rather than remaining as individual force commanders.[40]

The findings of the Singh committee were strengthened in terms of their acceptability by the outcome of the Gulf war. The shattering defeat inflicted by the US on the larger Iraqi armed forces—forces that, like the Indian military, relied heavily on Soviet equipment—was salutary. As one writer put it, 'It would be foolish [in the aftermath of the war] to ignore the advances of technology and allocate resources for maintaining large numbers of men with large quantities of obsolete equipment'.[41] Shortly after the war, Minister of State for Defence in the V.P. Singh government, Raja Ramanna, appeared to lend support to the approach adopted by the Singh committee by asserting that it would be necessary to trade off expenditure on manpower for the needs of modernisation.[42]

Table 1.12, below, indicates that capital costs were rising at a greater rate than other costs, as one would expect from a modernisation program. This trend was, however, reversed at the time of the tight budgetary circumstances that occurred in 1991-92, during which capital costs fell to a greater degree than other costs. This suggests that the modernisation program has been seriously set back by the economic crisis. It should also be noted, however, that 'capital' provides not just for weapons purchases but also for large building programs. It is likely that the latter suffered far more in the cuts than acquisition of weapons. The navy's ambitious port development program seems to have been particularly severely affected. The budget estimate for 1992-93 suggests that the government has again embarked on a pattern of allocating a growing share of total expenditure to capital. Preliminary estimates of the rise in inflation suggest that the capital allocation will, however, represent a fall of some three points in real terms. Overall, it seems likely that the modernisation schedule recommended by the Singh committee has fallen by the wayside because of the squeeze on funds.[43]

Table 1.12: Expenditure on capital in crore of rupees, capital expressed as a percentage of total current spending, and real percentage increases and decreases in capital spending and total spending, 1981-82 to 1992-93.

Year	Total capital	% Total	Capital real change	Total real change
1982-83	526.57	8.1	N/A	19.2
1983-84	596.01	8.5	5.3	0.1
1984-85	736.75	9.3	16.1	7.4
1985-86	967.36	10.1	25.7	14.9
1986-87	1298.49	10.3	26.8	24
1987-88	3107.63	21.6	121.1	5.5
1988-89	3782.93	23.6	13.3	3.7
1989-90	4221.77	24.3	3.9	0.6
1990-91	(RE)4737.56	25.1	1.8	-0.9
1991-92	(RE)4882.89	24.9	-5.7	-5
1992-93	(BE)5346.60	25.3	*-3	*-5.3

Sources: Defence Services Estimates for all years except 1992-93, which is taken from the 1992-93 Budget Papers; *Economic Survey 1990-91* for WPI. Totals are as in Table 2.7, above.
* Represents the author's rough estimate based on an estimated increase in the WPI of 13%.
Note: The sharp increase between 1986-87 and 1987-88 is explained by a different method of accounting for capital expenditure allowing for inclusion of aircraft engines and heavy vehicles over Rs200,000 in value.

One important restraint on the pace of modernisation throughout the 1980s was imposed by the sharp rise in personnel costs. This occurred despite the plateauing in the size of the armed forces at 1.265 million from the mid-1980s, a level which represented a rise from 1.104 million in 1981-

82. Within the 1981 to 1991 decade as a whole, it has been growth in the army that has represented most of this rise, with numbers in the navy also having risen from 47,000 to 55,000, while numbers in the air force fell marginally.[44] Thus while the parallel needs to modernise and reduce expenditure have conspired to place a cap on the rise in numbers of the armed forces, the government has not so far been able actually to reduce numbers to the degree it would have liked.

Moreover, real costs per serving individual have continued to rise significantly. In fact, between 1982-83 and 1991-92, the real cost per serving full time member of the armed forces, in pay and allowances, and including pensions of those no longer serving, rose from Rs13,658 to Rs23,237, which represents a rise of 70%.[45]

Since the costs of pensions and pay and allowances constituted 30% of total defence spending by 1992,[46] such a rise is more significant in terms of the loss of spending power of the defence rupee than is the fall in the value of the rupee against hard currencies, at least in terms of the decade of the 1980s when taken as a whole. The need to reduce expenditure on manpower by reducing numbers, therefore, is a paramount one if India is to achieve greater efficiencies in the management of its defence budget. This is especially so since India is generally assessed to have a high 'tail-to-teeth' ratio in the armed forces, and especially the army. One report noted that the number of non-combatant soldiers per division was 8829 for India, 2307 for Pakistan and 1274 for China.[47]

Given the comparative inelasticity evident in spending on manpower and capital in relation to total spending what, it might be asked, has been squeezed by the defence cuts? It would seem that the cuts have fallen most heavily on maintenance, running costs and training. Expenditure on the four heads that cover these areas for the navy together grew in the four year period between 1988-89 and 1991-92 by only 15.6% nominally, compared with a rise of nearly 20% for expenditure on the navy as a whole, notwithstanding the fact that the rapidly rising price of POL in the context of the Gulf crisis and the exchange collapse was included. The pattern is broadly similar for the other forces.[48]

Anecdotal evidence also lends credence to the view that maintenance and running costs are being seriously neglected. A magazine report in 1991 asserted that because of maintenance and training problems, the number of operational squadrons in the IAF had been reduced from 40 to 35 and flying time had been reduced by 30%, numbers of tanks per operational unit had been drastically reduced, sailing time in the navy for long cruises had been reduced by 30% and the frequency of divisional level army exercises had been reduced from one a year to one every two years.[49]   Anti-tank units now only get to fire one live missile every two years instead of one each year.[50]   As already noted, another report blamed the slippage in the maintenance schedule in part for the sinking of the corvette, INS *Andaman*, in 1990.[51] Other reports state that as many as 50% of the fighter planes in the air force have been grounded through a combination of defence cuts and the loss of spare parts as a result of the collapse of the former Soviet Union. Up to one quarter of the army's heavy equipment has been 'cocooned' under a chemical layer.[52]

The cuts have promoted something of a debate between those who advocate the US approach to its current round of military cuts—one that involves abolishing whole units on the basis that it is dangerous to erode the effectiveness of individual units by whittling away at their resources in a piecemeal way—and those who wish to see most if not all units retained.[53] This debate is about more than strategies for making cuts; it involves, by implication, respective positions on whether India should continue its rise to military power when the economy permits, or whether it should be content to place more resources into economic development while consolidating its defence forces into a smaller, more modern, structure. Those who would like to see a continuing rise to military power naturally tend to advocate the retention of the organisational infrastructure already developed against a time when it can again be built upon once resources permit. The debate thus represents the practical side of the 'guns or butter' debate that has emerged in India in recent years.

While the current financial squeeze has not so far resulted either in a marked reduction in numbers within the armed forces or radical change in the force structure, the government has been attempting to achieve at least some efficiencies. Even before the current round of cuts, the army had embarked on the process of reducing costs through better management of its bloated inventories of stores and materiel, particularly by means of computerisation.[54] The government is moving to reduce the number of army cantonments and military supply points, since they are essentially an outgrowth of the British need to control the countryside in the absence of the degree of mobility that potentially exists today. As we have noted above, the army's communications system has been modernised and computerised.[55] New methods of computer simulation are being introduced in order to reduce training costs.

`    `For all that the government is seeking to take some measures towards a more efficient use of resources, in the final analysis it has so far baulked at the prospect of making deep cuts in the structure of the military of the kind that would have long term implications. Indian leaders, and especially former Defence Minister Pawar, have made a series of strong statements to the effect that military modernisation must proceed despite the resources squeeze. In saying this, however, they also assert that technology and electronic warfare should be substituted for an ever expanding defence force.[56]

To the extent that cuts have been forced on the armed forces, these have fallen most heavily on the navy. The navy's ambitious scheme to command 20% of defence expenditure has been deflected and its bid for a 30,000 tonne plus aircraft carrier capable of taking conventional take-off and landing (CTOL) aircraft has been rejected in favour of a 15,000 tonne vertical-short take-off and landing (VSTOL) capable vessel, the timing of which is now uncertain.[57]

Prospects for defence exports

As the fiscal noose tightened around the Indian defence program, the government cast around for a means that would enable the continuing modernisation of the armed forces without placing excessive strain on the nation's economy. Defence exports provided a possible means.[58] Defence Minister Pawar hoped to quadruple the export industry to $120 million over the five years following 1991.[59]

Until 1989 India had not sought actively to export arms. Indian governments, with their Gandhian antecedents of non-violence, considered that the export of arms was not a morally worthy pursuit. In Stephen Cohen's words, India is too 'nice' a country to be successful in the export of arms.[60] Ever since Indian tanks ended up in South Africa at the height of the Apartheid regime, India has treated the matter of exports with care.[61] Unlike China, which sold to both sides, India refused to sell arms to the combatants in the Iran-Iraq war.[62]

There were also a number of bureaucratic impediments placed in the way of arms exports, such as a case by case clearance process that made the timely provision of arms difficult. It was only in 1991 that the Department of Defence Production and Supplies prepared a comprehensive list of items that could be exported without reference to it.[63] Nevertheless, even if an item is on this list there are a number of hurdles through which an exporter must pass. There is another list prepared by the Ministry of External Affairs, consisting of those countries to which India cannot sell. Even in the current more liberal climate for exports, the compilation of this list exhibits a rather stronger sense of scruples than the virtual open export policy apparently pursued by a country such as China.

Another important reason for India's failure to emerge as a significant exporter of arms is the restrictive nature of many of the licences under which it produces its arms. India was not permitted, for example, to export spares for the MiG-21 to Egypt after that country broke off relations with the Soviet Union.[64]   Since then, export of Soviet-licensed items has continued to prove difficult. It was only in 1990 that the then Soviet Union permitted India to export engines and spares for the MiG line of aircraft.[65]

Even now that the policy on sale of arms has changed, the approach seems still to be half-hearted. Coordination of overseas sales is in the hands of a body called the Projects and Equipment Corporation, within the Commerce Ministry. This body is reportedly extremely slow. It is also still very difficult for an importer to obtain information on Indian products because of the obsessive secrecy that surrounds Indian defence production. All information is held and released by a body with the Orwellian title of The Authority Holding Sealed Particulars.[66]

Added to the lack of basic coordination, will and direction in the sale of arms is the fact that India has decided to enter the arms market at a very difficult time. With the ending of the Cold War, arms from the former Soviet bloc and the West are literally flooding onto the market. At the same time, countries like Taiwan, Korea and Singapore are emerging as highly competitive suppliers in some areas. Moreover, as we shall see, India has so far failed in the production of non-licensed sophisticated weapons of the kind that might compete on the market, and it is still limited in the on-selling of its licensed products such as the T-72 tank and the Bofors field howitzer. If ever weapons such as the LCA go into production, they will be in competition with aircraft such as the F-16, which by that time (after 2000) will be well on into their production runs and relatively cheap.

All these factors together mean that Indian arms exports have been slow to take off. Export sales have been as follows: 1988-89—Rs45 crore; 1989-90—Rs80 crore; 1990-91—Rs80 crore; and 1991-92—Rs101 crore and 1992-93—Rs120 crore.[67] In terms of export performance, the DPSUs, with their more sophisticated structures have done far better than the ordnance factories. Sales from the DPSUs constituted over 90% of sales in 1988-89 and 76% of sales in 1989-90.[68]

One of India's difficulties is that it is restrained in sales to the most lucrative market of West Asia because of the preference in some nations in that region shown to Pakistan. Southeast Asia has therefore been targeted for sales, with a prominent Indian presence at various regional arms marts. Malaysia in particular has shown an interest in Indian equipment and maintenance facilities for the MiG-29, which it is to acquire from Russia. Indian commentators warn, however, that while India has had 'endless

enquiries' about sale of items, very few deals have actually been struck.[69]
Basically, with a defence bill of Rs21,000 crore and current exports of only
Rs120 crore, India has a great deal of ground to cover before Sharad
Pawar's dream of using exports to lighten the fiscal burden of defence can
be realised.

*

The foregoing discussion has attempted to shed light on the relationship
between the Indian economy, defence spending at the macro-level, and the
effects of economic stringency on the force structure. It has shown that
growth in real defence spending tracked closely the increased economic
growth rate experienced in the 1980s. Conversely, the fiscal stringency
experienced in the early 1990s caused a fall in real defence spending, but
not to the extent that has commonly been believed. What the squeeze
illustrates is that India will cling to the force structure dictated by the
continental imperative at the expense of the more expansionary vision
afforded by a navy. It also shows that India is, in the final analysis, most
reluctant to abandon its long-term aspirations to be a prominent regional
power. Rather, it has sought to retain its basic force structure to build on
when times improve.

Given the far-reaching program of economic reform, we can again
expect renewed real growth in defence spending in the later years of the
decade. Indeed, in the 1994-95 budget, defence spending was increased by
20% in nominal terms and about 13% in real terms. But as we shall see
when we come to examine India's domestic political, regional South Asian
and international circumstances in the following pages, it is likely to be
some time before increased spending will again translate into an increase in
force projection capability.

Endnotes

1   The term originated with Prof. Raj Krishna.

2   See for example, Amiya Kumar Bagchi, 'An Economic Policy for
the New Government', *Economic and Political Weekly*, Vol. XXV,
No. 6, 10 February 1990.

3   Montek S. Ahluwalia, 'India's Economic Performance, Policies and

Prospects', in Lucas and Papanek, *The Indian Economy*, pp. 351-353.

4   Bagchi characterised the Gandhi economic reforms as constituting 'import-led growth'.   See 'An Economic Policy for the New Government', p. 317.

5   *India Today*, 15 February 1991, p. 109.

6   Government of India, *Economic Survey 1990-91*, Table 7.6, p. 109.

7   Data from *Economic Survey 1990-91*, Table 7.6, p. 109.

8   B.B. Bhattacharya, *India's Economic Crises, Debt Burden and Stabilisation*, B.R. Publishing Corporation, New Delhi, 1992, p. 9.

9   *Economic Survey 1990-91*, Chart 9.10, opposite p. 169.

10   The story may be apocryphal, but the Janata party supposedly lost the 1980 election because of the soaring price of onions!

11   Bhattacharya, *India's Economic Crises*, Figure 1.2, p. 6.

12   Calculated from Tables 1.1 and 7.1, *Economic Survey 1989-90*.

13   *Economic Survey 1990-91*, p. 3.

14   Chart, *Far Eastern Economic Review*, 23 July 1992, p. 53.

15   'Fallout of Gulf crisis: Indian exports suffer', *Indian Express*, 27 September 1990.

16   Bhattacharya, *India's Economic Crises*, p. 1.

17   'Freeing India's Economy', *The Economist*, 23 May 1992, p. 22.

18   'Where India's reforms get stuck', *The Economist*, 22 January 1994, pp. 25-6.

19   'Foreign investments rising', *The Hindu* (International Edition), 18 December 1993.   It is interesting to note that figures for foreign investment for East Asia, which seem far higher than those for India, are often based on approvals rather than actual investment.

20   Australian Department of Foreign Affairs and Trade, *India: Country Economic Brief—May/June 1993*, p. 2; Prem Shankar Jha, 'Learning to Think Positively', *The Hindu*, 14 April 1993, p. 9.

21   Australian Department of Foreign Affairs and Trade, *India—Country Economic Brief, May/June 1993*, Department of Foreign Affairs and Trade, Canberra, 1993, p. 6.

22   Australian Department of Foreign Affairs and Trade, 'India's Economy at the Midnight Hour', p. 32.

23   For the Merril Lynch assessment see 'Indian economy likely to grow

8 p.c. next year', *Times of India*, 17 December 1991.

24   East Asia Analytical Unit, Department of Foreign Affairs, 'India's Economy at the Midnight Hour: Australia's India Strategy' (draft), Canberra, 1994, p. 2.

25   For example, an article in the *Washington Times* concluded that Indian defence spending fell by a massive 28% between 1990-91 and 1991-92, a figure that, while accurate, is misleading. See Brahma Chellaney, 'Military growth in India over; funds cut', *The Washington Times*, 7 August 1991.

26   See the author, 'Indian Defense Spending: Treading Water in the Fiscal Deep', *Asian Survey*, Vol. XXXII, No. 10, October 1992.

27   The paradox is explained by the fact that, for contract purposes, the rouble was fixed whereas the rupee was valued against a basket of hard currencies. See S.S. Anklesaria Aiyer, 'Rouble's Devaluation Coming: How To Cut India's Debt By Rs 37,500 CR.', *Times of India*, 8 May 1992.

28   Calculated from G. Balachandran, 'India's Defence Expenditure: Widely Varying Estimates, *Strategic Analysis*, Vol. 14, No. 9, December 1991, Table 3, p. 1053, using the ACDA figures, and *Economic Survey 1990-91*, Table 7.4, pp. S-85-6.

29   Manoj Joshi, 'Defence Demands', *Frontline*, 3-16 August 1991, p. 13.

30   'In Reverse Gear', *India Today*, 15 November 1991.

31   The author, 'Indian Defense Spending', *Asian Survey*, Vol. XXXII, No. 10, October 1992, pp. 936-9, gives an account of how this calculation is derived.

32   For example, using the official figures for 1988-89, the most recent year for which we have actual expenditure, defence spending was 2.9% of GDP *including pensions* according to Table 7.3, p. 102, Government of India, *Economic Survey 1990-91*.

33   Ravi Rikhye, 'Indian Defence Budget: Fact and Fantasy', *Economic and Political Weekly*, 29 April 1989, p. 907.

34   According to *Economic Survey 1991-92*, it fell from a high point of 3.4% of GDP in 1986-87 to 2.1% (BE) in 1991-92. See Table 2.3, p. 6 (English version).

35   IDSA, *Asian Strategic Review 1992-93*, p. 47. The IDSA calculations are based on somewhat different data than those given in

Table 1.11.

36   The Sri Lankan exercise reportedly cost $300 to $400 million annually.   See the evidence of Paul Kreisberg before the *US Subcommittee on Asian and Pacific Affairs, Committee on Foreign Affairs*, House of Representatives, March 1989, p. 668.

37   It should be recognised, however, that the shifts may be explainable in terms of how individual contract payments happened to fall in any one year or the stage in the life cycle of equipment that a particular force might happen to possess.

38   Lt Gen. K.K. Nanda (Ret'd), 'Cost Effective Defence', *Indian Defence Review*, January 1991, p. 81.

39   Manoj Joshi, 'Defence Demands', p. 12.

40   Joshi, 'Defence Demands; Change of Guard', *Frontline*, 31 July 1991, p. 56; K. Subrahmanyam, Theatre commands', *The Economic Times*, 20 July 1993.

41   Col. Arjun Katoch (Ret'd), 'AirLand battle—Its Future and Implications for Third World Countries', *Indian Defence Review*, October 1991, p. 50.

42   As interviewed in *Defense and Foreign Affairs*, see 'Boarding a Moving Train: India's New Minister of State for Defence, Raja Ramanna', *Defense and Foreign Affairs*, Vol. XVIII, April 1990, p. 46.

43   See Manoj Joshi, 'Defence Demands', *Frontline*, 3-16 August 1992.

44   Figures are based on *The Military Balance* for respective years.

45   Calculated using the numbers of serving members of the armed forces as given in *The Military Balance* for respective years, the Defence Services Estimates (actuals) for 1982-83 and the Budget Papers (revised estimate) for 1991-92. The real expenditure has been calculated from the index numbers for wholesale prices (average of weeks) at Table 5.1 in *Economic Survey 1990-91*, with the 1991-92 index assumed at 199.

46   Calculated using the figure for total defence spending given in Table 1.10, above.

47   Sub theme box on 'teeth to tail' ratio in Shekhar Gupta and Paranjoy Guha Thakurtha, 'Heading for a Crisis', *India Today*, 28 February 1989, pp. 94-95. We need to note here, however, that an Indian division is larger than a Chinese division.

48   Calculated from the *Defence Services Estimate for 1988-89* (actuals) and *Budget Papers* for 1991-92 (revised estimate).

49   'Chinks in the Armour', *India Today*, 15 November 1991, pp. 173-9.

50   'Anti-tank missiles hit 100 pc targets', *Hindustan Times*, 27 April 1992.

51   'In Choppy Waters', *India Today*, 30 September 1990, p. 145. In an interview with the author in New Delhi in 1991, Commander Uday Bhaskar of IDSA also pointed out that one of the reasons the vessel was lost was because the pumps were not working.

52   Christopher Thomas, 'India puts outlays on Army in mothballs', *The Australian*, 12 March 1992. See also 'India cuts arsenal', *Aviation Week and Space Technology*, 23 March 1992, p. 13.

53   Two advocates of the radical cutting approach have been Col Arjun Katoch (see 'Restructuring set-up', *The Hindustan Times*, 2 April 1992) and G.C. Katoch (a former financial adviser to the government—see 'Defence Expenditure—Some Issues', *Indian Defence Review*, January 1992). For a view that opposes any further cuts see C. Uday Bhaskar, 'No scope for Defence cuts', *Hindustan Times*, 1 April 1992.

54   See interview with the then Defence Secretary Seshan, in *Defense and Foreign Affairs*, Vol. XVI, No. 12, December 1988, p. 22.

55   *Asia-Pacific Defence Reporter*, June-July 1992, p. 25.

56   See a speech by Pawar, 'Nation can repulse Pak attack: Pawar', *Times of India*, 24 July 1991.

57   According to Manoj Joshi, this was one of the recommendations of the Arun Singh Committee. See 'Defence Demands', *Frontline*, 3-16 August 1991.

58   See interview with Sharad Pawar, 'We will sell guns', *India Today*, 15 November 1991, p. 174.

59   'India, South Korea look to Soviets', *Jane's Defence Weekly*, 14 September 1991, p. 488.

60   Quoted in 'Heading for a Crisis' by Shekhar Gupta and Paranjoy Guha Thakurtha in *India Today*, 28 February 1989, p. 97.

61   Amit Gupta, 'India and the Arms Bazaar of the Nineties', *Economic and Political Weekly*, 22 September 1990, p. 2129.

62   David Silverberg, 'India Faces Roadblocks in Export Drive', *Defense*

News, Vol 6, No. 46, 18 November 1991, p. 1 and p. 36.

63   *Asia-Pacific Defence Reporter*, April 1991, p. 22.

64   Amit Gupta, 'India and the Arms Bazaar of the Nineties', p. 2129.

65   *Vayu*, No. IV, 1990, p. 5.

66   Pravin Sawhney, 'India unlikely to meet arms exports target', *Times of India*, 20 January 1992.

67   IDSA, *Asian Strategic Review 1992-93*, p. 53.

68   Calculated from 'Industry builds up strength', *Jane's Defence Weekly*, 26 May 1990, p. 1039.

69   Pravin Sawhney, 'India unlikely to meet arms export target'.

4   Performance and Prospects

India's performance in defence production has been strong in certain areas such as space, missile production, some aspects of electronics and some areas of warship building. But overall it cannot be said to have lived up to the very large investment placed in it or the promise held out for it.

The histories of key high technology weapons projects such as the LCA and MBT illustrate many of the faults of Indian defence industry. The difficulties encountered within the industry include the failure to relate 'big science' to the productive side of the economy, excessively bureaucratic and cumbersome structures, the general malaise in the Indian public sector, difficulties in the management of the nexus between the military as end user and the R&D and productive units and unreal and costly expectations of indigenous design capabilities caused by the secretive nature of Indian organisations and lack of public scrutiny of programs.

Another problem is caused by the eclectic nature of India's acquisitions policy and the lack of harmonisation between schedules associated with indigenous production and technology imports, leading to a situation in which many important and costly items of equipment are left without the necessary offensive or defensive add-ons such as missiles and anti-missile defences. The procurement process as a whole is also excessively bureaucratic, unresponsive to needs on the ground and open to corruption.

But the crux of the problem is an organisational one. It relates to the lack of overall planning and direction, not just for the defence industries themselves, but for the entire security apparatus in India. This problem is a deep-seated one that goes to the heart of the way the Indian economy has been developed and the political context within which the security forces are required to function. India appears to be able to build some of the components of a modern defence-industrial base, but to have greater difficulty in making the system function as a whole. The Indian system can be likened to a computer network in which individual components function at times quite well, but which overall suffers from a series of 'inter-face' problems.

One of these is between the military and the DRDO. In order to address this problem, in the early 1960s the government detached semi-permanently 'military technologists' from the armed forces to assist the DRDO. It soon realised, however, that this would create a semi-permanent class of specialists, so rotations were made from the military throughout the DRDO.[1] Currently the interface between the DRDO and military seems to operate better in the case of the navy than the army, which in turn appears to relate better to its design and production units than the air force.

Although the situation is improving, these interface problems between the military and the defence production and R&D units are likely to persist. To an extent they are innate to the differences between the uniformed services and the bureaucracy as a whole. They also relate to the continuing preference on the part of the military for state-of-the-art weapons, a preference that is understandable in circumstances in which one's life might well depend on the possession of superior weapons. It is unlikely, however, that a nation such as India will be in a position to manufacture any major weapons platform in line with the state-of-the-art in the foreseeable future, except in circumstances in which there is a high import content. The mismatch between desire and capability will therefore continue to plague defence planning and production.

Another interface problem occurs between the private sector and the government-owned industries. It is also unlikely, however, that the private sector will be in a position rapidly to pick up the main burden of defence production in India, even if the government were willing to make more work available to it. This is not so much because the private sector's capabilities will be insufficient to meet the technologies and tolerances required, but more because there will not be the economies of scale for the private sector to undertake the massive R&D needed for a modern weapon system, unless India can export in quantity, which is unlikely.

Increasingly, however, there will be a role for the private sector in niche areas, component production and in the production of materiel and ordnance. Components and sub-assemblies in the field of electronics is a particularly promising area for more active private sector involvement. But it will be many years—if ever—before the private sector will be able to offer a panacea to the defence industries.

Despite these flaws in the way in which the Indian defence industries are organised, indigenisation is unlikely to be abandoned. Indeed, the effort to develop a self-sufficient defence-industrial base is likely to intensify. Scarcity of foreign exchange, the shock applied to the system by the collapse of the Soviet Union, and the attempts on the part of the United States to impose a nuclear freeze through banning exports of some high technology items, together act to ensure that the policy of indigenisation is secure. But while India will not abandon indigenisation, is it likely to succeed in its efforts?

The success of the economic transformation now occurring in India will be crucial in determining the extent to which India is able to place its defence-industrial base on a firmer footing. The re-casting of the philosophies underlying current economic organisation and practice into more dynamic and competitive forms is likely eventually to flow into the defence industries—at least to an extent and after a period of some delay. As already noted, it now seems more likely than not that the higher growth rates achieved during the 1980s will again be a feature of the Indian economy in the latter part of the 1990s. There is some prospect that this new growth will, *ipso facto*, be translated into increased military spending, as it was during the 1980s.

A difficult current account position will, however, likely continue to restrict the importation of the fore-front weapons systems and technologies needed for the indigenous industry. One estimate places outgoings for debt servicing at $9.8 billion for 1992-93 and $12 billion annually over the following four years.[2] These figures indicate that India will not be in a position to import arms on the scale of the 1980s during the 1990s, and especially now that the Soviet Union no longer exists to provide cheap imports. While these problems are likely to be offset to an extent by India's recent stronger export performance, given the overall situation with the current account and strong competing priorities, defence imports are likely to be restrained for several years. This combination of a growing economy and continuing difficulties in sustaining the importation of expensive weapons systems will tend to favour indigenisation strategies.

There is also reason to expect that the Indian defence industries will gradually gain in capability. As we saw from Table 1.7 (chapter 2 above), the share of defence production that is undertaken indigenously has risen substantially over the last two decades. While much of this production takes place in non-high technology areas, the growing role of domestic production progressively frees foreign exchange resources for the import of high technology items.

Moreover, while India has not performed well in areas such as the production of aircraft, it is able to perform creditably in some key areas that are likely to become more important to modern defence forces. These are electronics, including computation and the development of software, missile technology, sensing technologies and those aspects of electronics relevant to C^3I. Critically, India is also now able to participate in almost all aspects of the nuclear sciences necessary for the development of a comprehensive nuclear arsenal without substantial international assistance. This capability puts India in a class of its own in relation to other nuclear threshold nations. It remains an important question whether this 'bias of success' in favour of non-conventional weapons production will cause a commensurate bias in the development of India's force structure in years to come. That is partly a geo-political issue, and it will be addressed in the third part of this book.

There is also evidence that there is an increasing tendency for technological spin-offs to cross from one area of defence production and high technology activity to another, thus contributing to the development of significant synergisms. Some examples of this process at work include:

- the possible spin-off in guidance between the LCA program and the missile program, between the tactical missile program and the ballistic missile program and between the space program and ballistic missile program;
- the spin-off between the research sector in the materials sciences and the various weapons programs (examples are the development of high grade steels for warship building and maraging steel for missiles and nuclear weapons);
- the spin-off between the electronics program, and especially areas such as highly sophisticated software design, ASICS and parallel computation, and almost all areas of defence production, but especially in areas such as the military uses of space, cruise and ballistic missiles, precision guided weapons, sensing capabilities, SIGINT/ELINT capabilities and the development of nuclear weapons;
- the spin-off between the space and electronics programs and the C^3I requirements of the defence forces, a spin-off that could eventually lead to a significant multiplier effect within the broad parameters of existing budgets; and
- the potential spin-off arising from economic liberalisation, which could eventually improve the performance of leading defence production organisations such as HAL and BE.

Importantly, there is evidence that, far from having destroyed Indian indigenous capability, the collapse of the Soviet Union and consequent loss of access to Soviet supplies of spares and maintenance has actually stimulated the indigenous arms industry. There are a number of instances of the indigenous capability having been strengthened as a result of the loss of Soviet support. These include the establishment of a marine turbine overhaul centre (this type of propulsion unit was previously overhauled in the soviet Union) and the successful production of spare parts for SAMs and the full range of MiG aircraft, along with aircraft retrofitting and overhaul, which now makes HAL the only non-CIS company with this capability.[3] Limitations imposed by the US on the transfer of dual use technology because of its non-proliferation concerns have had a similar effect. One example is the creation of the successful program in parallel computation, which was a direct response to the US boycott, and which may eventually enable key organisations such as BARC to have full access to super-computer facilities.

Necessity being the mother of invention, India's access problems have precipitated a far more focused approach to the acquisition of indigenous capabilities. In order to progress indigenisation, resist any boycotts and mitigate the effects of the loss of Soviet support, the head of the DRDO, Abdul Kalam, established a self-reliance committee to determine what critical components, metals and other equipment should be maintained in stock, and what capacities should be developed indigenously. The organisation has indentified critical components in short supply, such as thermal-resist material and ASICS (shortages that developed following the cryogenic bans). It has identified public and private Indian and overseas firms capable of meeting these needs. Kalam has also submitted to government a plan to address the critical needs emerging in the aviation sector.[4]

The delay in the production of sophisticated indigenous platforms that has resulted from loss of Soviet support and the financial squeeze is not necessarily disastrous for India. Given the current structure of the Indian defence industries and the nature of the platforms currently in the inventory, there is considerable scope for India to achieve efficiencies through force multipliers such as enhanced EW capabilities and through retrofitting existing platforms, using a range of locally produced weapons and sensors and imports, which will increasingly be provided by Israel and the West rather than Russia. Thus, for example, we see the decision to upgrade 80-100 of India's more modern MiG-21s, possibly with assistance from Israel, and to install Israeli fire control systems in the Soviet T-72 tank.[5]

The logic of India's programs of retrofitting and acquisition of force multipliers arises out of the fact that its inventory contains some relatively modern platforms that are relatively poorly equipped. The MiG-29 (which is an older version without any EW capabilities), *Kashin* destroyers (which contain no CIWS or AMM capabilities) and *Mirage* 2000 fall into this category. Moreover, with India's gathering momentum in the production of tactical missiles and electronics, it will increasingly be able to undertake retrofitting and provide add-ons from indigenous resources. Already there is pressure from within the air force for acquisition of aerial re-fuelling capabilities and AWACS.[6]

Most importantly, while economic liberalisation will not in itself lead to a major transfer of production from the public to private sector, and while public sector activities might to an extent be shielded from any new efficiencies introduced as a result of liberalisation, it would be surprising if there were not at least some positive flow-on benefits to the defence industries as a result of the process of liberalisation. Furthermore, it would be a mistake to assume that because the current structures are inefficient by, say, OECD standards, India will not eventually achieve a significant capability. The counter-point is easily made by reference to the Soviet Union, in which the state sector managed to produce some highly competitive weapons systems. Although the efficiency of the Soviet defence industries probably left something to be desired, they seemed to work better on the whole than their civilian counterparts.

Moreover, with the exception possibly of the United States, in very few countries today are defence producers truly private. Rather, they are the subject of closed shops and considerable state support. In fact, the model of the Indian DPSU, provided it is further modified organisationally, could eventually form the basis of a reasonably efficient defence industry. The recent improvement in HAL, for example, is illustrated by the reduction in the loss rate of the Indian Air Force. In the late 1980s, the loss rate of the IAF was about three aircraft every 10,000 hours of flying time, which ranked as one of the highest rates in the world. As a result of unhappiness with this situation within the IAF, substantial organisational and quality control changes were made within HAL, and the loss rate has now been reduced to under one per 10,000 hours.[7] As we have seen, HAL is now working to rationalise its staffing and introduce new technologies and management systems.

Even the LCA, which is commonly thought of as a project with significant difficulties, may bring more net benefits to the wider defence industrial base than are apparent at first sight. At least some of the goals of the LCA project are unstated and go beyond the production of the LCA itself. They would include acquisition of CAD/CAM technologies that could be applied elsewhere, the building up of a body of expertise in aircraft design and manufacture that would, unlike in the case of the *Marut*, persist over the long-term, an understanding of a range of associated technologies that go along with the design of the fighter, including avionics and radar, which could assist in the upgrading of existing aircraft, technologies relating to guidance which might be used in ballistic missile design, propulsion technology, and the acquisition of various composite and other materials that would have a wide range of uses in the defence industries. While it might be argued that the construction of the LCA is an expensive and not particularly efficient means of acquiring these technologies, they are technologies that may well not be available on the open market for the purposes to which they might ultimately be put. This is not to argue that the main purpose of the LCA is to act as a 'stalking horse' for the acquisition of technologies for other purposes. It clearly is not. It is to point out, rather, that the difficulties associated with the LCA should be seen in a somewhat broader context in the final cost-benefit analysis of the project.

So how is India likely to stand in the matter of defence production one decade from now? It is most suitable to attempt to answer this question in terms of capabilities rather than what will actually have been produced and be part of the inventory. This is particularly the case since India's strategy, especially as it relates to the production of more sophisticated and expensive items, is one of developing capabilities and keeping them 'on the shelf', as it were, in case they are required. Ten years from now India will likely possess:

- the capability to produce a state-of-the-art main battle tank, including a number of key assemblies, and to up-grade the existing very large inventory of tanks;
- a wide range of skills to enable the continuation of a flexible regime of missile production, including an ICBM, an IRBM, and a range of tactical missiles;
- a comprehensive space program involving indigenously launched and built imaging satellites suitable for military use, highly sophisticated indigenously built communications satellites and a threshold capability to launch them indigenously, plus the attendant technologies relating to networking and targeting;
- a relatively sophisticated electronics and software design industry that could provide the basis for an effective system of C^3I (assuming adequate coordination of the military effort) and provide a wide range of electronics associated with sensing and weapons systems as well as SIGINT and ELINT functions;
- a developing capability in the production of military aircraft, but one that falls well short of the one possessed by leading nations in this area, combined with a wide range of associated technologies relating to the aerospace industry;
- near self-sufficiency in the nuclear sciences such that, should it decide to do so, India could produce a range of nuclear weapons, including possibly thermonuclear weapons, warheads capable of being delivered by ballistic missiles and possibly also MIRVs;
- The capacity to build and arm a wide range of warships, including

submarines; and

- an economy that is capable of meeting many of the needs of the defence industries and sustaining a significant defence industrial base, including in areas such as electronics, materials sciences, computation and engineering.

Finally, it needs to be emphasised that it would be a grave mistake in the case of all developing countries to compare their technological capabilities with those of developed countries such as the US or Japan, and thereby to find them wanting. Countries such as India may never catch up to these nations in terms of their technical capabilities in the defence industries. But as we shall see when we examine the geopolitical and geostrategic underpinnings of India in its region, such comparisons may become less rather than more relevant should developed nations such as the US continue to prefer to avoid any involvement militarily in regional affairs. Thus while India may never develop the stealth technology, for example, one must ask whether this is strictly relevant in circumstances in which its technological and productive capabilities are within the next decade likely to outweigh those of any other nation in the Indian Ocean littoral and immediate hinterland, with the possible exception of Australia.

But as well as assessing India's technological capability, there is another question we must address before we are in a position to understand the true import of India's rise to power and its true depth as a regional power. This is its ability to continue to develop as a power in circumstances in which both it and the region of which it is part face significant problems arising from the growing difficulty in the management of poverty, population and the resource base.

To date, India has chosen to emphasise its leading technologies, its capabilities in 'big science', in heavy industry and in the development of the kind of infrastructure that supports its continuing rise as a regional military power. Yet all the while it has suffered from growing instability within its own society. We must now ask whether this phenomenon will be powerful enough to deflect India in its rise to power.

Endnotes

1   Kapur, *Building a Defence Technology Base*, pp. 47-49.

2   'Tightrope Walking', *India Today*, 31 July 1992, p. 105.

3   A joint venture company between India and Russia to manufacture MiG parts has been set up at Bangalore. See 'India updates its

Russian fighters', *Aerospace*, June 1993, p. 56.

4 Vivek Raghuvanshi, 'India Accelerates Drive Toward Self-Sufficiency', *Defense News*, July 26-August 1, 1993, p. 1 and p. 29; 'Snags of Agni identified', *Times of India*, 13 January 1994.

5 Michael Dornheim, 'Industry Outlook', *Aviation Week and Space Technology*, 7 June 1993, p. 29.

6 Vivek Raghuvanshi, 'The Indian Air Force in Crisis', *Aerospace*, December 1993, p. 14.

7 Interview, Manoj Joshi, Canberra, 21 January, 1993.

Part 2

The Limits to Power

1   Instability and power

In the preceding chapters we described how India is gradually developing the basis to emerge as a significant technological and economic power. These advances must mature, however, in the complex political and social milieu that constitutes modern-day South Asia. Unless they are able to do so in a stable domestic and regional setting, they are unlikely to serve any useful purpose in terms of India's development as a power.

Unless India can be 'comfortable' in its own polity and in its own South Asian neighbourhood, it will be unlikely to seek to project its power or exercise its influence in more distant regions. Or if it were to make the attempt—perhaps to divert attention from domestic issues—it would likely be less effective in its efforts. Its security, organisational and economic resources would be severely over-stretched by domestic crisis. Its force structure and force location would also be arranged primarily to meet the local situation. Its standing in the hierarchy of nations would, moreover, be seriously compromised by political instability and by the human rights issues that arise out of such situations.

In order to build its power on a stable basis, India must first achieve a measure of political stability at the central level of government. Stability at the centre is required to meet the growing challenge to the integrity of the Indian Union from various sub-national, or peripheral movements. A strong central government is especially needed to ensure that the benefits of development are reasonably evenly spread. Unless a way can be found to improve circumstances in poorer regions, they are likely further to slide into states of chronic sub-regional crisis, in which a vicious circle is established between poverty, instability, the flight of capital and further neglect.

The task of ensuring stability at the periphery is, however, complicated by the fall in political standards and increasing volatility at the centre. That, in turn, owes a great deal to sub-national crises both in other South Asian nations and in India. Increasingly, domestic political crises in South Asian nations tend to 'wash back and forward' across the arbitrary and porous borders of the region, bearing with them the flotsam and jetsam of political discontent. Crisis at the periphery of nations can also run back up through the political system like a brush fire and contribute to instability at the centre, as happened when Mrs Gandhi was assassinated by Sikh separatists in 1984.

In terms of a study of a large nation's rise to power, these issues concerning the relationship between poverty and instability are not merely academic. Indeed, they go to the very heart of a key question in the analysis

of a large, populous and poor country such as India: does India's large
population stand as an asset in its rise to power, or does it, rather, act as a
sheet-anchor in that process? The answer to this question will depend to a
significant degree on how we interpret instability in India. In particular, we
need to know to what extent instability is driven by poverty or resource
scarcity and to what extent it is driven by other socio-political factors.
Depending on whether one ascribes a larger or lesser role in the current
malaise to cultural, social and political factors than to a growing squeeze on
a finite resource base, one will be inclined to be more or less pessimistic
concerning the nation's ability to contain and overcome the problem of
internal insecurity. Before examining the important issue of the causes of
instability, however, let us look briefly at its characteristics and extent.

The domestic character of instability

In South Asia, the problem of civil violence has in recent years emerged as a
more serious security issue than the problem of interstate warfare. The
breakdown in civil order is now the major destabilising factor in relations
between India and Pakistan. The serious terrorist bombings in Calcutta and
Bombay in 1993, which the Government of India attributed at the time to
Pakistani intelligence services, and the involvement of Pakistan in assisting
the separatists in the Indian state of Jammu and Kashmir, are cases in
point.[1]

The consequences of civil violence in terms of loss of life and property
have been far more serious in recent years than have the consequences of
war. The problem became so serious in India that President Venkataraman
warned specifically against it when opening parliament in 1991.[2] Yet
security analysts often downplay the issue of internal security in relation to
the issue of war.[3] While keeping in mind that statistics on loss of life in
civil unrest are often unreliable, it may be instructive to review some of
them, if only to give the reader an idea of the dimension of the problem in
relation to that of war.

An estimated 2-4,000 Sikhs were killed throughout India at the time of
Mrs Gandhi's assassination in 1984.[4] In the Indian state of Punjab, 3,500
were reportedly killed in civil strife in 1990 and over 5,000 in 1991.[5] One
estimate places the total number of deaths in the Vale of Kashmir since the
insurgency commenced in 1989 at 15,000 out of a total population of 3.5
million.[6] An estimated 5,000 persons have been killed in the state of Assam
since the commencement of separatist violence there in 1979.[7] In Bihar, an
estimated 1,500 people were killed between 1982 and 1987 in caste related
violence in the flood planes of the Ganges and other rivers. It is impossible

to estimate how many have been killed in Sri Lanka in the twin crises generated by the Janata Vimukthi Peramuna (JVP) and the Tamil separatists. One indicator of the intensity of the military campaign in the north is that, in the four months following the assassination of Rajiv Gandhi, the number of deaths within the Sri Lankan government forces and the Tamil Tigers was 4,000.[8] A United Nations investigation team reported that 12,000 persons were 'un-accounted for' in Sri Lanka between 1983 and 1991.[9] And in the Pakistani state of Sindh, according to government figures 1,640 people were murdered and 2,432 kidnapped during the two year period of the rule of Benazir Bhutto's Pakistan People's Party (PPP).[10] Even in New Delhi, which has historically been a stable, well-run capital city, there were a reported 384 kidnappings between January and July 1991.[11]

In contrast, the total number of soldiers killed in the 1965 war between India and Pakistan was about 6,000.[12] In the 1971 war, which was a particularly costly one for Pakistan, there were an estimated 5,000-10,000 casualties. Most of these, however, occurred in the civil strife in East Bengal province of Pakistan rather than in fighting with India.[13]

The statistics for violent deaths in South Asia must, of course, be taken in the context of the very high population of the region. As Austin and Gupta point out, when compared with some developing regions, South Asia has not been especially violent.[14] The point of citing such statistics, however, is not so much to establish that these societies are more violent by nature than others, but rather to establish that domestic violence has now become a far more significant problem in terms of numbers killed than violence *between* nations. It is, moreover, apparently an increasing problem.[15]

As Atul Kohli points out in his extensive study on what he calls 'India's growing crisis of governability', the rule of law, as it was understood during the later colonial and post-colonial period, has become in many areas virtually inoperative (see Map 2, below).[16] This state of affairs has pertained at various times in the border regions of Punjab and in parts of the Vale of Kashmir; but it is also prevalent in the Hindi heartland.[17] For example, large areas of central Bihar are dominated by caste-based private armies or by Naxalite-like groups.[18] In Sri Lanka, the Jaffna Peninsula, home to nearly a million people, has for a decade been virtually ruled by the Tamil Tigers. There the Tigers dispense justice, maintain a uniformed police force, gather taxes and run the schools and hospitals. In the Pakistani state of Sindh, the problems of kidnapping and armed robbery reached such intensity in 1991 that foreigners were not permitted to enter the state (except for urban Karachi) without an armed police escort. The Sindh robber gangs drew recruits from the unemployed and distressed tenant farmers of the feudalistic province. One gang has even set up an 'employment bureau' to recruit unemployed youth.[19]

Map 2: Areas of Disturbance in South Asia.

As well as becoming seemingly more violent, South Asia has also suffered from growing political volatility. Governments are now turned out of office by discontented voters with monotonous regularity. In India, for example, if we exclude the 1985 re-election of the Congress (I) government, an event that owed much to the massive sympathy vote for the party following the assassination of Mrs Gandhi, the last government to be re-elected for a second term was Mrs Gandhi's 1971 Congress government. Moreover, the last three governments in India have been minority ones. V.P. Singh's Janata Dal-led government (which was not a coalition in the strict sense) lasted barely a year. Chandra Shekha could muster only 10% of MPs in the lower house and depended on outside support from the Congress (I) party. He did well to last nine months. The present Congress (I) government of Narasimha Rao until recently commanded only 241 seats in the 532 member lower house and was dependent on support from minor parties for its survival. It escaped defeat in a censure motion in August 1993 by a mere 14 votes.

Instability is not only manifest in the level of violence in society and in political volatility, but also in the decline of political standards. Indeed, it would seem that the two phenomena are closely linked. An example may be found in south-western Uttar Pradesh, where gangsters for years were given virtual free rein because of the political patronage they enjoyed.[20] In that same state, the 1991 national election entailed the imposition of security 'on the scale of a military operation' to prevent the capturing of voting booths and limit election violence.[21]   One report estimated that 40 of the current Bihar parliament of 325 are gangsters-turned politician.[22]

The Bofors deal put corruption in India on a new level. Although the exact details of the deal are still not known, it seems likely that $25 million was given to Indian politicians and/or a political party in a secret and illegal commission.   Scandal also surrounds the large contract for the German Type-209 submarine. These and other instances of high-level corruption, or alleged corruption, are different in scale than anything that went before them. As illustrated by the fall of Rajiv Gandhi in 1989 to V.P. Singh, the man who challenged him on the corruption issue, they can also be highly destabilising.

The 'licence raj' as it operated until recently came to benefit certain large business houses through the pedalling of political influence. This process further undermined the integrity of the state. These conglomerates flourished in an environment in which access to production licences and imports were a 'licence to print money'. *The Economist* described this system as producing a 'rentier' class of businessmen, bureaucrats and politicians whose fundamental interests lay in constricting economic activity rather than in expanding it.[23] The taxation structure also contributed to a situation in which India came to be awash with so-called 'black' money, funds which exist in the cash economy to avoid tax. The prevalence of 'black money' only served to enhance the level of political corruption by making large amounts of 'hidden' money available to influence the political process.

The opportunities offered by a highly centralised economy also contributed to the erosion of values in the bureaucracy. Even the Indian Administrative Service, the re-incarnated Indian Colonial Service that was once considered the elite 'steel frame' of the administration under the British, has been seriously compromised as a result of political pressure, including threats of arbitrary transfer, and by the temptations held out by central command of the economic levers. The bloated bureaucracy has become an instrument of obstruction in the conduct of Indian affairs and there were widespread fears that Narasimha Rao's economic reforms would be derailed by its 'dead hand'.[24] Because of bureaucratic inertia, at the time of the 1993 Aid India consortium meeting in Paris, there was a staggering $17 billion in un-expended aid funds in the pipeline, money that was needed urgently in the social sector and for the development of infrastructure.

Politics in other parts of South Asia are no less seriously corroded. Although Zia-ul-Huq in Pakistan and General Ershad in Bangladesh were both able to retain government for a considerable period, they did so through use of the army. One is now assassinated and the other in jail. Zia's democratically elected successor, Benazir Bhutto, lasted only two years, and her successor, Nawaz Sharif, was dismissed by the president after a similar period, necessitating, ultimately, fresh national elections. Following these elections, Ms Bhutto was able to form a government only after substantial negotiation with minority parties and independents. In Bangladesh, President Ershad's successor, Begum Khalida Zia, must be considered to have an uncertain political future.

Given the extent of the problem of instability in South Asia and its important role in defining India's present strategic posture and future capabilities, an examination of the nature of instability within India and within the South Asian region emerges as an important task in the process of charting India's rise to power.

Endnotes

1   These examples are discussed in greater detail below.

2   'President calls for stern action', *Times of India*, 28 December 1991.

3   This point was made in an article by N.S. Saksena, who pointed out that while 1500 police had died in the line of duty over the previous three years, they were largely forgotten, whereas the 1000 who had died in the 1971 war with Pakistan were still remembered as heroes.

'Low Police Morale', *Times of India*, 1 October 1991.

4   For the higher figure see Rahul Bedi, 'India's Reluctant Police', *Jane's Defence Weekly*, 6 July 1991, p. 22.

5   Rahul Bedi, 'India's Reluctant Police'; and 'Gung—ho syndrome', *Times of India*, 9 February 1992.

6   Reuters News Service, Article number 000373859465, 13 December 1993.

7   D. Austin and A. Gupta, 'The Politics of Violence in India and South Asia: Is democracy an endangered species?', *Conflict Studies*, No. 233, Research Institute for the Study of Conflict and Terrorism, London 1990, p. 10. Note: the source of this quotation seems to be wrongly attributed by the authors. It presumably comes from the Indian fortnightly *Frontline*.

8   S.D. Muni, 'Sinhalas Not Keen On Resolving Conflict', *Times of India*, 22 October 1991.

9   'Sri Lankan abuses leave 12,000 missing', *The Australian*, 12 March 1992.

10   Ahmed Rashid, 'No law, no order', *Far Eastern Economic Review*, 24 January 1991, p. 24.

11   Y. Raj, 'West UP epicentre of Delhi abductions', *Times of India*, 17 September 1991.

12   K.C. Praval, *Indian Army After Independence*, Lancer International, New Delhi, 1990, p. 304.

13   Guy Arnold, *Wars in the Third World Since 1945*, Cassell, London, 1991, p. 467.

14   Dennis Austin and Anirudha Gupta, 'The Politics of Violence in India and South Asia', pp. 4-5.

15   Atul Kohli, *Democracy and Discontent: India's Growing Crisis of Governability*, Cambridge University Press, Cambridge, 1991, Figure 1.1, p. 7.

16   This quotation forms the sub-title to Kohli's work. See fn 15, above.

17   Haryana, Uttar Pradesh, Himachal Pradesh, Bihar, Madya, Pradesh and Rajasthan.

18   Kohli, *Democracy and Discontent*, chapter 8, and pp. 224-5; 'Bihar: Domain of the Dons', *India Today*, 31 January 1992.

19   'Pak dacoits set up job bureau', *Times of India*, 8 March 1992.

20   'Double Impact', *India Today*, 31 March 1992, pp. 70-73. In the 1993 state election in Southern UP one bandit stood for office (successfully as it transpired) in order to gain protection from a closing police dragnet. (Interview, election worker in that electorate, New Delhi, 1993.)

21   Manoj Joshi, 'The Gun Culture: Situation in UP, Gujarat', *Frontline*, 25 May-7 June 1991, p. 20.

22   'Bihar: Domain of the Dons', *India Today*, 31 January 1992, p. 59.

23   'A Survey of India', *The Economist*, 4 May 1991, p. 15.

24   For an interesting account of the decline of bureaucratic standards, including in the IAS, see Inder Malhotra, 'Sad plight of the Civil Services', *Times of India*, 6 February 1992. The author has also drawn on interviews with senior bureaucrats and journalists.

2   The Roots of Instability

Any examination of the causes of instability in India and South Asia is complicated by the fact that we are not dealing with a single large event such as a civil war, but rather with a slow accretion of violence and decay. In the words of V.S. Naipaul, India's problem is one of 'a million mutinies now'.[1] Although such events *appear* in the aggregate as a continuum, each one will have its genesis in circumstances which are highly specific. It is particularly difficult to establish in a general way why this type of violence is occurring.

At best, we can describe some of the broad economic, social, and political changes that constitute the background against which individual events are played out. While not ultimately satisfying in the interpretive sense, such an approach may at least serve the utilitarian purpose of answering the questions that inform the present study, namely: is such violence likely to increase, or can it, rather, be contained and eventually overcome? What will be the role of economic liberalisation in either intensifying grievances or in ameliorating them? And what are the long-term implications of such domestic and regional instability for the power projection capabilities of the largest regional actor, India?

Commentators on South Asia have provided comprehensive interpretations of the deteriorating political and internal security environment. These in the main tend to emphasise the challenge posed to the hierarchical social structure by education, democracy and the raising of expectations; changes in the village-based and caste-based production systems with the coming of modern markets and means of production; rapid improvement in communications, including a more active and extensive media; the breakdown of the 'Congress system'; and the obsession of the modern nation state with quantification, which is said to create the basis for comparison between castes and communities where none previously existed.[2]

These phenomena have together sharpened expectations about what democracy should deliver voters at the very time when the political system itself has fallen into decline. In the case of India, to a significant degree this decline has resulted from the loss by the Congress party of its predominant position. For its first 28 years, independent India experienced a chain of unbroken democratic rule by Congress. This record was based on the prestige inherited by Congress from the days of the freedom struggle, the very high profile of leaders such as Jawaharlal Nehru, the links of the party with regional figures of political note and a broad but successful voting combine.

Now, however, the Congress party's base is eroding, at least when viewed against the backdrop of the halcyon post-independence era. Organisationally, the party has been described as 'a disaster'.[3] The district offices are for the most part closed.[4] Elections for party positions at the district level have only recently been held after an interregnum of 18 years. Not surprisingly, after such a long period the elections proved highly divisive.[5] Rather than providing for a 'bottom-up' process, the party now consists of a system of loose and fluctuating alliances of convenience. Consequently there have been at least four major splits in the party since 1969. These factions have tended to re-group from time to time around the magic of the Gandhi name; but that name no longer exists in Indian politics.

Yet despite these manifest political problems and the obvious issue of rising expectations, it is also possible to discern a growing pressure on different groups to compete arising either from the deterioration of their objective circumstances, or at least the dissipation of expectations that might reasonably have been held by them in more hopeful times. In the final analysis, we are not simply dealing with a growing set of demands and expectations, but rather with an equation that has demand (expectation) on the one side and supply (available resources)[6] on the other. It is this relationship that we now turn to explore.

*

In seeking to draw attention to the role of resources in the current political malaise in South Asia, we certainly do not assert that disputes centring on scarcity can never be resolved through political or organisational means.[7] What we claim, rather, is that the greater the pressure on the resource base, the more drawn out, difficult, and possibly violent the resolution of issues becomes.

One problem with explanations that attempt to draw on resource scarcity is, however, that conditions *in the aggregate* do not actually appear to be getting worse. Despite the rapid growth of population in India, the problem of poverty is actually a diminishing one, at least when viewed in terms of real wages, production of grain *per capita* and percentages of those below the poverty line, if not the absolute number of those in poverty (which is rising to an estimated 400 million by 2000).[8] According to National Survey data, 48.3% of the population was below the poverty line in 1977-78, whereas only 25.8% was below it in 1989-90.[9] There is evidence, moreover, that at least in Green Revolution areas, the lot of ex-untouchables and landless labourers might be improving.[10] In these circumstances, one might ask, where is the deepening crisis? And why has a crisis arisen in Punjab, which is the most prosperous state in India?[11]

In addressing the paradox of increasing unrest in the midst of apparent increasing prosperity, it is necessary to explore aspects of poverty that go beyond the pitifully low minimum of calories by which poverty is traditionally measured in India. One reason for doing so is the body of work cited in footnote 2 in the present chapter, much of which suggests that *perceptions* of what life ought to be are as important as the actual physical indicators of what it has been. Here we need look no further than the process of politicisation, the spread of literacy and the associated phenomenal upsurge in access to various media. Each one of these factors conspires to extend aspirations beyond the limit of one or two meals a day.

Once expectations have been raised, what becomes especially important is access to employment. It is employment more than any other factor that represents the expanding range of the individual's aspirations. But the issue of employment extends well beyond the availability of jobs in the aggregate. The job seeker will be looking for employment in accordance with his or her social standing and educational level. In the case of Punjab, for example, there is discontent about jobs despite the fact that the state imports agricultural labourers from Bihar. For agricultural communities such as the Jat Sikhs, who happen to form the backbone of the *Khalistan* separatist movement in Punjab, there is a strong relationship between access to certain types of employment and access to land. It is not so much that work should be available, but rather that it should be a certain type of work as befits the member of a proud, landowning caste. Such appropriate work will often include a military or a government career, or a career in industry, but it will not include 'service' or agricultural labouring for someone else.[12] Moreover, perceptions of what constitutes appropriate work can change, even for the lower castes, as they have done for children of some labourers in Punjab and for graduate Harijan youths in Gujarat.[13]

What we are dealing with is thus not so much a diminution of resources in the aggregate for a particular group or community (although that certainly may be occurring in some cases), but rather an erosion of what was once a reasonable expectation of the ability to better one's lot, whether that expectation might have involved access to a government job, the ability to derive a higher income per family member from a fixed amount of land, or simply the ability to emigrate to greener pastures in one's own nation or abroad.

In the final analysis, however, this relationship between growing disorder and the changing resource base (in the widest sense of that term) can best be observed by studying individual examples of locally-based grievances. But first we shall examine the resource base in the aggregate.

Population, literacy, land and labour

The South Asian region contains more people living in abject poverty than any other region in the world.[14] In terms of providing adequately for these people, the nations of the region are required 'to run in order to stand still'. When India won independence its population was about 350 million. Today it would be approaching 900 million.   That fact represents the single greatest failure of independent India and the single greatest challenge faced by the nation.

In the first half of the 1970s, India was making good progress in controlling its population. Nearly three-fifths of the decline in the Crude Birth Rate which took place between 1961 and 1986 occurred in the early 1970s. At that time it appeared that India would meet its goal of attaining NRR=1 by the year 2000. With the ousting of Mrs Gandhi in 1977, however, government policy on birth control softened as it became apparent that the excesses of her government in implementing birth control during the Emergency had been an important factor in the way the country turned against her so sharply in the 1977 election.[15] The decline in the Crude Birth Rate stalled.   Following the release of the 1991 Census figures, the population growth rate still stands at a disappointing 2.1%. It is now expected that NRR=1 will not be achieved until between 2010 and 2015 and that India's population will top the billion mark by the turn of the century.[16]

The overall situation in India is, however, patchy, as illustrated by Map 3, below. The average annual population growth rate in the largest Indian state, Uttar Pradesh, is still high at 2.5%. The rate in the very poor state of Bihar, which has the second highest population, is about average for the nation. This fact is somewhat unexpected given the low level of education and extreme poverty of Bihar. The likely explanation is the high mortality rate.[17] We should therefore expect the population growth rates in this and similarly placed backward states to rise before they can fall. Since these backward states represent about 40% of the nation's population, the good progress achieved in the south and the richer northern states is likely to be largely negated in terms of the national figure. The longer-term prognosis for India is not entirely bad, however, since the rate of fertility has fallen overall from 5.3 to 3.9 in the decade of the 1980s.[18]   Elsewhere

Map 3: India: Differential population growth rates by state, as at the 1991 census.

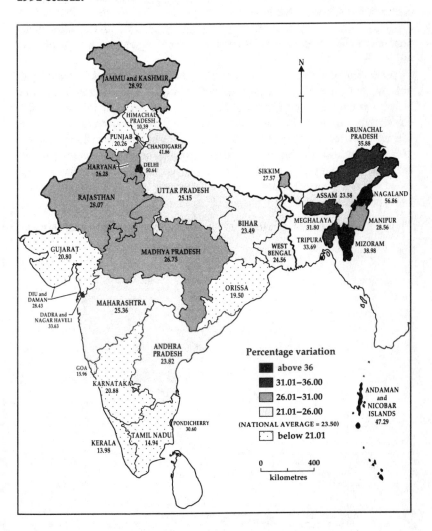

in South Asia, the continuing high rate of population growth is even more worrying. In Bangladesh the rate of growth is 2.4%. In Pakistan the population is still growing annually at the alarming rate of 3.1%.[19] This compares to an average for other low income countries of 2%.

Effective female literacy in Pakistan is only 19% and prospects for improvement are not good.[20]   Only 7% of Pakistani couples use contraceptives, one of the lowest levels of use in the world.[21]   Pakistan is expected to have 150 million people by the year 2000 and to more than double from its present population in the next 23 years to a total of 250 million.[22]

According to Leete and Jones, trends in Pakistan, Bangladesh and Nepal indicate that conventional demographic transition theories do not justify the belief that demographic transition to NRR=1 will occur at the early stage envisaged in more optimistic assessments.[23] They introduce an alternative scenario in which the population of South Asia would grow to 1.4 billion by 2000 and almost 1.8 billion by 2010.   Such a projection, were it to be realised, would have a snow-balling effect during the later years of the twenty-first century because the age structure by 2010 would contain exceptionally high child dependency ratios.[24]

Figure 2.1: Population projections for South Asia and China (millions).

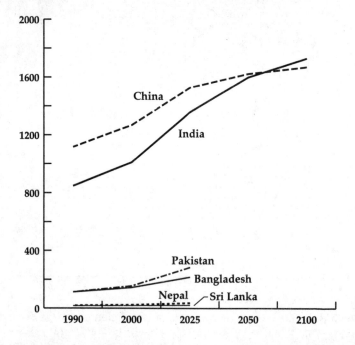

Source: R.A. Bulatao, et. al., *World Population Projections* (1989-90 ed.), Tables B-9, p. liv and B-5, p. xlviii, World Bank, Washington, 1990.

But even according to the more conservative projections of the World Bank and United Nations, the population of South Asia will have increased substantially, in fact to 1.8 billion (World Bank) or 2 billion (UN) by the year 2025.[25] Since the present population of South Asia is about 1.1 billion, the projections by Leete and Jones would involve finding jobs and food for 700 million additional people by the year 2010. Figure 2.1, above, provides the most recent World Bank population projections for South Asian nations. China is included for purposes of comparison.

Figure 2.2: HDI Ranking for South Asia and China, 1990.

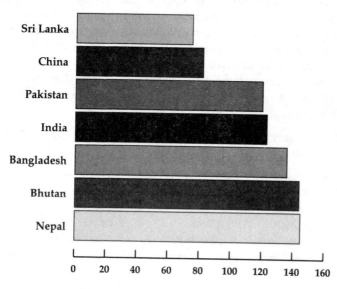

Source: Derived from UNDP, *Human Development Report 1991*, Oxford University Press, Oxford/New York, 1991, Table 1.2, p. 16.

One consequence of the large and rapidly growing populations in South Asia is that, with the exception of Sri Lanka, which has performed best in terms of limiting its population, all regional nations rank very low on the United Nations' Human Development Index (HDI).[26] The index is supposed to act as a rough comparative measure of the quality of life in all nations. To the extent that it measures the potential of the human resource to contribute to development, it is also an indicator of a country's potential for economic development. It thus becomes a crucial measure of the degree to which high population countries carry their populations either as an asset in terms of their capacity to contribute to development or as a burden. In Figure 2.2 above, countries are ranked according to their position on the HDI table.

The low rankings of the South Asian countries are in turn characterised by generally low expenditures in the social sector. Table 2.1 gives the percentage of the population below the poverty line and expenditure on public education and public health as a percentage of GNP. For the sake of comparison the percentage of expenditure on defence and data on China are included.

One point to note about the table is that the comparatively high expenditure on education in India has not yielded the results that China's lower level of expenditure has. The World Bank reports a literacy level of 73% for China and 48% for India (1990 figures). One explanation is that education expenditure in India has been heavily biased in favour of the tertiary sector because of the drive for technological self-sufficiency. Table 2.2, below, compares the education participation rates in India with several other Asian countries.

Table 2.1: Social expenditure compared with military expenditure for South Asia and China.

	% pop. below poverty line	% GNP spent on education	% GNP spent on health	% GNP spent on defence
Sri Lanka	-	2.4	1.7	5.7
China	10#	2.7	1.4	6.0
Pakistan	30	2.2	0.2	6.7
India	48*	3.4	0.9	3.5
B'desh	86	1.3	0.6	1.5
Bhutan	-	4.2	-	-
Nepal	60	2.1	0.9	1.5

Sources: UNDP, *Human Development Report 1991*, Tables 17 and 19.
Note:
\#   for rural population only.
*   does not correspond to the normal measure of poverty used in India.
@   represents the official figure. The actual amount spent would be higher.

Weiner and the Rudolphs argue that the Indian bias in favour of the tertiary sector has had disastrous results in terms of child welfare, public health, family planning and, ultimately, the battle against poverty.[27]

Newman points out that, even in recent years, the government has failed to comprehend the correlation between rural backwardness and bias towards the upper end of education.[28] Subramanian Swami's comparative study of development in China and India suggests that China has apparently managed a much higher growth rate in agriculture than India in part as a result of a larger investment in the social sector, including education.[29] The government itself admits to the tertiary bias, despite the fact that studies from all over the world point to higher social returns from primary education.[30]

Table 2.2: Education: gross participation rates by age cohort for selected Asian countries, by percent.

	Primary	Secondary	Higher
Pakistan	55	21	2
China	*118	39	2
India	92	41	9
Sri Lanka	*103	63	5
Bangladesh	60	18	5
Indonesia	*118	42	7
15 Asian LDCs	94	42	10

Source: World Bank, *Pakistan: Current Economic Situation and Prospects*, March 1991, p. 47.

* Due to the presence of over-age and/or underage students, participation rates can exceed 100% of the relevant age group.

Because of the apparent relationship between unemployment and political unrest, the excessive emphasis on the upper end of the education spectrum at the expense of the lower has important implications for internal security. The Indian five-yearly survey of organised sector employment growth for the years 1981-82 to 1986-87 indicates that the growth in the organised sector (the sector within which most graduates would expect to be employed) was only 2.3% in the public sector and actually fell by 0.3% in the private sector.[31] The somewhat perplexing aspect of these data is that total growth in output in the organised sector was over 7% during the decade of the 1980s, showing a significant inelasticity in the demand for labour.[32] The explanation would appear to lie in the nature of investment in the private sector, which was heavily biased in favour of capital-intensive activities.[33] Although this poor performance in the organised sector has been offset to an extent by a healthy growth rate in the unorganised sector, employment in that sector does little to alleviate the position of the educated unemployed.[34] The heavy reliance on the public sector for growth in organised sector labour has implications for the liberalisation process, since liberalisation is likely to involve a real decline in public sector employment.

It is this acute position of the more educated job seekers that contributed to the sharp reaction to the Mandal reforms that V.P. Singh attempted to introduce in 1990. Under these reforms, Singh attempted to reserve a further 27% of places in the government sector and in those private firms in receipt of government funding for members of the so-called 'other backward' classes, in addition to the 22% already reserved for 'scheduled' castes. This provoked 100-150 students into acts of self-immolation and attempted self-immolation. The intensity of this reaction might be considered surprising in view of the fact that only a few thousand jobs were at issue. As M.C. Datta and others have observed, however, it was not so much the jobs themselves which were seen to be at stake, but rather the principle of access by merit in ever-narrowing circumstances.[35]

But the problem of unemployment amongst educated youth is also an important contributing factor in separatist violence in rural areas throughout South Asia. In fact, it might well be the rural equivalent to the self-immolation wave that swept the northern cities of India in 1989. For example, it is widely recognised that the high rate of secondary and tertiary educated unemployed contributed substantially to the two episodes of violent unrest triggered by the JVP rebellions of 1971 and 1979 in Sri Lanka.[36] Similarly, Kohli argues that the presence of unemployed, educated Sikh youth is an important factor in the insurgency in Punjab.[37]

In terms of the more general problem of unemployment, the world Bank estimates that by the year 2000 about 70 million people will be added to the Indian labour force, necessitating an annual growth in employment of 3% between now and then if massive unemployment is to be avoided. Other estimates are, however, considerably higher. One is that India will need to find 109 million new jobs during the decade, necessitating an annual growth in employment of 5%.[38] According to Bhattacharya, 40 million new rural jobs and 11 million urban jobs are needed just to meet *current* needs, let alone to cater for new entrants to the labour market.[39]

An equally serious problem is posed by the 'miserably low levels of productivity and incomes' for many of those actually employed, particularly in the agricultural sector. It is estimated that an agricultural worker obtains on average only 150 days of work a year.[40] Such a low level of wages places enormous numbers of people below what must be considered a pitifully low definition of poverty.

But it is not just the landless of the lower castes who are now suffering in this way. There is also the problem of growing unemployment amongst the landowning castes and classes (many of whom are themselves educated) as the population increases beyond the point where land can be further subdivided and still be viable. Farm sizes overall are declining. The 1981 agricultural census, which is the most recent available, showed that average farm size was 1.84 hectares even then.[41] In the twenty years to 1981, the numbers of farmers owning under one hectare had grown from 31% of landowners to 57%.[42] The matter of land tenure is further complicated by the fact that even these small holdings are often highly fragmented and that consolidation is long overdue.[43] The Planning Commission estimates that the per capita availability of land will fall from 0.89 hectares in 1950 to 0.30 hectares by 2007.[44]

Because 75% of the labour force and 80% of those below the poverty line live in rural areas, the problems of unemployment and poverty should largely be addressed through rural policy.[45] Another reason for emphasising rural policy is that its neglect will further encourage large-scale migration to the cities, with all the problems that such migration entails. Yet it is precisely in agriculture that the record for employment growth has been weakest, at only 1% per annum.[46] In the words of the World Bank, 'agricultural policy is in crisis'.[47]

After rising steadily in the 1970s, real investment in the agricultural sector declined in the 1980s. Real investment in irrigation, for example, peaked in 1981-82 and real investment in agriculture as a whole actually fell between 1981 and 1991.[48] In part the reason was the expansion of recurrent expenditure in the public sector at the expense of capital expenditure. In the recent past agriculture was beset with a growing burden of subsidies, which acted as a drag on the rest of the economy. The subsidy regime tended to benefit the more wealthy and also to produce inefficiencies.[49] The perception of politicians that they can purchase rural vote banks has set up a vicious circle involving subsidies, inflation and subsequent price rises in the industrial sector.[50] Inefficiencies inherent in the subsidy regime and other factors mean that agriculture has an *effective* coefficient of protection of only 0.87, compared with 1.4 for industry.[51] This imbalance contributes to deteriorating terms of trade between the agriculture and industry and to the phenomenon of 'urban bias'.

There is evidence that in the home of the Green Revolution in north-western India, the application of inputs is reaching a point where further substantial increase in production is impossible. Irrigation, which is in any case far more extensive in the north-west than elsewhere, can only be expanded country-wide by a further 30%. In the wheat belt, HYVs already constitute 90% of production by area. In the case of rice, however, it is only

50%, and for dry land crops only 30%.[52] For South Asia as a whole, yields of rice are under half of those for Northeast Asia and well below those of Indo-China.[53]

Unless the Green Revolution can be promoted in the poorer eastern areas of the country, the prognosis for the agricultural sector being able to produce the required number of jobs over the long-term is not good. The evidence would suggest, however, that the spread of the Green Revolution has stalled.[54] One disturbing prospect is that progress is stalled in part because of the flawed agrarian structure in states such as Bihar, where the government's writ barely runs in large tracts of the countryside. In these circumstances, the basic conditions for a green revolution such as communications, co-operative societies and access to credit at reasonable rates is lacking.[55] In the case of Bihar, a vicious circle already appears to have been established. In the Ninth Five Year Plan, for example, allocations for infrastructure and the social sector will have to be cut because of Bihar's poor absorptive capacity.[56]

Moreover, it is the states that have failed to perform in agriculture that generally have the worst record in family planning. Because of the age structure of the population in these states, they can be expected to contain an ever increasing percentage share of the labour force. Yet they are the very states which have experienced the most significant lag in agricultural growth and absorptive capacity for agricultural labour.[57]

The government's strategy under economic liberalisation is to increase agricultural output by raising procurement prices, while at the same time reducing subsidies. This strategy is sound as far as it goes, but it will not assist in resolving the investment drought in agricultural infrastructure, and without more investment in infrastructure, particularly irrigation, gains in production will likely be limited.[58] A strategy of fostering small-scale, labour-intensive rural-based industries could also assist rural employment. But this strategy would also require significant investment in rural infrastructure.[59]

If some balance is required to this gloomy outlook, we might note that should the structural problems be overcome in the east, there is considerable potential for further growth in the output of rice. To a lesser extent, there is also scope to develop dry land agriculture in the rest of India.[60]

In comparative terms, India is not an especially densely populated country. It has, for example, considerably more arable land per capita of agricultural population than China.[61] But investment of both money and brainpower in agriculture will have to be high to achieve the levels of production that will continue to ensure adequate stocks of food grain. More importantly, it will be very difficult for agriculture to continue to provide sufficient employment for India's growing population.

In order to gauge the effects of the demographic trends outlined above on political processes and internal security, it is now necessary to look more closely at some of the individual sub-regional movements which together comprise the troubled situation in South Asia.

Transmigration, ethnicity, resources and unrest

In the following *tour d'horizon* we will only be able to do passing justice to the complex issues raised when we consider the relationship between resource scarcity and sub-regional expressions of unrest. One point that does emerge quite clearly, however, is the prominent role played by transmigration in upsetting the ethnic balance. Weiner estimates that since 1947, between 35 and 40 million people have moved across national boundaries.[62]

Transmigration is both triggered by resource scarcity and contributes to it. Often, too, it is government sponsored and sometimes it occurs despite the best efforts of governments. Often it relates to security problems in the source country or region. Sometimes it is encouraged by the fact that the borders of South Asia are essentially arbitrary ones imposed by a post-colonial settlement that paid little heed to the existence of trans-border communities. Map 4, below, illustrates the way in which a number of ethnic groups in South Asia are spread amongst several countries of the region.

This prominent role of transmigration in contributing to instability is evident in a number of sub-regions in South Asia. Map 3, above, which illustrates a very rapid population growth rate for the areas to the north-east of India, suggests that transmigration, predominantly from Bangladesh, is an important feature of the demography of the region. In Tripura and some other of the so-called 'seven sister' states of the north-east, the situation has reportedly reached 'alarming proportions' because the influx of Bangladeshis is pushing the tribals into 'decline' and politics into ferment.[63]

It is in Assam, however, that separatist violence associated with transmigration of Bengalis and Bangladeshis has especially been a feature over the last decade and a half. The situation in Assam offers a good example both of the importance of transmigration in causing unrest and of the complexity we immediately encounter when we try to assess what role resource issues play in triggering transmigration.

The migration of Bengalis into Assam, which has been a feature of the history of Assam over the past century, was caused by a multiplicity of

Map 4: Ethnic Groups and International Borders in South Asia

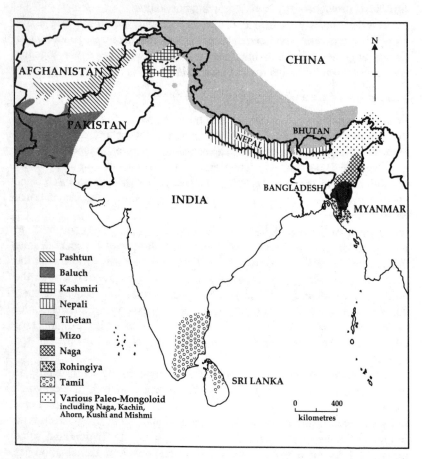

factors.   Prominent among these was over-population and associated scarcity of land in the source regions, particularly the very poor conditions in the province of Mymensingh in what is now Bangladesh.[64] In the post-partition period, communal conflict between Hindus and Muslims also played an important role in driving Hindus into India.[65] To complicate matters further, in earlier years there was a significant 'pull factor' at work in the form of jobs in the tea plantations or in the growing bureaucracy in Gauhati.

Within Assam, the arrival of migrants eventually intensified competition for scarce resources such as jobs in the bureaucracy and land.[66] The great pogrom of 1980 at Kamrup, in which 1,000 died, was basically directed at Muslim settlers from Mymensingh who occupied the *char*, or riverine lands. These lands had initially not been settled by the Assamese because they were considered too dangerous, but were left for the 'desperate' Bengalis. Now, however, with growing scarcity of land, the Assamese wanted the land back.[67] Jobs were equally important in the agitation, particularly as it found expression in the student body. One of the central demands of the predominantly student United Liberation Front of Asom (ULFA) was for greater access for Assamese for jobs in the bureaucracy, which was dominated by Bengalis.

Another area of growing unrest in India in which transmigration has played a powerful role is the great sickle-shaped locus of tribal populations in central India (see maps 2, above, and 5, below). Here the tribal populations of the region have been engaged in a quasi-Maoist agitation, known as Naxalism, focused on the loss of access to their traditional forests and lands.[68] Although the process of dispossession of the tribes has been a very long-term one, it was essentially a result of migration into the tribal areas of more powerful groups and economically more advanced peoples. These migrations had the effect firstly of pushing the tribals into the forested marginal land and subsequently eroding their base even within their forested fastness.[69]

The current predicament of the tribal populations is caused by the fact that the forest resource is itself in a state of serious decline. This decline is due to reckless exploitation by corrupt contractors, the building of large dams, the press of population and the development of mining and industrial sites (the tribal population happens to fall within the most mineral-rich part of India).[70] These developments have both attracted transmigrants and caused an erosion of the forest base from which the tribals derive their physical and spiritual well-being. This squeeze on the existence of the tribals has been exacerbated in recent years by the limited prospects for out-migration to act, in the words of Weiner, as a 'safety valve'.[71] The alienation of tribal land and destruction of the forests has resulted in the tribals joining the ranks of landless labourers, falling into the hands of money-lenders and subsequently often becoming bonded labourers.[72] As Calman points out, in response they have been progressively drawn into the Naxalite revolt.[73] The Ministry of Home Affairs report covering 1989-90 noted that in the course of that year there were 801 'extremist' Naxalite incidents causing 214 deaths. Most worrying, the movement was spreading

Map 5: Density of Tribal Population of India.

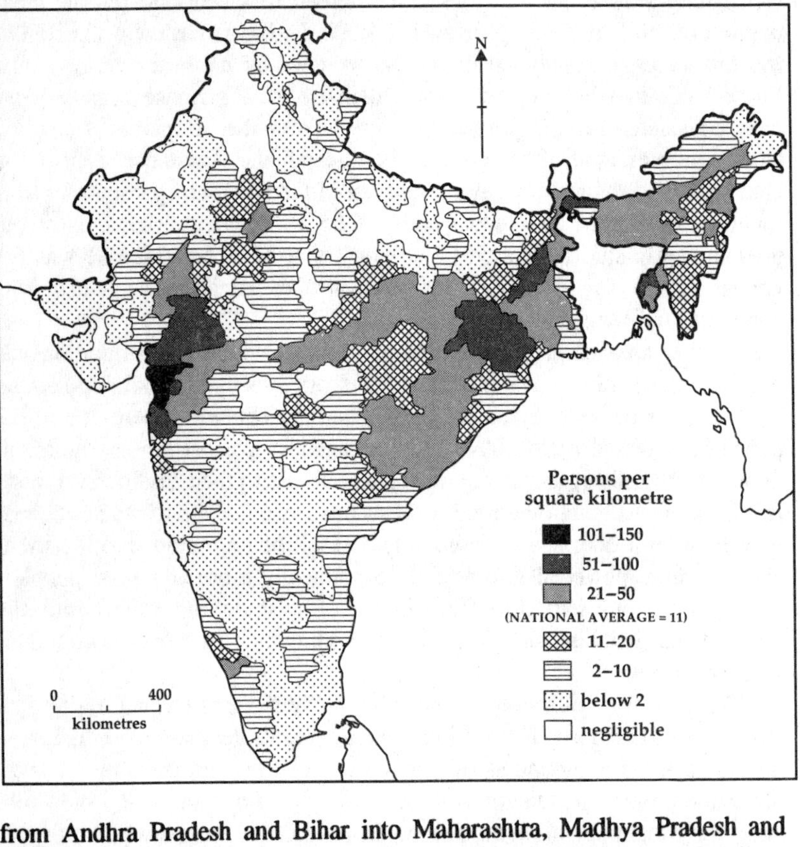

Persons per square kilometre
- 101–150
- 51–100
- 21–50

(NATIONAL AVERAGE = 11)
- 11–20
- 2–10
- below 2
- negligible

from Andhra Pradesh and Bihar into Maharashtra, Madhya Pradesh and Orissa.[74]   Recently the Commissioner for Scheduled Castes and Tribes, B.D. Sharma, noted that 'There is simmering discontent in almost the entire middle Indian tribal belt, particularly on the issue of land and forest'.[75]

Transmigration has also played a disturbing role in destabilising the small mountain kingdom of Bhutan. Bhutan is a relatively underpopulated nation, a fact which has attracted a steady stream of economic refugees from Nepal. The people of Bhutan, who are predominantly Tibetan Buddhists, number only between 400-600,000.   The conservative Bhutanese government fears that the local culture will be swamped by the influx of Nepalese, many of whom have been there for generations. Following unrest between the ethnic groups, large numbers of refugees have been forced to take refuge in Nepal. The issue has severely strained relations between the two hitherto friendly nations.[76]

As well as being caused by resource-related pressures and developmental factors, transmigration can also be facilitated by government policy. For example, government-sponsored transmigration was one of a number of factors in the build-up of tension between the Tamil and Sinhalese communities in Sri Lanka. Except around Trincomalee and on the Jaffna Peninsula, the Tamils were not in a majority in the north-east but were in a delicate state of equilibrium with Sinhalese and 'Moores' (Muslim Tamil speakers). From the 1950s on, however, the Sri Lankan government shifted Sinhalese from the populated south into the north-east as canal colony settlers in large irrigation schemes such as the Mahaveli scheme and gradually upset this balance.[77] This erosion of the ethnic balance has been an important factor in drawing Tamils living outside the Jaffna Peninsula into the separatist movement.

In contrast to the cases described above, security—in the form of the Soviet invasion of Afghanistan—was the major factor in driving up to 3.4 million Afghan refugees into the north-west of Pakistan. The location of the Afghan refugees is given at map 6, below.

Despite the fact that the refugees eventually came to constitute roughly 27% of the total population of the North-West Frontier Province (NWFP) of Pakistan,[78] the presence of what was at the time the largest single concentration of refugees in the world did not provoke directly serious unrest. One factor behind this tolerance may well have been the fact that the majority of the refugees were of similar Pushtun ethnic stock to their host community. What the case of the Afghan refugees suggests is that it is not transmigration *per se* that causes unrest, but rather the upsetting of balances that have often been built over many years into patterns of negotiation and accommodation between ethnic groups.

Although there were no direct large scale security problems generated by the presence of the Afghan refugees, there were a number of other negative influences. One was that the environment was adversely affected as a result of the influx of the refugees and their 3 million livestock.[79] There were also other less direct, but nevertheless even more serious consequences. These can be summed up in two words—guns and drugs. The gun and drug 'cultures' have had a highly negative effect on Pakistani society and politics. These negative effects are now starting to spread to India and other countries of South Asia.

The spread of drugs in Pakistan was closely linked with the requirement of the *mujahideen* in Afghanistan to finance the war against the Soviet Union. The eventual development of Pakistan as a major conduit for the

Map 6: Location of Afghan Refugees in Pakistan.

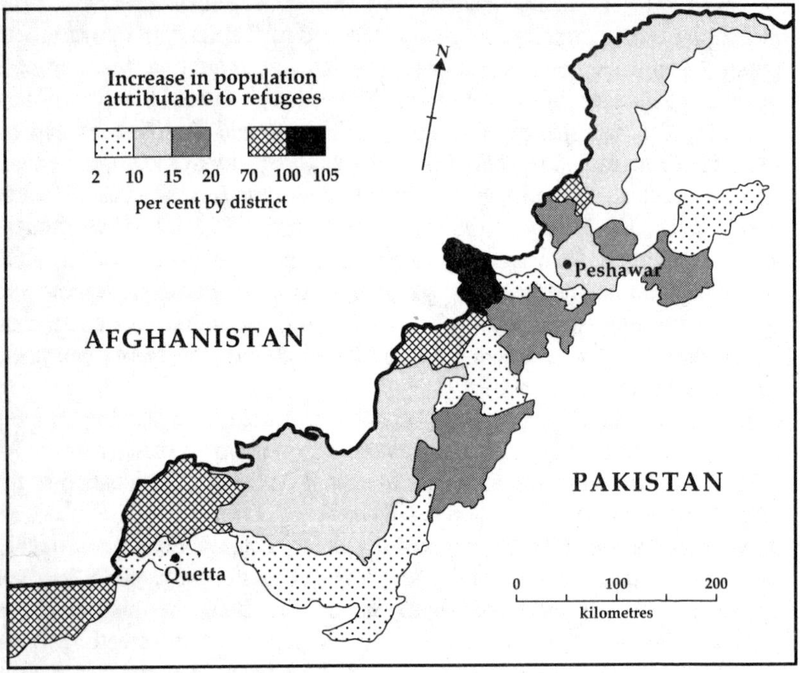

transfer of drugs from the growing areas (largely in Afghanistan) and the processing areas (mostly in the tribal agencies of Pakistan) to the West has brought about the influx of enormous amounts of money into Pakistan itself and the corruption of the political system. One estimate places the total annual value of the drug trade between $8 billion and $10 billion.[80] The amount of money involved helps explain the extent of drug-related corruption amongst Pakistan's politicians, police and military and the endemic violence in some areas of Pakistan, especially Sindh.[81]

The porous border between Indian Punjab and Pakistani Punjab was worked assiduously by the drug traders. The trade became closely linked with the separatist movement in Indian Punjab and an important source of finance for the militants. The Indian government was required to increase the presence of its paramilitary forces in the border areas, not just to counter the insurgency, but also to combat the drug trade. Drug trading and arms dealing are also closely linked.[82] Some militant groups have become little more than bands of smugglers.

India is also linked into the drug trade routes out of the 'Golden

Triangle'. As with the Punjab linkage, separatist insurgents are prominently involved in the trade through India's north-east. From the various land entrance points the drugs pass to maritime outlets, especially Bombay and Kochin. Bombay itself is increasingly emerging as a major global centre for the laundering of drug money.[83]

The war in Afghanistan has also contributed to a rapid increase in the numbers of sophisticated weapons in Pakistan. According to one estimate there are now one million unlicensed *Kalashnikov* rifles in Pakistan.[84] Such weapons find a ready use in the ethnic wars fought out in the cities of Sindh. They also provide an important source of supply for various insurgency movements in India, especially those in the border states of Punjab and Kashmir. In those states the list of weapons that are clearly by-products of the Afghan war include AK-47s, rockets and rocket launchers, mortars, cluster bombs, Chinese Type 56-1 assault rifles, Chinese Type-69 grenade launchers and grenades.[85] The supply of weapons is now spreading to other states in the north of India, especially Uttar Pradesh and Haryana.[86]

*

Another important aspect of transmigration that increasingly affects the whole of South Asia is the great one-way migrations that occur between the countryside and the cities. These migrations are driven by the extreme conditions and lack of investment in rural areas described above and by the 'pull' of jobs and better facilities offered by the cities.

The role of urbanisation in creating instability was highlighted starkly by the fact that the rioting following the destruction of the mosque at Ayodhya, in which perhaps 2600 died, occurred almost entirely in large urban centres. Moreover, those centres suffering the most rapid urbanisation, such as Surat and Bombay, seem to have experienced the rioting in greater intensity than other cities.

The 1991 census showed that the Indian urban population in large cities is still increasing rapidly, to a total of 217 million. More and more of this exploding urban population is confined to slums. It is estimated that, by the turn of the century, 32 million people will be living in the slums of India's large cities.[87] Table 2.3, below, gives an insight into the growth of some of South Asia's larger cities.

Until recently, the old Presidency cities of Calcutta, Bombay and Madras managed to retain their basic functional forms and social cohesion. Calcutta suffered a high level of violence in the 1960s and 1970s, in part as a result of the effects of a sudden and massive influx of Hindu Bengalis following partition and in part as a result of the Naxalite movement then prevalent. However, the city has since regained some of its equilibrium under the influence of the moderate Marxist government.[88]

Bombay, the second of the 'head link' cities of colonial times after Calcutta, has always been a city of migrants—Gujaratis, Konkanis, Maharashtrians, Marwaris, South Indians, Sindhis and northerners. Communal tension is certainly not new in this 'melting pot'. But despite this, Bombay has until recently maintained its cosmopolitan aura and commercial vigour. The two sets of riots following the destruction of the mosque at Ayodhya were of a different order of magnitude and viciousness than anything seen previously, however. In their form they resembled a 'pogrom' against Muslims rather than a 'traditional' riot.[89] One writer attributes the change in Bombay directly to the massive influx of people, the desperate search for jobs, housing, services and infrastructure and the extraordinarily high rents, which can reach Rs10,000 per square foot.[90]

Nor has Delhi escaped the problems associated with rapid urbanisation. Already it is reportedly the third most polluted city in the world.[91] Projections of the size of the city provided in Table 2.3, which would likely be very conservative, do not auger well for its future. Concern is frequently expressed in the Indian press about the unchecked influx of people to Delhi.[92] The BJP has made political capital out of the scarcity of water in the city, seeking to blame the neighbouring state of Haryana for the 'diversion' of the Jamuna waters.[93] Other cities such as Bangalore and Hyderabad which, like Delhi, were until recently well-run, peaceful cities, have been increasingly subject to tension, pollution and violence. Second-rank cities are also increasingly subject to communal tension. Notorious hotbeds of tension include Ahmedabad, Bhagalpore, the Varanasi-Allahabad belt, the Meerut-Aligarh belt, Agra and Jaipur.

Whether this deterioration is associated with a more general decline in communal relations or whether it in part relates to problems specific to rapidly expanding urban communities and the extreme conditions they spawn is difficult to say. But one first-hand account of the communal violence that occurred in Surat in the aftermath of the destruction of the Ayodhya mosque suggests a strong link between the violence, which had not previously been a feature of the city, and rapid urbanisation associated with industrialisation.[94] The situation in these rapidly growing secondary cities is exacerbated by infrastructure problems, especially relating to scarcity of water. Jaipur is estimated to have only sufficient water for 20 years and some cities, such as Rajkot, get only 20 minutes supply a day in the dry season.[95]

Table 2.3: Population and growth rates of major South Asian cities, with projections to the year 2000.

	POPULATION (millions)						AVERAGE ANNUAL GROWTH RATE (%)				
	1941	1951	1961	1970	1985	2000	1941-50	1951-60	1961-70	1970-85	1985-2000
INDIA											
Bangladore	0.41	0.79	1.21	1.62	3.73	7.67	9.27	5.32	3.76	5.56	4.81
Calcutta	2.17	2.70	2.93	6.91	10.29	15.94	2.44	0.85	1.51	2.65	2.92
Delhi	0.58	1.12	2.06	3.53	6.95	12.77	9.31	8.39	7.93	4.52	4.06
Greater Bombay	1.80	2.99	4.15	5.81	9.47	15.43	6.61	3.88	4.44	3.26	3.25
Madras	0.78	1.42	1.73	3.03	4.87	7.85	8.21	2.18	7.50	3.16	3.18
PAKISTAN											
Karachi	0.39	1.60	1.91	3.13	6.16	11.57	17.53	7.97	0.64	4.51	4.20
Lahore	0.67	0.85	1.30	1.97	3.40	5.93	2.69	5.29	5.15	3.64	3.71
BANGLADESH											
Dhaka	0.30	0.34	0.56	1.50	4.76	11.26	4.10	6.60	16.80	7.70	5.74

Sources:

1941-1961 figures:
INDIA: Census of India 1951, General Population Tables, Towns and Town Groups classified by Population in 1961 with variations since 1901.
PAKISTAN: '10 years of Pakistan in Statistics 1972-82', Federal Bureau of Statistics, Statistics Division, Government of Pakistan, Tables 2.6, Growth of Cities/Towns from 1901-1981.
BANGLADESH: 'Population Growth and Policies in Mega-Cities, Dhaka', Department of International Economics and Social Affairs, Population Policy Paper No. 8, ST/ESA/SER.R/69, United Nations, New York, 1987.

1970-2000 figures:
All cities -'Prospects of World Urbanization 1988', Population Studies No. 112, Department of International Economic and Social Affairs, United Nations, New York, 1989, Table 6, pp. 19-21.

In India, migration from rural areas is still relatively not as important a factor in the rate of urbanisation as it is in some other parts of the developing world such as South America. However, it is becoming increasingly so.[96]   Significantly, surveys indicate that in the case of migration from distant rural areas to cities, employment features highly as a motivating factor, while in the case of migration from a city's hinterland, education and other resource disparities are also important.[97]   Such data would suggest that as jobs in rural areas become ever more scarce and as disparities in resources between rural and urban areas increase, migration is likely to accelerate.[98]   It also suggests that the 'urban bias' evident in the allocation of subsidies and resources in the social sector are important factors in urban migration.

Nor is the problem of rapid urbanisation confined to India. Until recently, Karachi was one of the fastest growing cities in Asia. It was to Karachi that many of those who fled India on partition were drawn. This group, known as *Mohajirs*, rapidly came to outnumber the native Sindhis. With cash in hand as a result of selling up in India, they founded new industries and, like migrants the world over, quickly came to out-perform economically their hosts. Later, their success came to be resented by the Sindhi populace, more and more of whom had been forced into the cities because of the savage feudal conditions in the countryside.

The Afghan war brought with it the gun, drug and crime cultures now endemic in urban life in Karachi.[99] During the 1980s, the opponents of the *Mohajirs* used this new access to arms to transform themselves into armed criminal gangs. The resulting breakdown of civil society in Karachi has at times been almost total, with kidnappings of wealthy businessmen for ransom running at several a day. Perhaps 5% of the population is now addicted to heroin.[100] Karachi's neighbouring city of Hyderabad is also troubled by violence. At times the situation between warring factions in that city has degenerated to such an extent that the authorities had to cut off water supplies in an attempt to bring the city under control.[101]

*

As well as the cluster of problems around the issue of transmigration, a second set of problems occur when resource scarcity in a particular region results in a dependant population losing its source of livelihood and cultural continuity. As already noted, the tribal forest dwellers who inhabit the forest belt throughout central India have been severely affected in this way. Another example of the effect of resource depletion on ethnic tension may be found in the competition over the ever-diminishing resource of the *diara*, or flood plain riverine lands of Bihar. While this tension has been manifest for centuries as tension over caste *qua* caste, it has recently been intensified by the increase of population on an ever-diminishing resource as the *diara* has been subjected to the vicissitudes of ever longer floods.[102]

The clash between Tamil migrants to the city of Bangalore in the state of Karnataka and local inhabitants over the sharing of the waters of the Cauvery river provides a further example of a situation in which an absolute resource scarcity has occasioned unrest and loss of life. The Cauvery is the only large river flowing into Tamil Nadu and its delta waters the Thanjavur district, which is the 'rice bowl' of the state of 55 million. Since the upper riparian state, Karnataka, began to act in breach of the water-sharing arrangement between the two states, the traditional double crop of the delta has allegedly been reduced to a single crop.[103] When Karnataka was ordered to restore the cuts, riots against Tamils in Bangalore followed, some were killed, and thousands were forced to flee as refugees. The clashes caused by the need to relocate hundreds of thousands of people affected by the damming of the Narmada river provides another example of the way in which resource issues have directly impacted on security.

To a lesser degree, resource issues—particularly in relation to land and jobs—may be factors in the separatist movements in Punjab, Sri Lanka and Kashmir. Some caution is, however, warranted in these cases since a multiplicity of other factors are involved, such as loss of ability to achieve out-migration, political mismanagement on the part of central governments and religious, ethnic, linguistic and cultural differences.

Within the Northern Province of Sri Lanka, the district of Jaffna is 95% Tamil.[104] With the exception of the urban districts it is one of the more densely populated provinces, with 433 persons per square kilometre.[105] It is, however, located in the dry zone of the island and is heavily dependent on ground water irrigation.[106] Due to the squeeze on agriculture, the inhabitants of the peninsula have been forced to intensify cultivation and to cultivate even within the villages themselves.[107] Under the British, people from Jaffna—and indeed, Tamils more generally—found an outlet through education.[108] Within Ceylon, they entered the bureaucracy and professions in large numbers. This, and out-migration generally, afforded some relief from the build-up of population and lack of additional exploitable farming land.

With independence, however, the Sinhalese majority, many of whom were in poverty and unemployed following the rapid growth in population between 1946 and 1960,[109] used their political power to reduce Tamil influence within the bureaucracy and professions. The mechanisms by which this was done were the declaration of Sinhala as the sole national language (1956) and 'standardisation' (1971), under which Tamils were marked down in university entrance in relation to Sinhalese.[110] Outside employment was thus less available to the Tamils at a critical period. At the same time, overseas migration became more difficult as a number of countries, particularly within the European Community, began to close their doors to migrants.

It was the Jaffna Tamils and the poor of the peninsula who formed the rank-and-file of separatist organisations such as the Tamil Tigers.[111] Money is raised by the Tigers through collection of tax-like levies from the populace, allegedly from drug smuggling and arms dealing, and on occasion from mercenary activities. Wealthy Tamils in India, the West and Southeast Asia also provide the Tigers with considerable funds. The Tigers now provide what virtually amounts to a profession of arms to a number of otherwise disenfranchised young Tamils.

The role of resource-related issues in the insurgency in Punjab is more difficult to determine than it is in some of the cases discussed so far. Although it is evident that at least some of the excess labour caused by the plateauing of the Green Revolution has been picked up by small industries and that the lot of agricultural labourers might be improving, it is less clear that the children of Jat Sikh farmers have benefited from these trends.[112] Allowing for the fact that the data are inadequate, we might tentatively put forward the hypothesis that the family farm can no longer sustain the same degree of family labour as it used to. We also noted earlier that proud agriculturalist castes such as Jats are reluctant to work as agricultural labourers.

Land is only one of the inputs necessary for agriculture. More than almost any other Indian state, Punjab's 'miracle' of the Green Revolution has depended on irrigation. Yet the amount of new land brought under irrigation has plateaued, partly due to scarcity of river water. Some attribute this 'squeeze' on the supply of water to the fact that the state does not get its fair share of the river waters of the Ravi, Beas and Sutlej rivers. The Sikhs especially believe that this water is being unfairly channelled off into Haryana and Rajasthan.[113] It was for this reason that militants stopped work on the Sutlej-Yamuna Link Canal in 1990 after they had murdered a number of construction engineers.[114] Part of the problem derives from the rapid growth of New Delhi, for which water is being diverted from Punjab. The fact that the state of Rajasthan is both the driest in India and has a rapid growth of population has also brought pressure to bear on the government to supply that state with water. It is claimed that unless the water issue is quickly resolved, the excess use of sub-soil water (through tube wells) will render 66 of Punjab's 118 blocks 'dry' by 1996.[115]

It might also be the case that other traditional outlets for labour are increasingly denied to Sikhs. With independence and the revision of the theory of the 'martial' races, the percentage of Sikhs in the army evidently declined.[116] The decline in recruitment of Sikhs in the army may well be true of other professions such as the railways and the merchant marine. It is certainly true of police forces throughout India.[117] The British Empire also once provided a means by which Sikhs spread to far-flung corners of the globe wherever enterprise and the profession of arms were required. With the winding down of the Empire and the progressive tightening of migration provisions in Europe and North America, such avenues are now no longer so widely available.

This decline in employment opportunities outside Punjab is parallelled by the failure of the government to encourage industry within the state. Especially in the border areas, development of large-scale industry was prevented by the government's policy of not locating such industry in areas vulnerable to Pakistani land or air attack. While small-scale industry has flourished in the state, jobs in these industries might not be regarded as suitable by educated Sikh youth. As Amarinder Singh has observed, 'The primary problem [in Punjab] is one of an increasing population, unemployment and the consequent turning to separatist propaganda out of frustration'.[118]

The way in which this apparent squeeze on the traditional functions of Jat Sikhs is actually translated into an insurgency movement is less clear. At one time, a number of guerrilla groups appeared virtually drew sustenance from the movement for an independent *Khalistan*. Recruits—who mostly came from the Jat and Majhbi (ex-untouchable Sikh) castes—were reportedly offered a Rs3,000 minimum wage and an AK-47 semi-automatic rifle.[119] As with the Tamil Tigers, the majority of the insurgents were young, in fact mere teenagers. Funds to pay the guerrilla forces were derived from forcible and voluntary exactions from the Sikh populace, gun and drug dealing, kidnapping and contributions from overseas Sikh communities. But to draw firm conclusions along the lines that these young recruits were seeking outlets in light of loss of traditional avenues for employment is, perhaps, to 'draw a long bow.'

There has also been a general squeeze of agriculture in the confines of the Vale of Kashmir. The problem is exacerbated by the fact that there are few opportunities for employment of educated youth because of the lack of industry. The 3000-5000 armed insurgents appear to be generally well educated, but with few career prospects, which lends weight to the view that economic grievances are at least in part to blame for the problems of the valley.[120]

The picture in Kashmir is, however, even less clear than the one in Punjab. It is obscured by a range of factors that have contributed to discontent in the Valley. These include central government interference, corruption at the local level and the traditional dominance of the small group of Brahmin Hindus (the *Pandits*) over important parts of the bureaucracy. All these factors have contributed to growing Islamic fundamentalism in a population not previously noted for its strict adherence to Islam.[121]

*

What the above studies together suggest is that a purely political or social explanation of the deteriorating internal security environment in South Asia is not sufficient to explain the upsurge in these problems. In many cases, the issues of resources and their allocation appear to be closely inter-twined with political and ethnic issues.

Resource issues seem to impact more at the local than at the international level, however. Thus while the Cauvery dispute, a dispute *within* India, resulted in significant violence at the local level, the dispute between Pakistan and India—two traditional competitors—over the Indus waters, and the dispute between Bangladesh and India over the sharing of the Ganges waters, have not resulted in violence. But as we shall see in the following chapter, local level disputes can reverberate through the political system and impact nationally or even internationally.

While resource issues are often present as factors in sub-national tension, they do not always constitute the primary focus of discontent. Rather, ethnic or political differences themselves seem more often to provide the immediate catalyst. This subsidiary, or secondary role is suggested by the fact that, while the influx of 3.4 million Afghan refugees into Pakistan did not lead to wide-scale unrest, probably because the two communities were of similar ethnic and religious background, in the case of Assam, the differences in religion and ethnic background between the migrants and hosts has from the start caused problems.

Our discussion also highlights the role of unemployment in contributing to discontent. Progressively, the options for finding employment and a new life outside one's locality are narrowing. The 'chocks' of population are now wedged in tighter than they once were and it is now more difficult for those living on the margin to find more congenial circumstances elsewhere. The history of the tribal forest dwellers of India is a case in point. In earlier times, the tribals were able to retreat progressively to the forested backwaters when their forest life was threatened by newcomers. In later years they found work in tea gardens and other plantations throughout India. Now those solutions are denied them: with their backs to the wall they are standing and fighting.

There is evidence that a similar process is occurring internationally. The EEC, for example, has announced tough new guide-lines for migration. This reflects a reduction in migration opportunities throughout the entire developed world. According to official sources, illegal immigration into the European Community is consequently now occurring at a rate of 500,000 cases per year.[122]

This limiting of options seems to have affected communities at the periphery of the political mainstream particularly severely. Under the British, sub-national groups such as Sikhs and Sri Lankan Tamils tended to be inducted into the processes of government because the Raj perceived them to be its loyal supporters. Their services were in demand not just within their own regions but more widely throughout South Asia, and even the Empire. With independence, however, this outlet was gradually denied them, as democratic politics opened up more opportunities for mainstream communities.

Finally, given the rapidly growing populations in South Asia, it would seem reasonable to anticipate that the type of insecurity we have witnessed to date might intensify rather than diminish; or at the very least, that it will take many years to overcome. Furthermore, the evidence suggests that the various separatist and dissident movements throughout the region are increasingly tending to have an impact well beyond their own localities. It is this process of linkage that we now turn to examine.

Endnotes

1   V.S. Naipaul, *India: A Million Mutinies Now*, Rupa and Co, Calcutta, 1990.

2   While it is invidious to single out specific authors from a large body of high quality work in this area, the following are some of the writers who have been active in interpreting political change in India

broadly along these lines: F. Frankel, *India's Political Economy, 1947-77*, Princeton University Press, New Jersey, 1978; L. & S. Rudolph, *In Pursuit of Lakshmi: The Political Economy of the Indian State*; Kohli, *Democracy and Discontent*; M. Weiner, *The Politics of Scarcity: Public Pressure and Political Response in India*, University of Chicago Press, Chicago, 1962; Dipesh Chakrabarty, 'Political Hinduism and the Question of Ethnicity in India', abridged version of a public lecture given at the University of Melbourne, 24 April, 1991; Robin Jeffrey, *What's Happening to India?: Punjab, Ethnic Conflict, Mrs Gandhi's Death and the Test for Federalism*, Macmillan, London, 1986.

3   Kohli, *Democracy and Discontent*, p. 340.

4   J. Clad, 'Spinning wheels', *Far Eastern Economic Review*, 23 August 1990, p. 14. Clad quotes the newly published *Cambridge Encyclopedia of India*.

5   'Rao likely to be elected unopposed', *Times of India*, 3 February 1992. Despite the title, the piece is about the rifts occasioned in the party in states such as Kerala.

6   The term 'resources' is used here in its wider sense. It means the base for providing the populace with basic needs in food, land, education, jobs, water, fresh air and shelter. It has been used in preference to a term such as 'environment' in order to avoid some of the more complex ecological implications of that term and to enable inclusion of items such as public health, jobs and education that are not usually thought of as being included within the term 'environment'.

7   Amartya Sen's classic study of the 1943 Bengal famine illustrates the complex nature of the relationship between political organisation and what manifests itself as resource insecurity. He was able to show that the famine was, in fact, largely 'man made'. See *Poverty and Famines: An Essay in Entitlement*, Oxford University Press, Oxford, 1972.

8   Rudolphs, *In Pursuit of Lakshmi*, p. 10

9   S. Singh, M. Premi and A. Bose, *Population Transition in India*, B.R. Publishing Corp., New Delhi, 1989, Vol. I, p. 26. But some reports are higher. See '30 p.c. Indians below poverty line', *Hindustan Times*, 9 July 1992.

10   Nag, for example, found on his re-investigation of the village of

Manupur in the prosperous Ludhiana district of Punjab, that the degree of job security for unskilled labour had increased along with the number of brick houses owned by ex-untouchables. M. Nag and N. Kak, 'Demographic Transition in a Punjab Village', *Population and Development Review*, Vol. 10, No. 4, December 1984, p. 661.

11   Jeffrey, *What's Happening to India?*, p. xii.

12   For a good description of the Jats and their social order see M.C. Pradhan, *The Political System of the Jats of Northern India*, Oxford University Press, Oxford, 1966.

13   See the views of Nag's water-carrier caste informant. 'Demographic Transition in a Punjab Village', p. 668; Anil Pathak, 'Graduates labour to survive drought', *The Times of India*, 25 May 1992..

14   Although the World Bank asserts that South Asia contains only 30% of the world's population (a figure which appears to be incorrect), the Bank claims it contains almost half of those living in poverty. World Bank, *World Development Report 1990*, Oxford University Press, UK, 1990, p. 2.

15   M.H. Chaudhry, 'Fertility Behaviour in India, 1961-86: The Stalled Decline in the Crude Birth Rate' in Singh, Premi and Bose, *Population Transition in India*, pp. 89-102.

16   Mahinder D. Chaudhry, 'Population Growth Trends in India: 1991 Census', *Population and the Environment*, Vol. 14, No. 1, September 1992, p. 31.

17   This is suggested by the existence of an infant mortality rate estimated at 150 per thousand. See Arun Ghosh, 'Eighth Plan: Challenges and Opportunities - I', *Economic and Political Weekly*, Vol. XXVI, No. 3, 19 January 1991, p. 80.

18   'India "winner" in family planning', *Times of India*, 30 January 1992.

19   This finding is based on 1985-86 estimates. The 1991 census results were suppressed.

20   World Bank, *Pakistan: Current Economic Situation and Prospects*, March 1991, p. 14.

21   N. Sadiq, *The State of World Population 1991*, UNFPA, (no publisher or date provided), unpaginated statistical appendix titled 'Population and Social Indicators'.

22   All the foregoing data except current population is from World Bank,

Pakistan: Current Economic Situation and Prospects. The current population (and hence the doubling) is from the UNDP, *Human Development Report 1991*, Oxford University Press, Oxford, 1991, 'human development profile on Pakistan', p. 86. The *World Development Report*, Table I, p. 178, on the other hand, puts the population at 106 million for mid-1988. Even with an increase of 3.1% there is a discrepancy. The population for the year 2000 (150 million) has been estimated by the National Institute of Population Studies, Islamabad, and appears in their publication, *The State of Population in Pakistan*, Islamabad, November 1988, p. iii.

23   R. Leete and G. Jones, 'South Asia's Future Population: Are There Really Grounds for Optimism?' Unpublished paper, Demography Programme, Research School of Social Sciences, The Australian National University, p. 12.

24   Leete and Jones, 'South Asia's Future Population...', p. 17.

25   Leete and Jones, 'South Asia's Future Population...', p. 9.

26   The HDI is derived on the basis of indicators such as life expectancy, literacy, female-male disparities, wage rates, mean years of schooling, distribution of income, poverty, etc.

27   Rudolph, *In Pursuit of Lakshmi*, p. 298; Myron Weiner, *The Child and the State in India: Child Labour and Education Policy in Comparative Perspective*, Princeton University Press, Princeton, New Jersey, 1991.

28   R.S. Newman, *Grassroots Education in India: A Challenge to Policy Makers*, Sterling Publishers, New Delhi, 1989, p. 1.

29   Subramanian Swamy, *Economic Growth in China and India*, Vikas, New Delhi, 1989. China has also invested more in agricultural infrastructure, however.

30   Government of India, Ministry of Finance, 'Economic Reforms Two Years After and the Task Ahead' (Discussion Paper), New Delhi, 1993, p. 26.

31   World Bank, *India: 1990 Country Economic Memorandum*, Country Operations Division, India Country Department, Asia Region, World Bank, Vol. VI, Table 1.6, p. 14.

32   World Bank, *India: 1991 Country Economic Memorandum*, Country Operations Division, India Country Department, Asia Region, World Bank, Vol. 1, August 23, 1991, p. 2, Table 1.1.

33   UNIDO report on developing country performance in the 1990s, as reported in the *Times of India*, 1 April 1991.

34   World Bank, *India: 1990 Country Economic Memorandum*, para. 1.37.

35   Mrinal Chaudhuri Datta, 'Mandal and the Berlin Wall', *Seminar*, No. 377, January 1991, p. 58.

36   Peter Mares, 'Tearing itself apart', *Asia-Pacific Defence Reporter*, February 1991, p. 18.

37   Kohli, *Democracy and Discontent*, p. 355.

38   T.S. Papola, 'Unemployment, Poverty and Inequality', in M.S. Adiseshiah (Ed.), *Eighth Plan Perspective*, Lancer International, New Delhi, 1990, p. 216.   For a similar figure—endorsed by the approach paper for the revised Eighth Plan, see Arun Ghosh, 'A paper to ponder', *Frontline*, 20 December 1991, p. 111.   The discrepancy would seem to be due to the fact that the latter estimate includes those already unemployed.

39   D. Bhattacharya, 'Indian Economic Development', paper presented under the joint auspices of the Centre for Indian Studies (Sydney University) and the Business Council of Australia, 11 November 1988.

40   V.K. Ramachandran, 'IMF-style reform and the poor', *Frontline*, 6 December 1991, p. 35.

41   World Bank, *India: 1991 Country Economic Memorandum*, Vol. II, p. 2.

42   In 1961, the percentage of landowners who owned under 2.49 *acres* was 30.73%.   See P.K. Ghosh, *Developing South Asia: A Modernisation Perspective*, Greenwood Press, Westport, Connecticut, 1984, p. 32, Table 13.   By 1981, 57% of landowners owned under one *hectare*.   See *India 1991: Observer Statistical Handbook*, Observer Research Foundation, New Delhi, 1991, p. 69, 'Operational Holdings 1980-81'.

43   B.G. Verghese, *Waters of Hope: Himalaya-Ganga Development and Cooperation for a Billion People*, Oxford and IBH, New Delhi, 1990, p. 34.

44   Planning Commission, Government of India, *Eighth Five Year Plan 1992-97*, Controller of Publications, New Delhi, 1992, p. 33.

45   World Bank, *India: 1991 Country Economic Memorandum*, Vol. II,

p. 3.

46   Papola, 'Unemployment, Poverty and Inequality', p. 217.

47   World Bank, *India: 1991 Country Economic Memorandum*, Vol. II, p. 1.

48   Sunil Jain. 'Agriculture: Incomplete Initiatives', *India Today*, 15 February 1993, p. 109; Anon, 'Missing the wood for the trees', *Business India*, 29 March-11 April, 1993, p. 106.

49   World Bank, *India: 1991 Country Economic Memorandum*, Vol. II, p. iii.

50   *Times of India*, Editorial, 2 August 1991.

51   World Bank, *India: 1991 Country Economic Memorandum*, Vol. II, p. ii.

52   World Bank, *India: 1991 Country Economic Memorandum*, Vol. II, p. iv.

53   Chart on 'Social Indicators', *Far Eastern Economic Review*, 13 August 1992, p. 12.

54   World Bank, *India: 1991 Country Economic Memorandum*, Vol II, p. 7.

55   Verghese, *Waters of Hope*, p. 35.

56   'Bihar at bottom of economic graph', *Times of India*, 9 February 1992.

57   World Bank, *India: 1991 Country Economic Memorandum*, Vol. II, p. iv.

58   Ramesh Vinayak, Dilip Awasthi and Amarnath K. Menon, 'Agriculture: Incomplete Iniatives', *India Today*, 15 February 1993, p. 109.

59   World Bank, *India: 1991 Country Economic Memorandum*, Vol. II, p. 9.

60   World Bank, *India: 1991 Country Economic Memorandum*, Vol. II, p. 19. However, Dr Richard Shand, an agricultural economist who has worked extensively on South Asian agriculture told the author that he sees no early signs that dryland farming will be able fully to accommodate the expanding requirements of agriculture.

61   Nafis Sadiq (UNFPA), *The State of World Population 1990*, unpaginated Table under the title social indicators. India has 2.9 people per hectare of arable land in rural areas. China has 7.6

persons per hectares.

62 Myron Weiner, 'Security, Migration and Conflict in South Asia', *Defense Intelligence Journal*, Vol. 1, No. 2, Fall 1992.

63 'Infiltration posing problems for Tripura', *The Hindu*, 21 July 1992.

64 *Census of India, 1951*, Vol. XII, Part I-A, p. 72, as in M. Weiner, *Sons of the Soil: Migration and Ethnic Conflict in India*, Princeton University Press, 1978, p. 79.

65 This is indicated by the high numbers of Hindu arrivals. See Government of India, *A Portrait of Population, Assam, Census of India 1971*, Government of India Central Press, India, p. 106.

66 In the nineteenth century and early twentieth century there was a wave of migration of educated Bengalis moving in to service the growing Assamese bureaucracy in circumstances in which there were insufficient educated Assamese to fill the role.

67 Guha, 'Little Nationalism Turned Chauvinist: Assam's Anti-Foreigner Upsurge, 1979-80', *Economic and Political Weekly*, Special Number, Vol. XV, Nos. 41-43, p. 1707.

68 The name is derived from the original insurrection in 1967 in the district of Naxalbari in West Bengal.

69 Over many centuries the tribal populations were pushed into the forested marginal land by Aryans and other more powerful groups. See B.M. Boal, *The Konds: Human Sacrifice and Religious Change*, Aris and Phillips, UK, 1982, p. 107; Weiner, *Sons of the Soil*, pp. 154-5; and R.N. Pareek, *Tribal Culture in Flux: The Jatapus of Eastern Ghats*, B.R. Publishing Corp., New Delhi 1977, p. 192.

70 V. Das, 'Forests and Tribals of Jharkhand', *Economic and Political Weekly*, Vol. XXVI, No. 6, 9 February 1991; E. Verrier, *A New Deal for Tribal India*, Government of India, Ministry of Home Affairs, New Delhi 1963, pp. 54-5; Verghese, *Waters of Hope*, p. 387; and H. McDonald, 'Saint is dammed', *Far Eastern Economic Review*, 7 February 1991, p. 13.

71 Weiner is, however, cautious in attributing too much to the 'out-migration' safety valve. See *Sons of the Soil*, pp. 161-5.

72 Pareek, *Tribal Culture in Flux...*, pp. 184-6.

73 Weiner, *Sons of the Soil*, pp. 194-214; Leslie J. Calman, *Protest in Democratic India: Authority's Response to Challenge*, Westview Press, Boulder and London, 1985, p. 21; G. Parthasarathy, 'Roots of

Naxalism: The land question and law and order', *Frontline*, 14 February 1992, pp. 110-11.

74   Ministry of Home Affairs, Government of India, *Annual Report of the Ministry of Home Affairs for 1989-90*, New Delhi (n.d.), p. 4.

75   Quoted in B. Dogra, 'Tribal Discontent: Timely Warning', *Economic and Political Weekly*, Vol. XXV, No. 14, p. 710.

76   'Refugee crisis in Nepal', *The Hindu*, 17 August 1992.

77   See C. Manogaran, *Ethnic conflict and Reconciliation in Sri Lanka*, University of Hawaii Press, Honolulu 1987, pp. 90-91.

78   Calculation based on the 1987 figure of the population of the NWFP of 9.6 million, Government of Pakistan, Federal Bureau of Statistics, *Demographic Survey 1987*, Islamabad, p. 10.

79   'Warning Welcome', *Wall Street Journal*, 25 August 1987, p. 1 and p. 21; 'Afghan Refugees Burden Pakistan', *Wall Street Journal*, 23 June 1982, p. 31; T. Skogland, 'Ecology and the War in Afghanistan', in B. Huldt and E. Jansson (Eds), *The Tragedy of Afghanistan: The Social, Cultural and Political Impact of the Soviet Invasion*, Croom Helm, London 1899, pp. 175-96; and I. Cheema, 'Impact of the Afghan War on Pakistan', *Pakistan Horizon*, Vol. XLI, January 1988, pp. 29-29.

80   See Statement of Howard B. Schaffer, Deputy Assistant Secretary of State, Bureau of Near Eastern and South Asian Affairs, Department of State, before the Subcommittee on Asia and Pacific Affairs, House Foreign Affairs Committee of the US Congress, 8 March 1989, p. 557; ABC Radio program 'World Report', 24 October 1990; and M.K. Malik, 'Drug Menace in South Asia', *Regional Studies* (Pakistan), Vol. VIII, No. 3, Summer, 1990, p. 32.

81   ABC radio, 24 October 1990; Malik, 'Drug Menace', p. 39 and pp. 41-2.

82   'BSF plan to beef up border security', *Times of India*, 1 March 1991.

83   Christopher Thomas, 'Drug barons turn Bombay into money laundering centre', *The Times*, as in *The Australian*, 20 May 1993.

84   *Far Eastern Economic Review*, February 22, 1990, p. 28.

85   For example, the Government of India's *Annual Report of the Ministry of Home Affairs* for 1989-90 reported that during the year the BSF apprehended 74 'extremists' crossing the Punjab border and seized 71 AK-47s, 13 AK-74s, 9 rocket launchers, 64 rockets and

one MMG. See p. 12. Then Home Minister Mufti Mohammad claimed that land mines, tank mines, and rocket launchers had been discovered in the hands of the Kashmir rebels. 'Drive against Ultras to Continue: Mufti', *National Herald* (International Weekly), June 15-21 1990. See also J. Clad, 'Limits of tolerance', *Far Eastern Economic Review*, 17 May 1990, p. 11; and T.A. Davis, 'The killing season opens', *Asia-Pacific Defence Reporter*, Vol. XVII, No. 12, June 1991, p. 10.

86   Attacks in Haryana and Uttar Pradesh were carried out with AK-47s. See M. Srinivas, 'Spreading Fear', *Frontline*, 3 January 1992, p. 22. Such weapons would likely have originated in Pakistan and come via Punjab.

87   'Concern over rapid urbanisation', *The Hindu* (International Edition), 26 June 1993.

88   For an account of Calcutta's decline and revival under the Marxist government see Kohli, *Democracy and Discontent*, Chapters 6 and 10.

89   James Masselos, 'The Bombay Riot of January 1993: The politics of Urban Conflagration', paper read at a conference on *The BJP After Ayodhya*, Curtin University, Perth, July 1993.

90   T. Thomas, 'Bombay riot - 1: It had to happen', *Hindustan Times*, 24 February 1993. One of the factors behind the arson in the riots was apparently efforts by landlords to clear out squatters and fixed tenants from property so that it could be re-developed.

91   Michael Schuman, 'Unequal struggle', *Far Eastern Economic Review*, 19 September 1991, p. 48.

92   See for example, 'Caution against endless migration to Delhi', *The Hindu*, 4 October 1991; and 'Decentralisation the only answer', *The Hindu*, 2 August 1991.

93   'BJP says Haryana is not letting out water', *The Hindu*, 13 July 1991.

94   Sudhir Chandra, 'Of Communal Consciousness and Communal Violence: Impressions from Post-Riot Surat', paper read at a conference on *The BJP After Ayodhya*, Curtin University, Perth, July 1993.

95   See Bachi J. Karkaria, 'Still a watered down concern', *Times of India*, 20 July 1992; and 'Water resources in city will last only 20 years', *The Hindu*, 17 July 1992.

96   P. Visaria, 'Rural-Urban Disparities in India', in Indian Council of Social Science Research (Ed.), *Economic Development of India and China: A Comparative Study*, Lancer International, New Delhi, 1988, p. 82.

97   Visaria, 'Rural-Urban Disparities in India', Table 5, p. 89.

98   Visaria, 'Rural-Urban Disparities in India', Tables 7, p. 91; 8, p. 92; 9, p. 93; and 10, p. 95.

99   See A.S. Ahmed, *Pakistan Society: Islam, Ethnicity and Leadership in South Asia*, Oxford University Press, Karachi 1986, p. 32; and D. Brown, 'Military boots set rhythm in fun city of Pakistan', *Canberra Times*, 30 July 1990.

100   See K.M. Malik, 'Drug Menace in South Asia', *Regional Studies*, Vol. XIII, No. 3, Summer 1990, p. 32.

101   'PM fights demands for state of emergency', *The Times*, AFP, as in *The Australian*, 31 May 1990.

102   Centre for Science and the Environment, *State of India's Environment: Floods, Flood Plains and Environmental Myths*, Centre for Science and the Environment, New Delhi 1991, pp. 139-40.

103   'Hopes Hinge on Tribunal Award', *The Hindu*, 28 July 1991.

104   R.K. Dubey, *Indo-Sri Lankan Relations with Special Reference to the Tamil Problem*, Deep and Deep Publications, New Delhi, 1989, Appendix X, p. 203.

105   Central Bank of Sri Lanka, Statistics Department, *Economic and Social Statistics of Sri Lanka*, Vol. IX, December, 1986, Table 2.8, p. 12.

106   Morrison, Barrie, et.al. (Eds), *The Disintegrating Village: Social Change in Sri Lanka*, Lake House Investments Limited, Colombo, 1979, p. 150.

107   Morrison, *The Disintegrating Village*, p. 164.

108   See Mares, 'Tearing itself apart' p. 18.

109   K.M. de Silva reports that 14% of the work force was estimated to be unemployed by 1969-70. See *Managing Ethnic Tensions in Multi-Ethnic Societies: Sri Lanka 1880-1985*, University Press of America, Lanham 1986, pp. 166-67.

110   Mares, 'Tearing Itself Apart'. For a full statistical account of this

process see C. Manogaran, *Ethnic Conflict and Reconciliation*, Table 15 p. 121; Table 16 p. 123; Table 17 p. 125; Table 18 p. 128; and Table 19 p. 129.

111   The founder of the LTTE, Velupillai Prabhakaran, was himself a school dropout from Jaffna. He tended to recruit members of the lower castes.   See E. O'Ballance, *The Cyanide War: Tamil Insurrection in Sri Lanka 1973-88*, Brassey's, London 1989. p. 13.

112   J.R. Westley, *Agriculture and Equitable Growth: The Case of Punjab-Haryana*, Westview Press, Boulder, 1986, pp. 155-58, pp. 165-66, p. 182, and p. 267; M. Nag, 'Demographic Transition in a Punjab Village', p. 673.

113   Jeffrey, *What's Happening to India?*, pp. 160-61.

114   Dinesh Kumar, 'Militants' multiplying conduct codes ring alarm bells', *The Sunday Times*, 24 May 1992.

115   Amarinder Singh, 'Punjab Has Welcomed Army Deployment', *Times of India*, 17 December 1991.

116   M.L. Chibber, *Military Leadership to Prevent a Military Coup*, Lancer, New Delhi, 1986, Table 1.1, p. 40; Jeffrey, *What's Happening to India*, pp. 148-49; Lt. Gen. S.K. Sinha (Ret'd), 'Caste and the Indian Army', *Indian Defence Review*, July 1986, p. 81; interview, General A.M. Vohra (Ret'd), New Delhi, 10 October 1990.

117   Following independence, pressure was increasingly brought to bear on state governments to recruit locals into the state police. See K.F. Rustomji, 'The Paramilitary-Army Interface', *Indian Defence Review*, January 1991, p. 93.

118   Singh, 'Punjab Has Welcomed Army Deployment'.

119   See 'Militants Call the Shots in the Punjab', Dinesh Kumar, *Times of India*, 28 November 1990.

120   Davis, 'Kashmir: The killing season opens', p. 11.

121   The Pandits formerly constituted only about 3% of the population of the Vale of Kashmir, but according to some claims occupied about 90% of the positions in some central government institutions. See A.G. Noorani, 'Jagmohan turbulence', *Frontline*, 3 January 1992, p. 83.

122   'Alien Dirge', *The Sunday Times of India*', 8 March 1992.

3   Politics, Instability and the South Asian Setting

The failure of the nations of South Asia to come to grips with the related problems of high population growth rates, poverty and political instability, and the displacement of populations to which this failure has given rise, is in turn closely related to the failure of the region to develop a viable pattern of regional relationships. All too often domestic political problems become projected onto the regional stage. This process of projection occurs at a number of levels.

At one level, governments attempt to assist their nation building endeavours and to draw attention away from internal difficulties by pointing to traditional competitors. At its most obvious, this process may be observed in the competition between India and Pakistan, but it also occurs between other regional nations. Increasingly, however, this agenda, which has had to be pursued within restraints in order to retain its utility, is being 'stolen' by various chauvinistic elements. These subsequently 'up the ante' of the competition between nations and take it into realms which traditional elites would rather avoid.

At another level, the various problems that occur within nations, especially those relating to sub-national discontent as it occurs in border or peripheral regions described in the previous chapter, tend to 'wash back and forward' between the nations of South Asia and exacerbate existing chauvinistic tendencies. Thus the economic problems of Bangladesh have caused transmigration of Bangladeshis into India on a considerable scale. These migrations have triggered a chauvinistic response—a response that is encouraged by the BJP for its own political purposes. This use of chauvinism for political gain has in turn had a detrimental effect on relations between India and Bangladesh.

Traditional elites and regional competition

Elites in the constituent parts that emerged from the British colonial empire were initially faced with the challenge of forging nations from entities that were often highly disparate. One way round this problem of 'nation building' that has been utilised by political elites has been to emphasise the 'otherness' of neighbouring nations. Such a process, however, contains within it the germ of a significant problem: in seeking to define the neighbour as its principal competitor, a nation is inexorably led to a tighter definition of what constitutes its own nationhood. This in turn leads inevitably to the 'excising' of large minorities from the political mainstream.

In the case of India, the political purposes of the elites were initially served through the Congress party. The interests represented within Congress were, however, broad, reflecting the coalition of forces that had originally supported the nationalist movement. Such a combination, in conjunction with India's first-past-the-post voting system and the considerable prestige the party inherited from the long freedom struggle, meant that Congress was able to dominate the political scene for the first 20 years of independence.

A coalition of this nature, however, entailed that the party portray an inclusive, even eclectic, view of what constituted the essence of the Indian nation. This view was in turn expressed in the Gandhi-Nehru paradigm of how India should behave as an actor on the world stage.[1] The predominant paradigm during the years following independence comprised a mix of idealist and realist perspectives: but it was a mix in which idealism had the upper hand.

Although the moral precepts centring on non-violence developed by Mahatma Gandhi during the course of the long freedom struggle came to the fore on the world stage, in the narrower confines of the South Asian theatre, a kind of Monroe Doctrine inherited from the British Raj prevailed. On the world stage, India assumed the high moral ground. It abjured nuclear weapons, it came to see the colonising powers as the sources of war, and conversely, in Nehru's words, the developing nations as a 'moral makeweight to restore the balance of the world'.[2] Within this system, India was to be the first of equals and a leader in the Non-Aligned Movement (NAM), which was originally envisaged as a moral rejection of the power politics of the large, developed nations. In contrast, South Asia itself was conceived as falling within an Indian sphere of influence that precluded any involvement of significant external powers, protected behind the buffers of the Himalayas, the Hindu Kush and the surrounding oceans.

This essentially idealistic view of India's relationship with other developing countries outside South Asia was rudely shattered by the defeat of India in 1962 by a China that, according to the idealistic view then prevailing, should have been a brother Asian power ranged with India against the quasi-colonial powers and ready to resolve all issues through the principals of *panscheela*.[3] With the Indian defeat, the realist perspective moved to the fore. According to this view,

> ... after 40 years of Gandhian negation of power, the country has realised ... that unfortunately [in] the world as it exists today

military power counts ...[4]

This position has been summed up even more forthrightly by a leading defence official: ' ... weaklings are not honoured. So we should be strong'.[5]

Moreover, by 1969 the Congress hold on the electorate had begun to weaken. Mrs Gandhi had split the party in that year, and the split had necessitated that she enter into a strategic alliance with the Moscow-oriented Marxists, the Communist Party of India (CPI), in order to retain a parliamentary majority. In the early years of the 1970s her troubles deepened. She was forced to declare a state of emergency in 1975, and in 1977, for the first time ever, the Congress party was defeated in a national election.

Bhabani Sen Gupta has observed a strong link between the slump in the fortunes of the Congress party and the 'imperial or regnant' style in claiming that Congress alone was the party of the patriot.[6] Indeed, there are many instances of Congress using foreign policy issues to shore up its failing fortunes. The most obvious is Mrs Gandhi's decision to detonate a nuclear device in 1974, a decision made during a period of decline in her fortunes.[7]

As already noted, one means Mrs Gandhi used to deal with such problems was to encourage a view of India as the 'weak-strong state'.[8] Thus Mrs Gandhi and her son Rajiv chose to portray the Indian state as being weak and threatened from 'anti-national forces' and the 'foreign hand' (terms that were deliberately vague, but were implicitly taken to mean Pakistan and, on occasion, the United States). This 'weak' side of the equation was used in order to convey the impression that Congress was the only truly national party with a capability to prevent India being dismembered by 'anti-national' forces.

At the same time, India was portrayed as a nation that was rapidly developing the scientific and technical accoutrements of a regional superpower, such as self-sustaining defence industries, a nuclear industry, ballistic missiles, and the capability to develop a blue water navy. These ideas of power based on the new forms of technology accorded well with the aspirations of a rising, 'modern', predominantly Hindu middle class. They were made much of by Rajiv Gandhi's government in its campaign in the run-up to the 1989 election. The new instruments of war were given a somewhat vague Hindu identity—hence names such as *Indra*, *Trishul* and *Agni* for various pieces of lethal hardware. This paradoxical 'weak-strong' attitude to power was well expressed by Rajiv Gandhi's media minister, K.K. Tiwari, in 1989:

... [we]... must reach out to people and make them understand the gravity of the situation that the nation faces today ... [but equally] the heroic struggle of our people in the fields of science, technology, agriculture, industrialisation—should be projected.[9]

The nationalism that the Congress party hoped to employ, then, was one that was secular (although the party was not averse on occasion to playing the 'Hindu card' when it suited), that emphasised the new military, scientific and industrial power of India and the potential of the nation to be a regional great power, and that also portrayed a nation that required unity in the face of shadowy outside threats, particularly from Pakistan.

Pakistani politicians have been no less prone to use the competition with India to serve their own political purposes. Benazir Bhutto strongly attacked India over Kashmir when her first government was under threat from the military in the months before its dismissal. A decade before, her father raised invective against India to fever pitch in order to stave off the threat to his own government posed by the military. On the eve of the 1990 elections, when Pakistan faced considerable instability, the Chief of Army Staff, General Beg, blamed the Indian RAW for destabilising the nation, as did Benazir's successor, Nawaz Sharif.[10]

In order for the competition between India and Pakistan to serve its intended purpose, however, it has to be conducted within restraints. Total war would serve no purpose for the elites in either nation. For New Delhi, a full-scale war with Pakistan would achieve little unless India were able thereby to create a *cordon sanitaire* throughout the entire length of its border with Pakistan. Indeed, the last thing New Delhi would want would be to have to incorporate and hold territory containing millions more Muslims than it already possesses.

On their part, Pakistan's leaders are well aware that their nation would likely lose a war with India unless the latter were at the same time diverted on the border with China, an event that becomes less and less likely with the developing relationship between India and China. On both sides, the destruction imposed by full-scale war would cut directly across economic interests and political stability. There is, therefore, a sense in which the grandstanding which takes place in all regional countries for political purposes is seen by neighbours who are victims as just that—grandstanding. As Leo Rose has remarked, the conduct of relations with neighbours 'are both too important and too specific to be handled by [mere] slogan-mongering'.[11]

This need on the part of elites for at least some continuity and stability in the conduct of relations is evident in the way conflict is actually managed in South Asia. Conflicts between India and Pakistan have for the most part been conducted according to the kind of 'gentlemanly' norm, perhaps imagined but never wholly evident, in the high-noon of the Raj. The treatment of prisoners has, for example, been exemplary. After the fall of East Pakistan in 1971, the 91,000 West Pakistani troops captured by India were allowed for a time to keep their weapons so that they could protect themselves from the revenge of the Bengalis. And the age of chivalry was not dead: the senior-most Pakistani amongst the prisoners requested, like a captain leaving his sinking ship, to be the last to leave Indian soil.[12] Comprehensive sets of confidence and security building measures have also been established between the two, designed to prevent conflict from escalating.[13]

The long-running conflict over the Kashmir border also seemed until recently to be conducted according to certain unwritten rules. Except in the Siachen Glacier area (the one part of the border where there is no recognised 'line of control'), exchanges between Indian and Pakistani troops usually involved only small arms fire. Considerable efforts are made to settle outbreaks quickly between local commanders and 'hot lines' are in place at commander level. It has thus rarely been necessary to use the 'hot line' installed between the two Prime Ministers.[14] On those occasions when artillery duals have broken out, for example in September 1991 in the Poonch sector, the matter has been viewed very seriously indeed. Moreover, on each occasion when the two nations did actually go to war the conflict ceased after a short time. The longest the two have ever fought is three weeks in 1965.

The classic example of this tendency not to prosecute wars fully is India's failure to press home its strong advantage against Pakistan in 1971 and destroy once and for all its enemy's war-making potential. One Indian analyst, Ravi Rikhye, is scathing about this failure. Of the 1947-48 campaign he says 'It seemed that we were playing some gentleman's game of cricket'.[15]

But it would be misleading to exaggerate the point about the utility of war as a means of nation building. There are very real differences between India and Pakistan, not least the territorial dispute over Kashmir. Moreover, while it is true that competition between the two has been restrained, increasingly that restraint is being eroded by two parallel and inter-related developments. These are the growing pattern of sub-regional instability, cross border activity, transmigration and general unrest that we noted earlier and the increasing tendency in both nations for the agenda to be seized from traditional elites by religiously-based, chauvinistic forces.

Religious chauvinism and regional competition

The friction between India and Pakistan is to an extent synonymous with their very existence. As Mohammed Ali Jinnah, who is considered to be the founding father of Pakistan, said in an often-quoted remark: 'The Hindus and Muslims ... belong to two different civilisations which are based mainly on conflicting ideas and conceptions'.[16] This 'two nation theory', as it was known, was probably the single most important reason for the creation of Pakistan.

According to one line of argument, the two nation theory was itself propagated by the Muslim elites of the former British colony because they assessed that they would be better served by forming their own state, one in which they would play a prominent role. If this interpretation is correct, the process of creation has not only dictated that Islam has grown in importance in Pakistan as the elites that founded the nation have been progressively challenged from within, but it has also meant that, far from being a reformist state, the feudal nature of much of Pakistani society has remained virtually intact.[17] This persistence of feudal structures is especially evident in the provinces of Sindh, Baluchistan and the North-West Frontier; but it also exists to an extent in the more progressive and populous province of Punjab.

The need on the part of the governing elites to maintain their position in a quasi-democratic situation such as Pakistan's has meant that politicians, who are themselves not especially inclined towards Islam, have periodically moved close to the Islamic parties, which have from time to time exercised a balance of power.

In the case of India, the interpretation of Indian nationalism provided by Mrs Gandhi and Rajiv was ripe for exploitation and competition from another 'new' nationalism—that of the Hindu Right. Indeed, the idea of the 'weak-strong state' is often propagated by parties towards the extreme end of the political spectrum. If the Indian state were being undermined from without and within and if, at the same time, it was a show piece for the national 'genius', then it was but a short step to identify more precisely both the sources of threat and those of success.

This the BJP sought to do. The threat from outside was identified as resurgent Islam, especially as it was espoused by Pakistan, and more recently Bangladesh.[18] According to one sarcastic comment made in the context of the BJP's most recent campaign against migrants from Bangladesh: ' ... the foreign hand has now been identified.   It is emasculated, brown and very Bangladeshi'. And the BJP now refers to the 'silent demographic invasion' from Bangladesh.[19]   The RSS is concentrating its efforts particularly on the state of West Bengal, where it considers that the influx of Bangladeshis and the fear it generates give the BJP good prospects.   According to one estimate the RSS now has 7000 branches and 180,000 sympathisers in the state.[20]   Although the BJP continues to deny the point strongly, the corollary of this attitude to Muslims is that ' ... [it] leads to the view that all Muslims in India are "Pakistanis"'.[21]

Conversely, the source of India's successes are seen to reside in its Hindu character, or 'genius'. For example, when it was in power in Madhya Pradesh, the BJP re-wrote school textbooks to glorify Hindu science and mathematics and to reinterpret history.[22]   The weak-strong view of the Indian state propagated by the BJP is evident in the views of one party official on the question of nuclear weapons:

> We don't want to be blackmailed and treated as oriental blackies.
> Nuclear weapons will give us prestige, power, standing. An Indian
> will talk straight and walk straight when we have the bomb.[23]

Thus in the 1980s there evolved in India two competing versions of nationalism, one supposedly secular, but not entirely so, and the other supposedly 'Hindu'. But it is important to recognise that the seeds of the second are to be found in the first, and that the first is in turn the logical outcome of the destruction of the Gandhi-Nehru paradigm that sought to define the genius of India through its moral and spiritual qualities. Indeed, it is no accident that the BJP has argued consistently that the Nehru-Gandhi version of Hindus as humble people who would bare their back to the blows of the *lathi* (a view that is itself a parody) is in fact an aberration in Indian history and one that has fostered 'defeatism', 'pseudo-secularism' and internal division.[24]

Another acute, unresolved issue confronting theorists of the Indian nation concerned the South Asian entity itself. The British had always argued that there was no such thing as a unified *Indian* nation, but that they ruled a 'subcontinent' as diverse as Europe. Such views were anathema to the earlier nationalists because they were regarded as a manifestation of the British policy of 'divide and rule'. In response, the nationalists propagated a 'one nation' theory of Indian nationalism that was required of necessity to rest on a view that the cement of nation was its cultural unity, a unity that extended from the Hindu Kush to the Arakan Hills. As Nehru remarked on a visit to Colombo in 1945:

[The people of Ceylon] are culturally, socially and linguistically as much a part of India as any [Indian] province.[25]

In fact, Nehru's version of the one nation theory accords quite closely with one strand of RSS thought, according to which all the religions of the people of South Asia are subsumed within the cultural paradigm of Hinduism. On this basis, it was argued, South Asia should be formed into a loose 'confederation'.[26]

Such views about cultural unity were, however, increasingly challenged by powerful historical processes according to which, not just nations, but also sub-national groups, have sought to define themselves in ever more distinct ways from the mainstream. It would, for example, be totally unacceptable for a modern Indian leader to make a remark similar to the one Nehru made in Colombo.

Under these processes of historical and cultural re-definition, the people of Pakistan embraced Islam, at least in its outward manifestations, with increasing fervour; Sri Lanka sought increasingly to define itself as a Buddhist, Sinhalese nation; and in 1988, a hitherto secularly-inclined Bangladesh declared itself to be an Islamic nation.

This move towards a more rigid definition of nationhood has in turn affected the conduct of politics within India. Thus a powerful argument put forward by the Hindu Right for a Hindu nation states that, since some of the nations around India chose to separate from India by virtue of their religion and do not accord Hindus full citizenship rights on the grounds of religion, why should not India, which is 83% Hindu, declare itself to be a Hindu nation?[27]

But equally, the policies of the Hindu Right toward Muslims, and all that has flowed from them such as the destruction of the mosque at Ayodhya and the subsequent rioting, is starting to promote a Muslim backlash within India. Ironically, the growing tendency toward extremism within the Muslim community has the effect of turning the BJP accusations that Muslims constitute a 'fifth column' into a self-fulfilling prophesy.

Although a concern not to be branded anti-Indian, together with the fact that in most cases Muslims are a minority community at the local level and would suffer more than Hindus from any escalating cycle of violence, have acted to restrain the Muslim response, there were worrying signals from the community even before the destruction of the mosque that extremism was on the increase. The extensive bombings in Bombay and Calcutta in the aftermath of the January riots were seen as a manifestation of this Muslim response, provoking fears that 'India can become another Lebanon'.[28]

Increasingly Muslims, who are almost as diverse a community as Hindus, are defining themselves *qua* Islam rather than in terms of their narrower community.

The forces at work in this process of re-definition are not confined to India, but are running throughout the entire region of the so-called 'arc of crisis'. Islamic revivalism in Pakistan and Bangladesh cannot be explained in isolation from the phenomenon as it is occurring in neighbouring Southwest Asia; nor can Hindu revivalism in India be isolated from Islamic revivalism in South Asia.[29] As Rajni Kothari has pointed out in the context of India and Pakistan, 'There is a deep interface between the communal divide within the country and the international divide across the borders'.[30]

This relationship between what happens outside India and politics within is a two way process. The widespread rioting against Muslims following the destruction of the mosque at Ayodhya in turn caused a deterioration in relations not just between India and Pakistan, as might have been expected, but also between India and Bangladesh. In Dhaka, anti-temple riots occurred and the India Information Centre and Indian Airlines office were burned down. The role of the Muslim-oriented Jamaat-i-Islami was strengthened and the two nations entered a period of 'diplomatic war'.[31] Pakistan raised the mosque issue in the Organisation of Islamic Countries and the Gulf Cooperation Council. On its part, the Indian government has been forthright in blaming Pakistan, especially the Pakistani Inter-Services Intelligence Agency (ISI), for involvement in the bomb blasts in Bombay and Calcutta. The alleged involvement of Pakistan was taken so seriously that, according to 'unidentified US officials', preventive diplomacy was necessary on the part of the US in the aftermath of the blasts to restrain India.[32]

The malignant relationship between communalism and the conduct of India-Pakistan relations became particularly evident at the height of the BJP's Ayodhya campaign. In Pakistan, a religious party, the Jamiat Ulema Islam, mounted a country-wide agitation against what it described as the 'genocide' by Hindus against Muslims in India. In an obvious attempt to divert attention from Pakistan's own difficulties relating to its Gulf policy, the issue of Ayodhya was described by the Government of Pakistan as 'more important than Kuwait'.[33] Ironically, the BJP was quick to seize on such comments from Pakistan and to use them to blame Islamabad for the very violence which the party had helped precipitate.[34]

India and its neighbours thus seem to be locked into a mutually reinforcing set of chauvinistic constructs which have the effect of strengthening the exclusivist models of nation. What Golwalker once envisaged for the former British India (Hindustan) is now applied by the radicals within the Hindu movement exclusively to India. In Golwalker's words:

> Foreign nations in Hindustan must ... adopt the Hindu culture and language, ... or may stay in the country wholly subordinated to the Hindu nation, claiming nothing ... not even citizen's rights.[35]

These words have a disturbing resonance with a modern day slogan of the Hindu Right: 'If you wish to live in Hindustan, you will have to live like us [Hindus]'.[36]

This exclusivist philosophy is exposing a dangerous contradiction in the BJP's position: if India is to be Hindu in the exclusivist sense, where does that leave the peripheral areas of the nation, such as Kashmir, Punjab and the predominantly Christian north-east? And, more to the point, where does it leave India's 110 million strong Muslim community? For it was precisely to accommodate such diversity that the doctrines of 'one nation', secularism and cultural unity were developed in the first place.

Thus, although policies of fostering limited competition in the course of nation building might have had utility in the past, given current circumstances their utility is no longer so obvious. The quickening tempo of separatist movements on both sides of the border, the increased capacity of each to damage the other by fostering insurgency, and the way in which such issues have been seized upon by religious elements on both sides, mean that the stakes of the competition have been significantly raised. The nuclearisation of South Asia has also made the competition more dangerous.

In these altered circumstances, distinct dangers are inherent in any policy of using the Pakistan-India competition for internal political purposes. These occur not so much through what is said, which as we have noted is understood for what it is—mere posturing—but rather through what is done. The weight of evidence suggests that, under the first government of Benazir Bhutto, Pakistan at least attempted to curb direct aid to the separatists in Indian Kashmir.[37] But the ISI was evidently able to act independently of the government in a number of important respects, not least the arming of the *mujahideen* in Afghanistan.[38] The US State Department's Annual Report on Global Terrorism for 1991 cited Pakistan as a nation that was providing active support for the separatists in Kashmir.[39] Cross-border sniping and artillery duels are no longer simply a manifestation of latent tension; they increasingly appear to be used by Pakistan as cover for infiltration of insurgents into Indian Kashmir. In late 1991, border clashes in Kashmir began to escalate dangerously, and even included use of helicopter gunships by India, reportedly with 'devastating effect'.[40]

The modern reality of the differences over Kashmir lies not so much in any theoretical position that either side might espouse, but rather in the way in which the issue is now caught up in the politics of both nations. The elites who govern Pakistan would have great difficulty if it were perceived by the general populace that they were unable to protect the Islamic credentials of the nation, which is the very basis on which they claim its existence. In the case of India, loss of Kashmir would gravely damage the prospects of survival of the Congress government and would greatly strengthen the hand of the BJP. It is these internal difficulties that make the Kashmir dispute such an intractable one, and that in turn make a lasting rapprochement between India and Pakistan so difficult to achieve.

On its part, Pakistan has from time to time accused India of supporting separatists in Sindh, including through massive arms shipments. It also accuses New Delhi of attempting to destabilise its province of Punjab.[41] While the scale of the allegations involved tend to cast doubt on their detail, given the activities of RAW throughout South Asia over a considerable period of time, it would be most surprising if that organisation were not at least to a degree involved in fostering unrest in Pakistan.[42]

Such activities are not intended to provoke war; indeed they have become a substitute for an all-out war that neither side can afford. The fighting of proxy wars is a dangerous business, however. The degree of pain caused has to be finely calculated so as not to provoke the neighbour too far. When dealing with insurgents with their own agendas, such fine-tuning is often well-nigh impossible to achieve.

Along with the increase in the stakes of the competition for both sides, the rhetoric has increased in intensity rather than diminished. In 1990, the India Prime Minister, V.P. Singh, gave a clear message to Pakistan in the Indian parliament that, if India were forced to go to war as a result of Pakistan's assistance to the separatists in Kashmir, this time there would be no half measures.[43] In a similar vein the Indian Defence Minister, Sharad Pawar, warned Pakistan that India's response to any use of nuclear weapons would cause Pakistan to 'suffer for generations'.[44]

The relationship between deteriorating law and order and growing patterns of communal violence and chauvinism on the one hand and the damage it does to bilateral relations on the other is not confined just to the case of India and Pakistan. The temptation in South Asia for nations to 'fish in troubled waters' is encouraged by porous borders that bisect some of the diverse ethnic groups that make up the region and some of the more difficult terrain, and by the extensive pattern of transmigration already noted. The existence of these trans-border communities both facilitates and encourages destabilising activities on the part of the neighbour.

In terms of the dynamics of the India-Sri Lanka relationship, there was a close nexus between the late President Premadasa's need to cultivate the Buddhist clergy for his own political ends and his anti-Indian stance. Premadasa's use of Buddhism in politics in part derived from his need to foster unity and nationalism in the face of the menace of the JVP and the Tamil separatist movements, and in part from his need to maintain a conservative political line in order to accomplish unpopular economic reforms. In both cases, anti-Indian sentiment provided a useful rallying point for the nationalist cause.[45]

There are also persistent and probably well-founded allegations that the RAW was involved in fostering Tamil separatism in Sri Lanka during the early days of the movement. There is even a certain poetic symmetry in subsequent developments: the Rao government's decision not to attend the 1991 Colombo meeting of the South Asian Association for Regional Co-operation (SAARC) was essentially made in a fit of pique at the fact that the Premadasa government had been forced virtually to admit that it provided arms to the Tamil Tigers during the very time when Indian forces were fighting the Tigers at the invitation of the Sri Lankan government.[46]

Internal difficulties in the north-east of South Asia have also affected relations between neighbours in that part of the world. As well as playing on fears of economic migration from Bangladesh by asserting that there are now 15 million Bangladeshis in India, the BJP regularly publicises the plight of Hindus, Sikhs, Buddhists and Christians in Bangladesh.[47] Territorial and riparian disputes between India and Bangladesh have been intensified by domestic political considerations on both sides. For example, India's commitment of 16 years' standing to give the small corridor of Tin Bigha to Bangladesh was delayed for so long because of politicking by the BJP.[48]

Problems in the north-east are exacerbated by the general sensitivity of the whole area and by its remoteness from the rest of India. The region is separated from India by a very narrow neck of land just South of Sikkim known as the 'chicken's neck'. This was also the area in which the original Naxalite revolt took place, which was supported with weapons from China. The north-east constitutes a tangled skein of interconnecting alliances and cross-border activities involving separatist insurgencies, arms smuggling and drug smuggling from the Golden Triangle.[49] The steep and jungled terrain and the porous borders makes elimination of insurgency movements by military means alone well-nigh impossible.

Militant groups like the ULFA operate across the border between India and Myanmar. The Kuki tribal group, which also exists as a trans-border community and which has been forced out of Myanmar as a result of actions by the Myanmar military, is now at war with the Indian Nagas over territory and control of the drug trade.[50] Arms from China, which would have come via Myanmar, have been fuelling the conflict.[51] The outlawed National Socialist Council of Nagaland, which operates on both sides of the border, has also been pushed into India as the Myanmar military intensifies its campaign against it.[52] Thousands of Naga rebels are already reportedly seeking refuge from the Burmese military in India. There they place strain on the social infrastructure and form a potential focus for discontent amongst India's own Naga population.[53] Accusations have been levelled in the Indian Parliament that the ULFA is receiving help from Myanmar, Bangladesh and China.[54] India also accuses Pakistan of involvement in its north-east.[55] The way is potentially open for the sort of tit-for-tat fostering of insurgency movements that now exists in the western side of South Asia. So far, however, all of the nations bordering on the north-east have kept support of dissident movements in neighbouring countries to a manageable level: no doubt they are aware of their own vulnerabilities.

The porous nature of South Asia's borders also means that the various separatist and extremist groups have been more easily able to establish linkages between them. This process of linkage has in turn facilitated the spread of unrest from one sub-region of South Asia to another. It also has the effect of vitiating relations between regional governments, as one accuses the other of harbouring terrorists.

The insurgency organisation most commonly mentioned in relation to these cross-linkages is the Tamil Tigers. The Tigers are said to have been active in Maldives, Assam, Punjab and even Myanmar. Given the 'professionalism' of the Tigers as a terrorist group and especially their great 'dexterity' in the use of explosives, the prospect of linkages between them and Indian groups has been taken seriously by Indian security and intelligence apparatus. The Tigers were also thought for a time to be involved in arming and training the Naxalites in Andhra Pradesh, which was a neighbour state to their stronghold in Tamil Nadu.[56]

There are also concerns about links developing within India between the various separatist groups. Such links allegedly involve the ULFA, Sikh separatist groups, the Peoples' War Group (Naxalite) and the Jammu and Kashmir Liberation Front. The *Times of India* 'reliably' reported that efforts were underway to form a panel to bind these groups together.[57]

The Home Minister referred to a 'cross-pollenation with regard to methodologies, strategies and tactics' employed by the militants. The fact that the militants in Punjab have been forced 'onto the back foot' and are starved of weapons has had the effect of intensifying the links between them and militants in Kashmir, from whom they obtain weapons supposedly smuggled in over the more porous border between Indian Kashmir and Pakistani Kashmir.[58] A similar pattern has occurred in Kashmir, where groups like the pro-Pakistan Hizb-ul-Mujahedin have been forced out into Himachal Pradesh, where they are now attacking police.[59]

*

In South Asia, a pattern has emerged whereby sub-national insecurity is increasingly linked to a form of chronic regional insecurity. The mechanisms through which these linkages occur are various and complex. They involve a combination of the increasing tendency toward religious chauvinism, which itself feeds into and is fed by sub-national instability; the uncertain and incomplete nature of the entitities that were the inheritors of the British Raj, which dictated that elites turn increasingly to more rigid definitions of nation in order to engage in their nation-building endeavours; and the porous nature of the post-colonial borders and tangled skein of ethnic groups that surround the core areas of South Asia, which facilitates the spread of ethnic divisions and problems as well as the methodoligies of protest and dissent. In the next chapter we turn to consider how this growing pattern of dissent has affected the capabilities and standing of the foremost South Asian nation, India.

Endnotes

1   S. Gordon, 'Domestic Foundations of India's Security Policy', in R. Babbage and S. Gordon (Eds), *India's Strategic Future: Regional State or Global Power?*, The Macmillan Press, London, 1992. The use of such paradigms is intended to be heuristic.

2   Quoted in P. Gupte, *India: The Challenge of Change*, Methuen, London, 1989, p. 317.

3   These were five principles governing right conduct between the nations of the developing world that centred on resolution of

difficulties through discussion and compromise rather than conflict.

4   Speech of Admiral Nayyer (Ret'd) to the US Global Strategy Council Forum, Wednesday 27 September 1989, p. 53 (verbatim account by Neal R. Gross).

5   Interview with Abdul Kalam, at the time Head of India's missile program, *India Today*, 15 June 1989.

6   Babani Sen Gupta, *Economic and Political Weekly*, Vol. XXIV, No. 3, 21 January 1989, p. 121.

7   See the US Congress Staff Report (by Peter Galbraith), 'Nuclear Proliferation in South Asia: Containing the Threat', US Government Printing Office: Washington, 1988, p. 2.

8   L. & S. Rudolph, *In Pursuit of Lakshmi*: 1987, p. 1. They were referring more to India's general polity than to the conduct of its foreign relations. However, the two are, of course, closely related.

9   From an interview with K.K. Tiwari in *The Illustrated Weekly of India*, 28 May 1989, p. 17.

10 Kathy Evans, 'Pakistan reports plot to destabilise country', *The Age*, 3 October 1990; *Hindustan Times*, 6 October 1990, as in IDSA, *News Review on South Asia/Indian Ocean* (*IDSANR*), November 1990, p. 797. For the accusations on Sindh see *Jang*, 21 May 1990 as in *IDSANR*, July 1990, p. 496; for Punjab see 'RAW, KHAD agents involved in blasts, disruption', *Dawn*, 9 September 1990 as in *IDSANR*, October 1990, p. 746; and 'Trouble on the Home Front', *Asiaweek*, 12 July 1991, p. 27.

11 Leo Rose, 'India's Regional Policy: Non Military Dimensions', in S.P. Cohen (Ed.), *The Security of South Asia, American and Asian Perspectives*, University of Illinois Press, Urbana, 1987, p. 4.

12 See K.C. Praval, *Indian Army After Independence*, Lancer International, New Delhi, 1990, pp. 404-408.

13 Michael Krepon et. al., *A Handbook of Confidence Building Measures for Regional Security*, Handbook No. 1, Henry L. Stimson Center, September 1993; and Moonis Ahmar, *Indo-Pakistan Normalization Process: The Role of CBMs in the Post-Cold War Era*, ACDIS Occasional Paper, University of Illinois at Urbana-Champaigne, Illinois, 1993.

14 Pravin Sawhney, 'India, Pak Armies Showed Restraint', *Times of India*, 17 February 1992.

15 R. Rikhye, *The Militarization of Mother India*, Chanakya Publications, New Delhi, 1990, p. 7.

16 Quoted in Edward Duyker, 'The Kashmir Conflict: An Historical Overview', *The Indian Ocean Review*, Vol. 3, No. 4, December 1990, p. 1.

17 The foregoing interpretation of the creation of Pakistan, upon which the subsequent analysis of the existing structure of that nation depends, was given by Francis Robinson in *Separatism Among Indian Muslims. The Politics of the United Provinces' Muslims, 1860-1923*, Cambridge University Press, Cambridge, 1974. It is challenged by Gyanendra Pandey and his colleagues in the Subaltern Studies school of history. See for example Pandey's recent work, *The Construction of Communalism in Colonial North India*, Oxford University Press, New Delhi, 1992, p. 20.

18 For example, K.R. Mulkani, at the time a member of the BJP Executive, argued in 'The Hindu Confederacy', *The Illustrated Weekly of India*, 5-6 January 1991, pp. 22-23, that since Bangladesh and Pakistan are Islamic nations the 'Hinduisation' of India is inevitable.

19 W.P.S. Sidhu, 'Migrant Tinder-box', *India Today*, 15 February 1993, p. 71; Ashok Vyas, 'Caution on "demographic invasion"', *Hindustan Times*, 5 May 1992.

20 Malabika Bhattacharya, 'RSS a formidable force in Bengal, CPI tells CPM', *The Indian Express*, 29 December 1992.

21 Gyan Pandey, 'In Defence of the Fragment', p. 30.

22 Vinod Raina, 'Plurality Denied', paper delivered at a conference on *The BJP After Ayodhya*, Curtin University, Perth, July 1993; T. Jayaraman, 'Facing up to fraud', *Frontline*, 12 February 1993, p. 101.

23 Quoted in 'The Nuclear Risk Shifts to South Asia', *The New York Times*, 31 January 1993.

24 Raj Chengappa, 'Dangerous Dimensions', *India Today*, 15 February 1993, p. 66.

25 Quoted by B. Warraiwalla in *Illustrated Weekly of India*, 11-17 June 1989, p. 12.

26 See the quotation of Suryanarayan Rao in Raj Chengappa, 'Dangerous Dimensions', *India Today*, 15 February 1993, p. 66. See

also Walter K. Anderson and Shridhar D. Damle, *The Brotherhood in Saffron: The Rashtrya Swayamsevak Sangh and Hindu Revivalism*, Westview Press, Boulder and London, 1987, p. 77.

27   See Gyan Pandey, 'In Defence of the Fragment', p. 32. Item no. 11 from the referenced pamphlet gives a succinct statement of this position.

28   Statement of the Sheriff of Bombay quoted in Jefferson Penberthy, 'Nowhere To Turn', *Time*, 15 February 1993, p. 35. The Bombay bombings also, however, owed a great deal to the corruption, criminalisation and smuggling regimes that now flourish in and around Bombay.

29   See Yogendra K. Malik and Dhirendra K. Vajpayi, 'The Rise of Hindu Militancy: India's Secular Democracy at Risk', *Asian Survey*, Vol. XXIX, No. 3, March 1989, p. 321.

30   R. Kothari, 'Eroding the Republic', *Seminar*, No. 377, January 1991, p. 25.

31   Manash Ghosh, 'Spirit of Bengal', *The Statesman*, 8 April 1993.

32   See Anon, 'Bomb blasts: 12 détenus were trained in Pak.', *The Hindu*, 20 April 1993; R. Chakrapani, 'U.S. averted Indo-Pak clash after blasts', *The Hindu*, 16 April 1993; Anon, 'Pawar indicts Pak. for Bombay blasts', *The Hindu* (International Edition), 3 April 1993.

33   See 'Countrywide rallies against anti-Muslim riots in India', *Pakistan Times*, 22 December 1990 and 'Niazi says Babri mosque issue more important than Kuwait', *Nation*, December 30 1990, both in *IDSANR*, February 1991, pp. 87-8.

34   'Hindus accuse Pakistan of inciting Indian unrest', *The Australian*, 17 December 1990.

35   Quoted from *We or Our Nationhood Defined* in Swapan Dasgupta, 'BJP redefining "parivar" ideology', *The Times of India*, 19 May 1993.

36   Quoted in Gyan Pandey, 'In Defence of the Fragment', p. 34.

37   See an on-the-spot report titled 'Bhutto denies guns to Kashmiri refugees' by the respected correspondent Christopher Thomas in *The Times*, as in *The Australian*, 24 July 1990.

38   The ISI chose to channel US and Saudi arms to the fundamentalist *mujahideen* leader, Gulbuddin Hekmatyar. When Ms Bhutto came to power she attempted to break the monopoly of the ISI by sacking

the Head, General Gul, and installing her own man.

39 'Pak backing J&K ultras: US report', *The Hindustan Times*, 4 May 1992.

40 Manoj Joshi, 'An Indian dilemma', *Frontline*, 6 December 1991, p. 115.

41 See 'Trouble on the Home Front', *Asiaweek*, 12 July 1991, p. 27; *Dawn*, 9 September 1990 as in IDSANR, October 1990. p. 746; and 'India major arms pusher into Sindh: ex-ISI chief', *Nation* 19 January 1991, as in IDSANR, March 1991, p. 184.

42 For a detailed account of the activities of RAW in regional nations see Asoka Raina, *Inside RAW: The Story of India's Secret Service*, Vikas, New Delhi, 1981.

43 'Be ready for war with Pakistan: PM', *Sydney Morning Herald*, 12 April 1990.

44 Quoted in 'Indian threat "nuclear hint"', *The Australian*, 13 February 1992.

45 Seema Guha, 'Elite Conspires To Oust Premadasa', *Times of India*, 4 September 1991.

46 T.S. Subramanian and T. Abraham, 'Collapse in Colombo', *Frontline*, 6 December 1991, p. 24. For allegations of RAW's involvement in destabilising activities in Sri Lanka see Chapter 2, Part 3, below.

47 See the Editorial, 'Not well spoken', in *The Statesman*, 2 December 1991, on the tactics of BJP leader M.M. Joshi; and 'Deport Bangladeshis from India: BJP', *Hindustan Times*, 24 August 1992. The predecessor of the BJP, the Jana Sangh, used similar tactics to gain votes in Assam in the 1970s.

48 'Passage Pains', *India Today*, 15 December 1991, p. 83. This article puts the number of Indians in the area at 60,000. Others, however, put the number at 40,000. See *Times of India* Editorial, 13 February 1992.

49 See a report in *The Hindu* of 5 February 1991; B.W. Cloughley, 'India's stresses and strains', *Pacific Defence Reporter*, August 1985, p. 9; 'Burmese groups scale down support', *Times of India*, 25 October 1991; and R. Tomar, *India and South Asia: Problems of a Regional Power*, Parliament of Australia Background Paper, 22 November 1989, p. FA27.

50   Burmese dissidents are reportedly located in several main camps in India. Reports that they were being trained on Indian soil were denied by the Indians. See 'Rebels seek help from Myanmar', *Times of India*, 17 September 1991.

51   F. Ahmed and S. Das, 'Manipur: The hidden war', *India Today*, 30 June 1993, p. 69.

52   'Troops alerted on Myanmar border', *Times of India*, 12 February 1992.

53   'Beleaguered Nagas flee Myanmar' *Times of India*, 11 February 1992.

54   See 'No dialogue with ULFA: Chavan', *Times of India*, 17 September 1991; 'India concerned over Chinese arms supply to neighbours', Reuter News Service, 14 December 1991.

55   'Pak bid to destabilise N-E', *The Hindustan Times*, 23 May 1992.

56   For these allegations see *Times of India*, 8 January 1991, statement of PM Chandra Shekhar (later denied by the Tamil Nadu Chief Minister); *Times of India*, 10 January 1991; *The Hindu*, 21 and 22 June 1991 asserts that the central government in India is worried over attempts by the Tamil Tigers to smuggle arms into India because these might be used by the Naxalites in Tamil Nadu; Seized diaries show 'ULFA, LTTE links', *The Hindu*, 4 April 1991; 68 members of the LTTE were allegedly involved in the abortive coup attempt in Maldives in which 17 were killed (AP news flash, 10 August 1989 06:59); in September 1991 the BJP submitted a report alleging LTTE links with the People's War Group (*Times of India*, 12 September 1991). A member of the former DMK government was recently arrested for alleged support of the Tigers. Their activities in Tamil Nadu were evidently aimed at the creation of a 'greater Eelam' including parts of Sri Lanka and Tamil Nadu. See 'Conspiracy Surfaces', *India Today*, 15 December 1991, pp. 57-8.

57   'Punjab militants "pact" with ULFA', *Times of India*, 4 October 1991.

58   'Collect data to fight terrorism: Chavan', *Times of India*, 4 March 1992; Ajay Bhardawaj, 'Pak camps closed: BSF D-G', *Times of India*, 17 November 1992; 'Punjab militants reveal ISI links', *The Times of India*, 8 August 1992.

59   R. Vinayak, 'Spilling Over: J&K militants enter Chamba', *India Today*, 15 September 1993.

4   Consequences of Instability

Debased human rights

The need to involve the security forces more closely in the maintenance of civil order and to raise additional police and paramilitary forces to counter militants has inevitably eroded the quality of democratic life throughout South Asia.

In India, the government has introduced tough new laws and ordinances such as the Terrorism and Disruptive Activities Act (TADA). TADA allows for the arrest and detainment of any person for up to two years without charge, trial or access to legal counsel. In April 1993 the government extended the life of TADA by a further two years. In Kashmir, ordinances have been introduced under the Disturbed Areas Act that prevent the gathering of more than four persons and allow security forces to shoot to kill. (This latter provision is normally not made in India without reference to a magistrate.) The government is now seriously considering further strengthening the anti-terrorist provisions. Furthermore, the Indian Constitution provides for the dismissal of popularly elected state governments and the introduction of rule by the centre (known as President's rule). Punjab was under President's rule for almost five years and Kashmir has been for almost four years.

According to reports by external human rights groups, government forces have resorted to torture, extra-judicial killings in so-called 'fake encounters' with militants and sexual assault. Such measures are in part the result of frustration at a legal system that has proved virtually powerless to achieve convictions of arrested terrorists in situations in which witnesses are either intimidated or reluctant to testify on the grounds that they support the militants.[1] The US Congress, Asiawatch, the Commonwealth Law Secretariat, Amnesty International and Physicians for Human Rights have all commented adversely on the conduct of human rights in India. The US State Department's 1991 report on human rights accused government forces of misbehaviour in Kashmir.[2] Indian human rights groups such as the Committee for Initiative on Kashmir have also monitored the situation in Kashmir and produced reports that comment adversely on the Indian record.[3]

In response to growing concerns about human rights abuses, the US House of Representatives passed an amendment to the bill on military exchanges with India for 1992-93 which had the effect of demanding of the President that the military exchanges program should be designed so that it would inculcate an understanding of human rights issues within the Indian military. India 'angrily rejected' the amendment.[4] Nevertheless, the House of Representatives recently went one step further and banned India from the $340,000 military education scheme. More significantly, the House came to within 32 votes of cutting off aid to India entirely.[5]

India has defended its record by pointing out in international forums such as the United Nations that it is one-sided to criticise Third World nations for human rights violations while ignoring the outrages perpetrated by the insurgent groups.[6] India has also reacted by attempting to discredit the various reports and their authors.[7] It has counter-attacked against Pakistan by attempting to have it identified as a terrorist nation in the UN because of its support for the Kashmir and Punjab insurgents.[8] In general, the mainstream Indian media have supported the view that Kashmir is a special case because of the involvement of Pakistan, and that the nation needs to pull together in supporting the security forces.[9]

At the same time as causing an overall increase in the level of policing needed in society, the separatist and militant movements have also caused the introduction of new 'sophisticated' methods of combating terrorism and separatism. Israel has been involved in the introduction of these methods both in Sri Lanka and India.[10] In India, coordination is to be improved between the Intelligence Bureau and the state authorities. A comprehensive, computer-based data bank is being established to trace terrorists who move from one part of the country to another.[11]

Continuing accusations of human rights abuses prompted the government in 1993 to establish a Human Rights Commission. But from the first, the Commission was conceived of by the government as a means of diverting mounting international criticism of India's human rights record rather than as a genuine attempt to address the issue. In confirming the establishment of the Commission, the Home Minister, S.B. Chavan, said in the Lok Sabha that it was a means of correcting the 'distorted' picture of Indian human rights projected abroad.[12] One serious problem with the framework within which the Commission will operate is that it will have no mandatory investigative powers in respect of the military or paramilitary forces. It is free, however, to comment publicly on the actions of the military and the government.[13] India is also planning to set up a human rights cell in the army and introduce training about human rights into the services.[14]

Meanwhile, India is caught in a dilemma. It is true that the insurgents and militants are ruthless fighters who use any means at their disposal, including the murder of relatives of police, as happened in 1991 in Punjab.

The military and paramilitary feel that they are forced to fight 'with one hand behind their backs' by being bound to considerations of law when the insurgents are not. They deeply resent the activities of the human rights campaigners. The government, which is increasingly beholden to the army and paramilitary to maintain law and order, is reluctant to provoke them by allowing bodies such as Amnesty International or Asiawatch free access to disturbed regions. (The groups have now been allowed into India, but not to Kashmir). Without such access, however, accusations of human rights violations will persist and will remain unverified.

Meanwhile, use of draconian legislation, human rights abuses and the intensifying campaign against indigenous human rights groups to show them as somehow 'anti-national' mean that, in the words of Harsh Sethi, 'what we [Indians] are witnessing is a steady shrinkage of space for democratic dissent and differing political imaginations.'[15] It is inevitable that the fraying of India's otherwise admirable record on human rights (given the vast developmental issues it faces) will have further international repercussions, especially as India seeks to be more closely integrated into world forums such as the United Nations.

Retarded economic development

In matters of defence, management of macro-economic policy and management of foreign relations—what might be called 'high politics'—the functioning of governments has not been seriously impaired by the state of chronic instability emerging in South Asia. Rather, it is the capacity of governments to provide for change at the state and local levels that is being compromised by political and social instability. Where lack of effective government counts seriously is in those major programs in the social sector designed to improve life and public health, provide education, uplift the poor and reduce the population growth rate.

We have already noted that attempts to introduce the Green Revolution into the eastern areas of northern India have been adversely affected by lack of political stability. Major national programs designed to uplift the rural poor, such as the Integrated Rural Development Program (IRDP), National Rural Development Plan, Special Component Plan and the Rural Landless Unemployed Guarantee Program, have also suffered due to corruption and rank inefficiency.[16] Some put the losses in these schemes as high as one-third.[17] In the case of the most important scheme, the IRDP, 'none... [of the major studies of the program] claims any major reduction in the scope of Indian poverty through the programme'.[18] Even Rajiv Gandhi admitted that only 20% of IRDP funds actually filtered through to the people for whom they were intended.[19]

Chronic instability also feeds a vicious circle of underdevelopment and neglect. This happens in a number of ways. Firstly, at the sub-national level, there is a strong tendency for investment to shy away from those areas which are worst affected by such unrest. Throughout the province of Sindh, for example, law and order problems are now so extensive that foreign aid workers and investment are turning away. In 1990, Japanese investors and the Japanese government decided not to fund any more projects in Sindh. Since 53% of Pakistan's large industrial units are based in Sindh (most of them in Karachi) this is a serious problem for the whole of Pakistan.[20]

The same problem is also occurring in the Indian state of Punjab. As we have noted, the central government has diverted investment in heavy industry away from the state. But at the height of the insurgency even light industries, which had previously flourished, were being forced to leave.[21] In the Terai region of Uttar Pradesh, which is the 'rice bowl' of the state, prosperity has been set back by the fact that the Sikh separatists who infest the area have been extorting funds from the rice and sugar millers.[22] In Kashmir, the once flourishing tourism industry has been virtually destroyed. In Assam, a spate of kidnappings by the ULFA in the oil and tea industries, both of which are vital to India from the point of view of foreign exchange, have hampered investment and limited domestic supplies of oil.[23] In 1990 and 1991 India lost nearly one million tonnes of domestic production of oil, a serious matter in the context of the oil price rise associated with the Gulf crisis.[24] With proven reserves at 1200 million tonnes concentrated in Upper Assam, the potential economic losses from the insurgency in Assam are considerable.[25]

The growing pattern of violence in South Asia means that the region is to an extent now seen as a high risk area for investment. There is evidence that the instability following the destruction of the mosque at Ayodhya was one of the factors in the lack of investment in India in 1993, despite the liberalisation of the economy.[26] While by far the majority of South Asia is still relatively secure, the impression given by local level violence is the exact opposite. Once investment turns away, the problems of underdevelopment which contribute to the sense of grievance in the first place are exacerbated, thus contributing to a vicious circle of underdevelopment, violence and neglect.

Effect on military capacity

Effect on force structure

The instability evident in the South Asian region has created of India, which is the only regional nation of potential strategic reach, a country that is essentially inward-looking and regionally focused. India's security posture thus exhibits many of the characteristics of a continental nation. This fact is reflected both in the capacity and deployment of the military forces and, closely related to this, the conduct of foreign relations.

The effect regional instability has on military capability is, however, paradoxical. At the level of aggregate force acquisition, the competition between India and Pakistan has produced a regional arms race. According to some accounts, more arms entered the South Asian region in the 1980s than any other developing region in the world.[27] But in terms of force structure, deployment and strategy, the effect of chronic regional instability has been to cause both India and Pakistan to focus on sub-continental defence systems, border defences, and the maintenance of law and order at the expense of the acquisition of forces with significant strategic reach.

Nowhere is the emphasis on continental-type defence doctrine in South Asia more evident than in terms of the relationship between naval expenditure and expenditure on the other forces. In the case of India, expenditure on the navy has never risen above 14% of total defence expenditure, and for most of the nation's independent existence it has been well below that level. The army, on the other hand, has traditionally commanded the lion's share of the defence budget at about 62%.[28] In Pakistan, the same generally holds true.

In both countries, force structures have closely reflected the requirements of short border wars. For example, the Indian air force relies heavily on tactical fighters. It has no true long-range strike aircraft (the *Jaguar* does not really fall into that category) and has not yet developed an aerial re-fuelling capability for the *Jaguar*. Only eight of India's 88 *Jaguars* are dedicated to the maritime attack role.[29] The Indian and Pakistani armies contain massive amounts of armour capable of fighting in the plains of Punjab or deserts of Rajasthan (India has over 3,000 main battle tanks). By the same token, the training and strategy of the Indian army has until recently reflected the requirement of countering Pakistan in the plains and deserts and China in the mountains. Despite having to counter a long-running insurgency in the north-east, the Indian army was until recently not particularly well trained for jungle warfare, a fact that became all too evident during the Indian intervention in Sri Lanka.[30]

The major strategic concerns of India are also indicated by the location and basing policies of the military forces. The army is mostly located in north-central India or on the central rail links with that part of the country, or the west coast near Bombay, or else in the Himalayas, where 11 divisions of the total of 35 until recently confronted China. Three divisions were also until recently located in the north-east, where they were used in counter-insurgency work and as a counter to China (one was recently withdrawn for duty in Kashmir).

The air force is similarly located so as to be accessible to the western theatre, with additional squadrons located in Shillong and Bagdogra (presumably to protect disputed territory in Arunachal Pradesh), Bangalore and Hyderabad (where extensive aerospace industries works are located) and Bombay (again where there are valuable military-industrial assets).[31]

The activities of smugglers, especially those who introduced the plastic explosives used in the blasts in Bombay in 1993, and the Tamil militants, who previously passed with ease over the Palk Straits between Sri Lanka and India, have also caused a re-assessment of the role and structure of the navy. Contrary to the wishes of the former Chief of Naval Staff, Admiral Ramdas, who wanted to reverse the trend away from small ships and move back to the concept of a blue water navy, the government has now directed the navy to build more smaller ships in order to patrol the inner, or 'brown' waters. This policy has now been endorsed by the new naval chief, Admiral Shekhawat, who has referred to 'sudden unplanned commitment in internal security duties'.[32]

The increasing reliance on the army for the maintenance of internal security has meant that, despite earlier decisions to modernise equipment and reduce manpower, this has proved extremely difficult to accomplish. As already noted, the recommendation of the Arun Singh committee that manpower be traded for modernisation was not fully implemented.

With the increasing level of border-crossing, drug and gun running and internal unrest, all of the security forces of South Asia have been required to devote more of their resources to containing local and domestic threats. In Sri Lanka, the military has fought two major campaigns against the quasi-Marxist JVP, one in 1971 and the other in 1989-90. The second involved the formation of plain-clothed death squads known as the 'Black Cats', similar to those which exist in some South American countries. The prosecution of the civil war against the Tamil separatists has involved significant arms acquisitions, including from China, and a rise in the level of defence spending from 1% of GNP to 5.7%.[33]

India has had to deploy the army in aid of the civil authority for the maintenance of law and order increasingly throughout the decade of the 1980s. Since 1990-91, military assistance has been provided in the conduct of elections in Nagaland, Mizoram, Tamil Nadu, Uttar Pradesh and Punjab; to contain communal riots and other forms of civil disorder in almost every state and the Union territory of New Delhi; and to assist anti-insurgency operations consistently in Kashmir since 1989, extensively in Punjab under 'Operation Protection' (some reports put the deployment of actual soldiers into Punjab in 1991 as high as 115,000) and three times in Assam (under Operations 'Bhajang' and 'Rhino' and to control the Bodo agitation).[34] There are reportedly now 320,000 army men deployed in Kashmir in addition to 35,000 paramilitary. According to some accounts, 50% of army personnel are now deployed in aid of the civil authority.[35] These deployments for internal security purposes are already having an adverse effect on border security. For example, the withdrawal of border troops has caused additional infiltration of Bangladeshis into India.[36]

The fact that the government uses the military as a line of last resort means that it is often inserted into a situation in support of the civil authority with very little preparation or warning and with virtually no say in the management of crises on the ground. This in turn creates opportunities for friction to develop between the military and government. The military also dislikes its frequent use in support of the civil authority because it detracts from its proper role of defending the nation and, as noted above, distorts the force structure.[37]

The extent of the involvement of the army in maintaining internal security caused the former Army Chief of Staff, General Rodrigues, to complain that the army has been 'considerably overstretched' in countering insurgency in the last three to four years. He claimed that training standards for the primary military role had been affected and asserted that the army should be 'insulated' from internal security commitments.[38] However, because of the government's doubts concerning the capacity of the police and paramilitary forces, there is little chance of such insulation occurring, as evidenced by the massive deployment of the army into Punjab in late 1991 over the strong protests of General Rodrigues and other senior officers.[39]

This increasing use of the military in support of the civil authority raises the issue of the future loyalty and effectiveness of the military as an institution that increasingly stands as the only one capable of protecting the integrity of the Union.

The unity and loyalty of the security forces

Traditionally, the Indian military was one of the more isolated Indian institutions. It was generally kept apart from mainstream Indian society by professional codes of conduct and separate cantonment areas and schools. The use of the so-called 'martial races', particularly in the officer corps, also played a role in isolating the military from civilian life and making it a more loyal instrument of the government.[40]

During the post-independence period, however, an attempt was made to break the reliance on the martial races and to develop the military as a show case for 'secular' India. Moreover, there have recently been a number of incidents of poor discipline within the military. Taken together, these indicate that some of the general problems within Indian society may be starting to rub off on the military. For example, 'Operation Bluestar', the 1984 attack on the Golden Temple, was followed by a number of desertions and mutinies in some of the Sikh and mixed regiments. Following these events further pressure was brought to bear to 'secularise' the military and disband some of the Sikh regiments.[41]

Furthermore, the ethos, attitudes and social class of the officer corps is beginning to reflect more closely the general community. More officers are evidently now being recruited from what might loosely be termed the 'lower-middle class', and the army is no longer attracting India's 'best and brightest'.[42] Corruption is more pronounced in military life than it once was, reflecting patterns in Indian society as a whole.[43] Some officers have even been accused of selling their arms on the open market.[44] Where once the professionalism of the officer corps had meant that failure of promotion was accepted with forbearance, it is now commonplace to challenge supersessions in court and there are literally thousands of cases pending. Indeed, there appears to be considerable bitterness about perceived political and civilian administrative interference in the promotion process.[45]

These problems are compounded by increasing concern amongst the top brass about political developments in India. Progressive cuts in the defence budget over the four years prior to 1993-94 have contributed to a sense of neglect and poor morale.[46] The military believes that its operations have been unnecessarily 'curtailed' in Assam, Kashmir and Sri Lanka by excessive restraint imposed by politicians.[47] This tension was especially evident after the withdrawal from Sri Lanka, a venture that cost over 1000 Indian lives but achieved no lasting result. There was at one point evidently tension within the military over the policy of withdrawing troops from the Sino-Indian border.[48]

The military also laments the fall in the standard of probity in government and is frustrated by what it considers to be the inefficiencies inherent in rule by politicians. The BJP is attempting to play on such discontent. It favours better pension conditions for the military and supports ex-servicemen who have for a number of years been agitating over the issue of one-rank-one-pension (an issue relating to indexing of pensions). Although 'hot pursuit' of insurgents into Pakistan is not official BJP policy, most party members openly advocate such measures. The party calls for the military to be given 'nuclear teeth' and for the resumption of military modernisation, even though economic conditions are adverse. Ironically in view of the negative effect on security brought about by the destruction of the mosque at Ayodhya, the BJP seeks to convey the impression that it is a party of 'law and order', and it projects itself as the only exponent of true Indian nationalism.[49] A number of retired senior personnel have recently joined the ranks of the BJP, largely on the grounds of the party's law and order and nationalist credentials. Although it is difficult to confirm the point, RSS *swayamsevaks* (volunteers) are also said to be active within the top brass of the military and in the ranks of the intelligence services.[50]

For all these difficulties, according to Cohen '... the Indian political system [still] does not face the problem of a coup.'[51] Nevertheless, there are a number of dangers that fall short of a coup inherent in the increasing involvement of the military in support of the civil authorities, especially in the context of growing unrest associated with disputes between religious communities.

There is mounting evidence that the police and paramilitary, particularly in the north-west, are increasingly communalised, politicised and ineffective in combating India's growing problem of communal violence.[52] According to some reports, the RSS has made a special effort to target the police, and in some states such as West Bengal, has had some successes.[53] The military is concerned that the police in the north-east are giving up their arms to separatists without a fight.[54] It asserts that it has to do the job of the paramilitary and police, who have 'become alarmingly weak because of politicisation, political interference ... and the sycophantic attitude forced on its leadership.'[55] In a high-level report prepared by the army and Ministry of Defence, senior military officials were critical of the performance of the paramilitary, accusing them, virtually, of cowardice. According to the report,

> ... the paramilitary forces are fighting shy of carrying out operations in the night and insurgents and terrorists are exploiting the weakness.[56]

Even the government has doubts about the trustworthiness of the paramilitary, particularly in relation to its use in communal situations.

Because of these doubts it set up a 13,000 strong communally integrated Rapid Action Force that is specially trained to handle communal situations. There has even been a somewhat startling 'swap' in roles between the military and paramilitary, with those military divisions withdrawn from the border with China being re-assigned to internal duties, while new paramilitary forces are raised for duties on the border.

Conceivably, the military may have to become more actively engaged in confronting armed police and paramilitary forces themselves engaged in communal excesses. In Gujarat in 1985, the army had to be called out to quell unruly police engaged in communal rioting. The use of the military to quell an uprising in the Uttar Pradesh Provincial Armed Constabulary (PAC) is remembered with distaste by both sides.[57] In the 1990 riots in Aligarh associated with L.K. Advani's *Rath Yatra*, the army had to conduct a 'flag march' through an area of the city, following the reported active engagement of the PAC in rioting against Muslims.[58] In Kashmir in 1993 a serious police revolt had to be suppressed by the military, luckily without extensive loss of life. These are only several instances of a long list of such actions.[59] Today any violent confrontation might be far more costly than in the past, since the paramilitary and police are now more numerous and better armed.

In order to address this malaise, in 1993 the military made a bid to take over the paramilitary by transferring responsibility for it from the Home Ministry to the Ministry of Defence. This would have ensured a close involvement of the military in the training of the paramilitary and greater inter-changeability of personnel between the two.[60] In the ensuing 'turf war', however, the Minister for Home Affairs, S.B. Chavan, was able to prevail and retain control of the paramilitary.

In all the circumstances, the government would likely harbour doubts about whether the military would continue to allow itself to be used in such a way against the paramilitary and police, especially were a major show-down to be involved. Such doubts could explain the lengthy delay on the part of the government in despatching forces to deal with the impending demolition of the mosque at Ayodhya.[61] They could also explain the frequent use of outsider regiments, especially the Gurkhas, in riot control. According to Stephen Cohen, the numbers of Gurkhas in the military and paramilitary have recently risen—to a point where they now number about 10% of the total security forces (the percentage would be higher in the army).[62] If, indeed, regiments of Gurkhas are really being used because of fears about the reliability of mainstream regiments, it would amount to a return to a kind of martial races usage similar to that of the British.

In view of the growing influence of the BJP in the so-called 'cow belt' areas of the north-west, it is pertinent to ask what *is* now the communal composition of the military. Some argue that the martial races policy still persists in a *de facto* sense. They cite evidence suggesting that even as recently as the 1978-82 period, officer intake was heavily biased in favour of Punjab, Haryana and the western areas of Uttar Pradesh, from whence the martial races were traditionally drawn after 1857.[63] While it may still be true that the officer corps is drawn substantially from the north-west, it is by no means clear that the intake would now involve a high percentage of Sikhs. Rather, it would seem that more Jat Hindus and other Hindus from the north-west are being attracted to the military. In other words, the composition of the other ranks in the military might reflect quite closely the composition of the paramilitary, and even the police.

Yet the views of the officer corps and *jawans* (literally 'young ones' or other ranks) within the military on the emergence of a more 'Hindu' India remain an enigma. It would be strongly against Indian tradition for any such support to be expressed publicly within the ranks of *serving* members and any poll of their opinions is most unlikely. Probably, the officer corps itself maintains its professional demeanour; but it would be surprising if there were not some interest in the BJP, or in Hindu issues in general, amongst the soldiery, just as there has apparently emerged a Hindu bias in some of the police and paramilitary forces.

Attitudes within the military are relevant not just from the point of view of the military's role in supporting the civil authorities. The Indian army is a peasant army. It dispels into the countryside a constant stream of retiring soldiers who are literate and trained in the use of arms. The effect is multiplied many times in the case of the north-west, because recruiting is still heavily concentrated in that area. In the district of Meerut alone, 2.3 million persons are either ex-servicemen or their families.[64] Organisations based in the north-west such as the Bharat Kisan Union (Indian Farmer's Union) have made political capital out of conflating farmer's grievances with grievances relating to the position of ex-service personnel.

As for the top brass, while it grumbles discreetly about the government, it is not entirely happy with the machinations of the Hindu Right. Its basic aim is to keep the military from becoming politicised—and in Indian terms that now also means 'communalised'. Despite the claims of the BJP to be the party of law and order, its machinations have made the task of the military in support of the civil authority more rather than less difficult. For example, M.M. Joshi's *Ekta Yatra* march on Srinagar was strongly opposed by the military because it had the effect of further inflaming an already difficult situation.[65] The inflammatory behaviour of the BJP and RSS over the destruction of the mosque at Ayodhya, and the subsequent role of the religious chauvinist Shiv Sena in sparking riots in Bombay, can hardly be said to have contributed to the goal of stability.

If the army is considered the third line of defence, the paramilitary is the second, for they are in turn considered more reliable than the police. Increasing amounts of money have been provided to service the paramilitary forces.[66] In all there are 702,000 personnel now in the paramilitary, representing an apparent increase of 230% over the decade of the 1980s.[67] The Border Security Force (BSF) and Central Reserve Police Force (CRPF), each numbering 90,000, are the two largest of the paramilitary forces. The CRPF also includes a reserve force of 250,000 strong. Up to 70% of the CRPF have been engaged in fighting militants in Punjab and Kashmir alone.[68] The Rapid Action Force is a sub-unit of the CRPF. It will comprise more highly trained and educated troops than the rest of the CRPF.[69] The CRPF has also had to be re-armed with automatic rifles, machine guns and machine pistols in order to cope with the sophisticated weapons that flooded into India following the war in Afghanistan. The force is now actively seeking to obtain the new 5.56 mm weapons to be introduced into the army.[70] Of the remaining paramilitary forces, the Assam Rifles and Indo-Tibetal Border Police (ITBP) have grown rapidly. These units are closest to the military and are most actively engaged in filling the duties of the military divisions that have been moved elsewhere for internal duties.[71]

The problems of drug and gun smuggling have also caused the central government to devote additional resources to the paramilitary. Because of problems on the Punjab border, the BSF formulated an $18 million plan to raise an additional two battalions and to fence and mount floodlights along the border.[72] Due to the reluctance on the part of the military to become too closely involved in maintenance of security in Punjab following 'Operation Bluestar', the government also decided to raise a crack new paramilitary force, to be known as the National Security Guard. The new unit will eventually number 5,000 and have all the capabilities of the military. However, budget restrictions have delayed its formation.

The growing problem of smuggling of explosives, arms, gold and drugs, the need to prevent access of Tamil militants to their support bases in Tamil Nadu, and the growth of the economically exploitable maritime zones (EEZs), have all contributed to a rapid growth in size and capability of the coast guard. Ships are currently being commissioned into the force at a rate of about three a year. The fleet of *Dornier* aircraft and helicopters is to be expanded. A number of new coast guard bases have been built around the tip of the Indian peninsula, designed specifically to assist in the interdiction of traffic between India and Sri Lanka across the Palk Strait and Gulf of Mannar.

One reason for the rapid increase in the size of the paramilitary forces is the increasing demoralisation and corruption of the police forces. Because of the lengthy delays endemic in the judicial system, police are often encouraged to take the law into their own hands.[73] They are often poorly paid, ill-equipped and badly housed.[74] Moreover, because of pressure to provide jobs to people from the home state, state governments no longer follow the policy of recruiting police from outside the home state to ensure fair treatment between communities.[75] The police are consequently considered to be increasingly unreliable in combating communal violence. With the coming to power of a BJP government in Uttar Pradesh in 1991, the police were themselves reportedly frequently involved in communal violence against Muslims.[76] In Punjab, some of the police were at one stage closely aligned with separatist groups and were themselves accused of being involved with kidnap, extortion and corruption.[77] Both the paramilitary and the army consequently find themselves cast in the role of 'watching the watchers'.[78]

The demoralisation and increasing ineffectiveness of the police caused the Eighth Finance Commission to recommend that the central government provide an additional $104 million for the 1985-89 period to upgrade police forces, while the Ninth Commission recommended a further $13 million.[79] Since then, the spread of Naxalism and terrorism in areas such as the Terai region of Uttar Pradesh and Central India has prompted the central government to re-activate plans to co-ordinate with the states in a further major upgrading of police capabilities, including through the provision of sophisticated weapons.[80] In addition to these resources, the UP government has requested a further 25 companies of police from the central government.[81] The Maharashtra government is to spend an additional $6 million on upgrading the police and has approached the centre to have its police and paramilitary forces armed with sophisticated weapons.[82] Andhra Pradesh has even requested that its police be provided with MI-8 or MI-17 combat helicopters. Given the past history of unrest in the paramilitary and police, the Ministry of Home Affairs remains somewhat nervous about the arming of these forces to too high a level.[83]

The deterioration in law and order between and within countries of the South Asian region thus commands more and more of the planning effort, resources and focus of the regional nations. It means that the armed forces themselves have to be re-structured in order to conduct personnel-intensive internal security duties. It seriously sets back the process of military modernisation, because a 'machine-rich' environment that would enable greater force projection is not one that would be particularly useful in combating insurgency. Naval forces, which are usually considered integral to force projection, are severely restricted both on grounds of funding pressure within the other services, and particularly the army, and because of the patrolling needs associated with brown water protection.

Endnotes

1   In the Punjab district of Ferozepore, for example, there were over one period 279 killings but not one successful prosecution. See 'Sikhs worst hit in Punjab terrorism', *Times of India*, 6 March 1992.

2   'India likely to set up own panel', *Times of India*, 30 January 1992; Barbara Crossette, '2 Reports Find Wide Abuse by India in Kashmir', *The New York Times*, 8 November 1992; and P. Sharma, 'Ultras killed many in India: Amnesty', *Hindustan Times*, 9 July 1992.

3   Harsh Sethi, 'Human Rights in Kashmir: A Constricted Discourse', Information Unit on Militarisation and Demilitarisation in Asia (IUMDA), *Newsletter 4*, 1991, p. 61.

4   'India rejects US amendment on armed forces exchanges', *The Hindu*, 25 June 1991.

5   R. Chakrapani, 'US bars India from military education scheme', *The Hindu* (International Edition), 26 June 1993.

6   'Amnesty blind to crimes by terrorists', *Times of India*, 15 February 1992.

7   'Pak links of Asiawatch report', *Times of India*, 29 January 1992.

8   A former Jammu and Kashmir Governor, G.C. Saxena, blamed the situation on the 'state-sponsored terrorism' initiated by Pakistan. 'LAC mined to deter infiltrators', *Times of India*, 9 February 1992.

9   Sethi, 'Human Rights in Kashmir', pp. 61-2; Subhash Kirekar, 'An attempt to legitimise terrorist killings', *Times of India*, 10 February 1992.

10 'India may seek help on terrorism', *Times of India*, 22 February 1992.

11   'Collect data to fight terrorism: Chavan', *Times of India*, 4 March 1992.

12   Quoted by A.G. Noorani in 'Rights and wrongs: A commission and many omissions', *Frontline*, 27 August 1993, p. 38.

13   Noorani, 'Rights and wrongs', p. 39; Human Rights Commission: A Shackled Watchdog', *India Today*, 15 January 1994, p. 171.

14   Atul Aneja, 'Human rights cell in Army planned, *The Hindu*, (International Edition), 11 September 1993, p. 13.

15   Sethi, 'Human Rights in Kashmir', p. 65.

16   'RLEGP's execution comes under fire', *The Hindu*, 28 January 1992; and A. Ghosh, 'Eighth Plan: Challenges and Possibilities—III', *Economic and Political Weekly*, Vol. XXVI, No. 5, 2 February 1991, p. 197.

17   Marika Vicziany, 'India's Anti-Poverty Programmes, with Special Reference to the Untouchables', in *What's Happening to India—The Last Ten Years*, La Trobe University, Melbourne, 1986, p. 185.

18   Oliver Mendelsohn and Marika Vicziany, 'The Untouchables Today', in Jim Masselos (Ed.), *India, Creating a Modern Nation*, Sterling, New Delhi, 1990, p. 267.

19   A. Ghosh, 'Eighth Plan: Challenges and Opportunities—I', *Economic and Political Weekly*, Vol. XXVI, No. 3, 19 January 1991, p. 80.

20   S.A. Zaidi, 'Regional Imbalances and National Question in Pakistan', *Economic and Political Weekly*, Vol. XXIV, No. 6, 11 February 1989. p. 303.

21   'Terrorism: Intimidating Business', *India Today*, 30 April 1991, pp. 96-98; 'Punjab: Army Again', *Frontline*, December 1991, p. 13; and Alam Srinivas, 'High output mowed down by bullets', *Times of India*, 13 March 1992.

22   'Militants force out prosperity', *Times of India*, 8 February 1992.

23   'Terrorism: intimidating business', *Times of India*, 13 April 1991.

24   'Sticky Situation', *India Today*, 15 April 1991, p. 136.

25   'Looking for more oil in Assam', *The Hindu*, 19 September 1991.

26   See, for example, 'West finds Indian society violent', *Times of India*, 27 December 1993.

27   See 'Swords not ploughshares', *The Economist*, 23 March 1991, p. 52

28   Government of India, *Defence Services Estimates 1991-92*, Government of India Press, 1991, (Actuals for 1989-90). Note that these figures do not include items used in common between the services.

29   IISS, *The Military Balance 1991-92*, p. 163.

30   The Indian army was poorly equipped and trained for jungle warfare. Forays were made at company strength. Many lessons have since been learned, however. See 'Valuable War Lessons', *India Today*, 15 October 1989, pp. 106-7; and 'Sri Lanka Operation Dents Army Morale', *Observer News Service*, No. 55074, 26 September 1989.

31   There are also assets in Trivandrum and Coimbatore in the South. See Services location map, 'Growing security fears' *Jane's Defence Weekly*, 26 May 1990, p. 1025.

32   See 'India needs a strong navy: Shekhawat', *Times of India*, 2 December 1993.

33   See for example, Robert Karniol, 'Chinese weapons boost Sri Lanka, *Jane's Defence Weekly*, 15 June 1991, p. 1026; UNDP, *Human Development Report 1990*, Table 19, p. 156.

34   Steve Coll, 'India Deploys army in Punjab', *Washington Post*, 28 November, 1991; S.P. Baranwal (Ed.), *Military Yearbook 1990-91*, Guide Publications, New Delhi, 1990, p. 207 and *1992-93*, pp. 606-7.

35   Rahul Bedi says that there are four army divisions posted in Kashmir. See 'Conflict in Kashmir continues', *Jane's Defence Weekly*, 3 July 1993, p. 21. Other information comes from a non-disclosable source, New Delhi, December 1993. At least some of the troops located in Kashmir would still be deployed in the context of the Sino-Indian border dispute, however.

36   'Concern over Indo-Bangla border situation', *Times of India*, 14 February 1992.

37   Stephen Cohen, *The Indian Army: Its Contribution to the Development of a Nation*, Oxford University Press, New Delhi, 1990, p. 202.

38   Report of an interview in the army journal, *Sainik Samachar*, in the *Times of India*, 15 January 1992.

39   Rodrigues did, however, manage to ensure that the military was

largely confined to a back-up and logistical role in the latter operation in Punjab. Consequently, there were very few army losses in the operation. Interview with a senior bureaucrat, New Delhi, December, 1991.

40   Rudolphs, *In Pursuit of Lakshmi*, p. 87; Cohen, *The Indian Army*, pp. 45-56.

41   Unofficial accounts of the aftermath of 'Operation Bluestar' suggest that the mutiny amongst the Sikhs was far more serious than the government has ever made public and included a massacre of 400 non-Sikhs in the Bihar Regiment.

42   Cohen, *The Indian Army*, p. 216, p. 225 and p. 229.

43   Cohen, *The Indian Army*, p. 215.

44   N.K. Singh, 'The Army: Dangerous Dealings', *India Today*, 30 September 1993, pp. 77-8.

45   One ex-officer was so incensed about what he saw as corruption in promotion procedures that he wrote a book on the subject. See Brigadier Man Mobhan Sharma (Ret'd), *I Shall Not Volunteer: In Roads of Corruption in the Indian Army*, privately published, New Delhi, n.d.—c. 1992.   In December 1993 an officer shot himself when passed over for the position of Surgeon-General.

46   Some of these views are well summed up in a major piece on defence spending in *India Today*. See 'Defence: A Middle-Aged Military Machine', *India Today*, 30 April 1993, pp. 38-46.

47   See Mushahid Hussain, 'Indian Army's Changing Profile', *Regional Studies*, Vol. IX, No. 3, Summer 1991, p. 13.

48   Kanwar Sandhu, 'Confusion in Command', *India Today*, 15 April 1993, p. 148..

49   Seema Guha, 'Pragmatic approach needed for defence', *The Times of India*, 27 July 1991; ' "Ram raj" or "Imam raj" is the choice: Advani', *The Hindu*, 25 May 1991.

50   Mushahid Hussain, 'Indian Army's Changing Profile', pp. 11-12; Hamish McDonald, 'Ayodhya backlash', *Far Eastern Economic Review*, 14 January 1993; Robin Jeffrey, on the Australian Broadcasting Commission program 'Connections', 22 May 1991.

51   Stephen Cohen, *The Indian Army*, p. 222.

52   See for example R. McLean, J. McGuire and P. Reeves, 'The Communal Cauldron Boils Over: The Bharatiya Janata Party (BJP)

July-December 1992', paper delivered at the *After Ayodhya* conference, Curtin University, Perth, July 1993, p. 9; Ali Asghar Engineer, 'The Bloody Trail', *Economic and Political Weekly*, Vol. XXVI, No. 4, 26 January 1991, p. 155; Rahul Bedi, 'India's Reluctant Police', *Jane's Defence Weekly*, 6 July 1991, p. 22, and Stephen Cohen, *The Indian Army*, p. 203.

53   Malabika Bhattacharya, 'RSS a formidable force in Bengal, CPI tells CPM', *The Indian Express*, 29 December 1992.

54   Syed Zubair Ahmed, 'Arms surrender by police worries Army', *Times of India*, 28 December 1993.

55   Lt. Gen. S.C. Sardeshpande (Ret'd), 'Internal Violence and the Military', *Indian Defence Review*, July 1992, p. 29.

56   Quoted in T.A. Davis, 'Internal security deteriorating rapidly', *Asia-Pacific Defence Reporter*, August-September 1993, p. 11.

57   Khusro F. Rustamji, 'The Paramilitary-Army Interface', *Indian Defence Review*, January 1991, p. 92.

58   Ali Asghar Engineer, 'The Bloody Trail', p. 158.

59   Raju Thomas, *Indian Security Policy*, p. 84.

60   Currently, many army personnel join the paramilitary on retirement, but the reverse is not so common.

61   The central government's explanation for the initial delay is that it was in the jurisdiction of the state government to request assistance, and that the BJP government in UP did not do so. In fact, the government could have intervened under article 355 of the Constitution and had paramilitary troops posted around Faizabad ready to do so. The reaction of the paramilitary forces, which came close to mutiny in the earlier attempt on the mosque associated with Advani's *rath yatra*, could have alerted the central government to the danger of using troops once the mosque had been surrounded by the populace.   See Harinder Baweja, 'Wrong Man, Wrong Place, *India Today*, 31 December 1992, p. 48.

62   Stephen Cohen, *The Indian Army*, p. 211.

63   Apurba Kundu, 'The Indian Army's Continued Overdependence on Martial Races' Officers', *Indian Defence Review*, July 1991, Table 3, p. 73.

64   Lt Col Shyam Singh, 'Peasant Agitation and Internal Security', *Indian Defence Review*, July 1988, p. 134.

65   Altaf Hussain, 'Ire in the valley', *The Times of India*, 2 February 1992.

66   Commentary by Pushpa Saras, *All India Radio*, 3 March, 1992.

67   These figures are based on *The Military Balance* for respective years. We use the term *apparent* increase because the figures provided in the *Military Balance* actually fall in the early part of the 1980s after having been reported as static for five years. This suggests there may be a problem with the basis on which the figures are reported.

68   Sanjay Kaw, 'CRPF's glory a year older', *Times of India*, 30 August 1993.

69   'Riot-force undergo course', *Times of India*, 13 February 1992.

70   B.K. Karkra, 'Better Arms Vital For Fighting the Militants', *Times of India*, 10 February 1992.

71   'Jacob for curbs on para-military deployment', *Times of India*, 10 August 1992.

72   'BSF plan to beef up border security', *The Times of India*, 1 March 1991.

73   See for example K.F. Rustamji, 'The Paramilitary-Army Interface', pp. 93-94.

74   *Times of India* Editorial, 'Haryana Protest', 4 October 1991.

75   K.F. Rustamji, 'The Paramilitary-Army Interface', p. 91.

76   *India Today*, 15 December 1991, p. 62.

77   A.N. Sen, 'Combating Punjab Ultras', *Times of India*, 22 October 1991; 'Gill Returns', *India Today*, 15 December 1991; and 'Hitting Home', *India Today*, 15 November 1991, p. 75.

78   See for example Mark Tully and Satish Jacob, *Amritsar: Mrs Gandhi's Last Battle*, Jonathan Cape, London 1985, p. 120.

79   Government of India, *Ministry of Home Affairs Annual Report 1989-90*, Government of India Printer, New Delhi, p. 11.

80   'Centre revises plan for reserve units', *Times of India*, 3 February 1992.

81   'Terai: The new haven for militants, *Times of India*, 28 October 1991.

82   'The spreading dragnet of Naxalism', *Times of India*, 8 September 1991; 'MP not to call Army against Naxals', *Times of India*, 13

February 1991.

83   'Need for "an eye in the sky"', *Hindustan Times*, 5 April 1992.

5   Breaking the Vicious Circle

India and its South Asian neighbours are caught in a rising tide of political unrest. This tide frequently washes over international frontiers as a result of migration induced by economic or security factors, cross-border activities on the part of militant groups, the spread of weapons between countries and the highly lucrative trade in drugs.   It is adversely affecting relations between regional countries and creating a region of chronic instability. It is also turning away investment and retarding economic development.   The issue we need to explore in the context of India's rise to power is whether such problems are amenable to an early solution, or whether they are likely to continue to act as a restraint on India's development as a regional power.

There is considerable evidence that the failure of most countries in the region to invest adequately in the rural and social sectors and the consequent intensified competition for resources such as education, health, shelter, land and especially jobs, is an important contributing factor to the chronic instability of the region.   Not only are opportunities for employment narrowing at the local level, they are also narrowing nationally and internationally.   This diminishing access to employment has been experienced with special intensity by some minority groups, such as Sikhs and Sri Lankan Tamils.   These groups experienced more favourable circumstances during the colonial and immediate post-colonial period than they do now. Other communities, such as the tribal populations of central India, are experiencing hardship and loss of identity because resources of forest and land on which they depend are being increasingly denied them. Throughout South Asia, transmigration continues to upset relationships between different ethnic groups.

In order to address the growing problem of rural unrest and the threat of mass migration to the cities, India will need to devote more resources to the rural sector—to rural infrastructure, new investment in irrigation, agricultural research, rural literacy and basic health and population programs.

During the initial stages of the economic reform process, the government adopted a general program of cuts, including in the social and rural sectors. By the time of the 1993-94 budget, however, the government realised that such a strategy would lead to severe imbalances. It also assessed that it needed to provide largesse in the context of the important 1993 state elections. With the exception of the large poverty programs such as the IRDP, which the government considered to be ineffective because of the problem of 'leakage', New Delhi increased spending in health, family welfare (including family planning programs) and education, with a special thrust in basic literacy.[1] Overall, education spending rose by 37.6% and health by 60%. The basic literacy drive was extended to a total cover of 182 districts, with actual coverage of 43 million persons. Additional resources were devoted to solving the problem of female illiteracy. Rural infrastructure outlays were also increased, especially in irrigation.[2] Science and technology, including the space program, also did well, along with transport and energy. These new expenditures involved an increase in central plan revenue outlays of 32% for the 1993-94 year.[3]

These increases in revenue expenditure have, however, come at the expense of continuing restraint in capital expenditure, to the extent of a cut of 14% in 1993-94. These cuts were assessed by one leading business magazine to be at the expense of medium-term growth.[4] Moreover, at the time of writing there is evidence that the fiscal deficit projected in the budget of 4.7% is 'blowing out', raising the prospect of a tighter budget in 1994-95 and more exacting choices between expenditure in the social sector and on the infrastructure needed for growth.[5]

Nevertheless, as noted in Part I, the program of economic reform has also released a burst of internal investment which should effectively neutralise the dampening affect of cuts in government capital outlays. Furthermore, while the inflow of foreign investment has so far been restrained, India is now poised to receive a significant influx of foreign capital.[6] Overall, the prospects for renewed economic growth appear strong. Such growth, coupled with a continuation of increased government spending on basic requirements in the social and rural sectors should have a beneficial effect over the long-term.

But will this growth alleviate the jobs crisis in the short-term? And will it be even in its effects throughout the Indian Union? These are difficult issues. On balance, the answer to them would not appear to be as positive as India's sound basic economic indicators suggest.

With all its faults, the system of central planning in India did offer the government a kind of mechanism by which it could ensure that the various geographic areas of India were developed at least with a degree of balance. By its very nature, economic liberalisation dictates that resources will flow to those areas in which they can be utilised to maximum profit, which tends in general to consist of those areas in which the social and economic indicators are more promising in the first place. Vast tracts of the rural north-east and central India and some pockets in the south will tend to be left out of the development effort. Or even if they are not, disparities between wealthy and backward areas are likely to increase.

The Eighth Five Year Plan document recognised the problem of uneven development, both between sectors and regionally, associated with the liberalisation process. The basic strategy adopted in the Plan is to fill the gaps within the private economy, particularly through human resources development and support for backward areas, by means of creation of durable public works using employment creation schemes.[7] The Plan is to be financed by reducing non-productive government spending, especially in public enterprises, and by a 'critical' examination of defence, subsidies and establishment costs.[8]

If there is a weakness in this strategy, however, it lies in the area of infrastructure development, especially in transport, communications and the power sectors. The problem is that liberalisation entails that these sectors should be run on the basis of higher levels of cost recovery. Richer states will thus benefit over poorer. Industry will be attracted further to more wealthy areas and the problem of uneven development will be exacerbated. Basically, such problems cannot be dealt with through employment generation schemes and investment in the social sector alone, important as these are.

In terms of the issue of employment generation, our earlier discussion suggests that the problem will not necessarily be solved through liberalisation *per se*. We noted how investment in the private sector in the 1980s was particularly inelastic in terms of job creation and that most new jobs in the organised sector were produced as a result of public sector expansion (which will naturally stagnate or contract under a liberalising regime). We also demonstrated that the problem of unemployment was particularly evident in rural areas and that its solution would largely have to rest on rural policy and rural investment. While it is true to an extent that an expanding economy would enable greater government spending on work programs and the social sector in rural areas, it is unlikely that government spending in itself will prove adequate to supply the massive number of jobs needed in the sector, particularly since the current age structure in India will mean that many new participants will enter the workforce in the next two decades.

Such problems indicate that the process of development in India is likely to continue to be uneven and 'lumpy', at least in the short-to-medium term until some of the benefits of a liberalised economy can start to flow through to the general populace. These problems are also likely to be a feature of other South Asian nations. Thus the total regional environment is likely to remain difficult for some years.

Furthermore, there are important issues about the limits on growth imposed by environmental factors to be confronted by all nations with large populations of poor people. We have not considered such problems in detail because the issues surrounding them are vast and complex for a study such as the present one, focused as it is on security. But these issues are certainly worth considering in greater detail in another study, as some of the limited evidence we have presented illustrates.

Given the range of economic, internal political and regional South Asian problems confronted by India, it is likely that, for some time to come, resources and the organisational capacities of the elites will continue to be engaged in addressing such problems rather than focusing on the nation's wider power projection role. India will tend to be inward-looking, at least in its approach to security issues. Indeed, there appears to be a broader recognition of the fact that stable economic development is a necessary foundation for the development of a truly powerful nation and that, for a period at least, there may have to be some diversion of resources away from the accumulation of the 'raw apparel of power'.

In order to cope with internal and regional stresses, the Indian interpretation of democracy has become less 'liberal' than it has been at some periods in the past, particularly as it is interpreted in relation to the peripheral areas of the Indian Union. It is likely that central governments in India will continue to want to deal with separatist groups from a position of military strength rather than one of weakness. Already there is evidence that the principal thrust of Indian policy is to increase the effectiveness of the military response to insurgent and separatist movements rather than to negotiate politically on the issues involved, so that the 'backs of insurgency movements are broken' before the political process is set in train. This uncompromising approach is being exercised both in Punjab and Kashmir and is already having a deleterious effect on the conduct of human rights, especially in Kashmir.

At its heart, the relationship between population size and power in a nation like India cannot be reduced solely to the question of the size of the military that can be supported. There is no question that, given the resumption of a reasonable level of economic growth, India's economy could continue to sustain the current underlying expenditure on the military. If GNP growth resumes at the rate of 5-6% typical of the 1980s, as appears likely, military spending is likely eventually to rise in real terms also, if only to accommodate the demands of a military on which the government has become increasingly dependent. But this very dependency also has a limiting effect in terms of power projection because it entails that the government accommodate many of the personnel-related demands of the military at the expense of the capital demands. Rather than being dependent solely on the size of the military, therefore, the relationship between population size and power projection capability seems also to hinge on the nature of social relationships within a nation and the types of developmental policies that governments pursue.

The comparative advantages inherent in a large population, such as a large internal market and the capacity to develop a large economy, will thus not be fully realised for some time, until, for example, rural purchasing power is raised. As matters now stand, India experiences the *weaknesses* associated with a very large population, such as failure to break the bonds of poverty and pronounced dualism in economic development, rather than the *strengths*. These tend to exacerbate regional and ethnic unrest, raise the level of domestic and regional insecurity, and generally establish a vicious circle of poverty, violence and neglect. In the next part we examine how such stresses translate into policy as it relates to the external security environment.

Endnotes

1 Government of India, Ministry of Finance, *Economic Reforms Two Years After and the Task Ahead* (Discussion Paper), New Delhi, 1993, p. 27.

2 Budget speech of Finance Minister Monmohan Singh, as reported in full in *The Hindustan Times*, 28 February 1993, p. 11.

3 'Fiscal legerdemain', *Business India*, 15-28 March 1993, p. 50.

4 'Fiscal legerdemain'.

5 A.K. Battacharya, 'Actual budget deficit to double'. *Economic Times*, 10 January 1994.

6 'Indian firms can raise $5bn in 6 months, says banker', *Economic Times*, 21 December 1993.

7 Government of India, Planning Commission, *Eighth Five Year Plan, 1992-97*, Vol. I, New Delhi, 1992, Preface, pp. ii-iv.

8 Planning Commission, *Eighth Five Year Plan*, pp. v-vii.

Part III

The Context of Power

1   South Asia and the End of the Cold War

The gridlock imposed by the Cold War over South Asian relationships meant that an unprecedented number of lethal weapons were introduced into the region in the 1970s and 1980s.[1] The Cold War also contributed directly to the introduction of technology associated with nuclear weapons and the means to deliver them. The most obvious example was the case of Pakistan. Because the United States needed Pakistan as a front-line state in its efforts to dislodge the Soviet Union from Afghanistan, Washington turned a blind-eye to Pakistan's nuclear activities and continued to supply it with sophisticated conventional weapons throughout the 1980s.[2] Similarly, the close relationship that developed between China and Pakistan under the structure of the Cold War assisted the transfer of ballistic missiles, ballistic missile technology and possibly also nuclear weapons technology between the two.[3]

Although the Cold War intensified regional rivalries, it was local-level competition, and particularly the rivalries between India and Pakistan and India and China, that dictated the basic structure of relations in South Asia. These adverse relationships became tied into the Cold War environment through a complex quintet, according to which a Sino-Pakistani-US trio came to be ranged against a Soviet-Indian duo. At no point, however, was the structure ever a wholly rigid one. India, especially, sought room to manoeuvre between the superpowers; and the relationship between Pakistan and the US was not always as close as their respective strategic interests dictated. Moreover, since the early 1980s, India and China had been seeking guardedly to develop a *modus vivendi* that would enable them to pursue wider strategic objectives.

A decade earlier, however, the China factor had been a crucial determinant in the framing of the 1971 Indo-Soviet Treaty of Peace, Friendship and Cooperation, which came to be seen as the cornerstone of the relationship between Moscow and New Delhi. For many years it was part of China's strategy to build up Pakistan as a second front against India, just as it has been a basic element in Islamabad's strategy to use China to disperse Indian power away from its focus on Pakistan. According to one writer: 'It is not that China threatens South Asian security; it is that China diminishes Indian power'.[4] This ability on the part of China to act as a disperser of Indian power also explains the attraction China had for some of the smaller South Asian nations, such as Bangladesh and Nepal.

This strategic content to the relationship between Pakistan and China became evident in the 1965 Indo-Pakistan war. During that war, China manoeuvred on the Himalayan frontier and issued a number of ultimata threatening to attack unless India withdrew its troops from the border, thus pinning down Indian divisions and preventing their redeployment against Pakistan.[5]   As India began to contemplate engaging in hostile activities against Pakistan on the eastern sector early in 1971, it was fearful that China might seek to restrain its options by manufacturing an incident in the Himalayas that would have forced it to place additional resources in the north. New Delhi was also mindful that China provided a *kind* of nuclear umbrella over Pakistan, one that may have become relevant should war between India and Pakistan ever have escalated to the point where Pakistan's very survival was jeopardised. It was to counterbalance the role of China that India sought the insurance provided by the Soviet treaty.[6] And it was partly as a result of the 1971 treaty that Liu Shaoqui's earlier pledge to support Pakistan's territorial integrity was quietly put to one side during the 1971 war.[7]   It was also within that entangled context that Kissinger and Nixon decided to woo China using Pakistan as an intermediary. This policy in turn required that the US pressure India in the Bay of Bengal by means of the Seventh Fleet. This action was a decisive factor in the subsequent decision by India to develop the navy. It thus had far-reaching strategic consequences in the Indian Ocean.

But because of the growing dependence of India on the Western powers for trade and technology that we outlined in Part I, India could not afford to become too closely associated with the East Bloc powers, or too estranged from the West. New Delhi's subsequent approach to foreign relations to a significant extent came to be dictated by the *realpolitik* required both to maintain the 'special relationship' with Moscow and to ensure that the relationship with the West did not deteriorate to the extent that India became locked out in terms of its requirements in trade and technology. This strategy required what has been called a 'finely balanced' relationship between the superpowers.[8]

But such a strategy of balance was only evident in the later years of the 1980s. Earlier, India's substantial requirement for cheap Soviet arms meant that its version of non-alignment contained a decided pro-Soviet tilt. In practice, this policy forced India into some strange anomalies in the way it approached non-alignment.   When the Soviet Union invaded Czechoslovakia in 1968 and later invaded a neutral, and non-aligned Afghanistan in 1979, India raised not a murmur of objection.[9]

The Indian recognition of the Vietnamese-installed regime in Cambodia in 1980, while in part related to the need for continuing Soviet support, was at the same time a more tenable position for India to hold than the one on Afghanistan. The Vietnamese invasion had helped rid Cambodia of the genocidal Pol Pot regime. Furthermore, although New Delhi's decision to recognise was made shortly after Mrs Gandhi's return to power in 1980 and was thus perceived to be part of her return to a more pro-Soviet line than the one followed by her predecessor, Morarji Desai, it had as much to do with India's long-standing and independently-minded support for Vietnam as it did with the need to please Moscow. Nevertheless, in terms of international perceptions this differentiation was not really made at the time, thus underlining the considerable difficulty India has had in projecting an independent foreign policy, especially during the early years of the 1980s following the Soviet invasion of Afghanistan.

So strong were the imperatives dictating the relationship with the Soviet Union that Indian officials and politicians were slow to realise the full import of the changes introduced by Gorbachev in the latter part of the 1980s. Adherence to the old line on the Soviet Union was in part explained by fears in India of the emergence of a 'US-Pakistani-Chinese axis bearing down on its security interest ...'[10] These fears were in turn exacerbated by Washington's decision to sell $7 billion worth of F-16s fighters, AWACs, *Abrams* M1 tanks, naval warships and other lethal weapons to Pakistan. This decision was a factor in India's subsequent purchase of a whole range of new equipment from the Soviet Union.[11]

But even by 1986, the Gorbachev reforms were starting to affect India's relations with the Soviet Union in subtle ways. It was not so much that the East-West competition was less intense and that this meant that India was no longer able to benefit from arms deals, but rather that the geopolitical position was itself shifting.

From India's point of view, this shift in the role of the Soviet Union became most pronounced after the Brezhnev visit to New Delhi in November 1988, when the Soviet leader foreshadowed the impending rapprochement between the Soviet Union and China and suggested that India also seek better relations with Beijing.

Even before the 1988 visit, however, some of the practical benefits of the relationship for India were unravelling. One very important function of the Soviet Union had been the provision of satellite imagery for Indian intelligence purposes. On its part, India reportedly allowed Soviet technicians to gather signals intelligence (SIGINT) at Ludhiana and Bhatinda in Punjab. During the 1987 crisis over 'Operation Brasstacks', a crisis in which India and Pakistan came close to war, the Soviet Union had reportedly refused to make satellite imagery of Pakistani troop movements available to India.[12] Then, in a move 'long in the making', but one that nevertheless came as a profound shock to the Indian foreign policy-making establishment in New Delhi, Moscow voted in the United Nations in favour of a nuclear weapons free zone in South Asia, against what India believed to be its best interests.[13]

Even so, as late as 1990, the Indian MEA and the media establishment in New Delhi were able to characterise Prime Minister V.P. Singh's Moscow visit as an indicator that the relationship was still thriving, despite the prospect of India 'almost pleading' with the Soviet Union to remain friendly.[14] The apotheosis of this unreality came when the present Indian Prime Minister, Narasimha Rao, appeared to lend support to the 19 August 1991 coup attempt in Moscow.[15]

By this time it was becoming evident to those who cared to see in India that not only had the Soviet Union backed away from the strategic aspects of the relationship with India but, also, the economic aspects were serving India less well than previously. Concern centred on three areas. The first of these was oil. The Soviet Union had played a key role as a buffer for the Indian economy by supplying a considerable quantity of oil (up to one-sixth of the Indian requirement for imports) for payment through soft currency and barter. Under this arrangement, the Soviet Union also enabled India to import Iraqi crude oil with soft currency through third party agreements. By 1992, however, Russia was no longer honouring the arrangement because its own productive capability had been reduced and because it preferred to sell what oil it could spare for badly needed hard currency.[16]

Secondly, the new Russia was less important as a destination for Indian exports than the old Soviet Union had been. In 1986-87, 15% of India's exports had gone to the Soviet Union, but by 1991-92 only 9.1% went to Russia.[17] Moreover, the establishment of the rouble-rupee ratio at Rs30 to the rouble meant that, as the rouble went into 'free fall', trade with Russia was increasingly costly to India, to the point where it came to be artificially stimulated in 1989-90 and 1990-91 as a result of dealers on-selling Indian goods in hard currency markets at enormous profits. India thus built up a reserve of roubles that it could do little with, especially since Russia was by this time demanding hard currency for its oil and arms.

A third factor that contributed to the realisation in New Delhi that the Soviet Union (or later Russia) could no longer play its old strategic role was the loss of the special relationship in the supply of weapons and the consequent difficulties in access to repairs and spares we have already discussed in Part I. But the issue that finally 'broke the back' of India's strategic relationship with the Soviet Union was the 1991 Gulf war.

India and the 1990-91 Gulf crisis

Under the Cold War regime, it is doubtful either that Saddam Hussein would have invaded Kuwait or, if he had, that the issue would have been resolved in the way it finally was, by major war. Indeed, Saddam Hussein's misreading of the implications of the ending of the Cold War was a significant cause of the war. India too misread the new Soviet role.

Even though India had evolved basically successful strategies for countering Pakistan in the Southwest Asian region, Indian policy still tended to favour the more secular state of Iraq and the small, but oil-rich, state of Kuwait over the more powerful of the theocratic Gulf states, Iran and Saudi Arabia. Thus the Gulf crisis that emerged in 1990 found India with substantial joint venture commitments in Iraq to the value of approximately $500 million, 182,000 Indians working in Iraq and Kuwait and a significant percentage of its oil imports derived from those two nations. Ironically, New Delhi would likely have considered that this oil was more strategically secure than other Gulf oil, on the grounds that the latter might be subject to pressure from Pakistan.

The Gulf crisis thus placed India in considerable difficulties. Moreover, it came at a particularly dangerous political juncture. The BJP President, L.K. Advani, had commenced his *rath yatra*, or chariot pilgrimage, throughout India in order to raise consciousness over the mosque at Ayodhya. Feelings between Hindus and Muslims were at flashpoint. Relations with Pakistan had also deteriorated over Kashmir. At the same time, the two Indian governments in office during the Gulf crisis were both minority ones. The successor to V.P. Singh, Chandra Shekhar, commanded only 10% of seats in the Lok Sabha and depended on the goodwill of the Congress party to govern at all. Additionally, there were many entrenched bureaucrats who believed that the US position in the Gulf was morally reprehensible, and that the problem would never have arisen had the Soviet Union not withdrawn unilaterally from its role as a superpower. Therefore, despite the recognition in New Delhi of just how dependent India was on the coalition forces in the Gulf acting to keep the price of oil down, the V.P. Singh government felt unable to participate in the US-led action in the Gulf.

To add to New Delhi's discomfiture, Pakistan was itself a participant in the international task force. Although its troops were not to engage in fighting, they were stationed in Saudi Arabia as a back-up to Saudi troops who were at the front. Pakistan had made this commitment despite the fact that it caused considerable dissension at home, especially amongst the Islamic parties.

V.P. Singh therefore felt it was necessary to send his foreign minister, I.K. Gujral, to Washington to explain to the Americans why it was that India could not participate in the task force. Despite the fact that the US had made each nation's stance on the Gulf issue 'virtually a test of friendship', the US Secretary of State, James Baker, was reportedly understanding of the Indian position.[18]

It was a position, however, that became increasingly exposed, to the point where, under Chandra Shekhar, India agreed to allow US Gulf-bound *Starlifter* transport aircraft to stop at Bombay for re-fuelling. This decision received considerable criticism in the Indian press, however, and was generally unpopular with the public. The Congress party sensed in the situation an excuse to strengthen its own position and threatened to withdraw its support for Chandra Shekhar should the re-fuelling not cease. Chandra Shekhar had no choice but to stop the assistance to the US.

While the refuelling was not vital to the US from the logistical point of view, it was important to Washington at the time that the war in the Gulf be seen to be supported by leading nations of the developing world such as India.[19] Certain parties within the Pentagon were reportedly 'furious' at the Indian reversal, especially since the original re-fuelling agreement had been one negotiated by the Congress party.[20]

The Gulf crisis itself triggered a crisis in Indian foreign policy. Although some senior members of the Congress party, such as Sitaram Kesri, argued for an 'anti-imperialist' stand against the US position, the old shibboleths of the Soviet alliance, the NAM and even Third World unity, were generally seen for what they were, that is, as totally ineffectual in the world of the new order. As the lead of the *Times of India* put it,

> ... non-western nations [read India] will have to learn several searing lessons from operation Desert Storm. The first is the wholly ineffectual role of the Soviet Union in this conflict.[21]

Indeed, the majority of influential commentators in India noted that Indian foreign policy had been unable to serve the nation's vital needs, that it was too inflexible and too bound up in the past and that it depended on cliches such as 'friends with all and enemies with none'. They argued that however much a unipolar world order was to be deplored, it was a reality, and Indian policy makers did the nation no service by jeopardising its links with the most powerful nation in the world, by risking access to vitally needed cheap oil and by threatening vitally needed loans for economic reconstruction.[22]

The Gulf war also had the effect of causing India to feel far more exposed strategically than it had been. The way in which the war had been conducted illustrated both the redundancy of much of India's Soviet equipment and the out-dated quality of its battle doctrine. It demonstrated the value of the new arts and sciences of war such as the concept of the air-land battle, the importance of 'real time' intelligence, the value of so-called 'smart weapons' and of missile technology, and the importance of electronics generally in warfare. At the same time, it led directly to a tightening of the MTCR in order to prevent the spread of technologies such as the *Scud*-B IRBM. It re-focused the attention of the US and the UN on the importance of preventing the spread of nuclear weapons and other weapons of mass destruction. Indian commentators were quick to seize on these effects and to apply them to India's circumstances.[23]

The Gulf War thus entailed a fundamental shift in India's foreign policy and management of its military resources. As we have seen, it also had the effect of precipitating India into financial crisis because of the effect it had on oil prices. This latter development caused some commentators to conclude that the US intervention was a good thing as far as India was concerned, because the US and its allies had intervened to keep the price of oil down.[24] The contribution of the Gulf crisis to India's own balance of payments crisis, and the fact that the oil price rise was an important factor in India's having to go cap-in-hand to the IMF and World Bank for assistance, had the effect of further pushing India towards the major capitalist powers. As Dilip Mukerji put it,

> ... a country's access to multilateral institutions like the IMF is largely dependent on the goodwill of its largest shareholders, notably the US ... There is now no choice but to subordinate [the] political objective to the overriding need for financial resources.[25]

While it took the Gulf War and the attendant financial crisis to sheet home to the powers in New Delhi that the world order had changed profoundly, the logical outcome of this realisation—namely a shift in perspective towards the West and the US in particular—was both difficult, but also in some respects easy, to accomplish.

Indo-US relations

The difficulty arose from the many years during which Indian governments harboured feelings of suspicion about the motives of the United States for their activities in the Indian Ocean region, and the way in which governments chose to convey these concerns to the Indian people. The original strategic concerns that had motivated anti-US attitudes were real enough, in the sense that they related to real strategic issues such as the 1971 entry of the Seventh Fleet into the Bay of Bengal and the decision of the Reagan administration to supply $7 billion worth of sophisticated weapons to Pakistan. The interpretation that Indian governments placed upon these events, however, made little allowance for the wider US strategic interest in the Indian Ocean in relation to oil or the Cold War. Rather, US actions tended (perhaps understandably enough) to be seen as wholly motivated by 'anti-Indian' sentiment, or at least as 'a challenge to India's natural dominance of the [Indian Ocean] region'.[26]

We have earlier noted how Mrs Gandhi translated this anti-American position into a kind of shadowy fear of a 'foreign hand' (usually used to refer to the CIA or the Pakistani ISI). Mrs Gandhi was particularly active in propagating such views as an explanation for the necessity for her to impose a state of emergency between the years 1975 and 1977.[27] As one commentator put it: 'Having been fed on suspicion and envy, the Indian public may not be psychologically prepared for a rapprochement with the West'.[28]

This continuing fear and doubt about the regional role of the US has not been entirely removed from the Indian political lexicon. Admiral Kohli (Ret'd) was able to cite the US presence in the Indian Ocean as a justification for the Indian naval build-up as recently as 1989.[29] And parliamentarians, examining the purchase of sophisticated F-404 engines for India's indigenous fighter, feared that the US would use the engines to 'ransom' India over its security.[30]

In other respects, however, New Delhi was well placed to make the change to a more pro-Western and pro-US position. As we have noted in our discussion of technology transfer and the 'brain drain', the relationship between India and the United States is one that functions at many different levels. At the people-to-people level, it is assisted by mutual liberal attitudes on issues such as democracy, by the common use of English and by the 830,000 Indian's who have emigrated to the US and who have done exceptionally well there in the sciences, arts and business. These unofficial aspects of the US-Indian relationship have stood both Washington and New Delhi in good stead in terms of the mutual desire to find a new way forward with the ending of the Cold War. For example, the actual breaking of the ice between the two was accomplished at the academic and quasi-official level rather than officially. Without the valuable and long-standing contacts between the academics of both countries, the process of opening out a dialogue would have been far more difficult.

From Washington's perspective, the ending of the Cold War meant two things in terms of the relationship with New Delhi. First, Pakistan was no longer a front-line state in relation to the war in Afghanistan. Nor was it required as a conduit into Afghanistan that the US could use in its efforts to dislodge the Soviet forces. Secondly, India would no longer be seen as a potential surrogate for the Soviet Union in the region, nor as a means by which the Soviet Union might obtain state-of-the-art US dual use technology, either by stealth or other means. These developments allowed Washington for the first time to act according to its well-founded belief that India, not Pakistan, was the power of the future in South Asia, and even in the wider Indian Ocean region. As a US Congressman put it as early as 1989:

> The reality is that India is the dominant power [in the Indian Ocean] ... Living, if you like, with the Indian hegemony is the name of the game.[31]

A further consideration in Washington's calculations related to the type of world that was envisaged following the ending of the Cold War. In some respects, the Americans had been pushed unwillingly into an unchallenged global role by the rapid and unexpected collapse of the Soviet Union. The financial burden of the leadership role became all too evident in the 1991 Gulf war. The war as a whole was assessed to have cost the United States $40 billion. This amount was obviously unsustainable to a power that was concurrently seeking substantial cuts to the military to reap the 'peace dividend' and to become more economically competitive internationally. It was fortuitous, therefore, that Washington's allies in the Gulf venture were able on this occasion to come up with a handsome $54 billion in payments to the US for its role in the war.[32] But the question must have occurred in Washington: how would the costs of the leadership role be defrayed in any future crisis?

The idea of collective global security, and the associated idea of collective *regional* responsibility for regional security, provided one possible answer. The term used in Washington for this approach is 'burden sharing'. Washington's thinking on collective regional security was particularly evident in the management of the crisis associated with the break-up of Yugoslavia, which was initially seen by the US as a European problem.

The other active trouble spot during this period was the Middle East-Southwest Asian region. There, however, the role of Europe was far less pronounced and the role of the US commensurably greater. At the same time, the US was seeking to lessen its general presence in the Indian Ocean.

Patrolling into the Ocean by US battle groups was halved in the period following the ending of the Iran-Iraq war.[33]　Yet, simultaneously, the argument was increasingly put to the new administration that the command structure should be re-drawn to reflect the post-Cold War order, that such an order should be configured with the security of the Persian Gulf and the flow of oil from it uppermost, and that the security of the Indian Ocean was vital to this latter concern as the 'gateway' to the Gulf.[34]

The need to articulate a world order in which the US would play a leadership role and yet would not have to shoulder the bulk of the costs associated with playing world policeman was one factor in Washington's attempt in 1991-92 to build a network of regionally-based alliances such as the one centring on the ASEAN states in Southeast Asia.　In the Indian Ocean, any meaningful alliance with maritime capabilities would need to include India—or at the very least would involve a neutral India—since India was the most powerful maritime power in the region.　This position was summed up by a statement of the then US Under-Secretary of Defense Policy, Dr Fred Ikle:

> India could be a power that contributes to world stability as the United States will see it, ... a power with which we could work together much as we try to work together with other major powers now...[35]

The growing awareness in the US that the relationship with India might be important both in terms of over-all Indian Ocean security and in terms of narrower Gulf strategy came in the dying days of the Bush administration, which was a time of drift in US foreign policy.　The US position at the time was influenced by a series of pressure groups, the principal ones being within in the Pentagon, the Department of State, 'individual' operators within the military such as the Commander-in-Chief Pacific Forces (CINCPAC) and independent academics and quasi-independent think tank members.

Significantly, the initiative towards a closer relationship with India was eventually taken by CINCPAC, from Honolulu.　CINCPAC was charged with area command not only of the Pacific but also the Indian Ocean (excepting the area of the Gulf, which fell within the responsibilities of Central Command).　CINCPAC's responsibilities were thus not so much the fighting of any new war in the Gulf, but rather, protecting extended supply lines into the Gulf through the 'west about route'.　Perhaps CINCPAC also initiated the first round of high-level military contacts with India in part to build up its 'turf' in relation to its on-going competition with CENCOM for bureaucratic influence.[36] According to a CINCPAC study,

India's foreign policy has been steadily converging with US interests as a result [of the advent] of the bipolar era. For example, both share similar concerns with respect to international terrorism, the spread of AIDS, religious fundamentalism, illegal drug trafficking, support for human rights, *and unrestricted navigation in the Indian Ocean, and the adjoining Persian Gulf region*. [Emphasis added].[37]

Part of the difficulty of conducting strategy in the Indian Ocean from the point of view of the Western powers relates to the immense distances involved and the costs they generate. For example, sending a ship from the West coast of the US to the Persian Gulf takes about 45 days (or 90 days for the return trip). This is time added to patrolling. Both in time and space, littoral navies are estimated to have a 'three-to-one' advantage over external fleets.[38] India could potentially provide valuable assistance in any future activity in the Gulf, both in terms of its capability implicit in the size of its navy, but more particularly because of its role as an extensive land mass that juts down 2000 km into the Indian Ocean, located only 1,000 kilometres from the Straits of Hormuz. In this respect, it could play an important role in assisting an allied force to stage into the Gulf through the west about route and in the supply of such forces once there. Indeed, the US navy is understood to have made tentative 'probes' seeking visiting facilities at Indian ports to assist it following the loss of the Subic Bay base in the Philippines.[39]

While it is not certain that India will ever make its territory available in this way, such a role must inform at least part of the thinking in Washington about the future of Indo-US relations. At the very least, India is a power that it would be better to have in a supporting role in the Indian Ocean rather than in an oppositional role. In this sense, the US interest constitutes a kind of ill-defined 'insurance policy'.

There was another reason for US interest in India's Indian Ocean role. As the US generally disengaged from the Cold War, it was no longer cost effective in strategic terms for it to maintain the level of commitment in the Indian Ocean it had maintained previously, other than in respect of its Gulf interests. As a democratic and moderately powerful nation, India provided an excellent means of maintaining the *status quo*, within limitations, in the Indian Ocean.

This developing US compliance in an enlarged strategic role for India in the Indian Ocean was first given focus even before the ending of the Cold War proper. India's decision to send a peace-keeping force to Sri Lanka in

1987 was supported by the US. Washington's support was also forthcoming when India acted to restore order in Maldives in 1988 after a coup attempt. On that occasion, the US lent active support, probably through provision of overhead intelligence relating to ship movements and weather conditions. After the operation had been successfully concluded, President Reagan wrote to Rajiv Gandhi expressing 'appreciation' of the Indian action and saying it 'would be remembered as a valuable contribution to regional stability.'[40]

But there is also a further possible factor in the US strategic interest in India: the role of China. The Bush administration was becoming increasingly concerned about China's maverick role as an exporter of missiles and missile-related technology, possibly of nuclear technology, and of arms generally into troubled regions of the globe such as South and Southwest Asia. Moreover, at the very time that the US was seeking to reduce its presence in the Asian region generally, a cashed-up China was acquiring significant new capabilities from a Russia desperate for hard currency. Washington's Asian allies, particularly Japan and some of the ASEAN states, were also becoming concerned about China.[41] China's trade imbalance with the US continued to grow at the same time as Beijing refused to adhere to what the US saw as fair trading provisions, while enjoying most favoured nation trading status with the US. This imbalance contributed to fear and doubt about China, especially in the US Congress.

All of these concerns about China have helped, in a general and undirected way, to point US interests towards India as a possible future balance against China in Asia. CINCPAC in particular sought increasingly to build up relations with India as a possible means of balancing China. This tendency was also evident in the second of the so-called 'strategic dialogues' between the US and India, when a senior US official delivered a 'diatribe' against China. In a similar vein, it is reported that US Defence Secretary Richard Chaney warned his Indian counterpart, Sharad Pawar, against a return to the so-called *bhai-bhai* days of the 1950s, when India believed that China could do no wrong.[42]

But despite the imperatives leading both Washington and New Delhi towards a closer relationship, there are also a number of reasons why the relationship could not be taken as far or as fast as some would have wished.

Within India, the ruling Congress party was facing a political challenge from the BJP and the Left, which accused it of caving in to US pressure, exerted through the IMF and World Bank, to liberalise the Indian economy. These accusations of loss of independence in economic management fed into India's long-standing concern to assert its economic and strategic independence. Moreover, as the reform process bit home in terms of the suffering it imposed on the Indian people, the Congress became increasingly exposed to accusations that such suffering was caused by the US.

These feelings surfaced powerfully at the time of the first Indo-US naval exercise in May 1992. The exercise 'provoked outrage' amongst a number of Indian parliamentarians.[43] This reaction caused the Defence Minister, Sharad Pawar, to claim that the exercises were little more than a courtesy, that they were necessary to the navy's performance (the two points contradicted each other) and that henceforth exercises with foreign navies would be limited to one a year.[44]

The other major impediment to the relationship relates to India's position on nuclear proliferation. Having acted strongly against Pakistan's acquisition of a nuclear capability by cutting off the supply of arms under the military assistance program, the US felt that it was compelled to apply the same strictures to India.[45] Washington was also of the view that the nuclearisation of South Asia would go against its global anti-proliferation strategies and could speed up the process of proliferation in the sensitive Southwest Asian region, where Iran and Iraq are believed to be seeking nuclear capability, and where Kazakhstan and Israel already possess nuclear weapons.[46]

The Bush administration, however, eventually came to recognise that any attempts to force India to accede to the NPT would likely be counter-productive. The administration therefore moved in its dying days to recognise the nuclear status quo in South Asia by suggesting to the Indians in talks in November 1992 that they cap their nuclear program, the implication being that roll-back would not be pursued.

The Clinton administration initially drew back from the softer line taken by his predecessor. In August 1993, the US and a number of other Western nations issued what amounted to a joint *démarche* against India on the nuclear issue. Following this event, it became for a period more difficult for India to obtain finance through the IMF and World Bank for a number of proposals, particularly in the power sector.[47] The ban imposed by the United States on the export of cryogenic rocket engine technology from Russia to India—a move that outraged India—was also driven by Washington's non-proliferation concerns.[48]

Late in 1993, however, President Clinton began to move back towards the final position of his predecessor. He attempted to persuade Congress further to amend the Pressler Amendment to enable him again to offer to sell F-16 fighters to Pakistan. He hoped thereby to use the aircraft as a means to lure Pakistan out of its nuclear burrow and also, coincidentally, to ensure the continuing production run for the F-16.

In September 1993, the US jointly sponsored with India and a number of other nations a United Nations General Assembly (UNGA) resolution calling for negotiation in the Conference on Disarmament of a regime for the non-discriminatory banning of the production of fissionable material for weapons purposes.[49] The resolution, which was an amalgamation of Indian and Canadian drafts that had been circulating for some time, abandoned the principle contained within the Canadian draft that verification would imply adherence to the provisions of the NPT. The Canadian draft implied that India would either have had to accede to the NPT or else abandon its large commercial nuclear program, neither of which it was willing to do. Importantly, the wording of the new draft did not provide for retrospectivity, thus allowing potentially for the existence of capped programs in threshold regions such as South Asia, either on the basis of weaponisation or near weaponisation.[50]

Although Washington claims that, by supporting the implementation of a capped regime in South Asia it does not forego its position on 'roll-back', the reality is that, by working side by side with threshold powers such as India and Pakistan towards a cut-off regime that does not carry retrospectivity, the US will to an extent weaken the roll-back position and 'partially legitimise' the *de facto* situation in South Asia.[51]

While the United States is moving gradually to recognise the nuclear status quo in South Asia, there are still a number of remaining friction points between Washington and New Delhi. Kashmir is one of them.

Leading government figures in New Delhi were deeply angered by statements of the Assistant Secretary of State for South Asia, Robin Raphel, in October 1993, to the effect that there had been no legal or binding act of accession to the Indian Union on the part of Kashmir. The remarks were particularly worrying to India because they were made during the siege within the Hazratbal mosque, a time of flashpoint tension in Kashmir.[52]

Although Washington sought to clarify Raphel's statement by re-iterating the time-honoured formula that the issue should be solved according to the Simla Agreement (i.e. through bilateral negotiations), it also went beyond Simla by continuing to maintain that there was a problem between India and Pakistan and that it could only be solved according to the wishes of the people of Kashmir. Behind this policy shift lies growing fear in Washington that the Kashmir dispute could lead to war between India and Pakistan and that the war might take on a nuclear dimension—or at least that the dispute acts as a stimulant on the nuclear competition. In a sense,

Washington's new focus on solving the issue of Kashmir arises from the growing recognition that the nuclear genie is out of the South Asian bottle.

India's concern about Washington's stance *vis à vis* the India-Pakistan competition was sharpened by US moves to try to maintain some kind of relationship with Pakistan, even while it improved relations with India. In the context of its vital Gulf diplomacy, Washington could not afford to be seen as a power that lightly abandoned an ally. Even though military aid had been cut off under the Pressler Amendment, in May 1993 the US and Pakistan held joint naval exercises off the Straits of Hormuz, in a seeming effort to balance the exercise with India exactly one year before.[53] Later in 1993, the US administration began to bring pressure to bear on Congress to amend the Pressler Amendment to enable the President to supply arms to a nation in breach of the provisions of the Amendment, where the US national interest dictated. What it had in mind was to re-commence selling F-16 fighters to Pakistan. Again, this move was seen in New Delhi as a direct challenge to vital strategic interests.

There are also a range of 'second order' problems that have plagued the Indo-US relationship. These include friction over the international trading regime, and in particular over Indian patent law as it applies to the pharmaceutical industry and copyright law as it applies to computer software. In the face of the threat of sanctions under the US 'Super 301' provisions, India endeavoured to reach compromise solutions on both these issues, and they are unlikely in themselves seriously to destabilise the relationship. The trading situation was also somewhat eased by the settlement reached on the GATT round in late 1993, despite the fact that some tension still surrounds the issues of patenting of biological resources and textiles.

Tension has also been introduced into the relationship over a range of so-called North-South issues such as human rights and the environment. In the context of the 1987 Montreal Protocol negotiation on chlorofleurocarbons, and again during the UN's 1992 Earth Summit at Rio de Janeiro, India and China took a strong, generally anti-Western stand, notwithstanding the fact that New Delhi is a signatory of the Montreal Protocol.[54] And as we noted in Part II, the human rights issue, particularly as it relates to Kashmir, is likely to remain a troubling one for the Indo-US relationship.

Because of this range of concerns between the two nations, it is likely that the relationship will continue to develop at a measured pace. Unlike Pakistan, India is a substantial nation not directly threatened by any other nation. It thus does not have a natural propensity to seek out very intense relations with more distant large powers as a means of assisting security. It would prefer to continue to foster other relationships in order to achieve some kind of balance with the US rather than becoming 'over reliant' on Washington. It will not, however, allow the relationship to decline to its previous level. The fore-front role of the US in providing investment for India's liberalisation program (the US has supplied 48% of all foreign investment since 1991), its key role in trade and the continuing importance of US technology are in themselves sufficient to ensure India's continuing interest in the relationship, despite all the difficulties that it seems constantly to throw up.

The relationship with Moscow will continue to provide one means by which India can balance its relationship with the United States. Russia will also remain important from the point of view of servicing the extensive residual arms relationship. It is significant that during his 1993 visit to New Delhi, Mr Yeltsin himself was more outspoken about Pakistan than any Soviet leader was, even at the height of the Cold War. Furthermore, India and Russia were able to negotiate their way through the most difficult bilateral issue confronting the two: the question of India's rouble debt to Russia.[55] While falling short of a 'fair' rate of exchange, the compromise rate finally agreed, at twenty rupees to the rouble, appears to have advantaged India somewhat over the initial rate demanded by Russia.

As another means of achieving flexibility in international relations, India is endeavouring further to develop its relations with the two other leading global economic powers, Germany and Japan. In both cases, however, relations have not developed as well as might have been expected. As we have noted, the relationship with Germany earlier provided an important source of technology for India, including dual use technology in the space and nuclear industries. With the unification of Germany and the additional demands that it has placed on German capital, Germany has been less forthcoming in its aid and investment in India. With the ending of the Cold War, it has declared that its aid will be more closely linked to reduced military expenditure, the rejection of nuclear weapons and human rights.[56] As we discuss in greater detail below, Japan too is engaged in solving its own economic difficulties and is driven largely by imperatives in its more immediate region. These limitations on the economic relationship with Germany and Japan have tended to make India more reliant on the US than it would like.[57]

Endnotes

1 See Chapter 2, Part I, above.

2 For an extensive account of this process see Seymour M. Hersh, 'On the Nuclear Brink', *The New Yorker*, 29 March 1993.

3 Pakistani officials have confirmed the Chinese assistance to the Pakistani missile program. See 'China aided Pak missile programme', *Hindustan Times*, 25 March 1989. For the M-11 transfer see 'Pentagon sources', as quoted in *Jane's Defence Weekly*, as reported in the *Hindustan Times*, 10 October 1992; and *Times of India*, 27 June 1991. For accusations that China assisted Pakistan to develop its nuclear bomb see 'India may be threatened', *Times of India*, 27 June 1991; and M.K. Dhar, 'India concern over China move', *Hindustan Times*, 10 March 1993.

4 Steven I. Levine, 'China and South Asia', *Strategic Analysis*, Vol. XII, No. 10, January 1989, p. 1113.

5 Rosemary Foot, 'The Sino-Indian Complex and South Asia' in Barry Buzan and Gower Rizvi (Eds), *South Asian Insecurity and the Great Powers*, St Martins Press, NY, 1986, pp. 190-91.

6 Foot, 'The Sino-Indian Complex and South Asia', p. 191.

7 Surjit Mansingh and Steven I. Levine, 'China and India: Moving Beyond Confrontation', *Problems of Communism*, March-June 1989, p. 35.

8 Gregory Copley, *Defense and Foreign Affairs*, December 1988, p. 13.

9 Amin Saikal, 'The Regional Politics of the Afghan Crisis', in Amin Saikal and William Maley (Eds), *The Soviet Withdrawal from Afghanistan*, Cambridge University Press, Cambridge, 1989, pp. 56-7.

10 Jyotirmoy Banerji quoted in Ramesh Thakur, 'India as a Regional Seapower', *Asian Defence Journal*, No. 5, 1990, p. 14.

11 Thakur, 'India as a Regional Seapower'.

12 Amit Gupta, 'Fire in the Sky: The Indian Missile Program', *Defense and Diplomacy*, No. 10, 1990, p. 47.

13 A.G. Noorani, 'Soviet vote for NWFZ', *Indian Express*, 5 December 1991.

14 See C. Raja Mohan, 'Indo-Soviet relations—the return of common

264 India's Rise to Power

sense', *The Hindu* (International Edition), 18 August 1990.

15   Rao had characterised the coup as a warning to those who would pursue reforms too hastily. See Hamish McDonald, 'Looking for friends', *Far Eastern Economic Review*, 19 September 1991, p. 24.

16   R. Krishnan, 'Oil deal with Russia dries up', *The Hindu*, 15 October 1992.

17   Ministry of Finance, Government of India, *Economic Survey 1989-90* and *1991-92*, pi graph opp. p. 119 for 1989-90 and pi graph opp. p. 70 of English section for 1991-92.

18   'Gujral tells Baker: India hard hit by Gulf crisis', *Times of India*, 29 September 1990;   N.C. Menon, 'Indo-US differences removed: Dubey', *Hindustan Times*, 22 September 1990.

19   Jasjit Singh, 'Refuelling: A political gesture', *Frontline*, 2-16 March 1991. Singh points out that both *Starlifter* and *Galaxy* aircraft have the necessary range to fly from the US bases in the Philippines to the Gulf un-refuelled. The US also had refuelling facilities in Sri Lanka.

20   Interview, senior Australian defence official.

21   *Times of India*, Editorial, 18 January 1991.

22   It is difficult to encapsulate the very voluminous debate that unfolded at the time. A good range of opinion is to be found in 'Dangerous Liaisons', by Jyoti Malhotra, *Illustrated Weekly of India*, 16-17 February 1991, pp. 18-23. See also, Sunanda K. Datta Ray, 'India and the USA: Hoping to Shape the Peace', *The Statesman*, 3 February 1991; Inder Malhotra, 'Political Commentary: Posturing as Foreign Policy', *Times of India*, 14 February 1991; and Swaminathan S. Anklesaria Aiyer, 'Weaning US From Pakistan: New Opportunities Of The Gulf War', *Times of India*, 4 February 1991, p. 8.

23   See Manoj Joshi, 'The Indigenous Effort, *Frontline*, 13-26 April, 1991, p. 49; 'Pawar flays Pakistan', *Times of India*, 29 July 1991; and Jasjit Singh, 'Security in a Period of Strategic Uncertainty', in Jasjit Singh (Ed.), *Asian Strategic Review, 1991-92*, IDSA, New Delhi, 1992, pp. 23-25.

24   See Swaminathan S. Anklesaria Aiyar, 'Gains Of Stopping Saddam: India Needs Non-Cartelised Oil', *Times of India*, 22 January 1991.

25   Dilip Mukerjee, 'Challenge to Foreign Policy', *Seminar*, No. 337, January 1991, p. 53.

26   Ross Babbage, 'India's Strategic Development: Issues for the Western Powers', in R. Babbage and S. Gordon (Eds), *India's Strategic Future: Regional State or Global Power?*, Macmillan, London, 1992, p. 157.

27   See Francine Frankel, *India's Political Economy, 1947-1977*, Princeton University Press, Princeton, 1978, pp. 527-28; Robin Jeffrey, *What's Happening to India?*, p. 157.

28   Sunanda K. Datta-Ray, 'India and the USA', *The Statesman*, 3 February 1991.

29   Admiral S.N. Kohli (Ret'd), 'The geopolitical and strategic considerations that necessitate the expansion and modernization of the Indian Navy', *Indian Defence Review*, January 1989, pp. 37-8.

30   Starred question in the Rajya Sabha No. 24, to be answered on 27 March 1990 by Dr Raja Ramanna, supplementary question of Suresh Kalmadi, p. 34.

31   Statement of Congressman Leach, member of the Congress Subcommittee on Asian and Pacific Affairs, Committee on Foreign Affairs, House of Representatives, March 1989, p. 665.

32   See International Institute of Strategic Studies, *The Military Balance 1991-92*, as in *Asia-Pacific Defence Reporter*, 1992 Annual Reference Edition, p. 183.

33   US Senate Hearings Before the Subcommittee on Appropriations for 1991, Part 3, p. 394, US Government Printing Office, Washington DC, 1990.

34   P. Lewis Young, 'The United States Navy, the Indian Ocean and the Politics of Worldwide Command in a Post-Cold War World', *Asian Defence Journal*, No. 4, 1993, p. 7.

35   Quoted in Vice Admiral M.K. Roy, 'The Indian Navy from the Bridge', US Naval Institute *Proceedings*, Vol. 116/3/1045, March 1990, p. 74.

36   For an account of this competition see P. Lewis Young, 'The United States Navy ... ', *passim*.

37   Quoted in Selig S. Harrison and Geoffrey Kemp, *India and America After the Cold War*, Report of the Carnegie Endowment Study Group on US-Indian Relations in a Changing International Environment, The Carnegie Endowment, Washington, 1993, p. 9.

38   Anon, 'The LM2500 Demonstration', *Asia-Pacific Defense Forum*,

Winter 1991-92, p. 38; and Vice Admiral M.K. Roy (Ret'd), 'The Indian Navy from the Bridge', p. 74.

39   Rahul Bedi, 'Talks bring closer Indo-US ties', *Jane's Defence Weekly*, 8 February 1992, p. 187.

40   The letter is reproduced in the *Asian Defence Journal*, December 1988, p. 131. The US assistance is not detailed but is referred to in general terms in an article by Hamish McDonald titled 'Slow Speed Ahead', *Far Eastern Economic Review*, 10 October 1991, pp. 20-22.

41   See D. Ball, 'China's Disturbing Arms Build-Up', *The Independent Monthly*, February 1993; G. Segal, 'Russia and the Chinas—New Risks', *Jane's Intelligence Weekly*, September 1992, pp. 416-7.

42   When an Australian defence analyst questioned a senior CINCPAC Admiral as to why Washington was pursuing the Indian relationship, he was told, somewhat surprisingly at the time (this was in December 1991) that the US was 'extremely annoyed' with China. See also Manoj Joshi, 'Next door diplomacy', *Frontline*, July 1992, p. 36.

43   Hamish McDonald, 'Slow speed ahead', *Far Eastern Economic Review*, 10 October 1991.

44   'No move to cancel joint Indo-US naval exercises', *Times of India*, 7 May 1992.

45   'Pak. makes no secret of having n-bomb: Pressler', *The Hindu*, 27 January 1992; 'Pakistan admits to A-bomb capability', *The Sydney Morning Herald*, 10 February 1992.

46   Leonard S. Spector, *The Undeclared Bomb: The Spread of Nuclear Weapons, 1987-88*, Carnegie Endowment for International Peace, Bellinger, Cambridge, Mass., 1988, p. 15.

47   Manoj Joshi, 'US-led policy to eliminate India's defence autonomy', *Times of India*, 12 August 1993.

48   Conversation, US official, New Delhi, December 1993.

49   UNGA 48, *Resolution on the Prohibition of the production of fissile material for nuclear weapons or other nuclear explosive devices.*

50   Manoj Joshi, 'UN resolution on N-material gives leeway to India', *Times of India*, 3 December 1993; interview, Rakesh Sood, Joint Secretary, Ministry of External Affairs, New Delhi, December 1993.

51   Office of the Press Secretary, The White House, 'Fact Sheet on Non-Proliferation and Export Control Policy', Washington, 27 September

1993, p. 4.

52   According to one source available to the author, the Cabinet was set to downgrade relations with the US following Raphael's statement. However, Narasimha Rao drew Arjun Singh aside and it was decided to treat the issue in in a low-key manner. Indian therefore contented itself with sending an aid memoire to the US government.

53   'Joint US, Pak navy exercises in Arabian Sea', *The Statesman*, 9 May 1993.

54   Sumit Ganguly, 'South Asia After the Cold War', *The Washington Quarterly*, Autumn 1992, p. 179; 'Developed nations should meet costs: India', *The Times of India*, 3 April 1992.

55   Vanora Bennett, 'India, Russia end dispute', *The Sydney Morning Herald*, 30 January 1993.

56   See 'Germany reduces aid to India', *Times of India*, 3 April 1992; 'Bonn slashes aid to India', *Hindustan Times*, 3 April 1992.

57   For an argument in favour of balancing the US with Japan see Swaminathan S. Anklesaria Aiyer, 'Towards an Indo-Japanese alliance', *The Times of India*, 5 September 1993.

2   India and South Asia

South Asia has been aptly called a 'loveless hothouse where member states feed on each other's fears'.[1] While the Cold War was certainly a factor in creating such an atmosphere, as we noted in Part II, local factors, particularly religious and ethnic differences and the way that they are reinforced by resource issues, have been more important. We now turn to the substance of the different sets of relationships between South Asian nations and to an examination of the prospects for more harmonious regional structures to evolve now that the Cold War is over.

India's attempts to assert a regional management role

The nations that comprise the South Asian region have in many respects not had an easy passage to full independence since the departure of the British in 1947. In that period they have experienced a number of wars, including the India-Pakistan wars of 1947-48, 1965, and 1971, the Sino-Indian border war of 1962, the takeover of Goa by India in 1961, and the continuing civil war in Sri Lanka. Relations between India and all of its smaller neighbours have at one time or another been troubled.

One significant complicating factor in the basic structure of South Asia is the very great difference in size between India and its neighbours. As the Rudolphs have pointed out, the difference between India and its neighbours is far greater than the difference between the largest nation in any other region of the globe and its neighbours.[2] This difference in size has had the effect of creating fear and suspicion of India. Since the sum total strength of regional states would still be insufficient to balance India, the disparities in size prevent the formation of effective balances and alliances against India on the one hand (not least because geographically India lies at the centre of South Asia); but on the other, the disparity holds out the temptation to the smaller nations of the region to 'gang up' on India. Worse from the point of view of the well-being of the region as a whole, it tempts the smaller nations to form relationships with distant large powers that they assess are capable of providing backing against India.

At the same time, the predominance of India has drawn New Delhi into a strategy of attempting to deny the smaller nations of the region their relationships with distant powers in an endeavour to place a *cordon sanitaire* around South Asia and thus preserve Indian predominance. This strategy was clearly enunciated by Jawarlal Nehru, when he said of Nepal:

> Much as we stand for the independence of Nepal we cannot allow anything to go wrong in Nepal or permit that barrier [the Himalayas] to be ... weakened, because that would be a risk to our own security.[3]

The subsequent 'Indira doctrine', first formulated by Mrs Gandhi in 1983, was stated thus:

> India will neither intervene in the domestic affairs of any states in the region, unless requested to do so, nor tolerate such intervention by an outside power; if external assistance is needed to meet an internal crisis, states should first look within the region [that is, to India] for help.[4]

The embodiment of this policy of exclusion is most obviously to be found in the two treaties that govern India's relations with Nepal and Bhutan. The treaty with Nepal, originally signed in 1950 and renewed, after a period of friction, in 1990, stipulates under Article 7 that there should be no travel restrictions or restrictions over trade or commerce between the two nations. This gave rise to a situation in which over three million Nepalis, forced out of Nepal by deteriorating economic circumstances or attracted by the pull of opportunity, reside or work in India. On their part, Indians have come to control much of the contracting and commerce in Nepal, which is a source of friction against India. A close security relationship was also envisaged under the treaty and Nepal was expected to consult India on defence purchases.[5]

Under the 1949 treaty between India and Bhutan, India guaranteed not to interfere in Bhutan's internal affairs and Bhutan agreed to be 'guided by' India in its foreign relations. India also pays a subsidy to Bhutan, stations troops in western Bhutan, and maintains the road system. In the early 1980s Bhutan decided to test the boundaries of its autonomy with India. The King of Bhutan attended a NAM summit in his own right, where previously Bhutan had been represented by India. Bhutan also negotiated a separate border agreement with China. This shrewd move was seen as a veiled threat that Bhutan would move closer to China should India interfere too much in its affairs. While Bhutan has managed to establish some distance between itself and India, it would be a mistake to believe that it is now completely independent of India's influence. India can still 'lean on' Bhutan, as happened in the case of the 1991 SAARC summit, when the non-attendance of the King of Bhutan was thought to have been due to pressure from India.[6]

As a larger state, Nepal's position of subservience is less pronounced. In 1987, the then Panchayat government purchased a limited number of anti-aircraft guns from China, apparently in response to Indian violations of

Nepalese airspace by aircraft on reconnaissance over Tibet. Since India's main advantage against China is its superiority in the air, the influx of Chinese anti-aircraft defences into Nepal was interpreted as a provocative move by India, which saw China as attempting to build up a long-term relationship with Nepal and thus breaching Nehru's dictum cited above.[7] Nepal further aggravated the situation by imposing work permits on Indians employed in Nepal in contravention of the 1950 treaty.

In order to place pressure on Nepal, India refused to renew the trade and transit treaty and confined the border trade to only two points of access. This move placed a virtual stranglehold on the land-locked country. The economic damage that eventuated helped to provoke a political crisis in Nepal. The Palace, which had hitherto manipulated the political process through a form of controlled democracy relying on local-level elections, was forced to introduce full democratic elections, and the pro-Indian Nepali Congress Party was elected. Strictures on Indians working in Nepal were removed and the trade and transit treaty was renewed in 1990. The Nepali Congress party is, however, somewhat delicately placed. The Nepali Communist party did far better than anticipated in the national elections, and the forces of the Palace are also waiting in the wings. The relationship with India has become a domestic political issue and could eventually work to undermine the Nepali Congress party through a nationalist backlash. As with most of the other smaller South Asian nations, the issue of the relationship with India has become embedded in Nepali national politics.

The India-Nepal crisis had wider ramifications. After the initial transfer of arms, China backed away from further provocation of India and refused any further sales.[8] Beijing presumably had other agendas that did not involve military confrontation with India at that time. The international community, however, strongly supported Nepal's position. India was widely seen to be adopting 'bullying' tactics against its small land-locked neighbour, a country popular with tourists.[9] Bangladesh and Pakistan expressed sympathy and provided material support, Bangladesh in the form of badly needed petroleum and petroleum products. India had asserted its predominance, but at a price.

India's difficulties with Sri Lanka arose from a variety of causes. India believed that the United States was seeking to obtain basing arrangements in Sri Lanka at the superb natural harbour of Trincomalee. Trincomalee had been the most important naval base in the Indian Ocean in the Second World War. Left over from that conflict were an airstrip and a large petroleum tank farm. The latter was leased by a US firm, which the Indian government believed to be a front for US government interests. The United

States had also been using Sri Lanka to broadcast the Voice of America into the South Asian region. Moreover, the Sri Lankan government had, from about 1983 on, been consulting closely with Israel in order to gain experience in anti-terrorist operations and purchasing arms from Pakistan and China. It had also reportedly approached the United Kingdom, the United States, Pakistan and China in July 1983 for assistance in case India invaded. New Delhi saw such activities as being 'not friendly' to Indian interests.[10]

In Sri Lanka, President Jayawardena had been experiencing considerable difficulty in combating the Tamil Tigers and other Tamil separatist groups, not least because the separatists were being given arms and safe-haven in the Indian state of Tamil Nadu.[11] The Sri Lankan armed forces were at the time ill-constituted to counter such a force. In a desperate move, the ageing Jayawardena decided to seek assistance from New Delhi. In part, his strategy was determined by the reasonable belief that if India were engaged in assisting Sri Lanka to resolve the situation in its north, New Delhi could not, at the same time, countenance assistance to the Tigers from its own state of Tamil Nadu.

The Indian government, however, decided to use Sri Lanka's plight to bring pressure to bear on Colombo to resolve what New Delhi perceived to be its geopolitical concerns in the region. These concerns were fully reflected in the text of the exchange of letters that preceded the accord. The letters read in part:

> [The two nations] will reach an early understanding about the relevance and employment of foreign military and intelligence personnel with a view to ensuring that such presence will not prejudice Indo-Sri Lankan relations (2.1); [and]

> Trincomalee or any other ports in Sri Lanka will not be made available for military use by any country in a manner prejudicial to India's interest (2.2).[12]

In 1988, however, Jayawardena retired and was succeeded as President by the Prime Minister, Ranasinghe Premadasa. Unlike Jayawardena, who was one of a long line of high caste politicians, Premadasa was from the lower Hinna (washerman) caste. His rise to prominence had depended on his political skills as something of a 'street fighter' who had sought to cultivate Sinhala chauvinism and the Buddhist clergy to obtain his power base. For such a man, the accord with India was not acceptable. But Premadasa also had another problem. In 1989 the JVP mounted the second of its violent insurrections (the first had been in 1971, when India had assisted the Sri Lankan government with troops). A shadowy Maoist-cum-nationalist organisation, the JVP was making considerable capital out of the uneven treaty with India and the presence of Indian troops on Sri Lankan soil. For these reasons, Premadasa demanded that India withdraw immediately.

This Rajiv Gandhi refused to do. He argued that India had already lost over 1000 men in order to assist Sri Lanka, and that the political gains won as a result of the intervention, which included the negotiation of a viable federal system and the formation of a moderate coalition of Tamils, would be lost. He feared a blood bath in the northern province should India unilaterally withdraw. As a concession, he placed a time frame of seven months on the Indian withdrawal.[13] In December 1989, however, Gandhi lost power to V.P. Singh, who agreed on an immediate withdrawal. As Gandhi predicted, any gains won by the Indians were immediately lost, amidst considerable loss of life, including, eventually, his own.

As in the case of the dispute with Nepal, the tension over the withdrawal of Indian troops from Sri Lanka was widely interpreted as a case of bullying by India.[14] In this sense, the venture constituted a diplomatic *débâcle*. But the problem of the arrangement lay in the unequal nature of the accord between the two nations. Such an accord could not be acceptable to any self-respecting government.

The foregoing short survey of India's problems in imposing its own version of the Monroe Doctrine on South Asia illustrates the somewhat obvious point that in the case of smaller countries such as Bhutan the task is easier than in the case of larger ones like Nepal and Sri Lanka. In the case of Pakistan it is so difficult that it is has not proved to be possible at all. Indeed, one of the most important aspects of Pakistan's 'grand strategy' has been to use outside assistance in such a way as to make it quite impossible for India to impose its will in any matter whatsoever. This leads us to the second problem in South Asian relations—the intractable nature of the competition between India and Pakistan.

The Pakistan-India divide

The problem of Kashmir represents the embodiment of the differences between India and Pakistan. In essence, Pakistan's claim to Kashmir rests on its original claim to the Muslim majority portions of the former British India and the princely states it encompassed. Jammu and Kashmir contained at independence a 77% Muslim majority population (the Vale of Kashmir was 94% Muslim). India, on the other hand, claimed to be a secular nation. As such, it was quite possible for a Muslim majority state such as Kashmir to be a member of the Indian Union. Even so, certain allowances were made for Kashmir, which had a special status under the Indian Constitution that, among other measures, prevented outsiders from owning land. As far as those who espouse a secular polity for Indian are concerned, the removal of Kashmir from the Indian Union on the grounds that it is a Muslim majority state would be tantamount to an attack on the very secular basis of India's being. The advocates of the 'Hinduisation' of India argue that it is divisive to give special status to Kashmir. They want Kashmir's privileges removed. They too, however, are strongly opposed to any secession of Kashmir.[15]

The issue of Kashmir is greatly complicated by the way it is caught up in domestic politics on both sides. In Pakistan, the religious parties have for a number of years exercised a balance of power. The elites who govern Pakistan would have great difficulty if it were perceived by the general populace that they were unable to protect the Islamic credentials of the nation, which is the very basis on which Pakistan claims its existence. Similarly in the case of India, loss of Kashmir would gravely damage the prospects of survival of any government, given the fraught and narrowly fought elections upon which Indian democracy now depends. It is these internal difficulties that make the Kashmir dispute such an intractable one, and that in turn make a lasting rapprochement between India and Pakistan so difficult to achieve.

While India is by far the larger of the two nations, a kind of rough balance of power, in the widest sense of that term, has existed between them. This balance has depended on the way in which Pakistan has successfully sought to cultivate outside powers, consistently China and the oil-rich Islamic states of Southwest Asia and on occasion the US, as well as on the effectiveness of the Pakistani armed forces, particularly the army.

This series of relationships between Pakistan and its principal supporters has had two main effects in terms of defining the parameters of the military confrontation between India and Pakistan. First, it has enabled Pakistan to induct a range of sophisticated weapons; and secondly, it has dictated India's strategic posture, which has been fundamentally directed to the north and west, and which has needed to accommodate the possibility that in a conflict Pakistan and China might act in collusion.

Although in recent years it has become increasingly less likely that China would reactivate the Himalayan front in support of Pakistan (China is now described as 'carefully neutral' on Kashmir),[16] India has, until recently, had to allow for that possibility in its strategic planning. Another problem for India is that it costs five times as much to maintain a soldier on the

Himalayan frontier as it does to maintain one in the plains.[17]   Throughout most of the period of confrontation with China, India deployed 11 mountain divisions on the frontier, almost one-third of its land forces.   It also constructed an extensive system of roads up to the frontier in extremely difficult geographic circumstances, an exercise that consumed a substantial amount of resources.

On the other hand, with the exception of ballistic missile technology, the level of sophistication of the arms that China has provided Pakistan has not been high.   Items provided to Pakistan have included the Type 69-11 tank (modified with Chinese assistance), F-7P fighter aircraft (a derivative of the MiG-21) and the jointly-produced K-8 jet trainer, along with several smaller naval craft.

In contrast to the relationship with China, the relationship between the United States and Pakistan has provided Islamabad with its principal source of sophisticated weapons, as well as an important source of psychological and diplomatic backing against India.   Indian strategists sometimes claim that the reason for the relationship from Washington's viewpoint was to provide a check on India, but there is no evidence that this has ever been a major motive of the United States.   Rather, in both phases when the relationship was more intense (the 1950s and 1960s and the period between 1980 and 1990) Washington's principal intention was to provide a bulwark against Soviet expansion.   To the extent that it was believed in Washington that India was a surrogate for the Soviet Union in the Indian Ocean, then the desire to check Indian power may have been a motive for US assistance to Pakistan, but it was never the principal motive.

The strategic nature of the relationship between the US and Pakistan is indicated by the nature of the activities conducted by the US from Pakistani soil.   Pakistan provided an important base for US activities into the Soviet Union, such as the U-2 spy flight in which Gary Powers was shot down. The US also reportedly conducted signals intelligence monitoring from Pakistan up to 1966 and again from about the mid-1980s on.   From 1983, PC-3 *Orion* aircraft stationed in Pakistan were reportedly used to monitor the activities of Soviet SSBNs in the Indian Ocean.[18]

It was during the 1980s that the most significant transfers of weapons took place.   In seeking to establish Pakistan as a bulwark against Soviet expansion, Washington made available to Islamabad what would have amounted by 1994 to a $7 billion aid and military aid package.   Under these agreements, Pakistan obtained 51 F-16 fighters, sophisticated AA defences, radar-guided artillery and superseded destroyers armed with *Harpoon* missiles.   *Harpoons* were also provided for Pakistan's French submarines.

Pakistan has also sought to counter Indian power through its relationships with Gulf nations. Pakistan's Gulf strategy has consisted on the one hand of attempts to use Islam to co-opt the Gulf states diplomatically against India, especially on the issue of Kashmir, and on the other of developing economic and military ties through reciprocal arrangements designed to draw the Gulf states into the South Asian strategic ambit.

Of the two principal Gulf states, Iran and Saudi Arabia, Pakistan's relations have tended to be better with the Saudis. According to one observer, a symbiotic relationship has evolved between the two in which each is to a degree dependent on the other for its security, with Pakistan supplying manpower and expertise and Saudi Arabia supplying money.[19] In 1967 Pakistan and Saudi Arabia signed a defence pact, under which Pakistanis were to participate in the Saudi military modernisation program as advisers. In 1976 Pakistani troops formed part of the Saudi contingent of the Arab League in Lebanon. By 1979, 5,000 Pakistani troops were stationed in Saudi Arabia. A year later, the 1967 agreement was renewed and 3,000 Pakistani technicians and instructors were stationed in Saudi Arabia. In the 1980s Pakistan had an unequipped armoured brigade stationed in Saudi Arabia. Pakistanis reportedly performed security functions on the oil fields and provided officers both for the army and the National Guard. They were also active in Oman and the United Arab Emirates.[20] Pakistan withdrew its troops in 1988, but sent fresh ones in 1990 in the context of the Gulf crisis.

In return, the Saudis have reportedly funded Pakistan for the purchase of two squadrons of F-16 fighters from the United States, suggesting an interesting and little recognised three-way connection between Islamabad, Washington and Riyadh in the maintenance of Gulf security.[21] Saudi Arabia also funded the Hezbe Islami Afghan *mujahideen* group, the same group supported by the Pakistani ISI. The Saudis reportedly also provided more direct, if modest, assistance of a military nature in both the 1965 and 1971 wars with India.[22]

Support from Iran for Pakistan has been less consistent, principally because of the Shia-Sunni difference between the two populations and the feeling on the part of post-revolutionary Iran that Pakistan has been too close to Saudi Arabia and the US. Under the Shah, Iran provided assistance to Pakistan during the revolt in Baluchistan in the 1970s and also during the 1971 Indo-Pakistan war.[23] In 1989 the two nations signed a defence cooperation agreement that focused on joint military training and cooperation in defence production.

In the final analysis, however, support of a military nature for Pakistan from the Gulf has not been as forthcoming as Islamabad would have liked, considering that Pakistan is an Islamic nation confronting non-Islamic India.[24] According to the speaker of the Iranian Majlis, Iran has sufficient problems of its own, and does not wish to be dragged into the messy South Asian strategic milieu.[25] The same would no doubt be true of Saudi Arabia.

The India-Pakistan military balance

While on the surface it would appear from the order of battle that Indian forces are overwhelmingly superior to those of Pakistan, certain conditions have in the past tended to bring the capabilities of the two forces in an actual combat situation more closely into balance.

In some areas, Pakistan has managed to acquire capabilities of an order of those possessed by India, or even more sophisticated ones. For example Pakistan's standoff capability at sea provided by *Exocet* and *Harpoon* missiles is unmatched by anything in the Indian inventory. Its F-16s possess EW suites, whereas India's equivalent aircraft do not.

Moreover, as previously discussed, India has been required until recently to deploy 11 mountain divisions against China. Some of its airforce is also configured against China, for instance those squadrons stationed at Shillong and Bagdogra. As we have seen, in recent years, perhaps 50% of India's army has been occupied with internal peace-keeping duties. While this need to support the civil authority is also evident in Pakistan, the Pakistani military is not so extensively engaged in internal duties as the Indian military.

At sea, Pakistan has far less coastline to defend and only one major port, Karachi. But by the same token, this factor also enables India to 'bottle up' Pakistan's naval forces, as it did very successfully in the 1971 war. Pakistan is also vulnerable because of its lack of strategic depth, especially in the area opposite Rajasthan. It has long been a tenet of Indian strategy to cut Pakistan in two at this point; indeed this was one of the hypothetical goals of Operation Brasstacks in 1986, the massive multi-divisional exercise that led the two nations to the brink of war.

India would be the superior side in any war of attrition because of its greater industrial base. Pakistan seeks to counter this superiority by adopting the tactic of the short, sharp, surprise attack designed to achieve a strategic asset such as a part of Indian Kashmir, where India is perceived to be vulnerable in the Poonch sector, then sue for peace (the strategy of defence through offence). This strategy is essentially flawed, however, insofar as India would never concede loss of territory to Pakistan, a point that Pakistani strategist have increasingly come to recognise. On the other hand, India is vulnerable to Pakistan's tactic of waging war by proxy in Kashmir and Punjab.

With the loss of East Pakistan following the 1971 war, the new state emerged as a more easily defended entity than it had previously been. In the earlier phase of its existence, it suffered from the need to split its key Punjabi troops and to maintain long and costly lines of supply, whereas India benefited from interior lines. Now, however, its troops are ranged wholly along one frontier, whereas those of India are split between the Pakistani and Chinese frontiers. So while Pakistan suffers from a lack of strategic depth, it has at least the advantage over India of an undivided frontier.

Thus while India is clearly the superior power, it is not as superior as would appear to be the case from the order of battle. War with Pakistan could not be prosecuted without significant cost, a price that India can ill afford to pay given its current economic and political difficulties. Therefore, Pakistan is placed in a position in which it does not have to accede to Indian pressure in South Asia, which is precisely its principal goal. It can meanwhile 'turn up the heat' on India by assisting the separatist movements in Kashmir and Punjab. But this is a dangerous game, since while Islamabad might be able to assist the separatists, it cannot control them.

Furthermore, as shall become apparent from our discussion in the Conclusion of this work, Pakistan's ability to counter India is likely to be increasingly eroded as a result of loss of support of the United States, the strategic separation of Pakistan and China brought about by the Sino-Indian rapprochement and the increasing strain placed on Pakistan's economy as a result of its attempts to retain some kind of strategic parity with India. It is these economic developments above all that are pressing on all the nations of South Asia, as the region becomes increasingly isolated from the rapid developments occurring in the international trading regime. The question is, will this economic isolation eventually lead to a more accepting attitude to the principal instrument of regionalism in South Asia, the South Asian Association for Regional Cooperation (SAARC)?

Regional cooperation and SAARC

One of the factors currently pushing the nations of South Asia into closer association is the growing concern that the world is increasingly coalescing into trading blocks, and that South Asia will find itself shut out of this process and marginalised. SAARC is seen as one means of avoiding this marginalisation.[26]

The perpetual state of tension between India and Pakistan has, however, adversely affected India's relations not just with Pakistan but with other South Asian nations, and thus cast a shadow over the prospects of SAARC.[27] Moreover, although India has trading incentives to support SAARC, its attitude to the forum is ambiguous. It fears that SAARC may be used as a means by which the smaller states might gang up against it, or that Pakistan might use it to raise bilateral issues, such as when it raised the issue of Kashmir at the November 1990 meeting of the SAARC foreign ministers. India has also used the SAARC forum to 'punish' smaller states, as it did when it refused to attend the Colombo SAARC summit in 1991 and prevailed upon Bhutan to do likewise, thus scuttling the meeting. SAARC has repeatedly fallen victim to political difficulties within its member countries, as happened when the summit was twice postponed in 1993 due to the fall-out from the destruction of the mosque at Ayodhya.

Nevertheless, the forum has recently 'dipped its toe in the water' of regional trade reform. At the 1993 SAARC summit in Dhaka, a general framework was struck for a more liberal trading regime within a notional time-frame of three years. However, the measures involved would not give substance to a fully-fledged trading bloc, since they do not carry reciprocity.[28] The 1993 summit also agreed to establish a common fund for South Asia.

Some Indians are sceptical about the trading benefits that freer intra-SAARC trade would bring. They argue that the South Asian market is too small to make a significant impact on India's external trade. According to them, India should put the effort it has devoted to negotiating a more open market in SAARC into the far more lucrative markets of East Asia or North America.[29] On their part, the smaller SAARC nations fear that their economies would be dominated by India in any SAARC free trade association.

These doubts, along with the persistent ill-will between India and Pakistan and the way it impacts on relations between India and the other South Asian nations, mean that it may still be many years before SAARC starts to fulfil the role of a dynamic regional organisation in South Asia.

Endnotes

1   Rajni Kothari and R.K. Srivastava, 'Regional Co-operation in South Asia', in Evelyne Blamont (Ed.), *Regional Co-operation and Peace*,

International Social Science Council of UNESCO, 1989, p. 66.

2   L. and S. Rudolph, *In Pursuit of Lakshmi*, Table 1.

3   Quoted in O.P. Singh, *Strategic Sikkim*, B.R. Publishing Corp., New Delhi, 1985, p. 37.

4   Quoted in Mohammed Ayoob, 'India in South Asia: The Quest for Regional Predominance', *World Policy Journal*, Vol. VII, No. 1, Winter 1989-90, p. 124.

5   R. Tomar, *India and South Asia: Problems of a Regional Power*, Legislative Research Service of the Australian Parliament, Canberra, 1989, pp. FA27-28.

6   T.S. Subramanian and Thomas Abraham, 'Collapse in Colombo: Behind India's manoeuvre', *Frontline*, 6 December 1991, p. 24.

7   Tomar, *India and South Asia*, p. FA29.

8   See Bhabani Sen Gupta, *India Today*, 15 June 1989, p. 101.

9   Editorial, *The Independent* (London), 16 August 1989, as described in 'India dubbed a regional bully', *The Hindustan Times*, 17 August 1989.

10 These alleged grievances are laid down in V. Suryanarayan, 'India-Sri Lanka Accord and the Prospects for Security in South Asia' in K.P. Misra and V.D. Chopra, (Eds), *South Asia-Pacific Region: Emerging Trends*, International Institute for Southern Asia-Pacific Studies, New Delhi, 1988, pp. 128-32. See also Mohammed Ayoob, 'India in South Asia: The Quest for Regional Predominance', *World Policy Journal*, Vol.VII, No.1, Winter 1989-90, p. 123.

11 Denzil Peiris, in an article in *South* of March 1985, gives a detailed table purporting to show locale and details of training camps in Tamil Nadu. See 'Colombo Rides the Tiger', p. 14. See also J. Masselos, 'India: A Power on the Move', *Current Affairs Bulletin*, Vol. 64, No. 10, March 1988, p. 25; and Ayoob, 'India in South Asia', p. 123.

12 Suryanarayan, 'India-Sri Lanka Accord and the Prospects for Security in South Asia', p. 132.

13 Editorial, *Times of India*, 27 July 1989.

14 The Editorial of *The Guardian Weekly* of 23 July 1989 was, however, opposed to the view of India as a bully in Sri Lanka, arguing that the Sri Lankan government had been unable to bring the bloodthirsty Tigers to heel, and that there was now the prospect of a

more moderate Tamil position emerging in the north.

15   For the Hindu argument see Walter K. Anderson and Shridhar D. Damle, *The Brotherhood in Saffron: The Rashtriya Swayamsevak Sangh and Hindu Revivalism*, Westview Press, Boulder, 1987, p. 77. The secularist position is well summed up by Sisir Gupta, as quoted in Edward Duyker, 'The Kashmir Conflict: An Historical Overview', p. 4.

16   Selig S. Harrison and Geoffrey Kemp, *India and America After the Cold War*, Carnegie Endowment Study Group on US-Indian Relations, Carnegie Endowment, Washington DC, 1993, p. 10.

17   I am grateful to Dr Manoj Joshi for this information.

18   Anon, 'Strategy's friends', *Toronto Globe and Mail*, 16 December 1986, as in US Department of Defence, *Current News*, 31 December 1986, p. 14, quoting a source in the US State Department.

19   See B.A. Robertson, 'South Asia and the Gulf Complex', in Barry Buzan and Gower Rizvi (Eds), *South Asian Insecurity and the Great Powers*, p. 159.

20   The foregoing details are all from B.A. Robertson, 'South Asia and the Gulf Complex', pp. 171-2; and Business Recorder, 21 September 1990, as in IDSA, *News Review on South Asia/Indian Ocean*, Vol. 23, No. 11, November 1990, p. 819.

21   Amit Gupta, 'Fire in the Sky: The Indian Missile Program', *Defense and Diplomacy*, No. 10, 1990, p. 45.

22   S.N. Kohli, *Sea Power and the Indian Ocean*, McGraw-Hill, New Delhi, 1978, p. 135; B.A. Robertson, 'South Asia and the Gulf Complex', p. 170.

23   B.A. Robertson, 'South Asia and the Gulf Complex', p. 172.

24   See Jasjit Singh, 'India and Pakistan: A Small Window of Opportunity', *Times of India*, 22 March 1991.

25   Author's conversation with Dr Saeed Rajai Khorasani, Australian National University, 11 May 1991.

26   For example, Anon (President of ITC Global Holdings, Singapore), 'SAARC: Trading with the World', *Business India*, 29 March-11 April, 1993, p. 134.

27   For the intrusion of 'high politics' into SAARC see Mohammed Ayoob, 'India in South Asia: The Quest for Regional Predominance', p. 127.

28   S Kamaluddin, 'South Asia: Progress by Numbers: SAARC summit's belated step to lower tariffs', *Far Eastern Economic Review*, 22 April, 1993, p.17.

29   Rajiv Malik, 'Don't waste time on SAPTA!', *Business India*, 30 August-12 September 1993, pp. 49-50.

3   The Southwest Asia Nexus

From the security perspective, Southwest Asia is one of the more important focal points for India. The Straits of Hormuz, the vital strategic choke point of the Persian Gulf that carries a billion tonnes of crude oil annually, are located only 1,000 kilometres away. Pakistan, India's foremost rival, is contiguous with the Gulf. As we noted in the previous chapter, Pakistan's strategy is to broaden the South Asian strategic sphere to encompass Islamic Southwest Asia. Furthermore, Gulf oil and Gulf trade are vital to the well-being of the Indian economy.

In this chapter we examine New Delhi's endeavours to counter Pakistan's attempts to draw the states of Southwest Asia into its competition with India. We also look more closely at the economic relationships between South Asian nations and the Southwest Asian region. And we assess the effect of the emergence of the newly independent central Asian republics on the geopolitics of the region.

Although Pakistan has not been as successful as it would have liked in co-opting the Gulf powers into its strategic competition with India, to an extent at least, India feels constrained to 'factor in' Pakistan's relationships with Gulf powers in its own strategic calculations. There are several reasons why India regards itself as vulnerable in relation to the Gulf.

Competition between India and Pakistan in the Gulf has been in evidence for many years. In 1979, when there were riots between Hindus and Muslims in the Indian city of Aligarh, Pakistan attempted to pressure India in Saudi Arabia and other Gulf countries. It also sought to sabotage India's attempts to obtain financial assistance for the Rajasthan Canal from Saudi Arabia on the grounds that the canal would be a strategic asset.

The circumstances surrounding the Cold War, however, provided certain advantages to India in its efforts to counter Pakistan's initiatives in Southwest Asia. The professed secular character of India at that time and the leading role India played in the NAM gave New Delhi a ready-made means of distancing itself from the interests of the US and the West in the region, which were perceived to be aligned with those of Israel. These aspects of Indian policy also set India aside from the emerging tendency on the part of the Islamic revivalist forces in the region to juxtapose Islam with Western interests. In pursuit of these strategies, in the 1970s India successfully neutralised a burgeoning relationship between Pakistan and Iran by vastly increasing bilateral economic relations with Iran and conducting a 'diplomatic offensive of profuse mutual assurances'.[1] In 1982, Mrs Gandhi sent a series of diplomatic missions to the Middle East and

visited Saudi Arabia herself, where she reaffirmed India's support for the
Palestinian stand and argued for even-handed treatment between India and
Pakistan.[2] India was assisted by the fact that it had emerged as an important
market for the region's oil and a significant supplier of unskilled and skilled
labour.

**Figure 3.1: Numbers of Indian and Pakistani guest workers in the
'Middle East', 1975-1985, in thousands.**

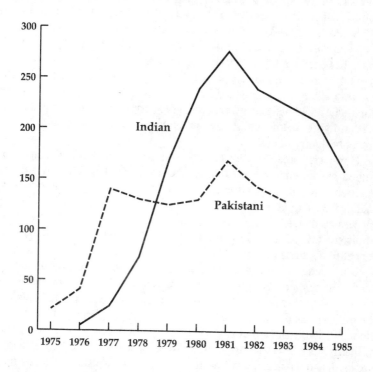

Source: Ian Seccombe, 'International Migration, Arabisation and Localisation in the Gulf
Labour Market', in G. Salame and G. Luciani, et. al. (Eds), *The Politics of Arab Integration*,
Croom Helm, London, 1988, Figures 8.2b and 8.2c, p. 162. Data relate to all countries in the
Middle East, not just the Gulf.

India's trade with OPEC, an organisation with most of its membership in
the Gulf-Southwest Asia region, matched the EC as a source of Indian
imports in the first half of the 1980s and was an important destination of
exports, commanding about 10 per cent of India's exports between 1980 and
1985. In the latter part of the decade, however, with the fall in the price of

oil and the success of India's efforts to produce more of its own oil, imports from the Gulf region fell from 25% of total imports to under 15%, and exports to Southwest Asia also declined to about 7% of India's total exports.[3]

As Figure 3.1, above, shows, the Gulf was also an important destination for Indian migrant labour, especially in the years during and immediately following the 1979-80 oil boom. It can be seen from this figure that the numbers of Indian guest workers tended to tail off more rapidly than the numbers of Pakistani workers in the years following the decline in the price of oil after about 1982. While it is difficult to interpret this greater decline, it may in part have related to the fact that the hold of Pakistan on the Gulf states has been stronger because it is an Islamic nation. Yet on the eve of the Gulf War in 1990, there were 182,000 Indian guest workers in Kuwait and Iraq alone, suggesting either that numbers of Indians working in the Middle East had built up again in the latter part of the 1980s, or that the data in the figure below constitute an underestimate. They do, however, probably signify trends.[4]

However, India's ability to counter Pakistan in the Gulf began to be eroded by the end of the 1980s as the situation in Kashmir deteriorated. Pakistan was able to point to a range of atrocities allegedly committed by Indian forces in Kashmir after 1990 and to have India condemned in a succession of OIC meetings. In response to what the then Indian Foreign Minister, I.K. Gujral, referred to as an 'orchestrated campaign', Iran cancelled a scheduled visit of Gujral.[5]

The events surrounding the Gulf war, especially the loss of Iraqi and Soviet oil supplies, also left India more exposed than ever on the issue of oil. The Gulf war found India facing a serious shortage of POL reserves for the military. India had derived 50% of its oil imports from Iraq and Kuwait alone.[6] Pakistan reportedly considered 'exploiting' this vulnerability militarily. Such was the fright occasioned in New Delhi that rationing was imposed and civilian stocks were drawn down in order to build up the military reserve of POL products. These measures proved so difficult to impose and so unpopular, however, that they were abandoned.[7]

Once the crisis in the Gulf broke, New Delhi embarked on a 'desperate' hunt for crude oil from non-Gulf sources. But India was restricted by the fact that Venezuelan and other crude oil was not suitable for its refining system. It again became heavily dependent on Gulf crude, especially from Iran, which it considered a more favourable source of supply than Saudi Arabia, which was thought to be too friendly with Pakistan.[8]

As the relationship between Islamabad and Washington began to crumble over the nuclear issue, Pakistan countered by seeking closer military ties with Iran. By 1991 Iran had started to rebuild its military resources, including with Chinese assistance, and Pakistan was regarded as a useful intermediary. The importance of the 'Iranian option' was demonstrated when a 100 person military delegation visited Pakistan early in 1991.[9] All of these events were un-nerving to India, which embarked on an ambitious round of diplomatic lobbying in the Middle East in order to deflect criticism in the OIC.[10]

Another aspect of India's concern about the Pakistan-Gulf nexus relates to the problem of missile and nuclear weapons proliferation. India feared that technology associated with Saudi CSS-2 'East Wind' IRBM (supplied by China), or with the array of missiles that are now believed to be in Iran or under development there, such as the 600 km modified *Scud*-C and the 1000 km *Tondar*-68, might find its way from Saudi Arabia or Iran to Pakistan.[11] Some Indian commentators also expressed concern that nuclear technology might flow from the former Soviet Central Asian Republics to Pakistan or Iran. Others in India believe that Saudi Arabia financed Pakistan for the production of an 'Islamic bomb'.[12]

Whether or not these concerns about Pakistan's Islamic connections to the west are based on a sensible assessment of reality, they have recently been sharpened by the sensitive issue of the emerging large-scale friction between Hindus and Muslims within India. In the aftermath of the destruction of the Mosque at Ayodhya in December 1992 and the rioting that followed, in which many more Muslims died than Hindus, a connection seems to have emerged between the perpetrators of the revenge bombings in Bombay and Calcutta and the Gulf, albeit not, apparently, at the official level within any Gulf country.[13] There has also been an unconfirmed report that a ship from 'North Africa' (possibly Libya) carrying explosives bound for India was stopped by the coastguard off Lebanon.[14]

Events in India following the destruction of the mosque have also affected India's relationships with Gulf nations. Although the problem has now been rectified, for a time it became difficult for non-Muslim Indians to obtain working visas to the Gulf.[15] Prime Minister Narasimha Rao was forced to cut short a visit to the Gulf in light of the political fall-out from the Ayodhya incident. In reaction to the events at Ayodhya, Saudi Arabia threatened to deport Hindu Indian guest workers.[16]

The deteriorating relationship between Hindus and Muslims within India and the effect it has had on India's relations with Islamic nations to the west, combined with the emergence of newly independent Islamic republics in Central Asia, gave rise to fears in India of the development of a huge trans-national Islamic identity. Indeed, some Indian commentators and politicians have tried to appeal to Washington by making it appear that India constitutes the only really powerful regional bulwark against the emergence of such a bloc. Commentators in the United States and US politicians such as Larry Pressler have picked up on this theme themselves.[17]

Even now, however, India is not without resources in dealing with the Southwest Asian region. There is a basic tension between Iran and Pakistan over the latter's desire to emerge as a conduit for the Central Asian Republics. As a predominantly Shia state, Iran harbours suspicions of Sunni Pakistan. These suspicions are enhanced by the competition between Iran and Saudi Arabia, a Sunni state with which Pakistan retains very close links. Pakistan's ambitious scheme to develop itself as an entrepôt into the Central Asian Region and an outlet for its oil are blocked by the on-going civil war in Afghanistan. The Central Asian Republics are divided ethnically and religiously between Shia and Sunni, which makes the emergence of an Islamic bloc unlikely, at least in the shorter term.[18]

India, moreover, has emerged as an important buyer of Iranian oil, and potentially as a significant source of repairs and maintenance for the Russian weapons systems to be acquired by Iran such as the *Kilo*-class submarines. An 'isolated and desperate' Iran is seeking a strategic dimension to the relationship, including naval cooperation, but so far India has not pursued this particular aspect of the relationship as vigorously as it might because of concerns about what it might do to the relationship with the United States.[19] Iran has even agreed to treat some of its oil sales to India on barter terms and to increase the amount supplied from two to three million tonnes.[20] For all these reasons, Pakistan has not been able to wean Tehran away from the relationship with New Delhi.

Even a smaller Sunni nation such as Oman has been disposed to maintain its links with New Delhi, possibly seeing in India a counterweight to the neighbouring Saudis, with whom Pakistan is closely linked.[21] Oman also is to be linked with the gas pipeline scheduled to be built between Iran and India. India is planning to develop an MOU with Oman, and possibly also with other Gulf states, to limit terrorism. Oman has called for the resolution of the Kashmir dispute along the lines of the Simla agreement, which is shorthand for maintaining neutrality in relation to the dispute.[22]

In Central Asia, India is fighting to retain the trade and barter links that existed with the region under the Soviet regime. The Presidents of Kazakhstan and Tajikistan have visited India and the Indian Prime Minister and Minister of State for External Affairs have visited three central Asian republics. In the large, oil rich state of Kazakhstan, many of these trading links have been resumed. The relationship with India is a non-threatening one as far as the current Kazakh regime is concerned, which is a secularly inclined one (38% of the population is ethnic Russian). In order to garner its own influence in Central Asia, Iran is seeking to build a railhead to the sea through its territory. India will be involved in the project as a joint venturer, thus picking up the idea once floated under the Shah. Iran's broad strategy would seem to be to head Pakistan and Turkey off in the Central Asian Republics by working with India to develop trade.[23]

Nevertheless, given the likelihood of continuing tension between Muslims and Hindus in India, India's diplomatic position *vis à vis* Pakistan in the Southwest Asian region must be considered more precarious than it once was. In recognition of its vulnerability, New Delhi has appointed a special minister of state in the ministry of Foreign Affairs, Salman Kurshid, charged with maintaining sound relations with the Gulf states.

Endnotes

1   Ashley J. Tellis, 'India's Naval Expansion: Reflections on History and Strategy', *Comparative Strategy*, Vol. 6, No. 2, 1987, p. 188.

2   *The Hindu*, 9 April 1982.

3   Fig. 3.2, below.

4   'Asian Flight: Wake Up', *The Economist*, 8 September 1990, p. 53.

5   Foreign Broadcasting Information Service from South and Southwest Asia, Daily Report for 26 January 1990, pp. 26-7.

6   *The Hindu* (International Edition), 25 August 1990, p. 3.

7   Shireen M. Mazari, 'US Intervention in the Persian Gulf: Strategic Implications for South West Asia', *Strategic Studies*, Vol. XIV, Nos. 1/2, Autumn/Winter, 1990-91, p. 54-5, incl. f.n. 2; conversation with Manoj Joshi, Canberra, November 1992.

8   'PM wants paper on Gulf options', *Times of India*, 28 November 1990; *Times of India*, 30 November 1990; and *Times of India*, 20 January 1991.

9   Ahmed Rashid, 'End of Empire', *Herald*, March 1991, p. 24.

10   'India moves to pre-empt Pak diplomacy in Kashmir', *The Hindu*, 25 May 1991.

11   For the views of a 'senior MEA official' see untitled report on India, *Asia-Pacific Defence Reporter*, Vol. XVII, No. 12, June 1991, p. 25.

For a comprehensive statement of India's concern see Ruchita Beri, 'Ballistic Missile Proliferation', in Jasjit Singh (Ed.), *Asian Strategic Review 1991-92*, Institute for Defence Studies and Analysis, New Delhi, 1992, pp. 168-204.

12   See Kesava Menon, 'Pak. mum on N-deal with Republics', *The Hindu*, 28 January 1992, p. 1; Anon, 'M-11 missiles to Pak: India may be threatened', *Times of India*, 27 June 1991. An Iranian nuclear delegation visited Kazakhstan, reportedly to obtain information on nuclear weapons. See a report of the BBC, as re-broadcast on the ABC program 'Foreign Correspondent's Report', 3 April 1993. See also reports of Reuters and *The Washington Post*, as in 'Iran in deal for nuclear weapons', *Sydney Morning Herald*, 13 October 1992.

13   Press reports at the time linked the apparent perpetrators of the bombings, the gangster family of Ibrahim Dawood, to Dubhai, where Dawood is based. Tim Mcgirk, 'India: US warns India over new terrorist danger', *Independent*, 17 March 1993, p. 17, (per Reuters news service).

14   'Ship with explosives to India intercepted', *Hindustan Times*, 29 March 1993.

15   Conversations, Indian diplomats, July 1993; T.N. Gopakumar, 'Happy days are here again', *India Today*, 15 June 1993, p. 30.

16   K.K. Katyal, 'PM puts off Yemen visit', *The Hindu* (International Edition), 19 June 1993; 'Plea not to deport Indians from Saudi', *The Hindu* (International Edition), 12 June 1993.

17   See Admiral K.K. Nayyer's speech to the US Global Strategy Council Forum, 27 September 1989, verbatim transcript prepared by Neal R. Gross, pp. 13-14 and pp. 20-21. For the emergence of an Islamic identity on a global scale see Pran Chopra, 'Foreign Policy in a Changing World', *Economic and Political Weekly*, Vol. XXVI, No. 14, 6 April 1991, p. 913. For a description of US views see Amin Saikal, 'Resurgent Islam not a unified enemy of the West', *The Canberra Times*, 20 January 1993, p. 11; and Robert Haupt, 'Front line now is between capitalism and Islam, *Sydney Morning Herald*, 11 May 1992, p. 15.

18   For an account of Pakistan's ambitions see 'Pakistan: Singapore of Southwest Asia?', 'Briefs', *East-West Centre Views*, July-August 1992, p. 3. On the divided nature of the republics see Amin Saikal,

'Resurgent Islam not a unified enemy of the West'.

19   Interview, Professor S.L. Rao, Director-General, National Centre for Applied Economic Research, New Delhi, December 1993.

20   F.J. Khergamvala, 'Stage set for stronger ties with Iran', *The Hindu* (International Edition), 24 July 1993.

21   India and Oman signed a defence cooperation agreement in 1993 and the Omani and Indian navies have exercised together.

22   F.J. Khergamvala, 'India seeks total relations with Oman', *The Hindu*, 5 June 1993; F.J. Khergamvala, 'Indo-Oman ties: Pak. not a factor', *The Hindu* (International Edition), 26 June 1993.

23   'India closing ranks with Central Asian Republics', *The Hindu*, 20 October 1992; 'India offered access to Muslim republics', *Times of India*, 10 August 1992; 'India to help Kazakhstan on economy', *Times of India*, 22 February 1992; 'Iran for Indian role in C. Asia', *Times of India*, 20 May 1992; and 'Tie-up with Iran in rail sector', *The Statesman*, 16 November 1993.

4   India 'looks East'

India's interest in Asian nations lying to its east has never been as strong as it has in those regions to its west. In part this attitude is cultural and historical: the great invasions of India all came from the west. India's introduction to modern technology was through the colonisation process, and it has until recently shared a 'love-hate' relationship with western technology. The conquests of Islam led to the development of a significant cultural affinity between north India and southwest Asia, one that involves language (Hindi and Urdu are significantly Persianised), art through Moghul miniature painting and other mediums, architecture, and food. The fact that political and cultural power tends to be located in the populous north, where the cultural connection with Southwest Asia is strongest, rather than in the south, through which the cultural links with Southeast Asia were originally extended, also gives rise to the perception of stronger linkages with nations to the west than to the east.

This lack of interest in the Asian continent to the east was not always a feature of Indian policy, however. India played an important role in Indonesia's independence struggle. Nehru believed India and China together constituted the great powers of Asia of the future. As such, he expected them to have a special relationship of brothers in the anti-colonial struggle. When Jo En-lai visited New Delhi in 1954, the term *Hindi-Chini Bhai Bhai* (Indians and Chinese are brothers) was coined to express the sense of brotherhood between the two nations. Like many world leaders since, Nehru even tended to romanticise China. This romantic anti-colonialism was encapsulated in the idea of *Panshcheela*, the five principles that were to govern relations between the two nations, enunciated in the form of a Sino-Indian agreement in 1954 and again at Bandung in a wider Asian context in 1955.

Nehru's romantic dream of an Asia of brotherhood was, however, rudely shattered by the Chinese attacks on the Himalayan frontier in 1962. With China removed from India's idea of Asia because of the confrontation between the two nations, New Delhi could no longer see any substance in an Asia strategy. Japan had been severely weakened by the Second World War. India regarded the smaller nations of Asia as technologically backward 'poor cousins', as, indeed, they then were. At the same time, tension with Pakistan quickly escalated in the post-independence years, drawing with it India's strategic gaze westward. When Pakistan lost East Bengal in 1971 this tendency was reinforced.

Thus a *de facto* 'look west' policy developed in Indian trade and strategy. This was until recently reflected in trading patterns, investment and technology transfers and in security concerns. If the west is taken to include Europe and North America, then the tendency runs deeper still. As Table 1.1 in Part I illustrates, foreign investment has been heavily weighted in favour of non-Asian nations. Figure 3.2, below, illustrates that India's trade is also substantially directed towards the oil-rich Middle East and the 'old' world of the industrialised North. Even today, India still gives considerable attention to its trading relationships with Europe and North America.

Figure 3.2: India's Direction of Trade: Changes Between the Sixth Plan (1980-85) and the Seventh Plan (1985-90), plan av. % share.

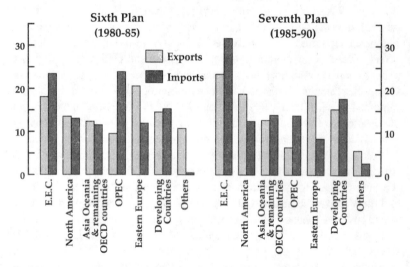

Source: Figure opposite p. 164, Government of India, Ministry of Finance, Economic Survey, 1990-91.

This policy of tying India's fortunes to the West is, however, under some pressure, with some advocating closer ties with Asia on the ground that it is the centre of growth in the world today.[1] They argue that India has been cut adrift from the East bloc for purposes of trade and caught in a world in which trading blocs are assuming greater importance. They also maintain that SAARC does not have the critical mass to provide for India's trading needs, even if the political climate were more favourable for regional trade.[2]

These views have been reflected in the policies pursued by the Ministry of External Affairs (MEA), which has been attempting to have India more closely associated with ASEAN and the Asia-Pacific Economic Cooperation forum (APEC), the loose formation that brings the nations bordering the Pacific together for trade-related discussions. Such trends are reinforced by the fact that one-third of India's trade is now with East Asia, a figure that is rising.[3]   Just recently, approved (as distinct from actual) Japanese investment in India has risen dramatically, from Rs50 million in 1990 on the eve of the liberalisation program to Rs6.1 billion in 1992.[4]   India's prospects in the regions to its east are examined in greater detail below.

India's relations with Southeast Asia

During the 1960s, Indonesia and Malaya were locked into competition over President Sukarno's policy of *Konfrontasi* (Confrontation), according to which Indonesia laid claim to parts of Malayan Borneo. At the same time, Indonesia supported Pakistan in the 1965 war with India, including through offers to send two submarines to assist Pakistan and by means of threats to seize Indian territory in the Andaman and Nicobar Islands as a diversion. Given this calculus, India and Malaysia drew together as natural allies and remained close in later years. Although India and Indonesia never became close, after the fall of Sukarno, and in the context of growing fears about the role of China in Southeast Asia, Indonesia softened its position on India.

Relations with Thailand, however, continued to be complicated by the role of China. India was a long-time supporter of Vietnam in the context of the Indo-China war. This support continued after the American withdrawal and the Vietnamese invasion of Cambodia. Bangkok's strategic perceptions were, however, shaped by Thailand's proximity to Vietnam, a nation that emerged from the war with the United States with battle-hardened land forces that were the largest in East Asia outside China. In order to check what the Thais saw as the threat from Vietnam, they developed a close relationship with China that involved the transfer of Chinese arms both to Thailand itself, and through Thailand to the principal Cambodian opposition groups, including the Kmer Rouge. Because of New Delhi's role in support of Vietnam and, by extension, the Soviet Union, India was viewed with some suspicion by Thailand. The feeling was mutual: the Thai move to create a deep water naval port on the Indian Ocean side of the Thai peninsula was regarded by New Delhi as a facility that might possibly be used by China.[5]

Despite differences in perspective on Indo-China, once it became apparent to New Delhi that the Association of Southeast Asian Nations (ASEAN) was being forged into a dynamic growth area of Asia, India sought association status as an observer. Malaysia, the ASEAN country with which India had closest relations, supported India's bid. Because of this support from Malaysia, and in the context of improved relations with Indonesia, the bid had some prospect of success. Yet at this point, New Delhi's strategic links with the Soviet Union and its friendship with Vietnam overrode any desire to be associated with ASEAN.

Shortly after the return of Mrs Gandhi in 1980, therefore, she decided to recognise the Vietnamese-backed regime in Cambodia. But New Delhi's timing could not have been worse. The announcement was made just prior to the visit of the then Foreign Minister and current Prime Minister, Narasimha Rao, to the ASEAN meeting at Kuala Lumpur that was to have endorsed India's observer status with the Association. Wisely, Rao found a diplomatic excuse to cancel the visit. This act on the part of India caused 'shock and anger' within ASEAN and gave the impression, however unfairly, that India was a virtual 'fellow traveller' of the Soviet Union.[6] When such a view became associated with the Indian naval build-up of the mid-1980s, it gave the impression to at least some of the ASEAN nations that India was a threatening power in the region.

Of particular concern on the part of the ASEAN nations was the fact that from 1972, India had been planning to upgrade significantly its military facilities at Port Blair in the Andaman and Nicobar Islands into a substantial joint services facility, subsequently known as FORTAN (for Fortress Andaman and Nicobar). This facility was opened in 1985. One outside commentator writing in *The Straits Times* likened it to a 'super and unsinkable aircraft carrier, only 80 miles west of the Straits of Malacca'.[7] Another non-regional commentator describes the facility as providing a 'fulcrum of control over access to the eastern entrances of the Indian Ocean ....'.[8]

To date the development of FORTAN has involved the construction of a 1300-1400 metre airstrip, communications facilities and a floating naval dry-dock, reportedly capable of slipping vessels of up to 15,000 tonnes. While *Jaguar* strike aircraft and *Bear* maritime reconnaissance aircraft can stage through the facility, contrary to some reports, they are not based there. BN-2 *Islanders*, *Dornier* Do-228 and *Fokker* F-27 aircraft operate from the facility in a maritime reconnaissance role, aimed primarily at preventing permanent settlement on the 500 plus islands (many of which are uninhabited) by Southeast Asian and Chinese fisher folk and their families, as well as poaching and smuggling. The importance of these anti-poaching measures in the overall defence configuration of the islands is illustrated by the fact that 'up to May 1990' over 200 poachers had been caught.[9]

Although Indian strike and long range maritime reconnaissance aircraft are not actually based at FORTAN, the increased range afforded by the facility gives India a maritime strike range into the Straits of Malacca and a maritime reconnaissance range well into the South China Sea. In practice, however, it would be unlikely that *Bear* MR aircraft would stage through the facility because their range is already sufficient to reach the South China Sea from their bases on the Eastern side of peninsula India.

There is no doubt that the development of the facility at Port Blair added to the anxiety on the part of the ASEAN nations about India's naval build-up. Concern was also heightened by a number of unsubstantiated rumours about New Delhi's intentions to develop an additional substantial base on Great Nicobar Island, only 80 nautical miles from the Indonesian island of Sumatra. Some of these reports claimed that the Indonesian Chief of Naval Staff and other Indonesian officials had raised the matter during a visit to New Delhi in 1989 and implied that it was as a result of Indonesia's expressions of concern that New Delhi decided to shelve plans to develop the facility.[10] Others, however, see other grounds for India abandoning the base plans, and it is doubtful whether they ever existed as a serious option.[11] Most likely, if such a base were ever under consideration, Car Nicobar Island, further to the north-west, would have been a more serious candidate, since it already contains a joint facility and would have been less vulnerable to attack. Moreover, cost rather than Indonesian pressure would almost certainly have been a primary motive for deciding not to build a new facility, were one under consideration. India is currently struggling to complete the far more important work at Karwar on the west coast of peninsula India, let alone develop a further facility on the Andaman and Nicobar Islands. At present, neither Malaysia nor Indonesia seems especially concerned about India's activities in the Andaman and Nicobar Islands, which they see as mainly concerned with maritime security.[12]

India's emergence as a significant actor in the region happened to correspond with a period of military modernisation in Southeast Asia.[13] The reasons for this build-up are subject to some debate, ranging from the requirement to modernise given approaching block obsolescence, to concern about China's military modernisation plans in the context of its claims in the South China Sea, where Beijing has recently reportedly built an airstrip on Woody Island in the Paracels capable of taking the new Su-27.[14] According to at least one interpretation, expressions of concern on the part of the ASEAN nations about India's role in the region offered at least some countries a means of 'masking' this build-up in circumstances in which regional tensions within ASEAN or expressed concern about China would not have been diplomatically acceptable.[15]

Whether ASEAN's concern about India was wholly genuine or not, during the years following 1988, India was subject to a range of criticism for its naval build-up from the nations of Southeast Asia and from non-official commentators in Australia. One of the stronger of these statements came from then Malaysian Defence Minister Rithaudeen, who said that while he had no evidence that India was building any large base in the Andaman and Nicobar Islands, 'we would still like to see an Indian assurance that it will not use force against neighbouring countries'. Australia's then Defence Minister, Kim Beazley, was more elliptical: he described the Indian naval build-up as 'intriguing'.[16]

The situation today, however, is a vastly altered one. One factor in the changing attitude to India on the part of ASEAN is that concern about India's military build-up has dissipated, largely as a result of the collapse of India's naval ambitions that has resulted from the financial squeeze it has suffered in recent years and the need to direct resources to brown water functions. While India's navy will be a somewhat better balanced one in the year 2000, with a better mix of offensive and defensive weapons, it will not, as can be seen from Table 3.1, below, be the significantly expanded navy that some regional nations feared in the 1980s.

India has also sought to deflect criticism of its position in the region by opening up the facility at Port Blair to visits from regional naval attaches and generally being more open about its military position.[17] In a 'bonanza' of exercising with the ASEAN nations and other regional nations such as Australia, India has now conducted naval exercises with Indonesia, Singapore and Australia and is scheduled to hold them with Malaysia and Thailand.[18]

Another factor in the new approach to India on the part of ASEAN is China's more open expression of its maritime claims in the South China Sea over the past three years. The forceful language in which China expresses these claims has had the effect of re-kindling old fears about China held by some ASEAN nations, especially Malaysia and Indonesia. If China's South China Sea claims were ever realised, they would take China's maritime territory almost right up to the Indonesian Island of Natuna, which is only several hundred kilometres from the Straits of Singapore, and to within about 70 km of the Malaysian state of Sarawak. In an uncompromising move, in February 1992 Beijing passed a law which had the effect of incorporating all the area of the claim into China's territory. In May 1992 China signed a lease with a US firm for oil exploration rights within the area claimed by Vietnam. China also issued an uncompromising statement on the claim on the eve of the 1992 ASEAN Post-ministerial conference in Manila, in which it warned against the 'internationalisation' of the dispute.[19]

As an expression of the radically altered circumstances between India and ASEAN, in March 1993 India was accorded sectoral dialogue status within ASEAN for the trade sector. Annual trade talks were also established. Targeted sectors for development include tourism, administration and management, trade and investment, computers and informatics, solar energy and environmental protection.[20]

Figure 3.3: India's foreign trade with ASEAN nations, 1979-1992, in millions of dollars.

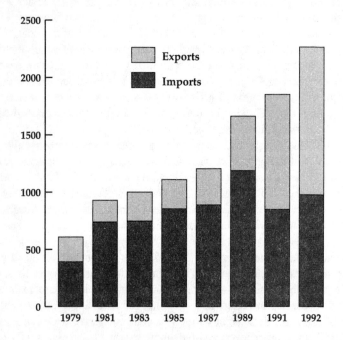

Source: IMF *Direction of Trade Statistics Yearbook*, various years.

Some observers believe that India does not have strong trading prospects in Southeast Asia. They argue that India is being blocked out of ASEAN trade on account of the very high Japanese and US investment in the region, which tends to favour trade with the investing nations.[21] It is also the case that India and the ASEAN nations compete in many areas of trade, particularly in agriculture, rather than being complementary to each other. Malaysia's Prime Minister Mahathir appeared to confirm that India was not welcome in ASEAN trade when he said that India would at no stage be allowed to participate in the proposed East Asian Economic Caucus.[22]

But other observers believe that there are good prospects for India in the Southeast Asian region. They point to the growing number of Indian joint-ventures in the region and to the 11% annual increase in two-way trade in recent years as India opens its markets to the world.[23] Probably, Indo-ASEAN trade will be restrained for a period. Once economic liberalisation takes root in India, however, it could grow substantially as Southeast Asia seeks to be part of a rapidly expanding market. Figure 3.3, above, provides an insight into India's trade with ASEAN in recent years.

Of the ASEAN nations, Singapore and Malaysia have made most effort to advance relations with India. Singapore is poised to undertake a substantial investment of the order of $500 million near Bangalore. Electronic warfare capabilities are also likely to provide an important dimension to the relationship. One of the reasons for Singapore's interest in India is to regain its competitive edge in software development. According to one highly reputable source, however, Singapore is also concerned to balance the growing economic power of China.[24]

In 1993 Malaysia signed a memorandum of understanding with India on military co-operation that opened the way for a wide range of joint activities in the areas of training and joint-production of military supplies. Items included an upgrade of Malaysia's L-70 AA guns, the supply of an oceanographic vessel and the possible sale of the Indian-made *Alouette* III helicopter and *Dornier*-228 aircraft.[5] Malaysia will also use India for pilot and ground crew training for the 18 MiG-29s it is planning to purchase from Russia, should that deal go ahead. It already works with India on the maintenance of its existing fleet of *Alouettes*. In addition, India trains Malaysian nuclear scientists at BARC. Following the humiliating collapse of the G-15 summit in November 1993, Prime Minister Mahathir of Malaysia and President Suharto of Indonesia were the only two G-15 leaders who undertook the journey to New Delhi.

Recently, Indian Prime Minister Narasimha Rao visited Thailand in an endeavour to improve the relationship as part of India's new 'Look East' strategy. India and Thailand undertook to raise bilateral trade from $400 million to $1 billion.[25] Somewhat surprisingly in view of the long-standing relationship between Thailand and China, Narasimha Rao was reported to have presented India as a possible counter-balance to China. The Thai response is not recorded, but it would likely have been guarded.[26] Rao was also reportedly concerned to ensure that Thailand shared India's concern about Chinese involvement in Myanmar. While it is unlikely that Thailand would ever publicly express such concern, there is some evidence to suggest that Bangkok is increasingly nervous about the extent of the influence, particularly in the economic sphere, that Beijing is exercising in Myanmar.[27] Rao also managed to find common ground with Thailand by propagating an 'Asian' approach to human rights.[28]

Given the expanding range of these strategic and economic activities between India and ASEAN, what are the implications for the three-way sets of relationships between India, the ASEAN nations and China? Can we say that there is a sense in which any of the nations of Southeast Asia are attempting to balance India and China strategically—as distinct from seeking a trading and investment balance—or that they are seeking India's backing against China?

It is most unlikely that the ASEAN nations would wish at this stage for India to be actively juxtaposed with China.[29] There are two reasons why this would not be advisable from their point of view. First, while India is still probably more powerful than China in conventional terms, regional nations assess that over the long-term China is likely to emerge as more powerful because of its far more rapid economic development. It is perceived to be a power of the future that it would not be wise to antagonise unnecessarily.

Secondly, it is by no means yet clear what sort of power China will develop into. Beijing may well choose to resolve outstanding disputes in a way that retains its internationalist credentials and good standing, depending on a number of factors in play at the time, such as the nature of the post-Deng political leadership. It would be foolish and premature on the part of ASEAN to develop relationships that appear to be designed to counter China until the issue of China's regional role is more clear. To do so might be to create the very insecurity that the relationship was intended to avoid. Any juxtaposition of India and China in the region would run directly counter to this strategy. But nevertheless, this may not always remain the case, depending on the way India's relations unfold with China and China's with ASEAN. The China factor thus emerges as an issue of considerable importance in defining the level of involvement of India in the waters that lie in the north-east of the Indian Ocean and in Southeast Asia.

Sino-Indian relations

In the past, the strategic spheres of India and China were separated from each other by the barrier of the Himalaya mountains and the great distance of the Sino-Indian border from China's heartland. Friction was generated between the two only at the remote border on the Himalayas. The one place other than the high passes in which their interests might have intersected—Southeast Asia—tended to be ignored by India because of its intense competition with Pakistan, its economic engagement with the US and Europe, and its strategic links with the East bloc powers.

The main thrust of India's strategy against China was designed to prevent the Himalayan barrier from being breached. The reason why Sikkim assumed such strategic significance to India in the 1970s before India's annexation was because the Tista river valley offered China a potential way down to the plains of India at the most vulnerable point, the so-called 'Chicken's Neck', or narrow strip of Indian territory separating Assam from Bengal.[30]

Today the Himalayan barrier is less relevant than it once was. Long range weapons systems such as intercontinental ballistic missiles and modern air, land, sea links and telecommunications now transcend such barriers. Economic globalisation also means that competition tends to be played out in the international marketplace rather than on distant frontiers. The growing multi-dimensional character of the two nations' armed forces associated with military modernisation means that potentially their strategic interests will intersect more widely, for instance in the waters surrounding Southeast Asia. The radical shift in India's strategic and economic circumstances in the aftermath of the Cold War has also caused New Delhi to pay more attention to the rapidly growing economies of Southeast and East Asia. The respective ambits within which India and China function are thus increasingly tending to intersect.

Whatever the shape of Sino-Indian relations in the future, the two nations will have more, rather than less, to do with each other. As the two mega-population powers of Asia, the manner of their interaction will be of profound importance for the rest of Asia. At the same time, in recent years the nature of the Sino-Indian competition has been shifting from one that involves specific friction points, particularly on the border, to one that is more general in nature and also, hopefully, more benign.

*

India's defeat in the 1962 border war with China bit deeply into the psyche of the newly independent nation. In Nehru's words, the defeat forced an 'agonising reappraisal of India's foreign policy.'[31] Prior to the war, Indian defence spending had never risen above 2% of GNP. After 1962 it rose rapidly, and remained in the vicinity of 3% thereafter, when it was not actually higher.

In recent years, however, there has been a profound change for the better in Sino-Indian relations, especially since Rajiv Gandhi's visit to Beijing in December 1988. There were two changes that made that visit possible.

First, China had come to understand that India was no longer a power to be pushed around on the border. This realisation came about when India effectively 'faced China down' during the Sumdorong Chu incident in 1986-87. China realised that, if it were to regain the initiative on the border, it would have to modify its strategy of placing military modernisation as only number four in priority of the four modernisations. This it did not wish to do at the time.[32] Moreover, Beijing had other, more pressing, strategic issues nearer the Chinese heartland, such as Taiwan and Hong Kong, to resolve.

A second factor in the improvement in Sino-Indian relations was New Delhi's loss of Soviet support against China. As noted, this backing, particularly through the 1971 Treaty, was an important element in the prevention of an active Sino-Pakistani combine operating against India. Although New Delhi could never be sure on the point, it also possibly provided a nuclear umbrella.

On the eve of the Gandhi visit to China of December 1988, Gorbachev had visited New Delhi, made it plain to Gandhi that Moscow intended to normalise its relations with Beijing, and advised Gandhi to do the same. Implicit was the message that should India get into difficulties with China, the Soviet Union could not afford to back it and would not do so.[33]

As well as the negative factor of the loss of Soviet support, India was set to achieve significant strategic gains by any improvement in the relationship with China. India's principal adversary was Pakistan, which had been closely backed by China for the past two decades. As we have seen, this backing was troublesome to India, not so much because of the arms and technology transfers it involved (although they were a factor), but more because of the requirement that it split its forces between the two fronts.

This 'peace dividend' derived from the rapprochement with China has already become apparent. Beijing now assumes a position of 'careful neutrality' on Kashmir, claiming that the issue should be settled by bilateral negotiation as specified in the Simla agreement of 1972.[34] China has even said that it would oppose any moves for independence for Kashmir because they could destabilise the border.[35] As a result of the improved relations with China, and also as a result of improved electronic and photographic surveillance by India over Tibet, India has been able to remove at least three of its 11 mountain divisions from the border facing China and could ultimately reduce the number of divisions in readiness for use against China to only five or six. (It has, however, sought to upgrade the remaining Border Security Force and Indo-Tibetan Border Police).[36] The ability to withdraw these troops has proved invaluable at a time when the Indian military confronts increasing problems maintaining the civil order.

On its part, China is mindful of its vulnerability in Tibet. There are 100,000 Tibetans resident in India who could potentially be used as a means to embarrass Beijing. So far, India's position on Tibet has been, at least from China's perspective, impeccably correct. Despite the fact that the Dalai Lama has recognised the McMahon Line, in the aftermath of the Tiananmen Square incident in 1989, India reiterated its position that Tibet is an autonomous region of China.[37] On the eve of Premier Li Peng's visit to New Delhi in 1991, India issued a strong statement to the effect that Tibet was an internal problem for China. Tibetans in New Delhi were closely monitored and controlled to ensure that Li Peng was not embarrassed. Nevertheless, the sensitivity of the issue for China was underlined by the fact that *before* the visit, the Chinese Ambassador issued what amounted to a stern and un-diplomatic warning to India to keep the Tibetans in line throughout the visit.[38] There was also a 'certain frostiness' on the issue of Tibet evident in the joint communique.[39] This attitude prompted some Indian newspapers to dub the Li Peng visit 'one-sided'.[40]

The most difficult issue confronting the two nations is the border dispute. Probably the most satisfactory solution that could be hoped for would be recognition of the Indian claim in the east and the Chinese claim in the west, which would correspond roughly to recognition of a border that would run along both the actual line of control and the Himalayan watershed. China has a strategic requirement for the territory in the unpopulated west, where a Chinese road connects Tibet and Xinjiang, while India has a significant population to protect in the eastern sector in the state of Arunachal Pradesh. Chinese control of Arunachal Pradesh would also leave the balance of India's north-eastern territory highly exposed.

In fact, China has on at least two occasions suggested such a swap or 'package proposal', once by means of a suggestion conveyed by Jo Enlai just before the 1962 border war, and again, under Deng Xiaoping in the border talks of 1983, when India refused the 'offer' for internal political reasons. By 1985 China had re-asserted its claims in the East and the opportunity was lost.[41] During the visit of Chinese Premier Li Peng to New Delhi in 1991, no substantial progress was made on the border. However, it was decided to improve the relationship in other areas while the problem was resolved and to raise the border negotiations to Foreign Secretary level. By November 1992, a series of confidence and security building measures had been agreed by the Joint Working Group on the border designed to reduce troop numbers, delineate the actual line of control (confusion around the line had been an important cause of the Sumdorong Chu incident) and hold regular meetings of military commanders.

India's rapprochement with China has corresponded with a period in its history when it is seeking a new international role for itself in the context of the declining relevance of the NAM and of growing fears about excessive US influence in a 'unipolar' world. So-called 'Third World issues', such as the environment and human rights, have emerged as important areas in which India and China share a common perspective. This factor has facilitated progress in the general relationship. For example, such issues comprised an important element in the communique issued during the Li Peng visit.[42] India also acted jointly with China on the Montreal Protocol on CFCs (1987), and again in the UN on the issue of a security zone for the Kurds in Iraq.

But such issues are essentially peripheral to a number of other concerns that still dominate the relationship. Commentators such as the noted journalist and academic, Inder Malhotra, question whether India might be returning to the bad old days of *Hindi-Chini bhai-bhai* attitudes, according to which China could do no wrong and during which India 'let down its guard'. Malhotra is not the only one who harbours such concerns.[43] Sunit Ganguly notes that 'Over the longer haul, Chinese and Indian interests are bound to diverge' and that the Sino-Indian relationship is 'inherently competitive'.[44] Noted Indian economist, Prem Shankar Jha, sees this competition in economic terms. According to him, 'the dark side' of the East Asian success story is that there will inevitably be losers and that India could be one of them.[45] It was partly in this vein that the Finance Minister, Manmohan Singh, brought a fresh burst of economic liberalisation to the Indian economy during the 1993 budget, one of his stated goals being to catch up to China's economic growth rate.[46]

Generally, too, it would appear that the military is more cautious about China than the civilian bureaucrats, especially those in the MEA. The military cannot forget that, at least in its own view, it was the blundering of the bureaucrats and politicians that led to India's humiliating defeat in 1962.[47]

Such vague and amorphous fears have recently been sharpened by the fact that China is using its substantial accumulation of hard currency to press ahead with military modernisation. The Chinese military budget reportedly grew in nominal terms by 50% over the last three years, which would amount to a substantial increase in real terms even allowing for the gathering pace of inflation.[48]

With the Chinese growth comes an impressive build-up of technology in nuclear weapons and ballistic missiles, naval construction, space and a number of other 'dual use' areas. Also—and this hurts India most of all since the Soviet Union was once its principal guarantor against China—a 'cashed up' China is entering the Russian arms market through the purchase of *Sukhoi*-27 long range strike aircraft, the S300 SAM, and possibly also Mig-31 multi-role aircraft and the *Kilo*-class submarine.[49] At the same time, China is apparently continuing to work closely with Pakistan on the development of ballistic missiles and in the supply of the M-11 short range missile.[50]

Although it was the Sino-Soviet rapprochement that opened the way for better relations between India and China in 1988, as far as India is concerned the new relationship between Beijing and Moscow also has a decided down-side. The strategic aspect of the relationship between India and the Soviet Union, as embodied in the 1971 treaty, is now no more. While it is doubtful whether the Soviet relationship ever afforded India an actual nuclear umbrella against China, the existence of the treaty would at least have introduced an element of doubt to Beijing's calculations.

India has persistently claimed that its nuclear program is related to China's as well as Pakistan's. Unless India can set aside its concern about China's nuclear weapons program, it will be unlikely to cap its own program at any level below that which would provide a threshold deterrence against China. To an extent, therefore, the shape of India's program is determined by that of China's program.

China appears to have adopted the strategy of modernising its arsenal within the parameters of the existing number of warheads: that is, about 300.[51] This modernisation program comprises conversion of intermediate range ballistic missiles (IRBMs)—of which China has about 60 (along with about four ICBMs)—to smaller, solid-fuelled, road mobile, stealth and electro-magnetic-pulse-protected vehicles to promote survivability and increased accuracy, weapons yield and penetrability.[52]

In pursuit of modernisation, China has conducted a number of nuclear tests despite the moratorium on testing now in place in all other nuclear weapons powers. China is unlikely to reduce its comparatively small arsenal of nuclear weapons unless the US and Russia first reduce theirs to a level well below the current START-II agreement of between 3000-3500 warheads, which does not seem likely.

Until recently, China adopted the position that its nuclear forces should not be considered as part of the South Asian nuclear equation on the grounds that its program is directed towards the large nuclear powers rather than towards India.[53] The implication is that it would not agree to modify its program as part of any new regime that might emerge in South Asia. It became clear from recent talks on the South Asian nuclear issue hosted by China that Beijing tends to view its role as a facilitator rather than as an active participant; it certainly did not envisage that it would itself put any concessions on the table.[54]

China's uncompromising attitude towards any linkage of its own program with India's was illustrated when it exploded its largest nuclear device ever at the very time India's then President was visiting Beijing. While it was doubtless not the intention of the Chinese deliberately to disturb President Venkataraman's morning *idli*, the timing did leave an unpleasant aftertaste, to the extent that New Delhi protested privately to Beijing.[55] That it did not protest publicly is probably due to its desire to have the West, and particularly the US, leave it alone to get on with its own nuclear activities and to the strong impetus to attempt to 'wean China away' from Pakistan strategically.

Irrespective of developments within China's own nuclear program, what of the possibility that the improving relationship between India and China might acquire sufficient momentum to ensure that there would be no remaining impetus on India to link its nuclear program to China's?

Such a proposition assumes that India's nuclear activities *via à vis* China are motivated wholly by the potential threat posed by the Chinese program. Although New Delhi has doubtless in the past had cause for concern about China's program, it is likely that India's own program is increasingly driven by 'deep-seated reasons of honour and equity' and the desire to raise its position in the 'hierarchy of nations'.[56]

An additional factor motivating India's program is that nuclear parity between India and Pakistan would benefit Pakistan far more than it would India. A Pakistani analyst, Mushahid Hussain, summed up the position succinctly: 'by going nuclear', he said, 'we [Pakistan] feel we have achieved a certain parity with India'.[57] If that parity could be further enforced by an international regime that entailed stabilisation of India's program at a level close to Pakistan's, rather than China's, India's status would be further eroded.

In fact, China's continuing modernisation of its nuclear arsenal presents New Delhi with a more favourable environment from the stand-point of international pressure in which to press ahead with its own nuclear plans.

The Chinese program offers 'cover' behind which India can pursue its wider objectives. It is likely, therefore, that India will publicly continue to assert that its policy of nuclear ambiguity is framed in the context of China, even though the relationship with China might continue to improve.

Another cause of disquiet in the part of India is China's support for Myanmar. Since 1990, there have been a number of unsourced reports about the relationship. These assert that Myanmar and China are developing a strategic relationship involving the creation of an extensive network of communications from the Southern Chinese province of Yunnan to Rangoon and Bassein, including four lane highways. They further claim that China has sold between $500,000 and $1.4 billion in arms to Myanmar, including F-6 or F-7 fighter aircraft, naval patrol boats, anti-aircraft guns and tanks. Most significantly, the reports state that China is assisting Myanmar to develop naval 'bases' on the islands of Hianggyi and Coco, the former being located at the mouth of the Bassein river, and the latter contiguous to India's territory on the Andaman and Nicobar Islands, and also at the 'deep-water' port of Thiwala, on the Irrawaddy Delta. Beijing is alleged to have an agreement with Rangoon that the bases can be used by China's blue water fleet staging into the Indian Ocean. The Coco Island site is also said to possess SIGINT and radar facilities that could be used by China to monitor shipping and India's missile tests into the Bay of Bengal. While it is likely that some kind of powerful electronic facility is being constructed on Coco, it is unclear exactly what its purpose is or whether it is being controlled by Myanmar or China.[58] On its part, China has denied that it has any agreement to use any of the facilities being constructed in Myanmar.[59]

Many of these reports seem to have originated in India, which would naturally be concerned about the possibility that the Sino-Myanmar relationship could take on a threatening dimension. In the words of Inder Malhotra, Myanmar has turned out to be 'a strategic extension of China'.[60] This kind of terminology represents an Indian mode of strategic thought that fears, above all, 'encirclement' by China as Beijing develops links with a number of surrounding nations such as Pakistan, Bangladesh, and now Myanmar. These fears recently surfaced when the leading Indian English language daily quoted a Chinese general, Cho Mam Qi, as saying that China needed to extend its naval power further south to check India's attempts to 'dominate' the Indian Ocean.[61]

Behind these fears lies the fact that any development of a strategic relationship between China and Myanmar would, from India's perspective, amount to a breach in the strategic barrier provided by the Himalayas.

Unlike India's Himalayan border with China, its extensive Myanmar border is highly permeable and subject to border crossing from insurgents on both sides. It was, for example, from across the Myanmar border that insurgency movements, including the revolt in Naxalbari, were fed with arms by China in the 1960s and 1970s. A further factor is that Myanmar and India share an at times troubled relationship. There was a period during which India not only harboured Burmese democracy dissidents but also allowed anti-SLORC propaganda to be broadcast from New Delhi. The broadcasting activities have now ceased, but dissidents still seek safe-haven in India.[62]

The Indian military has been especially persistent in raising the issue of the Myanmar-China relationship. The 1989-90 Ministry of Defence Annual Report noted that 'uncertain political conditions in Myanmar have obvious security implications for India'.[63] Perhaps, in part, this publicly expressed concern is a manifestation of the desire of the military to assert its relevance in an era of fiscal stringency and defence cuts.

India is also intent on further developing its relationship with ASEAN, and mutual concern about China's role in Myanmar provides a useful entrée into the Southeast Asian region. But there is also doubtless an element of genuine alarm in New Delhi about the evolving Sino-Myanmar relationship.

It is difficult to say whether China has any long-term strategic goals in Myanmar. It seems likely, however, that many of the claims that China and Myanmar have already developed a strategic relationship are exaggerated. Neither the Hianggyi Island site nor the Coco Island site seems particularly suited for a deep water port in terms of their topographical and oceanographic conditions.[64] (But this is not to argue that there is not Chinese activity by way of developing one or another of the Burmese deep-water ports.) In assessing whether there is currently a strategic content to the relationship, one also needs to ask what immediate gains China would make in developing such facilities in Myanmar, given the current limited capabilities of the Chinese navy and the demands on it nearer home. On the other hand, if China's immediate need were for a commercial deep water outlet, connected by road to Yunnan, then it would make far more sense to concentrate on the existing deep water sites of Bassein and Rangoon than to develop new sites away from existing infrastructure.[65]

Even if the reports about the Hianggyi and Coco 'bases' prove incorrect, that is not to say that the evolving relationship between Myanmar and China is not of concern. Weapons obtained from China include items that give Myanmar a capability beyond its immediate needs. The sales also give succour to the widely despised SLORC regime. Most importantly, they open out the possibility that a strategic dimension may eventually be accorded to the relationship, even though one does not currently exist.

Whether or not the Sino-Myanmar relationship yet involves an overtly strategic dimension, it is evident that the issue is a sensitive one for India and that it is already a factor in Sino-Indian relations. It is also evident that India has a strong interest in ensuring that regional pressure on the SLORC regime to modify its political stance and distance itself from China is stepped up.

India will also be watching closely China's activities in its own region on the basis that these will constitute a 'bell-wether' for China's behaviour in more distant regions. In particular, it will be concerned how China handles the South China Sea dispute and, to a lesser extent, the issue of the return of Hong Kong and the problem of Taiwan.

Yet it is basically too early to interpret China's moves on these issues. Is Beijing simply engaged in a particularly uncompromising form of negotiation in a situation in which a compromise will eventually be reached, or do its claims represent a genuine effort to force the issue, no matter what the cost in terms of China's international relationships? Given this degree of uncertainty, India, which certainly does not want to lose the benefits rapprochement has brought, has adopted a 'watch and wait' attitude to China. On this basis, it will be willing to pick up on any advance in the relationship offered; but nor will not let down its guard. In the words of one observer:

> The prospect of a restoration of a Sino-Indian relationship to an even keel is a reality ... [but] The heady post-colonial idealism has been replaced by a hard-headed pragmatism.[66]

India's relations with Japan

Generally, Japan is considered far more important by India than India is by Japan. Japan has been India's largest aid donor since 1986, and in 1991 Japan ranked third of India's export markets, whereas trade with India accounts for only 1% of Japan's total trade.[67] Japan's interests in South Asia have never been as strong as they have been in Southeast Asia and East Asia. There are a number of reasons why this is so. To an extent, Tokyo considers South Asia to be outside its own sphere. Furthermore, the great investment boom in East and Southeast Asia was a product of a particular phase in Japan's economic history. South Asia missed out on this boom because the nations of the region had failed to open their economies sufficiently to encourage Japanese capital. Japan is now linked to the economies of East Asia through a circular flow of goods, investment and technology. New investment elsewhere is restrained by the straitened economic circumstances through which Japan is now passing.

Following the spurt of economic liberalisation that occurred in India in the mid-1970s, Japan showed increased interest in the Indian market. It was in that era that a deal between the struggling Suzuki auto firm and the firm that eventually became Maruti had its origin. This deal still stands as the only major successful examples of Japanese-Indian collaboration.[68]

By the mid-1980s, with the new bout of liberalisation introduced by Rajiv Gandhi in 1985-86, there was an upsurge in technology transfers from Japanese to Indian firms, with the number of collaborations rising from 27 at the start of the 1980s to 780 in 1991. This process did not result, however, in significant Japanese investment, which has always been the key as far as Japan has been concerned to transfers of state-of-the-art technology. Whereas by 1991 Japan stood fourth after the UK, US and Germany in terms of technology transfers, it stood only ninth in terms of actual foreign collaborations.[69] As a result, Indian business has been generally critical of the relationship with Japan. The Japanese are tough negotiators with high expectations of the host country. While it is difficult to generalise in these matters, it seems that the Indian way of doing business is not entirely suitable from the Japanese point of view.

Nevertheless, the latest round of liberalisation does hold out some hope that the situation will improve. Liberalisation occurred simultaneously with a capital crisis in the West triggered by the collapse of the Soviet Union, the unification of the two Germanies and recession in the United States. In such a climate, Japan came to be seen as something of a panacea for India's economic ills.[70] This perception was sharpened by an early Japanese decision to make $400 million available to India to help with the process of economic adjustment, Japan being the only nation prepared to make an individual aid contribution of this order. The commitment was followed by a visit of a delegation comprising members of the Japan and Tokyo Chambers of Commerce, led by Dr Ishikawa, and a return visit by Indian Prime Minister Rao to Japan in 1992. However, neither visit was followed by a significant breakthrough in Japanese investment. As recently as November 1992, a Japanese business delegation expressed doubts about India as a venue for investment.[71]

Corporate Japan appears to have been of the view that the reforms in India did not yet go far enough, especially in relation to the equity provisions and the sets of bureaucratic controls surrounding investment. Japanese business was particularly critical of the propensity for Indian bureaucrats to change the ground rules under them. For some time now they have been locked out of investment in large World Bank funded infrastructure projects because of a bribery scandal involving a Japanese firm that led to the Indian's favouring Japan's rivals, South Korea, in the award of tenders.   Above all, they had doubts about the political commitment of India to the reform process and about stability in South Asia generally.[72] Because of these doubts, Japan tried at the time of the visit of the then Prime Minister, Mr Kaifu, in 1990, and following that visit, to channel its aid through the SAARC mechanism in order to foster regional unity, a proposition that India did not view at all favourably.[73] These doubts concerning the overall security environment in South Asia were sharpened by the events of December to April 1992-93 surrounding the destruction of the mosque at Ayodhya.[74]

India and South Asia will probably never enjoy a flood of Japanese investment of the order of the one that flowed into Southeast Asia. Most of Japan's interests are now in the East Asian area, which is extremely dynamic in relation to South Asia, and with which South Asia will have to compete for the investment Yen. In terms of the requirement for tie-ups with low cost, labour-intensive centres of manufacturing, the nations of Indo-China provide strong competition against India. That is not to say, however, that the rate of Japanese investment will not pick up, particularly if the world economy improves in the 1990s, and especially in niche areas requiring technologically competent labour such as software development, in which India has a comparative advantage. Indeed, there are signs that corporate Japan is now ready to commit a higher level of investment to India than in the past, with approved investment rising sharply in 1992.[75]

One concern of Japan's was the issue of nuclear proliferation. As a non-nuclear power Japan has a strong interest in preventing the spread of nuclear weapons and maintaining the integrity to the NPT. It has periodically tried to link the issue of its aid to India to India's attitude to the NPT, and the matter was discussed between Prime Ministers Miyazawa and Rao in June 1993. Increasingly, however, Japan is starting to share the Indian perception that the NPT is a flawed regime that needs radical surgery when it is renewed in 1995. Tokyo is now of the view that India cannot be held rigidly to the regime until it becomes more effective. Recent events in Iraq and North Korea, both of which are signatories of the NPT but nevertheless which have nuclear weapons programs, only lend weight to such views in Japan.[76]

Japan has also become increasingly interested in India's role as a power in the Indian Ocean. This interest derives from India's location astride the major tanker routes out of the Gulf, through the Malacca and Sundar Straits, and on to Japan.   Japan derives 71% of its oil through this route. Its economy would suffer a devastating blow if supplies should be interrupted for any lengthy period. India is perceived by Japan to be a basically *status quo* power in the Indian Ocean, one capable of contributing through its navy to the general stability of the area. As a wealthy nation, but one that has not extensively developed its military capabilities since the Second World War, Japan also has a basic interest in collective security through bodies such as the UN. It will prove increasingly difficult to finance such security, however. For example, Japan was required to pay $13 billion towards the Gulf task force in 1991. In such a world, nations such as India with large and professional armed forces will be increasingly valuable. The strategic link is, therefore, a rapidly developing one, which saw the Indian Chief of Army Staff visit Japan in 1991.[77]

This focus on Indian Ocean security on the part of an important East Asian nation such as Japan in turn suggests that we should look in a little more detail at India's perceptions about its emerging strategic role in the Indian Ocean.

Endnotes

1   See Malcolm Subhan, 'Sengupta returns with task half-fulfilled', *Economic Times*, 10 August 1993.

2   See for example Jagdish Bhagwati, 'Negotiating Trade Blocs', *India Today*, 15 July 1993, p.139.

3   Interview, Ashok Jha, Joint Secretary, Commerce Ministry, New Delhi, December 1993.

4   Japan Economic Research Institute, *The Liberalization of India's Economy and Japan's Contribution*, Tokyo, 1993, p. 15.

5   Then Thai PM Chatichai Choonhavan attempted to parry these fears on the part of India by claiming that the facility was intended for trade use only. See 'Thailand PM speaks of winds of change in S.E. Asian region', *The Hindu*, 1 April 1989.

6   D. R. Sardesai, 'India and ASEAN—An Overview', in S. Kumar (Ed.), *Yearbook on India's Foreign Policy, 1987/88*, Tata-McGraw Hill, New Delhi, 1988, p. 117.

7   Ross Munro, 'Indian naval build-up: mixed signals', *The Straits Times*, 31 January 1991.

8   Ashley J. Tellis, 'Securing the Barrack: The Logic, Structure and Objectives of India's Naval Expansion', in R. Bruce (Ed.), *The*

Modern Indian Navy and the Indian Ocean: Developments and Implications, Studies in Indian Ocean Maritime Affairs No 2, Centre for Indian Ocean Regional Studies, Curtin University, Perth, 1989, p. 35.

9   *Quarterdeck '90* (official magazine of the Indian Navy, (Ed.) Uday Bhaskar), 1990, p. 71. Poachers are seeking shells, shark and live crocodiles.

10   See Mohan Ram, 'Ruling the waves', *Far Eastern Economic Review*, 15 May 1986, p. 30; Anon, 'Major naval base takes shape in Bay of Bengal', *Aerospace*, April 1992, p. 7; C.V.C. Naidu, 'The Indian Navy and Southeast Asia', *Contemporary Southeast Asia*, Vol. 13, No. 1, June 1991, p. 81.

11   Ayoob mentions Indonesian pressure as a possible motive for abandoning the base, but thinks that strategic issues were also important. See *India and South East Asia: Indian Perceptions and Policies*, Routledge, London, 1990, pp. 42-43. Manoj Joshi doubts that the base was ever really an option since it would have been too vulnerable (Interview, New Delhi, December 1992).

12   Interviews: Maj. Gen. (Ret'd) Soebiyakto, Head, Institute of Strategic Studies, Jakarta, 12 September 1991; Sudartji, Institute of Strategic and International Studies, 13 September 1991; General Soedibyo, 13 September 1991.

13   For details of this modernisation process see Desmond Ball, *Building Blocks for Regional Security: An Australian Perspective on Confidence and Security Building Measures in the Asia/Pacific Region*, Canberra Paper on Strategy and Defence No. 83, Strategic and Defence Studies Centre, Canberra 1991, Table 1, p. 13; Table 2, p. 14; Table 3, p. 15; and Table 4, p. 17.

14   William Branigin, quoting Desmond Ball, 'As China Builds Arsenal and Bases, Asians Wary of "Rogue in the Region"', *Washington Post*, 31 March 1993.

15   Derek da Cunha, 'The ASEAN Armed Forces: A Case Study of Singapore and Malaysia', Institute for South East Asian Studies, workshop on Major Asian powers and the security of Southeast Asia, Singapore, December 1990, p. 15.

16   For the statements of Rithaudeen and Singapore's then Prime Minister Lee Kuan Yew see Michael Richardson, 'Southeast Asia Wary', *Pacific Defence Reporter*, February 1990, p 42. See also the

statement of the then First Deputy Prime Minister of Singapore, Goh Chok Tong, as quoted in the *Economist*, 3 March 1990; and the statement of Brig. Gen. Lee of Singapore, as in *The Sunday Times* (Singapore), 11 March 1990. Mr Beazley's statement was made in the Australian parliament on 28 March 1988. He also emphasised that India did not threaten Australia.

17   Admiral R.H. Tahiliani (Ret'd), 'Maritime Strategy for the nineties', *Indian Defence Review*, July 1989, p. 24.

18   Dinesh Kumar, 'Joint naval exercise with Singapore', *Times of India*, 11 February 1993, p. 1 and p. 3.

19   Harvey Stockwin, 'The Sea of Turbulence', *Times of India*, 9 August 1993.

20   Joint Press Release, New Delhi, 16-17 March 1993.

21   M.V. Bratersky and S.I. Lunyov, 'India at the End of the Century: Transformation into an Asian Regional Power', *Asian Survey*, Vol. XXX, No. 10, October 1990, p. 939; Reuters News Service, 10 January 1994 (ref: 000388539747).

22   'India can't be EAEC member, says Mahathir', *Times of India*, 30 January 1992.

23   See Mohammed Ayoob, *India and South East Asia*, pp. 15-16; Ganganath Jha, 'India's Sectoral Partnership with ASEAN', *The Indonesian Quarterly*, Vol. XX, No. 3, third quarter, 1992, pp. 304-7; Reuters News Service, 10 January 1994 (ref: 000388539747).

24   Discussion with a very senior Singaporean official, December 1993.

25   'India, Thailand to step up trade', *Hindustan Times*, 26 May 1989, p. 16.

26   'India Club', *Far Eastern Economic Review*, 22 April 1993, p. 9.

27   Richard Valladares, 'Rao visit to minimise "threat" of PRC presence in Burma', *Bangkok Post*, 10 April 1993; David I. Steinberg, 'Myanmar as Nexus: Sino-Indian Rivalries on the Frontier', *Terrorism*, Vol. 16, 1993, p. 3.

28   Rodney Tasker, 'Rao's Look-East Policy', *Far Eastern Economic Review*, 22 April 1993, p. 16.

29   As already noted, there is an element of a desire to balance China economically in the behaviour of Singapore.

30   There is also a strip known as the 'Chicken's Neck' in the western

sector.

31   Noor A. Hussain, 'India's Regional Policy: Strategic and Security Dimensions', in S. Cohen (Ed.), *The Security of South Asia, American and Asian Perspectives*, University of Illinois Press, Urbana, C. 1987, p. 31.

32   See Gary Klintworth, *India's China War: A Question of Confidence*, Strategic and Defence Studies Centre, Australian National University, Working Paper No. 124, Canberra, 1987, pp. 5-6.

33   This message was evident even as early as Gorbachev's 1986 New Delhi visit. See Gregory Austin, 'Soviet Perspectives on India's Developing Security Posture', in R. Babbage and S. Gordon (Eds), *India's Strategic Future*, p. 144; Surjit Mansingh and Steven I. Levine, 'China and India: Moving Beyond Confrontation', *Problems of Communism*, Vol. XXXVIII, March-June 1989, p. 40.

34   Selig S. Harrison and Geoffrey Kemp, *India and America After the Cold War*, The Carnegie Endowment, Washington DC, 1993, p. 10.

35   Ahmed Rashid, *The Telegraph* (London), as in Reuters News Service, 4 January 1994 (ref: 000385364215).

36   For the point about surveillance see Manoj Joshi, 'Shy hands across the Himalayas', *Asia-Pacific Defence Reporter*, April-May 1993, p. 15. For the estimate of post-reduction force levels see interview with Jasjit Singh, BBC monitoring service, 10 September 1993 (ref: 000324542697).

37   Foreign Broadcasting Information Service, Daily Report for South/Southwest Asia, 3 January 1990, p. 63.

38   S.P. Seth, 'China and India shuffle closer but rifts remain', *Canberra Times*, 9 January 1992.

39   Manoj Joshi, 'The Communique', *Frontline*, 3 January 1992, p. 10.

40   Raju Gopalakrishnan, 'Indian Premier Denies Talks with China One-Sided', Reuter Textline, 16 December 1991.

41   Mansingh and Levine, 'China and India: Moving Beyond Confrontation', p. 37.

42   Sumit Ganguly, 'South Asia After the Cold War', *The Washington Quarterly*, Autumn 1992, p. 179.

43   Inder Malhotra, 'India, China and the Real World', *Times of India*, 28 May 1992.

44   Sumit Ganguly, 'South Asia After the Cold War', p. 179.

45   Prem Shankar Jha, 'Stagnation and Sovereignty', *The Hindu*, 15 July 1992.

46   Although Singh's budget speech did not specifically refer to China, he seemed to have China strongly in mind. For the relevant extract see Hamish McDonald and Jaya Sarkar, 'India: The Money Juggernaut,' *Far Eastern Economic Review*, 11 March 1993, p. 16.

47   For one view on this see M.V. Bratersky and S.I. Lunyov, 'India at the End of the Century: Transformation into an Asian Regional power', p. 932. The 1988-89 *Annual Report* of the Ministry of Defence (which also would have been written in 1990) gives a somewhat more pessimistic view of Sino-Indian relations, pointing to China's continuing military modernisation (p. 4). In 1991, a senior military commander in charge of troops stationed on the Himalayan frontier that were evidently being 'thinned out', questioned strongly the policies of his superiors in New Delhi toward China. See Kanwar Sandhu, 'Confusion in Command', *India Today*, 15 April 1993, p. 148.

48   For the 50% figure see Desmond Ball, 'China's Disturbing Arms Build-Up', *The Independent Monthly* (Australia), February 1993, p. 23.

49   There has been a good deal of press publicity surrounding these activities by China, at least some of it speculative. For a more careful view see Gerald Segal, 'Russia and the Chinas—New Risks', *Jane's Intelligence Review*, September 1992, pp. 416-7. See also Tai Ming Cheung, 'Sukhois, Sams, Subs', *Far Eastern Economic Review*, 8 April 1993.

50   Douglas Jehl, 'China linked to missile sale', *The Sydney Morning Herald*, 7 May 1993. p. 9 (from *The New York Times*). See also Carol Giacomo, 'USA: US to warn China of possible sanctions', Reuters News Service, (ref: 000297324395), 20 July 1993. China claims the M-11 does not come within the provisions of the MTCR. In January 1993, however, the treaty was extended to cover missiles similar to the M-11.

51   R.S. Norris, A.S. Burrows and Richard Fieldhouse, *Nuclear Weapons Databook*, Volume V, *British, French and Chinese Nuclear Weapons*, Westview Press, Boulder, Colorado, 1994, p. 325 and p. 359.

52   Yan Kong and Tim McCarthy, 'China's Missile Bureaucracy', *Jane's Intelligence Review*, January 1993, p. 41.

53   China's response to the five power conference proposal was that it stood in relationship to the South Asian players in exactly the same relationship as the US and Russia, and that therefore, while it could act as guarantor for any outcomes, those outcomes would be tied strictly to South Asia and would not apply to China.

54   This position was suggested by the fact that the Chinese delegation did not appear to be especially well linked into the policy apparatus. See Jeremy J. Stone, *Journal of the Federation of American Scientists*, Vol. 47, No. 2, March/April 1994, p. 6.

55   The information about the private Indian protest comes from a confidential source. I am indebted to Professor Desmond Ball for the interpretation of China's considerations in testing while Venkataram was in Beijing.

56   Stone, *Journal of the FAS*, March/April 1994, p. 1.

57   Quoted in Edward Desmond, 'South Asia: The Nuclear Shadow', *Time*, 27 January 1992, p. 19.

58   Robert Karniol, 'Chinese puzzle over Burma's SIGINT base', *Jane's Defence Weekly*, 29 January 1994, p. 14.

59   The more recent of this spate of rumours seems to have originated from the Japanese Kyodo news agency and to have been picked up from there by the US newspaper, *The Estimate*, and from there to have been reported widely in a number of military magazines. For the Kyodo report, see Reuters news service, 18 September 1992, 'China: Govt allegedly helping Burma to build naval base'. For the *Estimate* report see 'Is China Building an Indian Ocean Base?', The *Estimate*, 25 September-8 October 1992, p. 2. Edward Neilan, citing Indian intelligence sources, also picked up the story in the *San Francisco Chronicle* on 27 February 1993. For the reference to Chinese assistance at Thiwala see Richard Valladares, 'Rao visit to minimise "threat" of PRC presence in Burma', *Bangkok Post*, 10 April 1993. Information available to the author suggests that the lower valuation on the arms transfers is the more accurate one.

60   Quoted in Ganganath Jha, 'India's Sectoral Partnership with ASEAN', *The Indonesian Quarterly*, Vol. XX, No. 3, third quarter, 1992, p. 303 and f.n. 12. Two newspaper reports, identical in detail, both sourced from 'Asian News International', Rangoon, were run in

the (Indian) *Observer* (3 May 1993) and the *Hindustan Times* (1 May 1993).

61   'China's plan to build up navy', *Hindustan Times*, 13 January 1993.

62   'India protests to Myanmar', *The Hindu*, 26 January 1992.

63   For the role of the military in promoting concern about Myanmar see Dinesh Kumar, 'Sino-Myanmar ties irk Delhi', *The Times of India*, 20 November 1992.   See also commentary on the Ministry of Defence, Annual Report 1989-90, as in 'Growing Security Fears', *Jane's Defence Weekly*, 26 May 1990, p. 1027.

64   I am indebted to William Ashton, a knowledgeable and well-placed observer of Burmese affairs for topographical and oceanographic information on the two islands and for some of the interpretation of China's role in Myanmar.

65   Ashton.

66   Manoj Joshi, 'Sino-Indian Detente', *Times of India*, 7 September 1993.

67   Japan Economic Research Institute, *The Liberalization of India's Economy and Japan's Contribution*, Tokyo, 1993, p. 15.

68   For a good account of the Suzuki-Maruti venture see Raja Venkataramani, *Japan Enters Indian Industry: The Maruti-Suzuki Joint Venture*, Radiant Publishers, New Delhi, 1990.

69   Kamalendra Kanwar, 'Winds of Change', in Kamlendra Kanwar (Ed.), *India-Japan: Towards a New Era*, UBS Publishers, New Delhi, 1992, un-numbered Tables on page 9.

70   See for example, 'Japan may give green signal by year-end', by Subir Roy, *Times of India*, 1 February 1992.

71   'Japanese wary of local lobbies', *Times of India*, 20 November 1992.

72   James Clad, 'Patience Sorely Tested', *Far Eastern Economic Review*, 24 January 1991, p. 42.

73   A. Madhavan, 'The Post-Cold War Equations', in Kanwar (Ed.), *India-Japan: Towards a New Era*, p. 51.

74   This was mentioned specifically in the Fukukawa report. See *The Liberalization of India's Economy and Japan's Contribution*, p. 12.

75   *The Liberalization of India's Economy and Japan's Contribution*, p. 15.

76   Manoj Joshi, Reaching out to Japan', *Frontline*, 17 July 1992, p. 16;

C. Raja Mohan, 'NPT: A Japanese Proposal', *The Hindu*, 13 August 1992.

77   Madhavan, 'The Post-Cold War Equations', p. 53.

5   India as an Indian Ocean Power

India's perceptions of its naval role

India's naval build-up provoked considerable speculation both within the nation and in the wider region. Some non-Indian commentators believed that India was seeking a power projection capability rather than establishing a defensive posture. This interpretation also gained currency in the context of the diminution of the superpower presence in the Indian Ocean region, a phenomenon that left the role of large regional navies such as India's more exposed to view. It is claimed that continued superpower withdrawal would, '*in extremis*, [lead to] a Southeast Asia dominated militarily by China to the East and India to the west'.[1]

In response to such views, a range of Indian commentators have sought to justify the expansion of the navy in defensive terms. It is worth considering this body of opinion in some detail, because it provides an insight into India's developing image of itself as an Indian Ocean power. The doctrine runs broadly as follows:[2]

Naval development in India represents, it is argued, not so much a build-up as a catching up process. After independence, the British themselves left blueprints for a larger navy for India. While these were incorporated into India's strategic planning, the effort needed in building up the army and air force after the *débâcle* of the 1962 border war with China pushed the earlier plans for the navy to one side. It was only in the latter part of the 1970s and the 1980s that naval growth could resume. The navy still constitutes less than 13% of defence spending. To the extent that expansion has occurred, it has done so not so much in terms of the percentage of total funds spent on the navy, but has resulted from the overall expansion of the defence 'cake' as the Indian economy has grown.

Because of its lack of a maritime tradition and maritime capability (caste strictures for half a millenium prevented the crossing of the 'black water'), it is further claimed, India was vulnerable to conquest from the sea, first by the Portuguese and then the British. Both Nehru and his grandson, Rajiv Gandhi, used such arguments for maintaining a large navy. Nowadays, India in its present form has a 7600 kilometre coastline, a two million square kilometre EEZ, 350 island territories, 10 major and 200 minor ports to defend.

. The Indian Ocean is rich in mineral resources such as polymetalic sulphide and manganese nodules, oil and gas. India derives over 60% of its indigenous oil off-shore, and its platforms are highly vulnerable. According to the Ministry of Defence, this dependence of India on the ocean will increase: '... it is anticipated that with the rise in population and depletion of land resources our maritime interests are likely to grow very significantly in future.'[3]

Apologists also argue that Pakistan, with a much smaller coastline and only one major port to defend, itself has a powerful navy, with an edge over India in some areas such as missiles (planes, ships and submarines are fitted with *Harpoon* and *Exocet* missiles, against which India has no equivalent). Twenty five percent of Indian trade is with West Asia (including oil), and must pass through SLOCs that could be threatened by Pakistan. Ninety seven percent of India's overseas trade (which constitutes 14.4% of GNP) passes over the Indian Ocean.

Finally, it is argued, India has already been threatened from the sea by extra-regional navies in the modern era. India's conduct of the 1971 war against Pakistan was materially altered by the incursion of the US Seventh Fleet into the Bay of Bengal, as Kissinger's account of the event makes clear.[4] It is often overlooked that this potentially posed a *nuclear* challenge to India, since the task force was nuclear-capable (hence, the argument runs, India's acquisition of a Soviet *Charlie*-class SSN). While India recognised that it could not match a power like the US in the Indian Ocean, it believed it could pose a threat to it, and thus obtain a measure of sea denial, at least in its own waters. Although China currently does not have the capability to stage into the Indian Ocean on a regular basis, it has from time to time shown an interest in doing so. It is these 'extra-regional' threats that explain the need for a blue water capability, including one or more aircraft carriers and SSNs. In order to secure sea denial up to the outer reaches of India's sphere of interest, especially against larger extra-regional navies, it is necessary to deploy naval forces capable of acting well beyond the EEZ. Even in terms of defending the Indian EEZ, Indian strategists have noted that a modern naval-air task force is capable of extending power more than 300-500 km ahead of itself, requiring a potential adversary to be engaged up to 1000 km from the coastline, which in turn requires 'organic' air cover (i.e. aircraft carriers).[5]

While the above arguments are the ones most commonly used in defending India's naval growth to foreigners, other types of argument that are less apologetic about India's expanding naval role also have currency. According to these arguments, India has no need to apologise to anyone about its 'large' navy, since maritime power is the substance of great power status. The apostle of this line of argument is the maritime historian, K.M. Panikkar. Even today, Panikkar is extensively used in teaching in Indian staff colleges. According to Panikkar, India prospered at those times when it used the seas extensively and stagnated when it did not.[6]   A modern extension of such arguments is derived from the Mahanist doctrine that it is through control of the sea that great powers derive their status. Navies, in the words of General Sundarji, are what 'have true strategic reach today, not armies and tactical airforces.'[7] Rikhye sums up the argument thus: 'Navies are symbols of power. We want to be a world class power, so we must have a world class navy'.[8]

The development of this particular line of argument has its direct antecedents in the proposition discussed earlier, namely that India has progressed from a paradigm that would view moral suasion as a significant factor in the international hierarchy of power, to one that holds that 'strength respects strength'.

A more recent variant on this line of argument seeks to justify India's large navy, in the words of retired Admiral Nayyar, by virtue of its role as 'protector' of the Indian Ocean. According to Nayyar, India has actively sought, in its dealings with Japan and the United States in particular, to project itself as the only *status quo* regional Indian Ocean power capable of maintaining the SLOCS in the Indian Ocean.[9]

With the political failure of the peace-keeping effort in Sri Lanka, however, India is more wary of pushing itself as the *sole* guarantor of regional peace and stability.   The recent much stronger emphasis on collective security, particularly through the auspices of the UN, offers a power such as India an excellent, and less risky, vehicle through which to undertake such a role. Hence the substantial Indian contribution to the UN exercise in Somalia (a naval vessel of the new *Kukri* class, a supply vessel and 3500 troops) and to the UN peace-keeping force in Cambodia (500 paramedical and other specialists). The spate of naval exercising witnessed over the past two years (there have been 10 over the last three years) links the Indian navy directly into this multi-national force role, since such exercises are significantly concerned with establishing the communications and techniques necessary to participate in joint naval task forces. Over time, the complexity of these exercises has been slowly building up.[10] The Indian navy has also had to work closely with Western navies in fulfilling its duties for the UN in Somalia.[11]

While the foregoing reasoning provides a thematic backdrop to much of the discussion on the Indian navy within India, that discussion is obviously shaped to a significant degree by the circumstances—both financial and strategic—in which India finds itself. Thus there have been a series of shifts in India's policies and attitudes within the broader parameters outlined above.

The period of optimism and growth in the Indian navy commenced with the 1978 Twenty Year Development Plan for the Indian navy. Even 15 years later the plan has not been made public, but its essential features are well-known. It involved a navy of literally hundreds of major combatants by the year 2000, along with nuclear submarines and up to three carrier battle groups. Such grandiose plans, to the extent that they were ever incorporated into an overall security doctrine, appear to reflect the 'wish list' of the navy on the one hand, and on the other a set of strategic and economic circumstances that no longer apply.

In particular, they were designed to counter a 'hostile' US after the 1971 entrance of the *Enterprise* task force into the Bay of Bengal and China, which was believed to be interested in gaining a naval foothold in the Indian Ocean. One analyst, Ashley Tellis, describes an essentially defensive posture of the 'ring fence', inherited from the British, as lying behind this perceived need to 'neutralise' the border-lands and adjacent oceans.[12]

Since India has no broad mechanism for strategic planning, these plans were never fully incorporated into the thinking of the bureaucratic and political elite in New Delhi that controls key departments such as the Department of Finance, the Planning Commission and the MEA. This allowed plans easily to be superseded by opportunistic purchasing and the seemingly more urgent demands of other arms of the forces.[13] Recently, even the more modest 1985 Fifteen Year Perspective Plan has been allowed to slip in light of difficult financial times and, as noted in Table 3.1, below, the projection of the Indian navy by the year 2000 does not show a significantly larger force, although it will be more modern and better balanced.

Interpreting the role of India's navy through its force structure

Because naval planning documents such as the ones brought down in 1978 and 1985 have never been made public, independent observers are unable to place them in their correct political and financial contexts, far less to appraise them critically. This lack of transparency has meant that many of the analyses of the future of the Indian navy in the Indian Ocean have been exaggerated through no fault of the authors. As we have seen, this tendency has generated fear unnecessarily in smaller littoral states as far off as Southeast Asia.[14]

India has, at least to an extent, learned that it has nobody but itself to blame for the fact that lack of clarity about its intentions has led to concern on the part of regional nations. The 1991 decision to open up the base at

Port Blair to visits from regional naval personnel and defence attaches was an attempt to bring greater transparency to Indian defence and allay regional concern. India still has some way to go in becoming more open about its naval plans, however. Part of the problem lies in the fact that there is still no viable and reasonably open planning process for the military as a whole.

The Indian Parliament itself, a body that has in the past acted as a mere rubber stamp to defence documents, is now seeking a larger role in the defence planning process. In 1992, the Estimates Committee of the Parliament conducted a lengthy enquiry into the Defence Services Estimates.[15] The replies of the Ministry of Defence (MoD) to the questions of this committee on the role and future of the navy are on the whole vague, even evasive. They do not instil in the reader any confidence that a process for the ordered development of the navy according to a sound assessment of security concerns has been put in train, or that the navy will not again enter an expansionist phase, as distinct from the current phase of force modernisation. While the present naval force is considered by the MoD to be 'commensurate with India's current maritime interests', the Ministry also states that the plans do not meet the needs of the future in light of (unspecified) increases in the force levels of 'India's potential opponents' and the growth in maritime interests due to 'the rise in population and depletion of land resources'.[16]

In the absence of any credible planning process for the navy, interpretation of India's future naval role in the Indian Ocean must rest substantially on an assessment of the level and type of resources currently devoted to the navy or definitely on the drawing boards, the strategies and doctrines currently in train, the basing provisions now in existence and planned, and the nature of the developing contacts with foreign navies.

Before we enter into this type of analysis, however, it should be noted that the absence of a well-considered plan for naval development has provided the navy both with opportunity and costs. Opportunity has come about when naval planners have 'seized the time' in order to purchase major vessels at bargain-basement prices. In both of the major instances where this has happened—the purchase of 24,000 tonne aircraft carrier HMS *Hermes* (now INS *Viraat*) in the aftermath of the Falklands War for a bargain-basement price and the provision of a package by the Soviet Union at very favourable terms that included five *Kashin* class guided missile destroyers and the lease of a *Charlie*-I class SSN—the result has been an upsurge in the level of regional doubt about India's intentions in respect of its navy. The acquisition of a two carrier fleet generated a whole host of speculative concern about India's intentions.[17]

Those seeking to gauge whether the Indian navy is basically defensive or is intended as an instrument of force projection also cite two other areas besides the existence of aircraft carriers and SSNs. One is the seemingly ambitious amphibious program. As in the cases of the aircraft carrier and SSN capability, such concern has been heightened by the absence of any security planning document explaining exactly what the capability might be for, or even its intended extent. Also, as with other aspects of naval development, the more extreme statements of India's intentions appear to bear little resemblance to a reasonable assessment of capabilities.

Currently, India possesses the capability to land 2195 troops and approximately 80 armoured vehicles, whereas to constitute a power with a real projection capability it would need the capability to land at least a division.[18] The present amphibious capability is provided by one LST (large landing ship), eight medium landing ships (LSMs) and seven smaller vessels (LCUs). There were plans to build an additional seven LSTs, which would enhance the amphibious capability to approximately 3,600 but, as with so much Indian naval planning, it is uncertain whether these plans are to be realised, at least in the foreseeable future. Still other reports state that India has plans to enable it to lift a division, and even an army corps. Although these reports have caused some alarm, they remain unsourced.[19] In keeping with its current capabilities, India recently formed two 1,000 man marine units for assault purposes and opened a joint-services amphibious warfare training school near Visakhapatnam. In 1989 it also staged a comprehensive marine exercise in the Andaman and Nicobar Islands. For all of that, India's amphibious capability remains modest. Its long-range air-lift capability is, however, somewhat more substantial in comparative terms. According to one source, the IAF has the third heaviest combat lift capability in the world after the US and Russia.[20]

Another area of naval development traditionally used by analysts as a means of assessing power projection capability is the capacity of a fleet to sustain itself at sea. In the case of India, this capacity is still fairly modest. It includes two fleet tankers, a submarine tender and a diving support ship. Although a dedicated support vessel is under construction, as yet the navy does not possess such a vessel. According to Admiral Tandon, existing capabilities give the navy only a reliable reach of 1400 km, which 'no nations' should grudge ...'[21] Another analyst maintains that this level of support would only enable the navy to stay at sea for 14 days and that it would require several months preparation to get to sea in the first place.[22] Some analysts maintain that the support service could be supplemented by India's large merchant marine, just as the British were able to supplement their forces using the merchant marine in the Falklands campaign.[23] This is a point that could, however, be made of many navies. To a degree, at least, the strategic intent of a navy needs to be judged by the force-in-being. Obviously, operations in distant waters are lower in Indian priorities at the moment than other areas of operation.

Table 3.1: Present and Projected Numbers of Major Vessels in the Indian Navy.

Vessel	Present No.	Building	Projected	Comment	2000
Carrier	2	-	1	projected unlikely by 2000	2
Destroyer	5	3	2	projected unlikely	8
Frigate	18	1	2	projected unlikely; x6 *Petyas* assumed inactive	13
Corvettes	18	15	8	projected unlikely	33
Landing craft	9	-	1	projected unlikely	9
LCUs	7	-	-		7
Mine-sweepers	22	-	-	4 old	18
Support	7	3	-		10
Submarines	17	1	2	x2 projected unlikely; x4 *Foxtrots* likely inactive	14
Total	103				114

Sources: Derived from Captain R. Sharpe (ed.), *Jane's Fighting Ships 1991-92*, pp. 259-74; 'First Indian-built Submarine Commissioned', *Indian Defence Review*, (4) 1992, p. 386.

When described in terms of current naval building programs and realistic projections of expected acquisitions, the Indian navy by the year

2000 looks very different indeed from the navy described in the Twenty Year Plan of 1978 and the 1985 Plan. The above table gives a projection of the navy by the year 2000. The projection indicates an interest in smaller vessels, particularly corvettes, that does not accord with the intention to gain a true blue water capability.

This brown water bias may to an extent reflect the capabilities of Indian ship-builders; but it doubtless also reflects the needs of the time for a more solid performance in coastal waters in the context of crises such as the one in Sri Lanka, which gave rise to the need to interdict traffic between Tamil Nadu and Sri Lanka, and growing problems relating to smuggling, piracy, poaching of fisheries and the general maintenance of maritime security within the territorial waters and EEZ. It also reflects the need to protect India's growing off-shore assets, especially oil and gas rigs, from possible attacks by a regional power such as Pakistan. The coast guard, which was founded in 1978, has grown to 37 patrol craft and 16 maritime reconnaissance aircraft today.[24]   This level of growth reflects similar concerns with brown water-type requirements, as does the creation of five small naval bases in Tamil Nadu to support the coast guard and navy in their efforts to interdict Sri Lankan separatists and smugglers.[25]

It is this brown water thrust that the outgoing Chief of Naval Staff, Admiral Ramdas, sought to reverse. Ramdas did not see it as a proper role for the navy to conduct the multiplicity of interdiction tasks associated with the management of India's regional situation, except in relation to Pakistan. Rather, along with most senior naval officers, he preferred that this role be carried out by an expanded coast guard, in much the same way as the army would prefer to see India's internal problems handled by re-invigorated police forces and paramilitary. Along the same lines, he argued that the development effort should be extended to 'blue water' capable ports, bases and vessels. His aim was to reverse a situation in which only one-third of the navy's vessels were considered 'ocean-worthy' to one in which there is a 'ratio of 60-40 in favour of large ships'.[26]

Essentially, what India confronts is a debate about a trade-off between the growing and manifest requirement for a brown water force and the distant prospect that a blue water force may be required for India's wider security. As is so often the case in defence resource debates, it is a question of trade-off between a demonstrated immediate need and a possible future requirement.

Even the blue water school is further divided into those who support carriers and those who oppose them. The pro-carrier group, which is the most influential and includes Ramdas and the current CNS, Admiral

Shekhawat, argues that in-depth defence requires 'organic' air cover. Implicit in this latter position is the possibility of power projection; however, the recent decision to build a small (15,000 tonne) vertical-short take off and landing (VSTOL) capable craft rather than a conventional take off and landing (CTOL) capable one, does limit the projection capability considerably. In fact, one of the arguments used against carriers is that a VSTOL capable force (which is the only kind India can afford) cannot project power near land against larger fixed-wing, land-based aircraft, that there are few targets away from land except extra-regional navies, against which the VSTOL capability is in any case largely ineffectual, and that, therefore, VSTOL capable carrier battle fleets provide a costly, highly vulnerable and not very useful force. Thus, the argument runs, without gaining any substantial power projection capability, India has been subjected to considerable criticism from other regional powers because it appears to be seeking a maritime power projection capability.[27] At present, it would appear that India is caught in a dilemma: whatever the efficiencies or otherwise of its aircraft carriers, it needs them if only for a platform for its existing inventory of 24 *Sea Harrier* VSTOL aircraft and for its *Sea King* ASW helicopters.

Naval basing and threat perception

Just as the structure of an evolving navy can inform us within limitations about its intended use, so too can the location of bases inform us about the perceptions of threat, even in the absence of an overarching threat assessment document. Again, however, the degree to which we can read threat perceptions into basing decisions is limited. One such limitation is imposed by the fact that, by their very nature, perceived threats from the sea are far more diffuse than threats from the air or land. A sophisticated modern navy can appear 'out of the blue', as it were, whereas air and land power are obviously more restrained in their range. A further limitation on interpretation applies to India in so far as the nation only has 10 major ports. Most of them, such as Bombay, are seriously under-developed and highly congested. It is therefore incumbent on Indian naval planners to make as much use as possible of all available space, irrespective of whether the location is optimum in terms of the interpretation of threat. Location of naval facilities can also be a confusing basis for determining threat perception, because in some circumstances, facilities tend to be located so as to avoid perceived threat (i.e. in a distant region from the perceived area of threat) rather than to counter the perceived threat. Finally, India's basing strategies have been complicated in the past by the need to separate Soviet-derived combatants from those derived from the West. Although this need no longer applies, given the long time-frame involved in developing basing resources and facilities, it still dictates to a significant degree the disposition of forces.

In the context of these restraints, what can the present and projected location of facilities tell us of Indian perceptions of the strategic role of the navy in the Indian Ocean? The locations of these facilities are given in Maps 7 and 8, below. In broad terms, the location of facilities indicates that the basic concerns and orientations are still westward, but that as resources expand, there is also a growing capability in the east, particularly to meet the requirement for the maintenance of maritime security, as distinct from defence of the nation.

Recent developments in naval basing provisions have taken place in an era of stringent cuts. For example, while 1.2 billion rupees were allocated to naval construction in 1991-92 under the budget, by the time the revised estimates had been brought down the amount had been reduced to half of that.[28] In these circumstances, it will be instructive to see how funds are actually being spent.

The data for 1991-92 and 1992-93 indicate that no individually recorded expenditure was made on FORTAN in the Andaman and Nicobar Islands, indicating the low overall priority attached to further development of the base in present circumstances. Both Bombay and the giant new base at Karwar, near Goa, were cut back radically as part of the economy measures, but Karwar suffered more than Bombay, being virtually put on hold. The failure to develop these facilities as scheduled, together with the already overcrowded situation in Bombay, is likely to impose an overall constraint on future expansion of the fleet. Some facilities designed to serve the wider naval role in the Indian Ocean, such as the maritime reconnaissance (MR) base at Arkonam, near Madras, the very low frequency (VLF) transmission station at Kattaboman in Tamil Nadu near the Southern tip of peninsula India, and the submarine and MR bases at Visakhapatnam, have proceeded more rapidly to implementation than some of the work on the west coast. The east coast works should be considered as generic to the fleet, however. The location of the VLF base at the southern tip of the land mass, where the peninsula is very narrow, and well to the south, enables a protected site (from Pakistan) to communicate within a wide range of ocean around the peninsula and well to the south of it into the international shipping lanes. The Bear-F MR aircraft located at Arkonam are not significantly affected by location in relation to their area of operation, since they have an 11,000 km range. The base also involved the extension of an existing disused runway.

Map 7: Maritime and communication facilities to the west of India

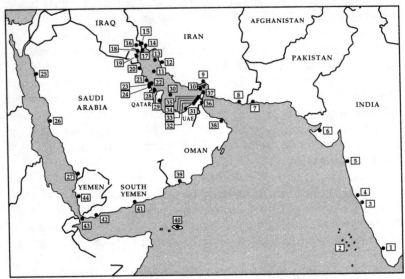

1 COCHIN
   - HQ, southern Naval Command
   - main training base
   - training school
   - air station "Garuda"
   - main base for helicopters
   - ship repair yard

2 LACCADIVE ISLANDS
   - facility for small vessels

3 KARWAR
   - Project Seabird
     (under construction)
   - 'proposed' HQ, eastern fleet
   - naval base
   - air station
   - dockyard

4 GOA
   - major air base
   - air station "INS Mansa"
   - main base for strike aircraft
     (carrier based)

5 BOMBAY
   - HQ, western fleet
   - major airforce combatants
   - dockyard
   - College of Naval Warfare

6 JAMNAGAR

7 GWADAR

8 SHAHBAHAR

9 BANDAR ABBAS

10 HENGHAM ISLAND

11 FARSI ISLAND

12 BUSHEHR

13 KARG ISLAND

14 BANDAR KHOMEINI

15 KHORRAMSHAR

16 AL BASRAH

17 FAW

18 UMM QASR

19 KUWAIT CITY

20 RAS AL MISHAB

21 AL JUBAYL

22 RAS TANNURAH

23 AL QATIF

24 AD DAMMAM
   - 22,000 & 62,000 ton
     floating docks

25 AL WAJH

26 JIDDAH
   - 16,000 & 45,000 ton
     floating docks

27 JIZAN

28 MANAMA

29 AD DAWHAH

30 HALUL ISLAND
   - platform, unconfirmed

31 ABU DHABI

32 DUBAYY
   - maintenance & repair capability

33 ASH SHARIQUAH

34 AJMAN

35 RAS AL KHAYMAH

36 AL FUJAYRAH

37 MASANDAM PENINSULA

38 MUSCAT
   - ship maintenance & repair
     capability

39 SALALAH

40 SOCOTRA

41 AL MUKALLAH

42 ADEN
   - 4,000 ton floating dock
   - 1,500 ton slipway

43 PERIM ISLAND

44 AL HUDAYDAH

Map 8: Maritime and communication facilities to the east of India

<table>
<tr><td>

1 PERTH
- "HMAS Sterling"
- major base (surface, sub.)
  (being further developed)

2 GERALDTON
- "Kojarena" satellite monitoring
  SIGINT station

3 NORTH WEST CAPE
- VLF comms. facility
- Learmonth airfield, MR re-fuelling
- HF transmitter/receiver

4 "EDINBURGH" MR BASE
- "Orions"

5 NURRUNGAR
- satellite comms. facility
  joint US/Australian

6 PINE GAP
- control station for
  SIGINT satellites
  joint US/Australian

7 JINDALEE
- Over-the-horizon radar

8 DARWIN
- air base
- patrol boat base
- "Shoal Bay" SIGINT and
  comms. facility

9 UJUNGPAN DANG
- HQ, maritime security elements,
  eastern fleet
- MR base

10 SURABAYA
- HQ, eastern fleet
- major combatants
- dockyard

11 JAKARTA
- "Tanjung Priok" Base
- HQ, western fleet
- major combatants

12 TELUK RATAI
- main naval base
  (under construction)

</td><td>

13 BELAWAN
- HQ, maritime security elements
  western fleet
- possible SIGINT site

14 COCOS IS. (AUST)
- 2400m runway
- staging of all military aircraft

15 CHRISTMAS IS. (AUST)
- 2100m runway

16 SABAH
- major new naval base
  (under construction)
- submarine support facilities
  (under consruction)

17 SINGAPORE
- "Brani" and "Tuas" naval bases
- US logistics contingent
- E-2C "Hawkeye" AEW

18 LUMUT
- HQ, Navy
- major surface combatants
- dockyard
- training

19 "BUTTERWORTH"
- joint Malaysian/Australian
  MR base, "Orions"

20 PHANG NGA
- main west coast
  naval base
- base for new helicopter carrier

21 SATTAHIP
- naval HQ

22 KAMORTA IS. (INDIA)
- naval base
- communications facility
- airstrip

23 CAR NICOBAR IS. (INDIA)
- 1500m runway
- possible visits of "Jaguar" &
  "Bear" aircraft
- squadron of Mi-8 helicopters

</td><td>

24 PORT BLAIR (INDIA)
- "INS Utkrosh"
- 3300m runway
- floating dry dock
- major surface combatants (stage)
- "Jaguar" & "Bear" aircraft (stage)

25 COCO IS. (MYANMAR)
- alleged patrol boat base

26 HIANGGYI IS.
- alleged new patrol boat base
  (being built with Chinese
  assistance)

27 CHITTAGONG
- "BNS Issakha"
- dockyard

28 CHARBATIA (CUTTACK)
- airbourne SIGINT base

29 VISAKHAPATNAM
- HQ, eastern fleet
- main sub. base
- sub. school (1991)
- MR aircraft base (1991)
- major surface combatants
- dockyard

30 ARRAKONAM
- "INS Rajali" (1992)
- naval/air base
- 4.5km runway
- "Bear" MR aircraft

31 RAMANATHAPURAM
- "INS Kattabomman"
- VLF submarine comms. facility

32 TRICOMALEE
- deep water anchorage
- "China Bay" naval/air station

MR - maritime reconnaissance
SIGINT - signals intelligence
ELINT - electronic intelligence
VLF - very low frequency
HF - high frequency
comms. - communications facility

</td></tr>
</table>

Furthermore, the location of the submarine base at Visakhapatnam (and consequent upon this the submarine training school in 1991) is in part an historical reflection of the fact that the original submarines were of Soviet origin. This would appear to be borne out by the fact that the four non-Soviet origin vessels are primarily based at Bombay. Some expenditure was also incurred in Cochin, probably reflecting the plan to establish the Southern Command as the seat of naval training.[29]

What this pattern of development seems to indicate is that the basic thrust of naval interest is still to protect the waters surrounding peninsula India. Unless there were a proven level of new activity on the part of China, it is unlikely that there would be any significant development of facilities in the Andaman and Nicobar Islands in the foreseeable future. Those facilities that already exist in the Andaman Sea seem to be mainly focused on maritime surveillance and the maintenance of maritime security. This is not to say that strategic concerns have not been involved in site location in the East. As we have already noted, the entrance of the US Seventh Fleet into the Bay of Bengal in the context of the 1971 war with Pakistan was a traumatic event for India. It is significant that work on FORTAN first commenced the year following the US 'intrusion'.

In recent years, concern about the US has been increasingly supplanted by concern about China, not that China currently has the desire or capability to range into the Indian Ocean effectively. But if it were ever to gain that capability, the facilities in the east, and especially those on the Andaman and Nicobar Islands, would play a crucial role in monitoring entry through the Straits of Malacca and, if necessary, interdicting.

India's navy in wider strategy

The debates and residual plans discussed above suggest a number of features about the development of India's navy not included in the range of explanations given by Indian commentators we have canvassed so far.

To begin with, India as a nation is by no means resolved that it wishes to be a true naval power. Much of the debate on the issue has been conducted within circles with an interest in naval matters. As such, it is not fully reflected in wider strategic thinking in New Delhi. Depending on circumstances, India seems to fluctuate between somewhat grandiose schemes of naval expansion and a more realistic appreciation of the appropriate overall role of the navy in security policy.

Although the lack of a comprehensive strategic role for the navy has provided opportunities that a more disciplined approach to planning might have thwarted, it has also presented a severe problem for the navy in the context of the current fiscal stringency being imposed on the military in general. Given the increasing demands on the army for internal duties and on the airforce in the context of approaching block obsolescence of much of the aircraft inventory, and given the fact that the voices of the army and airforce in New Delhi are stronger politically than those of the navy, as already noted, the navy has tended to suffer marginally greater cuts than the other forces in the context of tight budgets.

These developments suggest that India still has a fundamentally 'continental' strategic outlook, one that is impressed upon it by wider regional circumstances and by the lack of stability and confidence within the Indian polity. India still seems to lack the resources and confidence to play a full hand of sea-going capabilities and to range abroad. Until India's internal circumstances and the circumstances in its South Asian neighbourhood improve, therefore, it will prove very difficult for the nation to be able to fulfil the role of a true Indian Ocean power, in the sense of one with a capability for exercising independent action anywhere in the Indian Ocean region sufficient to affect outcomes in the way New Delhi would like.

A supplementary interpretation of this failure to persist in the development of the navy is that India is a nation that does not yet fully possess the 'will to power', in the sense that it is not yet ready to lay down plans and make the long-term sacrifices that would be necessary for it to emerge as a true regional power in the Indian Ocean, let alone a world power. Such an interpretation would fit well with the evidence about the pursuit of India's nuclear program. While India detonated a nuclear device as early as 1974, it has not developed the nuclear option as a currency of power, but prefers to maintain an ambiguous stance.

So what, then, is the true extent of India's naval power in the Indian Ocean? Writing prior to 1986, Raju Thomas characterised the Indian navy as one with 'essentially only a brown water capability'.[30] In terms of acquisitions, not a great deal has changed since that time. Nevertheless, although there are clear limitations on India's role as an Indian Ocean power when viewed in global terms, it is still a powerful nation *in Indian Ocean littoral terms*. It can impose its will at sea in its own region of South Asia, should it choose to do so. It would have no difficulty in ranging into the Southwest of the Indian Ocean and intervening for a limited period should it be required to do so by events in one of the Indian Ocean island states. It has significant resources in the Bay of Bengal through its facilities in the Andaman and Nicobar islands and on the eastern side of peninsula India. These resources enable it to stage major surface combatants, *Jaguars* and

Bears into the eastern reaches of the Indian Ocean and to exercise sea denial in those waters except in the case of the sole remaining superpower, the United States. It can engage in maritime reconnaissance in an arc extending for 11,000 kilometres out into the Indian Ocean. It could interdict SLOCs well to the South, should it ever for some reason choose to do so, provided it was not opposed by a superpower.

It could not, however, easily accomplish any of the following tasks. It could not easily sustain a carrier battle group at sea for an extended period in distant waters. Nor could it act independently in the enclosed waters of the Persian Gulf or Straits of Malacca, where its forces would be highly vulnerable to land-based air forces and missiles. It does not yet have a comprehensive range of anti-missile defences, including close-in defences or an anti-missile missile. Unlike some other regional powers such as Pakistan and Australia, it does not yet possess submarine borne *Harpoon* missiles or an equivalent missile. It does not yet have a comprehensive system of overhead monitoring in place that would enables it to obtain real time intelligence relating to the more distant waters surrounding it. In essence, it still remains a South Asian power. As an Indian Ocean power it is still a power in the making.

Endnotes

1   Ross Munro, 'Indian naval build-up: Mixed signals', *The Straits Times*, 31 January 1991.

2   The following is taken from a variety of sources, including: 'More for the Navy: Interview with L. Ramdas', *Frontline*, 20 December 1991, pp. 7-8; Transcript of a speech by Admiral Nayyar (Ret'd) to the US Global Strategy Council, Washington DC, 27 September 1989; Admiral S.N. Kohli, 'The geopolitical and strategic considerations that necessitate the expansion and modernisation of the Indian navy', *Indian Defence Review*, January 1989, pp. 33-45; Admiral R.H. Tahiliani (Ret'd), 'Maritime strategy for the nineties', *Indian Defence Review*, July 1989, pp. 19-30; Rear Admiral R. Tandon, 'The Maritime Priorities of India', *Conference on Maritime Change, Issues for Asia*, Sydney, Australia, 21-22 November 1991.

3   Ministry of Defence statement to the Parliamentary Estimates Committee (1992-93), Nineteenth Report, Presented 20 August 1992, Lok Sabha Secretariat, New Delhi, p. 29.

4   Henry Kissinger, *White House Years*, Little, Brown and Co., Boston,

1979.

5   Jasjit Singh, 'Indian Ocean and Indian Security', in S. Kumar (Ed.), *Yearbook on India's Foreign Policy 1987/88*, Tata-McGraw Hill, New Delhi, 1988, p. 133.

6   Admiral S.N. Kohli (Ret'd), The geopolitical and strategic considerations that necessitate the expansion and modernization of the Indian Navy', *Indian Defence Review*, January 1989, p. 33.

7   K. Sundarji, 'Stretching the Defence Bucks', *India Today*, 31 December 1991, p. 158.

8   Quoted in Nicholas Nugent, 'The Defence Preparedness of India: Arming for Tomorrow', *Military Technology* (MILTECH), No. 3, 1991, p. 30.

9   Interview with the author, New Delhi, December 1990. See also, Vice Admiral M.K. Roy, 'The Indian Navy from the Bridge', *Proceedings*, March 1990, p. 74.

10   Interview, senior British naval official involved with exercises with India in 1992. See also Rear Admiral K.R. Menon, 'Maritime Developments and Opportunities: South Asia', paper delivered at the conference, *Australia's Maritime Bridge into Asia*, 17-19 November 1993, p. 1.

11   Admiral Menon, 'Maritime Developments and Opportunities', p. 4.

12   Ashley J. Tellis, 'India's Naval Expansion: Reflections on History and Strategy', *Comparative Strategy*, Vol. 6, No. 2, 1987, p. 189.

13   Onkar Marwah, 'India's Strategic Perspectives on the Indian Ocean', in L. Dowdy and R. Trood (Eds), *The Indian Ocean: Perspectives on a Strategic Arena*, Duke University, Durham, 1983, pp. 312-13.

14   Marwah, 'India's Strategic Perspectives', p. 315.

15   Lok Sabha Secretariat, New Delhi, 'Ministry of Defence—Defence Force Levels, Manpower, Management and Policy', Lok Sabha, New Delhi, August 1992.

16   Lok Sabha Secretariat, 'Ministry of Defence—Defence Force Levels, Manpower, Management and Policy', p. 29.

17   See for example, Michael Richardson, 'East Asia and Western Pacific Brace for an Ascendant India', *International Herald Tribune*, 4 October 1989, p. 1 and p. 7.

18   India was eventually able to move over 50,000 troops to Sri Lanka.

However, the insertion of troops and equipment was conducted by stages.

19   John Jordan, 'India: The Indian Navy—Major Expansion Ahead', *Jane's Intelligence Review*, Vol. 3, No. 7, July 1991, p. 293.

20   Ramesh Thakur, 'India as a Regional Superpower', *Asian Defence Journal*, No. 5, 1990, p. 5.

21   Admiral R. Tandon, 'The Maritime Priorities of India', paper delivered at a conference on 'Maritime Change: Issues for Asia', Sydney, Australia, 21-22 November 1991, p. 25.

22   Ravi Rikhye, 'Nobody asked me, but ...', *Proceedings*, March 1990, p. 77.

23   Tellis, 'Securing the Barrack', p. 33; A.W. Grazebrook, 'The Indian naval build-up: Has Defence Central "got it all wrong"?', *Pacific Defence Reporter*, February 1990, pp. 14-15.

24   IISS, *The Military Balance 1992-93*, London 1992.

25   *Asia-Pacific Defence Reporter*, November 1991, p. 38.

26   See a report of a speech by Admiral Ramdas, *Asia-Pacific Defence Reporter*, June 1991, p. 25.

27   For arguments against carriers see Vice Admiral S.N. Mookerjee (Ret'd), 'Indian Naval Development—Need for Review', *Journal of the U.S.I. of India*, Vol. CXIX, April-June 1989, No. 496, pp. 151-7; and Pravin Sawhney, 'The Blue Water Argument', *Business and Political Observer*, 2 August 1991. For arguments in favour see Admiral S.N. Kohli, 'The geopolitical and strategic considerations that necessitate the expansion and modernization of the Indian Navy', *Indian Defence Review*, January 1989, pp. 41-42; Admiral R.H. Tahiliani, (Ret'd), Maritime strategy for the nineties', *Indian Defence Review*, July 1989, p. 28. For a short summary of the debate see John Jordan, 'India: The Indian Navy—Major Expansion Ahead', *Jane's Intelligence Review*, July 1991, Vol. 3, No. 7, pp. 296-7.

28   Government of India, *Expenditure Budget 1992-93*, (no pub. details given), Demand No 22, p. 47.

29   *Defence services Estimates, 1993-94*, Demand No. 22, p. 86.

30   Thomas, *India's Security Policy*, p. 156.

Conclusion

Conclusion

Changing attitudes to power

It is unlikely that South Asia will emerge as a significantly more stable region for some years to come. The fractured and highly complex entities that comprise the region are required to undergo substantial political, economic and social change at a time of considerable global flux. Patterns of instability evident at the local level reverberate throughout national and regional systems and are in turn affected by change imposed from outside.

As a large, heterogeneous nation with at least 300 million people living in poverty and shared borders with all of the nations of the region, India is particularly vulnerable to domestic and regional South Asian instability. The sense of vulnerability to which these circumstances give rise greatly complicates India's image of itself as a power and raises a number of concerns. Is India a large, powerful nation, or one that is threatened and weak? Is it more secure now that it has achieved a measure of rapprochement with China, or does China's phenomenal economic growth pose a long-term threat to its security in view of its own halting progress? Does the more robust form of Islam that has emerged in some neighbouring countries constitute a potential source of insecurity, especially in light of emerging internal tensions focusing on religion? And how can separatist forces be contained, especially when assisted from outside?

These and similar uncertainties mean that the 'weak-strong' paradigm through which India tends to view itself as a power, and the somewhat chaotic policy directions that are associated with it, will likely continue to be a feature of Indian strategic thinking for some time. The emergence of weak minority governments and the unstable domestic political situation generally also contributes to the lack of planning and strategic direction.

It would be wrong to assume, however, that the way in which Indians think about higher strategy is incapable of change. The collapse of the Soviet Union and ending of the Cold War administered a profound shock to the Indian world view. Although appropriate re-interpretations of India's place in the world have not yet been constructed in the aftermath of that event, certain trends in Indian security thinking are already evident.

The perspective on what constitutes power has broadened to incorporate competition in the international marketplace and international peace-keeping activities as well as the more traditional emphasis on purely military power. What has been referred to as India's 'great pontifications' on moral issues have also largely been set aside.[1]

This broadening of the concept of power away from an emphasis on purely military power to a more multi-dimensional interpretation brings with it the means to develop a role outside the difficult South Asian milieu. It could also eventually provide a renewed sense of confidence. But it would not be entirely correct to portray India as an emerging liberal democracy of internationalist inclination. Issues such as human rights and the environment that have their genesis in problems generated within South Asia complicate India's global role and tarnish its image, at least in the West. Power projection capabilities India has acquired in the South Asian strategic context, but which are applicable further afield (nuclear weapons are a case in point), command the attention of India's more distant neighbours. Attitudes towards, and positioning within, neighbouring 'security complexes', especially Southwest Asia and the Gulf, are to a significant degree defined by tensions within India between Muslims and Hindus and by the nature of the competition with Pakistan.

Moreover, the great political debate in India between the secular parties and the Hindu Right has effected an important change in national self-identity, particularly amongst the rising middle class. This dialogue about the nature of the Indian nation is set firmly within the South Asian regional context. In this context India is increasingly differentiated from surrounding Muslim nations by changing perception of Islam and of Hinduism. These shifting perceptions are driven by the symbiotic nature of the antagonisms within the region.

The religious debate in India has essentially been a debate about the nature of Hinduism—about whether it is a religion of the strong or the weak. Because of this fact, the debate about religion and the debate about the nature of the Indian nation have run a close parallel course. Thus we find many of the adherents to the BJP position in politics also to be adherents of a view that places India at the centre-stage of a wider region in traditional power projection terms.

For example, even L.K. Advani, a moderate in BJP terms, maintains that India should build a fleet sufficient to control the Indian Ocean 'from Singapore to Aden', a position that was written into the party's manifesto at the time of the 1991 national election. Thus, too, the party advocates that the military should be given 'nuclear teeth', that the process of military modernisation should press ahead despite India's economic problems and that the nation should 'stand by' persons of Indian origin abroad.[2]

While such views suggest the possibility of a more forthright India in terms of the way it views power and its place in the world, the emergence of such a nation is by no means a foregone conclusion. It would be dependent on a number of accompanying conditions. It would assume, for example, that the BJP would not be constrained in the exercise of its policies in the same way as the current government is constrained. It would be predicated on the BJP or a similar party actually coming to power. And above all, it would rest on the assumption that Indian power is on an upward trajectory, one built on the progressive realization of a more stable Indian entity. Let us address the latter of these issues first—for without stability there can be no real power for India—and then turn to the issue of the Hindu Right.

Stability and power

Speculation about the future of the Indian Union gained credibility following the collapse of other multi-ethnic states such as the Soviet Union and Yugoslavia. The issue of the survival of the Indian Union can perhaps best be addressed by reference to what Marxists used to refer to as 'state power'; that is, the mechanisms available to the state such as constitutional provisions and political means, the army, the police, the public service, the intelligence services, influence over the media and all the other means at the disposal of the state to protect itself and maintain its power, legitimacy and integrity.

Indian state power is extensive. It is also derived from the political mainstream in terms of attitude, culture and interest, a mainstream that far outweighs those interests—usually separatist but not exclusively so—that state power is used to contain. It would thus be unlikely that any separatist or revolutionary movement could overthrow state power, provided, of course, the centre holds. Moreover, India's enormous size and diversity mean that any unrest at the margin usually remains just that, essentially a movement at the margin of the Indian mainstream, rather than one that threatens the foundations of the Indian state. The fact that India is a democracy can also assist the re-incorporation of dissident areas into the national mainstream, as is apparently occurring in Punjab.

But how secure is the centre itself, keeping in mind that the Soviet Union also had enormous state power at its disposal, but nevertheless collapsed from the centre? Given the array of political, social and economic problems sketched out in the foregoing chapters, can we expect that the Indian political centre will hold? Even if the centre does hold, will it corrode in such a way that the nation becomes incapable of playing *any* sort of regional role for a significant period; or will India, rather, gradually emerge with governments that are more, rather than less, able to cope with the complexities of governing such a large, multi-ethnic state and at the same time projecting power onto the regional stage.

Even if a prolonged crisis at the centre were to precipitate some kind of greater involvement on the part of the military, a presidential-style coup or a new state of emergency, the government at the centre would still wish to apply state power in a way that supported the continuation of the Indian Union. Moreover, should a government be in such a state of disarray that political direction of its processes becomes impossible, then the bureaucracy, perhaps in association with the Presidency, would likely assume the role of directing and maintaining state power. Unlike the former Soviet Union, the last thing the Indian centre would ever do would be to 'give the game away' of its own accord. In saying this, we do not imply that there might not in future be some adjustment to India's present boundaries, for example relating to Kashmir or to the border with China.

If anything, the cement binding the Indian union has become stronger in recent years. This cement is constituted from the growing sense of nation evident amongst a rapidly expanding and increasingly cosmopolitan middle class. This class recognises very well that its best interests lie in the continuing integrity of the Union. Far from strengthening the separatist movements that plague India today by providing a model for change, the collapse of other multi-ethnic states such as the Soviet Union and Yugoslavia stands as an awful example to Indian elites of what not to do. Moreover, the situation in India is very different from the one that existed in the Soviet Union or Yugoslavia. In those nations there was never any Soviet or Yugoslav nationalism in the sense that there is an Indian nationalism.

While cataclysmic collapse may never eventuate, what of the possibility of slow decline in the ability of the centre to shape events according to its wishes, such as we are apparently already seeing. Will such a trend continue and, if so, what would that portend?

In the subtitle to his recent work Kohli refers to India's '*crisis* of governability'. He makes it clear in the body of the text, however, that the thesis of slow decline is nearer to his position than the one of sudden collapse. In his words,

> ... the "system" in India can continue to function but ... if it does so without major changes, its level of performance will remain quite low and will probably decline even further.[3]

According to Kohli, we thus have the prospect not so much of a crisis, but rather of the continuation of the type of 'muddling through' mentality that was described in the earlier part of the work.

Ultimately, however, continuing decline is likely to result in a 'corrective', either in the form of a reassertion of centralised authority—whether through a 'constitutional coup', as occurred in 1975 or some other means of usurpation or part usurpation of the democratic process—or else a cleansing of the democratic process itself. The latter would appear to be more likely than the former: as a democracy, the ability for peaceful renewal constitutes India's great strength.[4]

That is not to say that the period of instability in India will not be long and hard, and that it will not affect India's ability to move forward rapidly in its quest for the status of larger power in the region. It is to make the point, rather, that it would be a grave error of judgement simply to 'write India off' because of the difficulties through which it is passing or to underestimate the commitment to the continuation of the Indian state on the part of a large and growing number of people.

Moreover, since Kohli completed the work referred to above, what he characterised as India's 'half-hearted liberalisation' has been pushed forward dramatically.[5] Liberalisation offers the prospect of higher levels of growth and possibly also reduced levels of poverty, should the pattern in East Asia be repeated in South Asia. It may also eventually entail the revitalisation of the near-moribund Indian bureaucracy as ideas concerning efficiency are imported from the private to the public sectors and as large public sector undertakings are forced to compete in the marketplace or close their doors. Already this process is in train in some Indian ministries such as Finance and Commerce. Liberalisation also offers the prospect of expanded state revenues based on a larger economy. These revenues can be used to ameliorate adverse conditions in the social sector, without which the Indian nation cannot truly progress.

But at the same time, liberalisation confronts India directly with the need to manage politically a process in which differentials between rich and poor will increase rapidly and in which corruption in Indian will become more brazen and visible. Moreover, liberalisation will entail massive expenditure on the infrastructure necessary to support growth. This will in turn involve an intense competition for funds between infrastructure and the needs of the rural and social sectors. Progress in the social sector is also likely to be slow because of years of neglect. No matter how successful the family planning programs are in years to come, there will be a distorting effect for a number of years resulting from the low age structure of the population arising out of past failures. Continuing high population growth will to an extent offset any gains in the provision of jobs and services in the social sector. All these problems may well need to be resolved against an unstable political background as minority governments struggle for survival.

Thus it will probably be many years before the situation in the poorer areas of the countryside can be ameliorated and the associated problems of political instability and the drift to the large cities addressed. In this sense, and in the context of shifting relativities caused by economic liberalisation, the 1990s are likely to be India's 'dangerous decade'.

Crucially, the need to manage change on a massive scale is occurring at the very time when the Hindu Right has mounted a major challenge to the post-independence political settlement as embodied in the Congress party. In some ways, the process of economic reform has actually assisted the BJP. Following the 1991 economic reforms, the BJP attempted to make political capital not just out of the reform process itself and the costs it imposed on ordinary Indians, but also from what it asserted was the connection between the dictates of Washington and the demands of the IMF and World Bank. The BJP has also made considerable political play out of its opposition to the Dunkel proposals within the current GATT round, under which, it falsely claims, subsidies would be further reduced to farmers. This line of attack is part of a broader strategy to garner support outside the cities.[6] Party ideologues such as Govindachariya have given protectionism intellectual gloss by developing concepts of the 'new' *swadeshi* and village level control of economic life.[7]

Yet if India is to aspire to the status of a significant international power, which is one of the few foreign policy precepts upon which all of the members of the Hindu Right are apparently in agreement, it has to develop a multi-dimensional perspective on power, one that would enable it to garner the necessary foreign investment in order to acquire state-of-the-art technologies sufficient to develop a strong economy and sophisticated and self-sustaining defence industries. This fact is not lost on the moderates within the BJP, who are well aware of the dangers inherent in any return to autarky. L.K. Advani and A.B. Vajpayee have concluded that the social dislocation and potential damage to India's foreign and economic interests evident since the mosque incident cannot be accommodated in the Indian polity over the long-term. According to them, the party must dispense with the more exclusivist doctrines of M.M. Joshi and the 'sanghis' and develop a means to accommodate Muslims and other minorities.[8] In a recent address to the Confederation of Indian Industry, Advani informed his audience that the BJP was 'fully committed to the policy of deregulation, decontrol and debureaucratisation of the economy'.[9]   But the question remains: can Advani deliver on behalf of the 'internationalist' interests?

The generally poor showing of the BJP in the four state elections that took place in November 1993 illustrates that, in the final analysis, the pursuit of more robustly Hindu policies was not sufficient to guarantee re-election. Theoretically, the perception that the policy of forthright Hinduism has failed should strengthen the hand of the moderates in the party and help them to shape more reasonable policies.

Moreover, while there are few restraints on the way governments behave at the regional level, a BJP government at the centre, should one ever come to power, would be subject to many of the restrictions on policy experienced by the government of Narasimha Rao. India has progressed far down the path of economic reform and is dependent upon the support of the international community. It could prove difficult to step back from the broad program of economic reform. While it is certainly true that involvement in the international economy creates tension domestically, it also creates its own momentum and support base the longer it remains in place. For example, a number of Indian industrialists, who were initially sceptical about the reforms because of concern about competition from multinationals, have swung in strongly behind the reform process.[10]

In any case, in terms of its foreign and security policies, the platform of the BJP is in many respects not all that different than that of Congress. A 'blue water' navy has been on the drawing boards at least since 1978; it is just that the nation cannot afford to pay for it. Even in the nuclear sphere, the line of activity followed by the present government offers no 'restraint' on the eventual outcome India would achieve in terms of its accession as a nuclear power. Indeed, it is difficult to see that Indian foreign and security policies, as they relate to the wider global theatre outside South Asia, would be significantly altered in *their formal content* by a BJP government.

It is, rather, in terms of the effect of changes *within* the Indian polity and the implications of India's relations with its immediate neighbours that we should look in examining the implications of the coming to power of a BJP government. It is in terms of the growing intensity of the linkages between internal politics and neighbourly relations throughout South Asia and between South and Southwest Asia that the policies of the parties on the Hindu Right toward minorities and the effect that such policies have on communal relations that the coming to power of the BJP would be especially important. It is, moreover, in terms of such policies that a moderate, central leadership would have most difficulty in imposing its will over the grass-roots supporters of the party.

For those observers of India's rise to power from a more distant vantage outside of the South Asian region, the coming to power of the Hindu Right would likely have little immediate impact. Indeed, to the extent that the rising level of communalism that seems to be associated with the Hindu Right's quest for power causes additional friction within India and between India and its South Asian neighbours, Hindu politics could well delay the emergence of India as a significant regional power rather than enhance its prospects of achieving that goal. This delaying tendency would be particularly pronounced should India enter into a period of violence and counter-violence between Hindus and Muslims on a large scale. Any such development would be, quite literally, catastrophic for the Indian polity as we know it, and would set back economic and social progress for many years.

In any case, recent trends suggest that a 'three way split' between the BJP, the Congress and the Left parties is, perhaps, a more likely outcome than a government dominated by the Hindu Right.[11]   This suggests a continuing period of minority governments and 'hung parliaments' that could itself be destabilising, or alternatively, a Left-Centre alliance.

Initially, a Left government or a Left-Centre alliance would entail lower defence spending, attempts to improve relations with India's neighbours, increased spending in the social sector and a *partial* winding back of the process of economic liberalisation, particularly as it relates to the domestic economy.

The extent of the current program of reform, the dependency of India on the international financial institutions, the increasing internationalisation of the Indian economy and the reality of the government's growing dependency on the security forces to maintain law and order would probably mean, however, that compromises on these policies would quickly eventuate, just as they did after the initial periods of government of both the Janata Party in 1977 and the Janata Dal in 1989.

What we can anticipate, therefore, is the continuation of a political process that is still fundamentally about gaining access to power within a basic liberal-democratic framework rather than about creating profound, revolutionary change. We can also expect that while the economic reform process might be adjusted at the margin, it will be unlikely to be substantially dismantled.

Although the Hindu Right has so far been unsuccessful in its drive for power, we should not lose sight of the fact that the debate it has generated along the way about the nature of Hinduism and the Indian state has *already* altered profoundly the way Indians think of their nation and its role in the world. The idea of nation is now more closely aligned with a perception of its Hindu character. Hinduism itself has come to be seen as a more proactive and forthright religion. But at the same time, there has been a growing perception amongst more sophisticated observers that India's future power will rest as much on its internationalist skills (what has been referred to as the 'software of globalisation'), economic management and access to international technology as it will on the possession of raw military power and the will to use it.

The economy, technology and power

The process of economic reform is likely in time to advance India significantly as an industrial power. It is also likely to affect the level of technology India is able to import. Greater foreign equity will lead to access to higher grade technology; greater foreign competition within the economy will necessitate such access if Indian firms are successfully to compete. But this process will not happen quickly, principally because of the foreign investment 'drought' in which India finds itself, the somewhat uncertain nature of the political commitment to reform and the possibility of bouts of instability.

Economic reform is likely to tie India more tightly into the international financial sector, to which it requires access in order to fund the massive outlay needed to develop the infrastructure on which higher economic growth will ultimately depend. Growth of exports and imports already evident under the new regime will lock India ever more tightly into world markets, and this in itself is likely increasingly to dictate the pace and direction of future economic reform.

An important associated issue is the degree to which the economic reform process is likely to flow into the defence industries and bring about a more capable and substantial production base.

The general industrial base is likely to develop significantly in the following areas as a result of liberalisation: minerals and metals, electronics, engineering, transport, chemicals and power generation. Because of the strategic nature of these industries, progress in them will have a significant positive effect on the development of the defence industrial base. India also has potential as a civil shipbuilder once liberalisation has achieved efficiencies in the ferrous metals sector and the shipbuilding sector itself.

In many of the older, more traditional, defence industries there appears to be no substantial commitment to end the insulation currently in place between them and the private sector. It is unlikely that they will become significantly more productive in the short-term. The DPSUs, however, have better prospects. The DPSUs will likely become more closely tied in with the private domestic and international economies as they devote more of an expanded productive capacity to producing for these economies. Already this process is evident in the aerospace industries, electronics and to a lesser degree shipbuilding. In order to compete in the private sector in a liberalised environment, the DPSUs will need to achieve greater efficiencies. Again, as in the case of HAL, this process is already in train. There is no reason why the DPSUs should not eventually be capable of producing some sophisticated systems quite successfully. Moreover, as the benefits of economic liberalisation start to flow into the private sector, the possibility of a productive interface between the two sectors should grow substantially. Developments in some strategic industries providing dual use technologies, such as computers and some areas of the materials sciences, will prove to be especially relevant. Overall, however, the Indian defence industries will remain substantially in the public sector because demand will be insufficient to justify development and production in the private sector.

India's performance in the production of more sophisticated weapons platforms and systems has been at best mixed. Projects such as the LCA will, however, likely have at least some flow-on effect into the defence industries as a whole, both in terms of management systems and technology. Indeed, the scope for cross-fertilisation in areas such as CAD/CAM, materials sciences, guidance, EW and propulsion should not be underestimated. In a sense, this process might be seen as India 'cannibalising' its own projects. To the extent that this occurs, the 'success' or 'failure' of those projects should not necessarily be judged solely in terms of their immediate utility. However, it will be many years before India will have the capability to produce a front-line fighter, and it may still abandon the LCA project entirely.

On the other hand, some of the synergisms implicit in a number of areas of Indian military and civilian technological capability may start to come together sooner than expected. These relate to areas such as computation and electronics, space, the nuclear sciences, the material sciences and ballistic missiles. The drawing together of these skills could see India develop some relatively sophisticated capabilities relating to the military uses of space, sensing, ballistic and tactical missiles, and nuclear weapons sometime early next century.

But the problems India confronts in terms of its C^3I capabilities do not relate only to the development of hardware. They also relate to the lack of organisational capacity within the armed forces and the civil areas of government that support them. There appear to be no early signs that India has decided to come to grips with its shortcomings in the area of overall organisation and higher direction of the armed forces. Until this problem can be overcome, India's military capabilities in the context of modern warfare are likely to be less than those suggested by the inventories at its disposal.

In terms of the economic base that might support a reassertion of military modernisation in India, it seems likely from past experience that the Indian economy is set to regain at least the underlying growth rate of 5% experienced in the 1980s, and quite possibly a higher rate. But the question remains: would any such renewed growth automatically translate into a period of more rapid growth in real military spending, as happened in the 1980s, or might priorities now be different in light of the new internationalist perspective on what constitutes power and of other perceived needs for government spending introduced as a result of growing pressures in the social sector?

Military modernisation and geopolitics

Should the opportunity again arise in terms of renewed economic growth, it seems likely that the process of military modernisation will again pick up pace in India; only this time, modernisation will likely concentrate rather more on quality than quantity. There are several reasons to expect that modernisation will be resumed.

First, as noted in Part I, the structure of defence cuts to date does not indicate any substantial reassessment of India's strategic circumstances, such that military modernisation has been taken off the agenda. Given the extent of the decline in defence spending in real terms, the cuts are neither substantial nor deep. Rather, they seem to be designed to maintain the basic fabric of the force structure so that, resources permitting, modernisation can again resume on the basis of that structure.

A second factor that could tempt India to continue to modernise is that much could be achieved within the broad parameters of existing defence budgets. A strategy for achieving modernisation that relies on force multipliers and retrofitting happens to suit the current Indian inventory and force structure. It also suits the stage India has reached in its own productive capabilities. The very fact that India's large fighting forces are currently inefficient by Western standards provides the basis for an effective expansion in capability at minimum cost. Because India has a number of relatively under-equipped, relatively modern platforms, it can achieve significant gains by means of weapons and sensor refits, refits that it will be increasingly able to accomplish through indigenous technology.

It is most unlikely that modernisation would again entail the kind of overall growth witnessed in the 1980s, however. Financial pressures imposed by modernisation—especially given the ever-rising cost of sophisticated military equipment—could even entail a reduction in force levels in the air force and stagnation in the navy. Rather, India will tend to 'fill the gaps' in the current force structure and achieve force multiplication. Efforts are likely to focus on areas such as achieving enhanced C^3I capabilities, aerial refuelling, placement of more sophisticated weapons—particularly home-built missiles—on existing platforms, modernisation and retrofitting of existing platforms, greater mobility generally, further computerisation of management and training, better service integration and training, further development of war-fighting doctrine, an improved EW capability, and so on. In all of these processes, the new relationships with the Western powers, and especially the US and Israel, are likely to prove increasingly important.

A third factor that will continue to drive military modernisation is that, at base, India does not believe that its geopolitical circumstances have become more benign or are likely to become so over the short-to-medium-term.

Although predominant in South Asia, India's preeminence remains checked by a Pakistan that is still capable of inflicting significant damage by means of proxy war. While China has to an extent separated itself strategically from Pakistan and acted to reduce border friction with India, the latent competition between India and China remains a factor in strategic thinking in New Delhi and China's new accession to power remains troubling. Moreover, as China gains access to more sophisticated military technologies it will likely pass these on to Pakistan, thus compensating Islamabad *to an extent* for loss of US support.

Nor has India been able entirely to neutralise the linkages between Pakistan and the oil-rich states of the Gulf and Southwest Asia. The communal difficulties between Hindus and Muslims within India mean that the possibility of a strategic nexus developing between South and Southwest Asia remains a troubling one. India's growing reliance on Gulf oil to fuel its expanding industrial base also leaves it potentially vulnerable.

Over the longer term, however, the ability of Pakistan to act as a check on Indian power may well be eroded. Pakistan has been affected more severely than India by the end of the Cold War. While India has lost access to cheap Soviet arms, Pakistan has suffered a near total embargo of US military aid. As the smaller power, it was more dependent on the client relationship than was India; as the smaller economy, it is also less able to fill the gap through indigenous production of weapons. Its vulnerability to US pressure was illustrated by Islamabad's apparent decision to scale down assistance to the Kashmiri separatists in order to avoid being labelled a state in support of terrorism by Washington.[12]

Moreover, Pakistan confronts some very serious economic difficulties over the longer term in its efforts to maintain parity with India. Pakistan currently devotes 25% of government spending to the military, in circumstances in which debt servicing requirements have been rising rapidly. In 1979-80, military spending and interest constituted 32.5% of government outlays, whereas by the budget estimate of 1992-93 they had risen to a total of 47.8%.[13] Given the enormous problems Pakistan faces in the social sector discussed in Part II, a continuation of a situation in which nearly half government spending is hypothecated to defence and debt servicing would not appear to be sustainable over the longer term. Moreover, as already noted, Pakistan's circumstances are greatly complicated by India's successful efforts to 'wean China away' from it strategically.

These developments mean that the military competition with India may well become unsustainable by the end of the century. In these circumstances, Pakistan would likely be forced to confront the prospect of abandoning its efforts to retain its approximate parity with India, at least in terms of conventional weapons. This would facilitate a solution to the Kashmir problem, probably on the basis of the present line of control. Given the way in which the Kashmir issue is caught up in the internal politics of both nations, however, any such development might still be a number of years away. Nor would the process of transition from one policy to another on the part of Pakistan necessarily be a smooth one: it could involve a prolonged period of instability or even another war.

Any easing of tension with Pakistan would enable India further to cut military spending, since its problems with its two principal protagonists of past years—Pakistan and China—would have been ameliorated.

But would India actually respond to more peaceful circumstances in South Asia by substantially reducing expenditure on the military? Might it not take such an opportunity to re-focus its force structure on power projection capabilities such as a blue water navy, long range aerial capabilities, an amphibious capability and perhaps also strategic nuclear weapons? Certainly, these capabilities have been on India's drawing boards in the past; it is just that current circumstances have forced the nation into a defensive, essentially continental, mould in which other priorities take precedence.

At this juncture, all we can do is put such questions 'on notice'. Given India's current circumstances and restraints, any decision to re-focus on force projection capabilities is not imminent. It is impossible to know from this limited vantage what kind of government might be in power in New Delhi at the time and what new pressures might be brought to bear on that government. All we can say is that such capabilities have been on the agenda in the past.

It is unlikely now that India will emerge in the present decade as a power with a true Indian Ocean-wide reach. While its fleet will likely be better balanced, especially in its defensive capability and the modernity of its major platforms, it will not be significantly larger. Nor will it possess a significant amphibious capability. Indeed, there will likely be continuing pressure on the navy to expand its brown water capability at the expense of blue water forces for some years to come.

Although India is likely to seek to improve its capability to monitor naval and maritime traffic in the waters to the north-east of the Indian Ocean, provided that tension does not rise sharply between India and China, it is unlikely that there will be further major developments of the facilities in the Andaman and Nicobar Islands. The current state of India's finances and the greater perceived need to undertake major developments in the west, such as the Karwar facility, effectively act to constrain India from further developing its assets in the north-east, except in terms of the monitoring role.

But in three areas—nuclear weapons, ballistic missiles and the military uses of space—capabilities may well rise, giving India the possibility of a strategic reach it has never previously enjoyed, at least in the more abstract sense that the possession of nuclear weapons entails. This development is likely to occur in a *de facto* way by the end of the century, even if India has not graduated as a nuclear weapons power in the formal sense. But the real issue is not so much whether India will openly 'go nuclear'. Rather, it is whether the potential for a nuclear arms 'race' in South Asia, and possibly also nuclear competition between China and India, can be contained.

Our guess—and it can be no more than that—is that while the nuclear situation might ultimately stabilise, it will stabilise at a level at which India will have a threshold deterrence capability against China, which will be somewhat higher than the level implied by a 'stable' South Asian equation. Perhaps India might stabilise its force at about 80-100 weapons (or the equivalent in fissionable material, depending on the status of its nuclear program at the time). A ceiling at this level would depend, however, on

Pakistan agreeing to stabilise its force at a somewhat lower level so that India would not face the problem of Pakistan 'catching up'.

In fact, Pakistan would likely favour a stable nuclear equation in South Asia. It is estimated that Pakistan can produce only at sufficient for two to three additional weapons per year and that it currently has sufficient fissionable material for between seven and 15 weapons.[14]   Pakistan, therefore, might have only a maximum of about 20 weapons before it would be required to cut off production under any stabilised regime that might be established. Indeed, in the absence of a cut-off, India would actually further increase its 'lead' over Pakistan. Under a stabilised regime, on the other hand, Pakistan would have achieved a kind of rough strategic parity with India even were India itself to cap its program at a level that provided a threshold deterrence against China. In the words of one Pakistani analyst: 'by going nuclear, we [Pakistan] feel we have achieved a certain parity with India.'[15]

While there are obviously limits on the 'usability' of nuclear weapons, it nonetheless seems to be the case that their possession, particularly associated with the kind of strategic capability that India would likely have, does accord the possessor at least some strategic leverage and at least some new status in the 'hierarchy of power'. In the case of India, any new status dependent on a local level South Asian situation of mutual deterrence would not likely be all that significant. But should India obtain greater numbers of nuclear weapons (say 100 or the equivalent in fissionable material) along with an IRBM/ICBM capability, such that it could aspire to a threshold deterrence capability in relation to China, then the situation would change dramatically. With such a capability, India would be perceived to be a power with an Asia-Pacific strategic reach.

India as a global power

India's more outward perspective and less moralising and judgmental posture has enabled New Delhi to become constructively involved in a range of international undertakings. Integral to this new approach has been a more substantive role in the United Nations, a body within which India sees itself playing a potentially larger role, perhaps as a member of an enlarged Security Council. Also inherent in the new position is a much stronger interest in Indian Ocean security from the regional perspective. With the ending of the Cold War, India now finds itself not only accepting a role in the Indian Ocean for extra-regional navies, but actually contemplating joint activities with them in the context of multilateral task force membership.

India's entry into world markets is also likely to continue to give an internationalist dimension to its perception of power. That is not to say that international trade necessarily produces harmony or reduces tension; indeed, in terms of the politics of liberalisation *within* India it might do the exact opposite. But it will mean that India will have a much stronger interest in being actively involved in a much larger range of international forums in order to assert its position. It will, in short, be far more outward looking than was evident under the old, autarkic, policies of the last four decades.

As a manifestation of this new, more outward-looking, perspective, India has emerged as an important player in a number of international conventions in the area of disarmament. Notable amongst these is the Chemical Weapons Convention (CWC) and the new moves to set in place a register of arms acquisitions. On these issues, India has been able to present itself as an international 'good citizen'.

There are, however, a number of other issues about which India will not find itself in such harmony with the developed world. One is the issue of nuclear weapons. India will also tend to side with other Asian nations against the West on issues such as the environment and human rights. On these issues, it is likely to assume a so-called 'Asian' position, that is, one that holds that it is not within the rights of the Western democracies to impose their will on the developing world in such matters.

What we are likely to see, therefore, is an evolving, pragmatic, foreign and security policy that works at a number of different levels. At one level, India will ensure that it acts to secure its fundamental economic and security interests through its relationships with the United States and other Western powers. At another level, however, it will assume a more typically 'Third World' position—but never to the extent that it would jeopardise its fundamental interests as they relate to the West.

A longer term perspective

According to a longer term perspective, India is clearly the power of the future in the Indian Ocean region. It is the only power with the size, technological capability, industrial depth and potential strategic reach to fulfil this role. Its potentially large internal market gives it the possibility to develop and maintain a much wider range of technologies than nations with smaller populations. Such technologies will increasingly provide the basis for military and economic power. Moreover, unlike the Pacific, where a number of large powers vie for influence, India stands virtually alone in the Indian Ocean as the one power having such a potential.

Because of the restraints on India's rise to power imposed by instability in India's domestic and regional South Asian environments, however, India's emergence as a 'true' Indian Ocean power is likely to be a subject for consideration in the twenty-first rather than the present century. India at the moment is 'treading water' in terms of its acquisition of raw military power. At the same time, it is seeking to develop a more comprehensive definition of what constitutes power, a definition linking it more tightly into the international framework. For the lesser nations of the region, this latter development can only be counted a plus: it should be strongly encouraged since it will likely have the effect of tempering Indian power once that status is achieved.

This lesson in particular needs to be noted by the United States. The difficulties with the US over the cryogenic rocket engine deal and Kashmir and Washington's new flirtation with Islamabad, when combined with the failure of India's efforts to be more closely involved in APEC and the collapse of the G-15 summit, left India feeling somewhat isolated at the end of 1993. Indians were again saying, as they did in past years: 'we are a large nation, sufficient unto ourselves.'

At the moment, India still operates within what might be called a 'weak-strong paradigm' in terms of the perception of its own rise to power. In this, it is somewhat different than China, a power that seems more comfortable with its destiny as the 'Middle Kingdom'. Indeed, as an Asia-Pacific power, as distinct from an Indian Ocean one, India may well start to lose power in comparative terms in relation to nations like China rather than gain it. But should this occur, it would for many years only have limited relevance in the Indian Ocean context, a theatre in which the East Asian powers will be unlikely to seek a highly active role, unless perhaps in the context of a new Gulf task force. India's broad strategy will be increasingly designed to keep the East Asian powers, and especially China, out of the Indian Ocean, just as it was designed to keep the superpowers out during the Cold War years. If it is successful, as an Indian Ocean power India it is likely to stand very exposed to view in years to come. If it is not successful, the region to the north-east of the Indian Ocean is likely to emerge as a venue for naval and other forms of competition between India and China. Although such an outcome is feared by India, it is by no means certain; and in terms of China's capability, it is still a distant prospect.

For Southeast Asia, China is undoubtedly the more important power. The primary aim of the ASEAN nations will be to reach an accommodation with China. If this does not prove possible, they would be looking to Japan, the US and, increasingly, India to balance China's power. Already there are signs that they are seeking to engage India economically and diplomatically (although not yet strategically) as a potential balance to China.

In trade, India is likely for a time to have a somewhat difficult passage in East and Southeast Asia. This is a highly diverse, competitive region, a region that has already progressed significantly as an economic unit. But as the Indian market expands and Indian competitive capabilities develop, the economic linkages are likely to begin to grow more rapidly.

India will need to recognise that its economic future lies in eclectic and opportunistic trading policies in a variety of regions. In this process of recognition, it should not lose sight of the longer term possibilities in its own South Asian back yard. In particular, the linkages that could develop between South and Southwest Asia should some of the regional differences in South Asia become less pronounced show promise. Following a visit from South Africa's Foreign Minister Botha, India has started to talk about an Indian Ocean trade bloc.[16] It is doubtful, however, whether the concept would have either the support of the ASEAN nations or the 'critical mass' in economic terms necessary to make it a success. Rather than focusing on a particular region, India will need to develop as an opportunistic and pragmatic world trading nation.

Despite the many difficulties that cloud India's relations with the Western democracies, these relationships are likely to increase in importance rather than diminish. The relationship with the United States has, for India, considerable potential. The Gulf war impressed on India the important role of the United States in maintaining global supplies of cheap oil. The US is India's most important trading and investment partner and an important potential source of dual use technologies. But each side is likely to proceed with caution. India is quite simply too large a power ever to want to be 'the most allied ally', as was Pakistan. There are also a number of very real issues to resolve between the United States and India. But given the ending of the Cold War, the process of economic liberalisation in India, the unresolved issues evident in the Sino-US relationship and the perceived need on the part of the US to ensure the continuing viability of the Indian Ocean as a back door into the Gulf, a closer relationship with India has considerable attraction for Washington. While the US will continue to work to restrain the spread of nuclear weapons in South Asia, it is unlikely to allow India's nuclear weapons aspirations to stand in the way of a stronger relationship between the two.

India thus emerges as a power with literally enormous potential in the Indian Ocean region. There are many synergisms in the Indian system as currently constituted. But there are also many constraints, not least the somewhat unsure and halting sense of nation and flawed organisational capacity that result from the tensions inherent in Indian society. Once such problems are worked through—and the process of liberalisation both assists and complicates that process—India could emerge with unexpected rapidity as a significant power in the Indian Ocean region sometime in the first quarter of the twenty-first century. While India will continue to be overshadowed by China and Japan as an Asia-Pacific power, its position in the vast region that lies between the Middle East and the newly prosperous nations of East Asia will become increasingly prominent.

Endnotes

1   Sridhar Krishmnaswami, 'Getting closer to ASEAN', *The Hindu*, 18 April 1993.

2   Bharatiya Janata Party, *Towards Ram Rajya*, Friends Publishers, New Delhi, 1991, pp. 36-37.

3   Atul Kohli, *Democracy and Discontent*, p. 383.

4   As democracies, both Italy and Japan have had the means to address entrenched political corruption within the existing political framework. A nation like Iran under the Shah was unable to achieve peaceful reform.

5   Kohli, *Democracy and Discontent*, pp. 305-38.

6   Staff reporter, 'BJP makes inroads into Jat heartland', *The Hindu*, 20 April 1993.

7   A good account of the economic policies of the BJP is contained in a paper by Salim Lakha. See 'The BJP and the Globalisation of the Indian Economy', paper delivered at the *After Ayodhya: The BJP and the Indian Political System* conference, Curtin University, Perth, July 1993.

8   Swapan Dasgupta, 'BJP redefining "parivar" ideology', *The Times of India*, 19 May 1993.

9   Anon, 'Industry turns out BJP's surprise ally', *Indian Express*, 28 April, 1993. See also an interview with Advani, 'I am all for liberalisation', *Economic Times*, 10 August 1993.

10   'Manmohan must stay: industrialists', *The Hindu* (International Edition), 1 January 1994.

11   See for example Rajni Kothari, 'Beyond Congress and the BJP', *Times of India*, 13 August 1993. These trends were evidently reinforced by the outcomes of the 1993 state elections, and particularly by the emergence of the Harijan-Sudra alliance in Uttar Pradesh.

12   'Pakistan yielded to U.S. pressure', *The Washington Times*, 26 August 1993.

13   Government of Pakistan, Finance Division, *Economic Survey 1991-92* (Statistical Supplement), Islamabad, 1992, Table 8.4 p. 164. I am indebted to Muhammad Khan of the National Centre for Development Studies, ANU, for drawing this situation to my attention.

14   In December 1992 the NBC network, in a highly credible report apparently based on intelligence sources, said that Pakistan had seven nuclear weapons in could assemble in a matter of hours. See 'Pakistan said to have seven nuclear bombs', *Washington Times*, 2 December 1992. The CIA is reported to have believed in 1992 that Pakistan could assemble about 15 weapons. Interview with Oehler by Bill Gertz, 'India, Pakistan cited in spread of nuclear arms', *Washington Times*, 31 October 1992.

15   Quoted in Edward Desmond, 'South Asia: The Nuclear Shadow', *Time*, 27 January 1992, p. 19.

16   Reuters News Service, 14 January 1994, (ref: 000391639547).

Appendix 1

The foreign purchase by type of weapon, 1970-90.

**(a)   major conventional weapon
deals by type of weapon
1970-90**

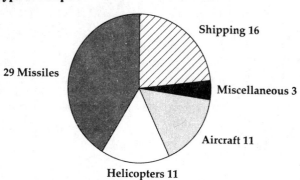

29 Missiles

Shipping 16

Miscellaneous 3

Aircraft 11

Helicopters 11

(b)   by country of origin

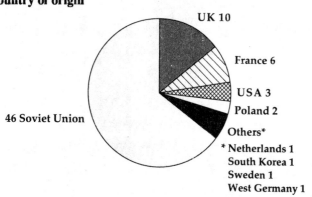

UK 10

France 6

USA 3

Poland 2

Others*

46 Soviet Union

* Netherlands 1
South Korea 1
Sweden 1
West Germany 1

(c) **licenced production by
type of weapon**

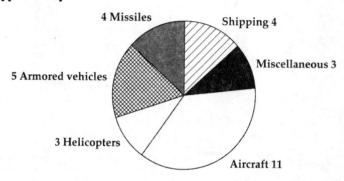

(d) **licenced production by
country of origin**

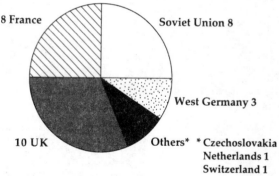

Source: US Congress Office of Technology Assessment, *Global Arms Trade*, Government
Printing Office, Washington DC, 1991, p.155, as from SIPRI.

Select Bibliography

Monographs

Ahmed, A.S., *Pakistan Society: Islam, Ethnicity and Leadership in South Asia*, Oxford University Press, Karachi, 1986.

Albright, David, Frans Berkehout and William Walker, *World Inventory of Plutonium and Highly Enriched Uranium 1992*, SIPRI, Oxford University Press, Oxford, 1993.

Anderson, Walter K. and Shridhar D. Damle, *The Brotherhood in Saffron: The Rashtrya Swayamsevak Sangh and Hindu Revivalism*, Westview Press, Boulder and London, 1987.

Anderson, W. and N.H. Dupree (eds), *The Cultural Basis of Afghan Nationalism*, Pinter, London, 1990.

Anthony, Ian, *The Arms Trade and Medium Powers: Case Studies of India and Pakistan 1947-1990*, Harvester Wheatsheaf, UK, 1992.

Ardeshir, M.S. (ed.), *Eighth Plan Perspectives*, Lancer, New Delhi, 1991.

Arnold, Guy, *Wars in the Third World Since 1945*, Cassell, London, 1991.

Asia and Pacific Review 1988, (9th Ed.), World of Information Press, Essex, U.K., 1987.

Ayoob, Mohammed, *India and South East Asia: Indian Perceptions and Policies*, Routledge, London, 1990.

Babbage, R. and S. Gordon (eds), *India's Strategic Future: Regional State or Global Power?*, The Macmillan Press, London, 1992.

Bakshi, Lt. Col. G.D., *Mahabharata:*
A Military Analysis, Lancer International, New Delhi, 1990.

Ball, Des, *Building Blocks for Regional Security: An Australian Perspective on Confidence and Security Building Measures in the Asia/Pacific Region*, Canberra Papers on Strategy and Defence No. 83, Strategic and Defence Studies Centre, Research School of Pacific Studies, Australian National University, Canberra, 1991.

Ball, Desmond and Helen Wilson (eds), *Australia and Space*, Canberra Papers on Strategy and Defence No. 94, Strategic and Defence Studies Centre, Research School of Pacific Studies, Australian National University, Canberra, 1992.

Ball, Desmond and Helen Wilson (eds), *New Technology: Implications for*

Regional and Australian Security, Canberra Papers on Strategy and Defence No. 76, Strategic and Defence Studies Centre, Research School of Pacific Studies, Australian National University, Canberra, 1991.

Ball, Desmond, *The Intelligence War in the Gulf*, Canberra Papers No. 78, Strategic and Defence Studies Centre, Research School of Pacific Studies, Australian National University, Canberra, 1991.

Ball, Desmond, *Signals Intelligence in the Post-Cold War Era, Developments in the Asia-Pacific Region*, Regional Strategic Studies Program, Institute of Southeast Asian Studies, Singapore, 1993.

Baranwal, Jayant (ed.), *Military Yearbook 1991-1992*, Guide Publications, New Delhi, 1990.

Baranwal, S.P. (ed.), *Military Yearbook 1990-91*, Guide Publications, New Delhi, 1990.

Baruah, S.L., *A Comprehensive History of Assam*, Manoharlal, New Delhi, 1985.

Bharat Electronics Limited, *37th Annual Report 1990-91*.

Bharatiya Janata Party, *Towards Ram Rajya*, Friends Publishers, New Delhi, 1991.

Bhattacharya, B.B., *India's Economic Crises, Debt Burden and Stabilisation*, B.R. Publishing Corporation, New Delhi, 1992.

Blamont, Evelyne (ed.), *Regional Co-operation and Peace*, International Social Science Council of UNESCO, 1989.

Boal, B.M., *The Konds: Human Sacrifice and Religious Change*, Aris and Phillips, U.K., 1982.

Boserup, Ester, *Population and Technology*, Blackwell, Oxford, 1981.

Bruce, R. (ed.), *The Modern Indian Navy and the Indian Ocean: Developments and Implications*, Studies in Indian Ocean Maritime Affairs No. 2, Centre for Indian Ocean Regional Studies, Curtin University of Technology, Perth, 1989.

Buzan, Barry and Gower Rizvi (eds), *South Asian Insecurity and the Great Powers*, St Martin's Press, New York, 1986.

Buzan, Barry, *A Sea of Troubles? Sources of Dispute in the New Ocean Regime*, Adelphi Paper No. 143, International Institute for Strategic Studies, London, 1978.

Calman, Leslie J., *Protest in Democratic India: Authority's Response to Challenge*, Westview Press, Boulder and London, 1985.

Cambridge Encyclopaedia of India, Francis Robinson (ed.), Cambridge University Press, Cambridge, 1989.

Centre for Science and the Environment, *State of India's Environment: A Citizens' Report: Floods, Flood Planes and Environmental Myths,* Centre for Science and the Environment, New Delhi, 1991.

Chibber, M.L., *Military Leadership to Prevent a Military Coup,* Lancer, New Delhi, 1986.

Cohen, S.P. (ed.), *The Security of South Asia: American and Asian Perspectives,* University of Illinois Press, Urbana, 1987.

Cohen, S.P., *The Indian Army: Its Contribution to the Development of a Nation,* Oxford University Press, New Delhi, 1990.

Cohen, S.P. (ed.), *Nuclear Proliferation in South Asia: The Prospects for Arms Control,* Westview, Boulder, Colorado, 1991.

De Silva, K.M., *Managing Ethnic Tensions in Multi-Ethnic Societies: Sri Lanka 1880-1985,* University Press of America, Lanham, 1986.

Dibb, Paul, *The Soviet Union: The Incomplete Superpower,* Macmillan, London, 1988.

Dowdy, L. and R. Trood (eds), *The Indian Ocean: Perspectives on a Strategic Arena,* Duke University, Durham, 1983.

Dubey, R.K., *Indo-Sri Lankan Relations with Special Reference to the Tamil Problem,* Deep and Deep Publications, New Delhi, 1989.

Economist Intelligence Unit (Great Britain), *India, Nepal Country Report,* No. 2, Economic Intelligence Unit, London, 1989.

Englemann, P. and C. Manthey, *15 Years of Bilateral Cooperation in Science and Technology between the FRG and the Republic of India,* Forschungzentrum Julich Gmbh International Bureau, Köln, 1990.

Frankel, Francine, *India's Political Economy: The Gradual Revolution,* Princeton University Press, New Jersey, 1978.

Gallagher, J., G. Johnson and A. Seal, *Locality, Province and Nation: Essays on Indian Politics, 1870-1940,* Cambridge University Press, Cambridge, 1973.

Gaur, Madan, *India 40 Years After Independence: Witness to an Unmitigated Anarchy,* Press and Publicity Syndicate of India, Bombay, 1988.

Ghosh, P.K., *Developing South Asia: A Modernisation Perspective,* Greenwood Press, Westport, Connecticut, 1984.

Gordon, Sandy, *The Search for Substance: Australia-India Relations into the Nineties and Beyond*, Australian Foreign Policy Publications Programme, Australian National University, Canberra, 1993.

Gupte, P., *India: The Challenge of Change*, Methuen, London, 1989.

Harrison, S., *In Afghanistan's Shadow: Baluch Nationalism and Soviet Temptations*, Carnegie Endowment, New York, 1981.

Harrison, Selig S. and Geoffrey Kemp, *India and America After the Cold War*, Report of the Carnegie Endowment Study Group on US-Indian Relations in a Changing International Environment, The Carnegie Endowment, Washington, 1993.

Hindustan Aeronautics Limited, *Annual Report for 1990-1991.*

Hoking, Brian and Michael Smith, *World Politics: An Introduction to International Relations*, Harvester Wheatsheaf, New York, 1990.

Huldt, B. and E. Jansson (eds), *The Tragedy of Afghanistan: The Social, Cultural and Political Impact of the Soviet Invasion*, Croom Helm, London 1989.

Indian Council of Social Science Research (ed.), *Economic Development of India and China: A Comparative Study*, Lancer International, New Delhi, 1988.

International Institute for Strategic Studies, *The Military Balance*, Brassey's, London, Various Years.

Jane's Radars and Electronic Warfare Systems, 1992-93, (Fourth Edition), Jane's Information Group, UK, 1992.

Japan Economic Research Institute, *The Liberalization of India's Economy and Japan's Contribution*, Tokyo, 1993.

Jeffrey, Robin, *What's Happening to India? Punjab, Ethnic Conflict, Mrs. Gandhi's Death and the Test for Federalism*, Macmillan, London, 1986.

Joshi, Mahesh, *Assam, The Indian Conflict*, Prachi Prakashan, New Delhi, 1981.

Kanwar, Kamalendra (ed.), *India-Japan: Towards a New Era*, UBS Publishers, New Delhi, 1992.

Kapur, B.D., *Building a Defence Technology Base*, Lancer International, New Delhi, 1990.

Kennedy, G., *The Military in the Third World*, Duckworths, London, 1974.

Kennedy, Paul, *The Rise and Fall of Great Powers: Economic Change and Military Conflict from 1500 to 2000*, Fontana Press, London, 1989.

Kissinger, Henry, *White House Years*, Little, Brown & Co., Boston, 1979.

Kohli, Atul, *Democracy and Discontent: India's Growing Crisis of Governability*, Cambridge University Press, Cambridge, 1991.

Kohli, S.N., *Sea Power and the Indian Ocean*, McGraw-Hill, New Delhi, 1978.

Krepon, Michael et.al., *A Handbook of Confidence Building Measures for Regional Security*, Handbook No. 1, Henry L. Stimson Center, September 1993.

Kumar, S. (ed.), *Yearbook on India's Foreign Policy 1987-88*, Tata McGraw-Hill, New Delhi, 1988.

Kureshy, K.U., *A Geography of Pakistan*, Oxford University Press, Karachi, 1977.

Lucas, R.E.B. and G.F. Papanek, *The Indian Economy: Recent Developments and Future Prospects*, Boulder, Colorado, 1988.

Manogaran, C., *Ethnic Conflict and Reconciliation in Sri Lanka*, University of Hawaii Press, Honolulu, 1987.

Manor, J., *Sri Lanka in Change and Crisis*, Croom Helm, London, 1984.

Masselos, Jim (ed.), *India, Creating a Modern Nation*, Sterling, New Delhi, 1990.

Matthews, Ron, *Defence Production in India*, ABC Publishing House, New Delhi, 1989.

Mellor, John W. (ed.), *India: A Rising Middle Power*, Westview Press, Boulder, Colorado, 1979.

Metcalf, T.R., *Modern India: An Interpretative Anthology*, Macmillan, Toronto, 1971.

Misra, K.P. and V.D. Chopra (eds), *South Asia-Pacific Region: Emerging Trends*, International Institute for South Asia-Pacific Studies, New Delhi, 1988.

Morrison, Barrie et.al., (eds), *The Disintegrating Village: Social Change in Sri Lanka*, Lake House Investments Limited, Colombo, 1979.

Mulkani, K.R., *The RSS Story*, New Delhi, 1980.

Murty, T.S., *Assam: The Difficult Years*, Himalayan Books, New Delhi, 1983.

Naipal, V.S., *India: A Million Mutinies Now*, Rupa and Co., Calcutta, 1990.

National Institute of Population Studies, *The State of Population in*

Pakistan, Islamabad, November 1988.

Nayar, Lt. Gen. V.K. (ret'd.), *Threat from Within: India's International Security Environment*, Lancer, New Delhi, 1992.

Newman, R.S., *Grassroots Education in India: A Challenge to Policy Makers*, Sterling Publishers, New Delhi, 1989.

Nixon, Richard M., *Seize the Moment: America's challenge in a one-superpower world*, Simon and Schuster, New York, 1992.

O'Ballance, E., *The Cyanide War: Tamil Insurrection in Sri Lanka 1973-88*, Brassey's, London, 1989.

Observer Research Foundation, *Observer Statistical Handbook*, Observer Research Foundation, New Delhi, 1991.

Pandey, G., *The Construction of Communalism in Colonial North India*, Oxford University Press, New Delhi, 1992.

Pareek, R.N., *Tribal Culture in Flux: The Jatapus of Eastern Ghats*, B.R. Publishing Corp., New Delhi, 1977.

Pradhan, M.C., *The Political System of the Jats of Northern India*, Oxford University Press, Oxford, 1966.

Praval, K.C., *Indian Army After Independence*, Lancer International, New Delhi, 1990.

Raina, Asoka, *Inside RAW: The Story of India's Secret Service*, Vikas, New Delhi, 1981.

Rikhye, R., *The War That Never Was*, Prism

India Paperbacks, New Delhi, 1989.

Rikhye, R., *The Militarization of Mother India*, Chanakya Publications, New Delhi, 1990.

Robinson, Francis, *Separatism Among Indian Muslims: The Politics of the United Provinces' Muslims, 1860-1923*, Cambridge University Press, Cambridge, 1974.

Rosen, George, *Democracy and Economic Change in India*, University of California Press, Berkeley and Los Angeles, 1967.

Rudolph, Lloyd I. and Susanne Hoeber Rudolph, *In Pursuit of Lakshmi: the Political Economy of the Indian State*, University of Chicago Press, Chicago, 1987.

Saikal, Amin (ed.), *Refugees in the Modern World*, Canberra Studies in World Affairs No. 25, Department of International Relations, Research

School of Pacific Studies, Australian National University, Canberrra, 1989.

Saikal, Amin and William Maley (eds), *The Soviet Withdrawal from Afghanistan*, Cambridge University Press, Cambridge, 1989.

Saxena, R.P., *Tribal Economy in Central India*, K.L. Mukhopadhyay, Calcutta, 1964.

Sen, Amartya, *Poverty and Famines: An Essay in Entitlement*, Oxford University Press, Oxford, 1972.

Sharma, Brig. Man Mohan, (Ret'd), *I Shall Not Volunteer: In Roads of Corruption in the Indian Army*, privately published, New Delhi, circa 1992.

Singh, Jasjit, (ed.), *Asian Strategic Review 1991-92*, Institute for Defence Studies and Analysis, New Delhi, 1992.

Singh, O.P., *Strategic Sikkim*, B.R. Pub. Corp., New Delhi, 1985.

Singh, S., M. Premi and A. Bose, *Population Transition in India*, Vol.1, B.R. Pub. Corp., New Delhi, 1989.

Smith, Chris, *India's Ad Hoc Arsenal: Direction or Drift in Defence Policy?*, SIPRI (through Oxford University Press), Oxford, 1994.

Spector, Leonard, *The Undeclared Bomb: The Spread of Nuclear Weapons 1987-88*, Carnegie Endowment for International Peace, Ballinger, Cambridge, Massachusetts, 1988.

Stern, Robert W., *Changing India: Bourgeois Revolution on the Subcontinent*, Cambridge University Press, Cambridge, 1993.

Swamy, Subramanian, *Economic Growth in China and India*, Vikas, New Delhi, 1989.

Tanham, George K., *Indian Strategic Thought: An Interpetive Essay*, Rand Corporation, Santa Monica, California, 1992.

Thakur, Ramesh and Carlyle Thayer, *Soviet Relations with India and Vietnam*, Macmillan, UK, 1992.

Thapar, Romila, *A History of India*, Vol.1, Penguin, Middlesex, UK, 1969.

The United States and India in the Post-Soviet World: Proceedings of the Third Indo-US Strategic Symposium, National Defense University, Washington DC, 1993.

Thomas, Raju G., *India's Security Policy*, Princeton University Press, New Jersey, 1986.

Tomar, R., *India and South Asia: Problems of a Regional Power*, Legislative Research Service of the Australian Parliament, Canberra, 1989.

Tully, Mark and Satish Jacob, *Amritsar: Mrs Gandhi's Last Battle*, Jonathan Cape, London, 1985.

United Nations Development Program (UNDP), *Human Development Report 1990*, Oxford University Press, Oxford, 1990.

United Nations Development Program (UNDP), *Human Development Report 1991*, Oxford University Press, Oxford, 1991.

US National Science Foundation, *Indian Scientific Strengths: Selected Opportunities for Indo-US Cooperation*, Washington DC, 1987.

Venkataramani, Raja, *Japan Enters Indian Industry: The Maruti-Sazuki Joint Venture*, Radiant Publishers, New Delhi, 1990.

Verghese, B.G., *Waters of Hope: Himalaya-Ganga Development and Cooperation for a Billion People*, Oxford and IBH, New Delhi, 1990.

Weiner, Myron, *The Politics of Scarcity: Public Pressure and Political Response in India*, The University of Chicago Press, Chicago, 1962.

Weiner, Myron, *Sons of the Soil: Migration and Ethnic Conflict in India*, Princeton University Press, Princeton, 1978.

Weiner, Myron, *The Child and the State in India; child labor and education policy in comparative perspective*, Princeton University Press, Princeton, New Jersey, 1991.

Westley, J.R., *Agriculture and Equitable Growth: The Case of Punjab-Haryana*, Westview Press, Boulder, 1986.

Wirsing, R.G., *The Baluchis and Pathans*, Minority Rights Group Report No. 48, Minority Rights Group, London, 1987.

Wolferen, Karel van, *The Enigma of Japanese Power*, Macmillan, London, 1989.

World Bank, *1991 Country Economic Memorandum on India*, May 1990, Vols.I & 2.

World Bank, *India: Recent Developments and Medium-Term Issues*, Vol.1, April 1988.

World Bank, *World Development Report 1990*, Oxford University Press, Oxford, Oxford, 1990.

World Bank, *Pakistan: Current Economic Situation and Prospects*, March 1991.

Sadiq, Dr. N., *The State of World Population 1991*, United Nations Population Fund (UNFPA) - document undated and without publication details.

Wriggins, W. Howard (ed.), *Dynamics of Regional Politics: Four Systems on the Indian Ocean Rim*, Columbia University Press, New York, 1992.

Articles, journals, working papers, etc.

'A case lost', *Frontline*, 3 January 1992.

A-PDR Newsletter', *Asia-Pacific Defence Reporter*, Vol. XVIII/XIX, No. 12/1, June-July 1992.

Abraham, Itty, 'India's Scientific Enclave: Civilian Scientists and Military Technologies', *Armed Forces and Society*, Vol.18, No.2.

Aggarwal, Yogi, 'Supercomputer race: Indian efforts yield results', *Frontline*, 27 August 1993.

Ahluwalia, Montek, S., 'India's Economic Performance, Policies and Prospects', in R.E.B. Lucas and G.F. Papanek, *The Indian Economy: Recent Developments and Future Prospects*, Boulder, Colorado, 1988.

Ahmar, Moonis, *Indo-Pakistan Normalization Process: The Role of CBMs in the Post-Cold War Era*, ACDIS Occasional paper, University of Illinois at Urbana-Champagne, Illinois, 1993.

Ahmed, A.S., 'The Politics of Ethnicity in Pakistan Society', *Asian Affairs*, Vol.XXI, Part 1, February 1990.

Ahmed, F. and S. Das, 'Manipur: The hidden war', *India Today*, 30 June 1993.

Albright, David and Mark Hibbs, 'India's Silent Bomb', *Bulletin of the Atomic Scientists*, Vol. 48, No. 7, September 1992.

Albright, David and Tom Zamora, 'India, Pakistan's nuclear weapons: all the pieces in place', *Bulletin of the Atomic Scientists*, Vol.45, No.5. June 1989.

Ali, Akhtar, 'A Framework for Nuclear Agreement and Verification', in Stephen Cohen (ed.), *Nuclear Proliferation in South Asia: The Prospects for Arms Control*, Westview, Boulder, Colorado, 1991.

Anon., 'Major naval base takes shape in Bay of Bengal', *Aerospace*, April 1992.

Anon., 'Pakistan receives more China-made missiles', *Aerospace*, January 1993.

Anon., 'The LM2500 Demonstration', *Asia Pacific Defense Forum*, Winter

1991-92.

Anon., (President of ITC Global Holdings, Singapore), 'SAARC: Trading with the World', *Business India*, 29 March - 11 April 1993.

Anon., 'Improved Prithvi missile launched', *International Defense Review*, No. 8, 1992.

Anon., 'Israelis negotiate US $1bil deals in India', *Aerospace*, November 1992.

Anon., 'Missing the wood for the trees', *Business India*, 29 March-11 April 1993.

Anon., 'Two Refugee Camps and an "Unpatriotic" Journalist', *Economic and Political Weekly*, XV/16, 19 April 1980.

'Arms and the Businessman', *Business India*, 25 June-8 July 1990.

Arunachalam, V.S., 'Defence, Technology and Development: an Indian Experience', D. Ball and H. Wilson (eds), *New Technology: Implications for Regional and Australian Security*, Canberra Papers on Strategy and Defence No. 76, Strategic and Defence Studies Centre, Research School of Pacific Studies, Australian National University, Canberra, November 1989.

Asia and Pacific Review 1988 (9th Edition), World of Information Press, Essex, UK, 1987.

Asian Defence Journal, quoting letter from President Reagan to Rajiv Ghandi, December 1988, p.131.

'Asian Flight: Wake Up', *The Economist*, 8 September 1990.

Austin, D and A. Gupta, 'The Politics of Violence in India and South Asia: Is democracy an endangered species?', *Conflict Studies*, #223, Research Institute for the Study of Conflict and Terrorism, London, 1990.

Austin, Gregory, 'Soviet Perspectives on India's Developing Security Posture', in R. Babbage and S. Gordon (eds), *India's Strategic Future, Regional State or Global Power?* The Macmillan Press, London, 1992.

Awanohara, Susumu, 'In the melting pot', *Far Eastern Economic Review*, 26 April 1990.

Ayoob, Mohammed, 'India as Regional Hegemon: External Opportunities and Internal Constraints', *International Journal*, Vol. XLVI, No. 3, Summer 1991.

Ayoob, Mohammed, 'India in South Asia: The Quest for Regional Predominance', *World Policy Journal*, Vol.VII, No. 1, Winter 1989-90.

Babbage, Ross, 'India's Strategic Development: Issues for the Western

Powers', R. Babbage and S. Gordon (eds), *India's Strategic Future: Regional State or Global Power?'*, The Macmillan Press, London, 1992.

Bagchi, Amiya Kumar, 'An Economic Policy for the New Government', *Economic and Political Weekly*, Vol. XXV, 10 February 1990.

Balachandran, G., 'India's Defence Expenditure: Widely Varying Estimates', *Strategic Analysis*, VOl.XIV, No. 9.

Ball, D., 'China's Disturbing Arms Build-Up', *The Independent Monthly*, February 1993.

Baweja, Harinder, 'Wrong Man, Wrong Place', *India Today*, 31 December 1992.

Bedi, Rahul, 'India's Reluctant Police', *Jane's Defence Weekly*, 6 July 1991.

Bedi, Rahul, 'Talks bring closer Indo-US ties', *Jane's Defence Weekly*, 8 February 1992.

Bedi, Rahul, 'Indian arms buys defy cash shortfall', *Jane's Defence Weekly*, 8 May 1993.

Bedi, Rahul, 'Conflict in Kashmir countries', *Jane's Defence Weekly*, 3 July 1993.

Bedi, Rahul, 'Collaboration invited for LCA programme', *Jane's Defence Weekly*, 29 January 1994.

Beri, Ruchita, 'Ballistic Missile Proliferation', in Jasjit Singh (ed.), *Asian Strategic Review 1991-92*, Institute for Defence Studies and Analysis, New Delhi, 1992.

'Bharat Electronics - a growing force in India', *Defence*, Vol.I, No. 2, 1990.

Bhattacharya, D., 'Indian Economic Development', paper presented under the joint auspices of the Centre for Indian Studies (Sydney University) and the Business Council of Australia, 11 November 1988.

Bhimali, Shefali, 'Reluctant Reformers', *India Today*, 15 September 1993.

Bhuskute, B.V., 'Tribals, Dalits and Government Lands', *Economic and Political Weeky*, Vol.XXIV, No.41, 21 October 1989.

'Bihar: Domain of the Dons', *India Today*, 31 January 1992.

'Boarding a Moving Train: India's New Minister of State for Defence, Raja Ramanna', *Defense and Foreign Affairs*, Vol. XVII, April 1990.

Bobb, Dilip and Amarnath K. Menon, 'Chariot of Fire', *India Today*, 15 June 1979.

'Bofors: What do the new revelations mean?', *Frontline*, 13 March 1992.

Bowonder, B. and Sunil Mani, 'Government Policy and Industrial Development: Case of Indian Computer Manufacturing Industry', *Economic and Political Weekly*, Vol. XVI, No.8, 23 February 1991.

Bratersky, M.V. and S.I. Lunyov, 'India at the End of the Century: Transformation into an Asian Regional Power', *Asian Survey*, Vol. XXX, No. 10, October 1990.

Bussert, Jim, 'Sonars of the Indian Navy', *Jane's Intelligence Review*, November 1992.

Bussert, James C., 'India's Navy Blends Eastern and Western Ships Systems', *Signal*, Vol. 48, No. 4, December 1993.

'Census 1991: India's Stagnant Status', *Frontline*, 13-16 April 1991.

Chakrabarty, D., 'Political Hinduism and the Question of Ethnicity in India', *Public Lecture, University of Melbourne*, 24 April 1991.

Chandra, Sudhir, 'Of Communal Consciousness and Communal Violence: Impressions from Post-Riot Surat', paper read at a conference on *The BJP After Ayodhya*, Curtin University, Perth, July 1993.

'Change of Guard', *India Today*, 13 July 1990.

Chaudry, M. H., 'Fertility Behaviour in India, 1961-86: The Stalled Decline in the Crude Birth Rate', in S. Singh et.al., *Population Transition in India*, Vol. 1, B.R. Pub. Corp., New Delhi, 1989.

Chaudry, Mahinder D., 'Population Growth Trends in India: 1991 Census', *Population and the Environment*, Vol.14, No.1, September 1992.

Cheema, P.I., 'Impact of the Afghan War on Pakistan', *Pakistan Horizon*, Vol. XLI, January 1988.

Chellaney, Brahma, 'Regional proliferation : issues and challenges', in Stephen Cohen (ed.), *Nuclear Proliferation in South Asia: The Prospects for Arms Control*, Westview, Boulder, Colorado, 1991.

Chengappa, Raj, 'Dangerous Dimensions', *India Today*, 15 February 1993.

Cheung, Tai Ming, 'Sukhois, Sams, Subs', *Far Eastern Economic Review*, 8 April 1993.

'Chinks in the Armour', *India Today*, 15 November 1991.

Chisti, Sumitra, 'Indo-Soviet Economic Relations', in S. Kumar (ed.), *Yearbook on India's Foreign Policy 1987-88*, McGraw-Hill, New Delhi, 1988.

Chopra, Pran, 'Foreign Policy in a Changing World', *Economic and Political Weekly*, Vol.XXVI, No.14, 6 April 1991.

Clad, James, 'Limits of Tolerance', *Far Eastern Economic Review*, 17 May 1990.

Clad, James, 'Paradise Abroad', *Far Eastern Economic Review*, 26 April 1990.

Clad, James, 'Patience sorely tested', *Far Eastern Economic Review*, 24 January 1991.

Clad, James, 'Power mid poverty', *Far Eastern Economic Reveiw*, 7 June 1990.

Clad, James, 'Short-term suitors', *Far Eastern Economic Review*, 26 April 1990.

Clad, James, 'Spinning wheels', *Far Eastern Economic Review*, 23 August 1990.

Clad, James, 'Status Symbol', *Far Eastern Economic Review*, 26 April 1993.

Clad, James, 'Technical Knockout', *Far Eastern Economic Review*, 7 June 1990.

Cloughley, B.W., 'India's stresses and strains', *Pacific Defence Reporter*, Annual Reference Edition, 1988.

Cloughley, Brian, 'Indian subcontinent: a year of man-made and natural disasters', *Pacific Defence Reporter*, 1989 Annual Reference Edition.

'Cocking a Militant Snook', *India Today*, 31 October 1991.

Confederation of Engineering Industry, Petition to the Government of India, 1990.

'Conspiracy Surfaces', *India Today*, 15 December 1991.

Copley, G.R., 'South Asia: Zone of the New Great Powers', *Defense and Foreign Affairs*, Vol.XVII, No. 5-6, May/June 1989.

Copley, Gregory, 'Pakistan on the Brink', *Defense and Foreign Affairs*, Vol.XVII, No. 4, April 1989.

Copley, Gregory, 'The Pragmatic Approach', *Defense and Foreign Affairs*, Vol.XVIII, No.4, April 1990.

Copley, Gregory, Interview with Dr Arunachalam, 'Unrestrained Ambition', *Defense and Foreign Affairs*, Vol. XVIII, No. 4, April 1990.

Copley, Gregory, Interview with Rajiv Gandhi, in 'India: A New Great

Power Arrives', *Defense and Foreign Affairs*, Vol. XVI, No.12, December 1988.

'Country Report on India', *The Economist*, 4 May 1991.

'Countrywide rallies against anti-Muslim riots in India', *Pakistan Times*, 22 December 1990.

Da Cunha, Derek, 'The ASEAN Armed Forces: A Case Study of Singapore and Malaysia', *Workshop on major Asian powers and the security of Southeast Asia*, Institute for South East Asian Studies, Singapore, December 1990.

Dali, Norliza, 'India to pursue an atomic weapons programme', *Asian Defence Journal*, No. 3, 1993.

Dali, Norliza, 'India's Budget Boosts Space Programme Spending', *Asian Defence Journal*, No. 4, April 1993.

Dali, Norliza, 'New Delhi begins operating another nuclear reactor', *Asian Defence Journal*, October 1992.

Dantes, Edmond, 'Missiles in Gulf Buoy India's Development Drive', *Defense News*, 25 February 1991.

Das, V., 'Forests and Tribals of Jharkhand', *Economic and Political Weekly*, Vol.XXVI, No.6, 9 February 1991.

Datta, Mrinal Chaudhuri, 'Mandal and the Berlin Wall', *Seminar*, #377, January 1991.

Davis, T.A., 'Internal Security deteriorating rapidly', *Asia-Pacific Defence Reporter*, August-September 1993.

Davis, T.A., 'The killing season opens', *Asia-Pacific Defence Reporter*, June 1991.

'Defence Demands', *Frontline*, 3-16 August 1991.

'Defence Expenditure - Some Issues', *Indian Defence Review*, January 1992.

'Defence: A Middle-Aged Military Machine', *India Today, 30 April 1993.*

Defense and Foreign Affairs, Vol. XVIII, No. 4 April 1990, Interviews with V.P. Singh and Raja Ramanna.

Desai, Ashok V., 'Technology Acquisition and Application: Interpreting the Indian Experience', in R.E.B. Lucas and G.F. Papenk, *The Indian Economy: Recent Developments and Future Prospects*, Westview Press, Boulder, Colorado, 1988.

Desmond, Edward, 'South Asia: The Nuclear Shadow', *Time*, 27 January 1992.

Dogra, B., 'Tribal Discontent: Timely Warning', *Economic and Political Weekly*, Vol.XXV, No.14, 1990.

'Double Impact', *India Today*, 31 March 1992.

Duyker, Edward, 'The Kashmir Conflict: An Historical Overview', *The Indian Ocean Review*, Vol. 3, No.4, December 1990.

Economist, The, 4 May 1991.

Engineer, Ali Asghar, 'The Bloody Trail', *Economic and Political Weekly*, Vol.XXVI, No. 4, 26 January 1991.

Fairclough, A.J., 'Policy Challenges of the Environment', *The Washington Quarterly*, Vol.14, No.1, Winter 1991.

'First Indian-built submarine commissioned', *International Defence Review*, No. 4, 1992.

Foot, Rosemary, 'The Sino-Soviet Complex and South Asia', in Barry Buzan and Gower Rizvi, *South Asian Insecurity and the Great Powers*, St Martin's Press, New York, 1986.

'Freeing India's Economy', *The Economist*, 23 May 1992.

Frontline, 20 December 1991, interview with Indian CNS Admiral Ramdas, p.7.

Furniss, Tim, 'India aims for polar launcher', *Flight International*, 3-9 June 1992.

Ganguly, Sumit, 'Ethno-Religious Conflict in South Asia', *Survival*, Vol.35, No.2, Summer 1993.

Ganguly, Sumit, 'South Asia After the Cold War', *The Washington Quarterly*, Autumn 1992.

Gearing, Julian, 'Russian connection revitalized', *Asia-Pacific Defence Reporter*, June-July 1993.

George, Paul, *Indian Naval Expansion*, Working Paper No. 32, Canadian Institute for International Peace and Security, February 1991.

Ghosh, Arun, 'A paper to ponder', *Frontline*, 20 December 1991.

Ghosh, Arun, 'Eighth Plan: Challenges and Opportunities - I', *Economic and Political Weekly*, Vol. XXVI, No. 3, 19 January 1991.

Ghosh, Arun, 'Eighth Plan: Challenges and Opportunities - III', *Economic and Political Weekly*, Vol. XXVI, No. 5, 2 February 1991.

Ghosh, Arun, 'Eighth Plan: Challenges and Opportunities - IV', *Economic and Political Weekly*, Vol. XXVI, No. 8 23 February 1991.

'Gill Returns', *India Today*, 15 December 1991.

Gordon, S., 'Domestic Foundations of India's Security Policy', in R. Babbage and S. Gordon (eds), *India's Strategic Future: Regional State or Global Power?*, The Macmillan Press, London, 1992.

Gordon, S., 'Indian Defense Spending: Treading Water in the Fiscal Deep', *Asian Survey*, Vol. XXXII, No. 10, October 1992.

Govindarajulu, V., 'India's S&T Capability: SWOT Analysis', *Economic and Political Weekly*, Vol. XXV, Nos. 7 and 8, February 17-24, 1990.

Grazebrook, A.W., 'The Indian naval buildup: Has Defence Central "got it all wrong"?', *Pacific Defence Reporter*, February 1990.

'Growing security fears', *Jane's Defence Weekly*, 26 May 1990.

Guha, A., 'Little Nationalism Turned Chauvinist: Assam's Anti-Foreigner Upsurge 1979-80', *Economic and Political Weekly*, Special Number (Vol.XV, Nos. 41-43), 1980.

Gupta, Amit, 'Fire in the Sky: The Indian Missile Program', *Defence and Diplomacy*, No.10, October 1990.

Gupta, Amit, 'India and the Arms Bazaar of the Nineties', *Economic and Political Weekly*, Vol. XXV, 22 September 1990.

Gupta, Amit, 'India's Mixed Performance', *Defense and Diplomacy*, Vol. 7, No. 5, May 1989.

Gupta, Bhabani Sen, *Economic and Political Weekly*, Vol.XXIV, No.3, 21 January 1989.

Gupta, Bhabani Sen, *India Today*, 15 June 1989.

Gupta, Shekhar and Paranjoy Guha Thakurtha,'Heading for a crisis', *India Today*, 28 February 1989.

Hill, Stephen and Shantha Liyanage, 'The Status of Indian Science and Technology Capabilities', *paper prepared for the Australian S&T mission to India*, July 1990.

Hill, T.R., 'Hills of Hatred', *Frontline*, 20 November 1992.

'Hitting Home', *India Today*, 15 November 1991.

Hull, Andrew, 'The Role of Ballistic Missiles in Third World Defence Strategies', *Jane's Intelligence Review*, October 1991.

Hussain, Mushahid, 'Indian Army's Changing Profile', *Regional Studies*,

Vol.IX, No. 3, Summer 1991.

Hussain, Norr A., 'India's Regional Policy: Strategic and Security Dimensions', S. Cohen (ed.), *The Security of South Asia, American and Asian Perspectives*, University of Illinois Press, Urbana, C. 1987.

Hyman, Anthony, 'Back from the Brink', *The Middle East*, July 1990.

IDR Research Team, 'Weapons and equipment state; are we getting our money's worth?', *Indian Defence Review*, July 1988.

IDSA News Review on South Asia/Indian Ocean, various issues.

'IMF-style reform and the poor', *Frontline*, 6 December 1991.

'In choppy waters', *India Today*, 30 September 1990.

'In deep waters', *Sunday*, 18-24 November 1990.

'In Reverse Gear', *India Today*, 15 November 1991.

'Indi-US defense relations thaw', *International Defense Review*, Vol. 23, No. 8, 1990.

'India builds by numbers', *Jane's Defence Weekly*, 16 January 1993.

'India Caged. A Survey: Plain Tales of the Licence Raj', *The Economist*, 4 May 1991.

'India Club', *Far Eastern Economic Review*, 22 April 1993.

'India Country Survey', *The Economist*, 4 May 1991.

'India cuts arsenal', *Aviation Week and Space Technology*, 23 March 1992.

'India deploys new missile at border', *Asian Defence Journal*, No. 7, 1993.

'India evaluates new Soviet fighters - LCA may be axed', *Aerospace*, August 1991.

'India faces critical spares shortage of Soviet arms (sic)', *International Defence Review*, Vol. 12, 1991.

'India's ASWAC spotted in the open', *Jane's Defence Weekly*, 14 August 1993.

'India updates its Russian fighters', *Aerospace*, June 1993.

'India's Last Chance Aircraft - The LCA!', *Vayu Aerospace Review*, No.IV, 1990.

'India, South Korea look to Soviets', *Jane's Defence Weekly*, 14 September 1991.

'India: Third stage of launch vehicle for polar satellite successfully tested', *India Today*, 15 December 1991, p.62

'Indian major arms pusher into Sindh: ex-ISI chief', *Nation*, 19 January 1991.

Indian Trade Journal, 8 February 1989, pp. A446-447.

'Indo-US defense relations thaw', *International Defence Review*, Vol. 8, 1990.

'Industry builds up strength', *Jane's Defence Weekly*, Vol.13, No.21, 26 May 1990.

Jain, Sunil, 'Agriculture: Incomplete Initiatives', *India Today*, 15 February 1993.

Jayaraman, T., 'Facing up to fraud', *Frontline*, 12 February 1993.

Jeffrey, Robin, 'Political Admirals: A Neglected Aspect of the Growth of the Indian Navy', in Robert Bruce (ed.), *The Modern Indian Navy and the Indian Ocean: Developments and Implications*, Studies in Indian Ocean Maritime Affairs No. 2, Centre for Indian Ocean Regional Studies, Curtin University of Technology, Perth, 1989.

Jha, Ganganath, 'India's Sectoral Partnership with ASEAN', *The Indonesian Quarterly*, Vol.XX, No.3, third quarter, 1992.

Jones, Rodney W., 'Old Quarrels and New Realities: Security in Southern Asia after the Cold War', *The Washington Quarterly*, Winter 1992.

Jordan, John, 'India: The Indian Navy - Major Expansion Ahead', *Jane's Intelligence Review*, Vol.3, No.7, July 1991.

Joshi, General, Interview, *India Today*, 15 July 1993.

Joshi, Manoj, 'An Indian dilemma', *Frontline*, 6 December 1991.

Joshi, Manoj, 'Change of Guard', *India Today*, 31 July 1991.

Joshi, Manoj, 'Coping with pressures', *Frontline*, 20 November 1992.

Joshi, Manoj, 'Defence Demands', *Frontline*, 3-16 August 1991.

Joshi, Manoj, 'India's "Technology Demonstration" Strategy', draft paper delivered at the Research School of Pacific Studies, Australian National University, Canberra, November 1992.

Joshi, Manoj, 'Next door diplomacy', *Frontline*, July 1992.

Joshi, Manoj, 'Reaching out to Japan', *Frontline*, 17 July 1992.

Joshi, Manoj, 'Sea Power', *Frontline*, 20 December 1991.

Joshi, Manoj, 'Shy hands across the Himalayas', *Asia-Pacific Defence Reporter*, April-May 1993.

Joshi, Manoj, 'The Communique', *Frontline*, 3 January 1992.

Joshi, Manoj, 'The Gun Culture: Situation in UP, Gujarat', *Frontline*, 25 May-7 June 1991.

Joshi, Manoj, 'The Indigenous Effort', *Frontline*, 13-16 April 1991.

Joshi, Manoj, 'Undersea Thrust', *Frontline*, 20 December 1991.

Kalam, Dr. Abdul - report of statement, *Pacific Defence Reporter*, Vol.XVI, No.11, May 1990.

Kamaluddin, S., 'South Asia: Progress by Numbers', *Far Eastern Economic Review*, 22 April 1993, p.17.

Karniol, Robert, 'Chinese weapons boost Sri lanka', *Jane's Defence Weekly*, 15 June 1991.

Karniol, Robert, 'Chinese puzzle over Burma's SIGINT base', *Jane's Defence Weekly*, 29 January 1994.

Katoch, Col. Arjun (ret'd), 'Airland Battle - Its Future and Implications for Third World Countries', *Indian Defence Review*, October 1991.

Kaye, Lincoln, 'Problem program', *Far Eastern Economic Review*, 2 March 1989.

Klintworth, Gary, 'China's Relations with Russia and India: Letting Bygones be Bygones', paper prepared for the *UN Conference on National Security and the Building of Confidence Among Nations in the Asia-Pacific Region*, Kathmandu, 1-3 February 1993.

Klintworth, Gary, *China's India War: A Question of Confidence*, Working Paper No. 124, Strategic and Defence Studies Centre, Research School of Pacific Studies, Australian National University, Canberra, 1987.

Kohli, Admiral S.N. (ret'd), 'The geopolitical and strategic considerations that necessitate the expansion and modernization of the Indian Navy', *Indian Defence Review*, January 1989.

Kong, Yan and Tim McCarthy, 'China's Missile Bureaucracy', *Jane's Intelligence Review*, January 1993.

Kothari, R., 'Eroding the Republic', *Seminar*, #377, January 1991.

Kothari, Rajni and R.K. Srivastava, 'Regional Co-operation in South Asia', in Evelyne Blamont (ed.), *Regional Co-operation and Peace*, International Social Science Council of UNESCO, 1989.

Kundu, Apurba, 'The Indian Army's Continued Overdependence on Martial Races' Officers', *Indian Defence Review*, July 1991.

Lakha, Salim, 'India aims for an Electronics Revolution: Growth of Computer Software Industry'. Unpublished paper.

Lakha, Salim, 'The BJP and Globalization of the Indian Economy', unpublished paper from the *'After Ayodhya' conference*, Curtin University, Perth, July 1993.

Lawler, Andrew, 'Indian Deal with Russia Brings US Reproaches', *Defence News*, 11-17 May 1992.

Leete, R. and G. Jones, 'South Asia's Future Population: Are There Really Grounds for Optimism?', unpublished paper, Demography Programme, Research School of Social Sciences, The Australian National University.

Leopold, George, 'U.S., India Discuss Nuclear Material Ban', *Defense News*, November 23-29 1991.

Levine, Steven I., 'China and South Asia', *Strategic Analysis*, Vol.XII, No.10, January 1989.

'Logging on to India's Potential', *India Today*, 15 May 1992.

Lyon, Peter, 'South Asia and the geostrategics of the 1990s', *Contemporary South Asia*, Vol.1, No.1, 1992.

Madhaven, A., 'The Post-Cold War Equations' in Kanwar (ed.), *India-Japan: Towards a New Era*, UBS Publishers, New Delhi, 1992.

Mahalingam, Sudha, 'Computer Industry in India: Strategies for Late-Comer Entry', *Economic and Political Weekly*, Vol.XXIV, No.42, 21 October 1989.

Majeed, Akhtar, 'The Indian Ocean: A Hotbed of Regional Rivalries', *Armed Forces Journal International*, October 1990.

Maley, W., 'Afghan Refugees: From Diaspora to Repatriation', in Amin Saikal (ed.), *Refugees in the Modern World*, Canberra Studies in World Affairs No. 25, Department of International Relations, Australian National University, 1989.

Malik, J. Mohan, 'Central Asia Astir', *Pacific Research*, Vol.5, No.2, May 1992.

Malik, J. Mohan, 'Chinese Debate on Military Strategy: Trends and Portents', *Journal of Northeast Asian Studies*, Summer 1990.

Malik, J. Mohan, 'Missile Proliferation: China's Role', *Current Affairs Bulletin*, Vol. 67, No.3, August 1990.

Malik, M.K., 'Drug Menace in South Asia', *Regional Studies* (Pakistan), Vol.VIII, No.3, Summer 1990.

Malik, Yogendra K and Dhirendra K. Vajpayi, 'The Rise of Hindu Militancy: India's Secular Democracy at Risk', *Asian Survey*, Vol.XXIX,

No.3, March 1989.

Mama, Hormuz P., 'Progress on India's new tactical missiles', *International Defense Review*, No. 7, 1989.

Mama, Hormuz P., 'Improved Prithvi missile launched', *International Defense Review*, No. 8, 1992.

Mama, Hormuz P., 'India's naval future: fewer ships, but better', *International Defense Review*, No. 2, 1993.

Mama, Hormuz P. and Ramon Lopez, 'India's Advanced Light Helicopter', *International Defense Review*, No. 9, 1989.

Manchanda, Rita, 'Heavy-water drought', *The Far Eastern Economic Review*, 31 August 1989.

Mansingh, Surjit and Steven I. Levine, 'China and India: Moving Beyond Confrontation', *Problems of Communism*, Vol. XXXVIII, March-June 1989.

Marwah, Onkar, 'India's Strategic Perspectives on the Indian Ocean', in L. Dowdy and R. Trood (eds), *The Indian Ocean: Perspectives on a Strategic Arena*, Duke University, Durham, 1983.

Masselos, J., 'India: A Power on the Move', *Current Affairs Bulletin*, Vol.64, No.10, March 1988.

Masselos, J., 'The Bombay Riot of January 1993: The Politics of Urban Conflagration', paper read at a conference on *The BJP After Ayodhya*, Curtin University, Perth, July 1993.

Mathews, Jessica Tuchman, 'Redefining Security', *Dialogue*, No.1, 1990.

Matthews, R., 'The Development of India's Defence-Industrial Base', *The Journal of Strategic Studies*, Vol.12, No.4, December 1989.

Mazari, Shireen M., 'US Intervention in the Persian Gulf: Strategic Implications for South East Asia', *Strategic Studies*, Vol.XIV, Nos.1/2, Autumn/Winter, 1990-91.

McCarthy, Tim, 'India's missile program: Part I', *Asian Defence Review*, September 1993.

McDonald, Hamish, 'Ayodhya backlash', *Far Eastern Economic Review*, 14 January 1993.

McDonald, Hamish, 'Indian Computing Power', *Far Eastern Economic Review*, 17 December 1992.

McDonald, Hamish, 'India: Iron Rations', *Far Eastern Economic Review*, 2 September 1993.

McDonald, Hamish, 'Looking for Friends', *Far Eastern Economic Review*, 19 September 1991.

Mcdonald, Hamish, 'Price of self-reliance', *Far Eastern Economic Review*, 10 December 1992.

McDonald, Hamish, 'Saint is Damned', *Far Eastern Economic Review*, 7 February 1991.

McDonald, Hamish, 'Secret shoppers', *Far Eastern Economic Review*, 29 October 1992.

McDonald, Hamish, 'Slow Speed Ahead', *Far Eastern Economic Review*, 10 October 1991.

McDonald, Hamish and Jaya Sarkar, 'India: The Money Juggernaut', *Far Eastern Economic Review*, 11 March 1993.

McLean, Doug, John McGuire and Peter Reeves, 'The Communal Cauldron Boils Over: The Bharatiya Janata Party July - December 1992'. Draft paper for the conference, *The BJP After Ayodhya*, Curtin University, Perth, July 1993.

Mehta, Ved, 'The Mosque and the Temple: The Rise of Fundamentalism', *Foreign Affairs*, Vol.72, No.2.

Mendelsohn, Oliver and Marika Vicziany, 'The Untouchables Today', in Jim Masselos (ed.), *India, Creating a Modern Nation*, Sterling, 1990.

Milhollin, Gary, 'India's missiles: with a little help from our friends', *The Bulletin of the Atomic Scientists*, Vol.45, No.9, November 1989.

Mookerjee, Vice Admiral S.N., (ret'd.), 'Indian Naval Development - Need for Review', *Journal of the U.S.I. of India*, Vol.CXIX, No.496, April-June 1989.

'More for the navy: interview with L. Ramdas', *Frontline*, 20 December 1991

Mukerjee, Dilip, 'Challenge to Foreign Policy', *Seminar*, No. 337, January 1991.

Nag, M. and M. Kak, 'Demographic Transition in a Punjab Village', *Population and Development Review*, Vol.10, No.4, December 1984.

Nagarj, K., 'The "missing" women', *Frontline*, 25 May 1991.

Naidu, C.V.C., 'The Indian Navy and Southeast Asia', *Contemporary Southeast Asia*, Vol.13, No.1, June 1991.

Nanda, Lt.Gen. K.K. (ret'd), 'Cost Effective Defence', *Indian Defence Review*, January 1991.

Nayar, Baldev Raj, 'A World Role: The Dialectics of Purpose and Power' in John W. Mellor (ed.), *India: A Rising Middle Power*, Westview Press, Boulder, Colorado, 1979.

'New Delhi begins operating another nuclear reactor', *Asian Defence Journal*, October 1992.

'Niazi says Babri mosque issue more important than Kuwait', *Nation*, 30 December 1990.

Noorani, A.G., 'Jagmohan turbulence', *Frontline*, 3 January 1992.

Noorani, A.G. 'Rights and wrongs: A commission and many omissions', *Frontline*, 27 August 1993.

Nugent, Nicholas, 'The Defence Preparedness of India; Arming for Tomorrow', *Military Technology*, No. 3, 1991.

Ormston, R., *The Growth of the Indian Navy: What is India Up To?*, unpublished sub-thesis, Strategic and Defence Studies Centre, Research School of Pacific Studies, Australian National University, Canberra, 1991.

'Pak warned on Amanullah's threat', *Times of India*, 23 January 1992.

'Pakistan: Singapore of Southwest Asia?', 'Briefs', *East-West Centre Views*, July-August 1992.

Pande, Arvind, 'International Competitiveness and the Indian Steel Industry' in *Metals in India's Development: The Vision of Jawaharlal Nehru*, Ministry of Mines and Steel, Government of India, New Delhi, 1989.

Pandey, Gyan, 'In Defence of the Fragment: Writing about Hindu-Muslim Riots in India Today', forthcoming: *Economic and Political Weekly*

Papola, T.S., 'Unemployment, Poverty and Inequality', in M.S. Ardeshir, *Eighth Plan Perspective*, Lancer International, New Delhi, 1990.

Parthasarathy, G., 'Roots of Naxalism: The land question and law and order', *Frontline*, 14 February 1992.

'Passage Pains', *India Today*, 15 December 1991.

Patel, Surendra J., 'Main Elements in Shaping Future Technology Policies for India', *Economic and Political Weekly*, Vol.XXIV, No.9, March 1989.

Pawar, Sharad, interview in 'We will sell guns', *India Today*, 15 November 1991.

Pedersen, G., 'Afghan nomads in exile: patterns of organization and reorganization in Pakistan', in W. Anderson and N.H. Dupree (eds), *The Cultural Basis of Afghan Nationalism*, Pinter, London 1990.

Peiris, Denzil, 'Colombo Rides the Tiger', *South*, March 1985.

Penberthy, Jefferson, 'Nowhere to Turn', *Time*, 15 February 1993.

Perkovich, George, *Revamping South Asian Nuclear Policy*, MIT Centre for International Studies Seminar Report, 17 February, 1993.

'Petrol: The Coming Crunch', *India Today*, 15 June 1990.

Prakash, Sanjiv, 'Indian Defense: A conscious Attempt at Pragmatism', *Defense and Foreign Affairs*, Vol.XVIII, No.4, April 1990.

'Principal Indian Defence Manufacturers', *Defense and Foreign Affairs*, Vol.XVIII, No.4, April 1990.

'Principal Indian Defense R&D Establishments', *Defense and Foreign Affairs*, Vol.XVIII, No.4, April 1990.

'Problems of Parity', *India Today*, 15 February 1992.

'Punjab: Army Again', *Frontline*, December 1991.

Quarterdeck '90, (official magazine of the Indian navy) 1990, p.71.

Raghavan, S.V.S., 'The Permit Raj Must Go', *India Today*, 15 June 1990.

Raghuvanshi, Vivek, 'Russians ship arms to Asian powers', *Defense News*, October 11-17 1993.

Raghuvanshi, Vivek, 'Indians Propose Joint Ventures', *Defense News*, October 11-17 1993.

Raghuvanshi, Vivek, 'India Accelerates Drive Toward Self-Sufficiency', *Defense News*, July 26-August 1, 1993.

Raghuvanshi, Vivek, 'The Indian Air Force in Crisis', *Aerospace*, December 1993.

Rai, Saritha, 'Software: People at a Premium', *India Today*, 15 May 1992.

Raina, Vinod, 'Plurality Denied', paper delivered at a conference on *The BJP After Ayodhya*, Curtin University, Perth, July 1993.

Ram, Mohan, 'Ruling the Waves', *Far Eastern Economic Review*, 15 May 1986.

Ramachandran, V.K., 'IMF-style reform and the poor', *Frontline*, 6 December 1991.

Rao, Brigadier B.N., 'Defence Production and the Private Sector', *The United Services Institute Journal*, April-June 1991.

Rasgotra, M.K., *Inaugural Admiral R.D. Katari Memorial Lecture*, London, 16 October 1991.

Rashid, Ahmed, 'No law, no order', *Far Eastern Economic Review*, 24 January 1991.

Ravi, K., 'The Military Implications of India's Space Programme: Some Observations', *Defense Analysis*, Vol.5, No.3, 1989.

'Raw, KHAD agents involved in blasts, disruption', *Dawn*, 9 September 1990.

Reed, Arthur, 'Hindustan Aeronautics: A Force to be Reckoned with in the World of High-Tech Aerospace', *British Aerospace Quarterly*, Summer, 1992.

Richardson, Michael, 'Southeast Asia Wary', *Pacific Defence Reporter*, February 1990.

Richelson, Jeffrey T., 'US Space Reconnaissance After the Cold War', in Desmond Ball and Helen Wilson (eds), *Australia and Space*, Canberra Papers on Strategy and Defence No. 94, Strategic and Defence Studies Centre, Research School of Pacific Studies, Australian National University, Canberra, 1992.

'Riding New Highs', *India Today*, 15 November 1991.

Rikhye, Ravi, 'Indian Defence Budget: Fact and Fantasy', *Economic and Political Weekly*, 29 April 1989.

Rikhye, Ravi, 'Nobody asked me, but...', *Proceedings*, March 1990.

'RMAF to get Indian air force help', *Asian Defence Journal*, No. 4, 1992.

Robertson, B.A., 'South Asia and the Gulf Complex', in Barry Buzan and Gower Rizvi (eds), *South Asian Insecurity and the Great Powers*, St Martin's Press, New York, 1986.

Rose, Leo, 'India's Regional Policy: Non Military Dimensions', in S.P. Cohen (ed.), *The Security of South Asia; American and Asian Perspectives*, University of Illinois Press, Urbana, 1987.

Rose, Leo, 'United States and Soviet Policy Toward South Asia', *Current History*, Vol.85, No.509, March 1986.

Rowlands, Ian, 'Building International Regimes', *The Washington Quarterly*, Vol.14, No.1, Winter 1991.

Roy, Vice-Admiral M.K., 'The Indian Navy from the Bridge', *Proceedings* (U.S. Naval Institute), Vol.116/3/1045, March 1990.

Rustamji, K.F., 'The Paramilitary-Army Interface', *Indian Defence Review*, January 1991.

Saikal, Amin, 'The Regional Politics of the Afghan Crisis', in Amin Saikal and William Maley (eds), *The Soviet Withdrawal from Afghanistan*, Cambridge University Press, Cambridge, 1989.

Sandhu, Kanwar, 'Confusion in Command', *India Today*, 15 April 1993.

Sandhu, Kanwar, 'MBT Arjun: On Course, Finally', *India Today*, 15 July 1993.

Sardesai, D.R., 'India and ASEAN - An Overview', in S. Kumar (ed.), *Yearbook on India's Foreign Policy, 1987-88*, Tata McGraw Hill, New Delhi, 1988.

Sardeshpande, Lt.Gen. S.C. (ret'd), 'Internal Violence and the Military', *Indian Defence Review*, July 1992.

Sawhney, Pravin, 'The Blue Water Argument', *Business and Political Observer*, 2 August 1991.

Scalapino, Robert A., 'National Political Institutions and Leadership in Asia', *The Washington Quarterly*, Autumn, 1992.

Schuman, Michael, 'Unequal Struggle', *Far Eastern Economic Review*, 19 September 1991.

Segal, Gerald, 'Russia and the Chinas - New Risks', *Jane's Intelligence Review*, September 1992.

Sen, Goel and Sengupta, 'Growth of the Indian Steel Industry' in *Metals in India's Development: The Vision of Jawaharlal Nehru*, Ministry of Mines and Steel, Government of India, New Delhi, 1989.

Sengupta, Prasun, 'China Expands Air Forces', *Military Technology*, No. 8, 1992.

Sengupta, Prasun, 'India develops new satellites, launchers', *Aerospace*, September 1990.

Sengupta, Prasun, 'Indian satellites find military uses', *Aerospace*, April 1992.

Seshan, Defence Secretary, interview in *Defence and Foreign Affairs*, Vol.XVI, No.12, December 1988.

Sethi, D.S., 'Non-Ferrous Metals—The Indian Scenario', in *Metals in India's Development: The Vision of Jawaharlal Nehru*, Ministry of Mines and Steel, Government of India, New Delhi, 1989.

Sethi, Harsh, 'Human Rights in Kashmir: A Constricted Discourse', *Information Unit on Militarisation and Demilitarisation in Asia (IUMDA) Newsletter 4*, 1991.

Sharma, Dhirendra, 'India's Lopsided Science', *The Bulletin of the Atomic*

Scientists, Vol.47, No.4, May 1991.

Sharma, Pranjal, 'Systems Failure', *India Today,* 15 November 1992.

'Shattered Silence', *India Today,* 31 December 1991.

Sidhu, W.P.S., 'Migrant Tinder-box, *India Today,* 15 February 1993.

Silverberg, David, 'India Faces Roadblocks in Export Drive, *Defense News,* Vol.6, No.46, 18 November 1991.

Silverberg, David, 'India Pushes Indigenous Combat Aircraft Despite Delays', *Defense News,* 18 November 1991.

Silverberg, David, Interview with Arunachalam, *Defense News,* 24 February 1992.

Singh, Jasjit, 'Refuelling: A political gesture', *Frontline,* 2-16 March 1991.

Singh, Jasjit, 'Indian imperatives: the strategic challenges', *Frontline,* 13-16 August 1991.

Singh, Jasjit, 'Indian Ocean and Indian Security', in S. Kumar (ed.), *Yearbook on India's Foreign Policy 1987/88,* Tata McGraw Hill, New Delhi, 1988.

Singh, Jasjit, 'Security in a Period of Strategic Uncertainty', in Jasjit Singh (ed.), *Asian Strategic Review 1991-92,* Institute for Defence Studies and Analysis, New Delhi, 1992.

Singh, N.K., 'The Army: Dangerous Dealings', *India Today,* 30 September 1993.

Singh, Lt.Col. Shyam, 'Peasant Agitation and Internal Security', *Indian Defence Review,* July 1988.

Singh, Ravinderpal, 'Indo-Soviet Military Cooperation: Experiences, Trends and Opportunities', *Strategic Analysis,* December 1990.

Singh, Ravinderpal, 'Trans-Century Technologies', *Strategic Analysis,* Vol.XIV, No.4, July 1991.

Singh, Sanjay J., 'Indian Ocean Navies Learn from War', *Proceedings,* March 1992.

Singh, Lt.Col. Shyam, 'Peasant Agitation and Internal Security', *Indian Defence Review,* July 1988.

Sinha, Lt.Gen. S.K. (ret'd), 'Caste and the Indian Army', *Indian Defence Review,* July 1986.

Skogland, T., 'Ecology and the War in Afghanistan', in B. Huldt and E. Jansson (eds), *The Tragedy of Afghanistan: The Social, Cultural and*

Political Impact of the Soviet Invasion, Croom Helm, London 1989.

Smith, Chris, 'Indecision may clip LCA's wings', *Jane's Defence Weekly*, 12 August 1989.

'Social Indicators', *Far Eastern Economic Review*, 13 August 1992.

Sohrabji, Sunita, 'Is the spree over?', *India Today*, 15 January 1994.

'Soviets offer Sierra SSN but Indians eye Oscar SSGNs', *Navy News and Undersea Technology*, 6 May 1991.

'Speak softly and carry a big stick', *Aerospace*, June 1992.

Spellman, Anthony, 'Asians Attracted by Russian Deals', *Armed Forces Journal*, May 1993.

Srinivas, M., 'Spreading Fear', *Frontline*, 3 January 1992.

Srinivas, M.N., 'Social Change in Modern India: Chapter 1, "Sanskritization"', in T.R.Metcalf (ed.), *Modern India: An Interpretative Anthology*, Macmillan, Toronto, 1971.

'Steel: A New Sheen', *India Today*, 31 August 1990.

'Sticky Situation', *India Today*, 15 April 1991.

Stone, Jeremy J., *Journal of the Federation of American Scientists*, Vol.47, No.2, March/April 1994.

Subramanian, T.S. and T. Abraham, 'Collapse in Colombo: Behind India's manoeuvre', *Frontline*, 6 December 1991.

'Succession Storm', *India Today*, 31 October 1990.

Sundarji, K., 'Stretching the Defence Bucks', *India Today*, 31 December 1991.

Suryanarayan, V., 'India-Sri Lanka Accord and the Prospects for Security in South Asia' in K.P. Misra and V.D. Chopra (eds), *South Asia-Pacific Region: Emerging Trends*, International Institute for Southern Asia-Pacific Studies, New Delhi, 1988.

'Swords not ploughshares', *The Economist*, 23 March 1991.

Tahiliani, Admiral R.H. (Ret'd), 'Maritime Strategy for the Nineties', *Indian Defence Reveiw*, July 1989.

Tandon, Rear Admiral, 'The Maritime Priorities of India', in Ross Babbage and Sam Bateman (eds), *Maritime Change, Issues for Asia*, Allen & Unwin, Australia, 1993.

Tanham, George, 'India's Strategic Culture', *Washington Quarterly*, Winter, 1992.

Tasker, Rodney, 'Rao's Look-East Policy', *Far Eastern Economic Review*, 22 April 1993.

Tellis, Ashley J., 'Securing the Barrack: The Logic, Structure and Objectives of India's Naval Expansion', in R. Bruce (ed.), *The Modern Indian Navy and the Indian Ocean: Developments and Implications*, Studies in Indian Ocean Maritime Affairs No. 2, Centre for Indian Ocean Regional Studies, Curtin University of Technology, Perth, 1989.

'Terrorism: Intimidating Business', *India Today*, 30 April 1991.

'Terrorists must be rooted out from Tamil Nadu: Joshi', *The Hindu*, 16 December 1991.

'Testing reaction', *Far Eastern Economic Review*, 8 June 1989.

Thakur, Ramesh, 'India as a Regional Seapower', *Asian Defence Journal*, No.5, 1990.

'The Drowning Villages,', *Frontline*, 20 December 1991.

'The Bloody Trail,', *Economic and Political Weekly*, Vol.XXVI, No.4.

'The Elephant Awakes,', *The Economist*, 23 May 1992.

'The Generosity of the Poor', *The Economist*, 25 January 1992.

'The Jane's Interview', *Jane's Defence Weekly*, 6 November 1993.

'This is the wrong way', *India Today*, 30 April 1993.

Thomas, Raju, 'US Transfers of 'Dual Use' Technologies to India', *Asian Survey*, Vol.XXX, No.9, September 1990.

'Tightrope Walking', *India Today*, 31 July 1992.

Todd, Daniel, 'Naval Shipbuilding: prerequisite for rising powers?', *International Defence Review*, No.3, 1991.

'Trouble on the Home Front', *Asiaweek*, 12 July 1991.

'Unrestrained ambition', *Defense and Foreign Affairs*, Vol.XVIII, No.4, April 1990. Interview with Dr Arunachalam.

'Valuable War Lessons', *India Today*, 15 October 1989.

Venkatanarayanan, R., 'Iron and Steel—Planning for the Next Decade' in *Metals in India's Development: The Vision of Jawaharlal Nehru*, Ministry of Mines and Steel, Government of India, New Delhi, 1989.

Vicziany, Marika, 'India's Anti-Poverty Programmes, with special reference to the Untouchables', in *What's happening to India?: the last ten years*, conference papers, La Trobe University, 1986.

Vinayak, Ramesh, Dilip Awasthi and Amarnath K. Menon, 'Agriculture:

Incomplete Initiatives', *India Today*, 15 February 1993.

Vinayak, R., 'Spilling Over: J&K militants enter Chamba', *India Today*, 15 September 1993.

Visaria, P., 'Rural-Urban Disparities in India', in Indian Council of Social Science Research (ed.), *Economic Development of India and China: A Comparative Study*, Lancer International, New Delhi, 1988.

Wariavwalla, Bharat, 'The Big Bully?', *Illustrated Weekly of India*, 11 June 1989.

'We will sell guns', *India Today*, 15 November 1991.

Weiner, Myron, 'Security, Migration and Conflict in South Asia', *Defense Intelligence Journal*, Vol.1, No.2, Fall 1992.

What's happening to India?: the last ten years, conference papers, La Trobe University, 1986.

'Where India's reforms get stuck', *The Economist*, 22 January 1994.

Wriggins, W. Howard, 'South Asian Regional Politics: Asymmetrical Balance or One-State Dominance?', in Howard W. Wriggins (ed.), *Dynamics of Regional Politics: Four Systems on the Indian Ocean Rim*, Columbia University Press, New York, 1992.

Young, P. Lewis, 'The United States Navy, the Indian Ocean and the Politics of Worldwide Command in a Post-Cold War World', *Asian Defence Journal*, No.4, 1993.

Zaidi, S.A., 'Regional Imbalances and National Question in Pakistan', *Economic and Political Weekly*, Vol.XXIV, No.6, 11 February 1989.

Official sources

Australian Department of Foreign Affairs and Trade, *India—Country Economic Brief, May/June 1993*, Department of Foreign Affairs and Trade, Canberra, 1993.

Australian Department of Foreign Affairs and Trade, East Asia Analytical Unit, *India's Economy at the Midnight Hour: Australia's India Strategy*, Australian Government Publishing Service, Australia 1994.

Australian Nuclear Science and Technology Organisation, *Newsletter*, June 1991.

Balachandran, G., *Submission to US Department of Commerce*, 21 July

1992.

Bhattacharya, Debesh, 'Growth and Distribution in India During the Last Four Decades', paper provided for the *Standing Committee on Foreign Affairs, Defence and Trade of the Australian Senate's Inquiry into Australia-India Relations*, 11 July 1989, Commonwealth Government Printer, Canberra, 1989.

Central Bank of Sri Lanka, Statistics Department, *Economic and Social Statistics of Sri Lanka*, Vol.IX, December 1986.

Council for Scientific and Industrial Research, *Status Report on Science and Technology in India 1988*, Government of India, Publications and Information Directorate, New Delhi, 1988.

Council for Scientific and Industrial Research, *Status Report on Science and Technology in India; 1990*, Government of India, Publications and Information Directorate, New Delhi, 1990.

Current News Supplement (US Department of Defence), 31 December 1986, p.14.

Current News Supplement (US Department of Defence), 21 May 1991, p.B14.

Dibb, Paul, *Review of Australia's Defence Capabilities*, Australian Government Publishing Service, Canberra, 1986.

Foreign Broadcast Information Service, *Daily Report for South/Southwest Asia*, 3 January 1990, US Government Printing Office, Washington DC, January 1990.

Galbraith, Peter, 'Nuclear Proliferation in South Asia: Containing the Threat', staff report to the *Committee on Foreign Relations of the US Senate*, US Government Printing Office, Washington DC, 1988.

Government of India, *Census of India 1951*, Vol.XII, Part 1-A, Government of India Central Press, India.

Government of India, *A Portrait of Population, Assam*, Census of India 1971, Government of India Central Press, India.

Government of India (Commercial), *Report of the Comptroller and Auditor General of India*, Part VIII, HAL Ltd., New Delhi, 1987.

Government of India, *Defence Services Estimates* (various years), Government of India Press.

Government of India, Department of Atomic Energy, *Annual Report 1989-90*, New Delhi, 1990.

Government of India, Department of Electronics, *Annual Report 1989-90*, New Delhi, 1990.

Government of India, Department of Space, *Annual Report 1989-90*, New Delhi, 1990.

Government of India, Directorate of Advertising and Visual Publicity, *Eighth Five Year Plan: Thrust and Objectives*, Government of India, New Delhi, 1992 (pamphlet).

Government of India, *Economic Reforms Two Years After and the Task Ahead* (Discussion paper), New Delhi, 1993.

Government of India, *Expenditure Budget 1992-93*, Demand No. 22.

Government of India, *India: Yearbook 1991*, Department of Information and Broadcasting, New Delhi, 1992.

Government of India, Ministry of Commerce, *Indian Trade Journal*, 8 February 1989.

Government of India, Ministry of Defence, *Annual Report 1989-90*.

Government of India, Ministry of Defence, *Statement to the Parliamentary Estimates Committee* (1992-93), Nineteenth Report, 20 August 1992, Lok Sabha Secretariat, New Delhi.

Government of India, Ministry of Finance (Economic Division), *Economic Survey* (various years), Government of India Press, New Delhi.

Government of India, *Ministry of Home Affairs Annual Report for 1989-90*, New Delhi.

Government of India, Planning Commission, *Seventh Five Year Plan 1985-90*, Controller of Publications, New Delhi, 1984.

Government of India, Planning Commission, *Eighth Five Year Plan 1992-97*, Controller of Publications, New Delhi, 1992.

Government of India, *Senior Executives of Public Sector Undertakings*, Centre of Publications, Government of India, New Delhi, October 1991.

Government of Pakistan, Federal Bureau of Statistics, *Demographic Survey 1987*, Islamabad.

Government of Sri Lanka, Department of Census and Statistics, 'Agricultural Holdings', *Statistical Abstract of Ceylon, 1949*.

Kemp, Geoffrey, testimony before the US Congress *Subcommittee on Asian and Pacific Affairs, Committee on Foreign Affairs*, House of Representatives, March 1989.

Kreisberg, Paul, evidence before the US Congress *Subcommittee on Asian and Pacific Afairs, Committee on Foreign Affairs,* House of Representatives, March 1989.

Leach, Congressman, statement, US Congress *Subcommittee on Asian and Pacific Affairs, Committee on Foreign Affairs,* House of Representatives, March 1989, p. 665.

Lok Sabha Secretariat, *Ministry of Defence - Defence Force Levels, Manpower, Management and Policy,* Lok Sabha, New Delhi, August 1992.

Nayyer, Vice Admiral (ret'd), *Statement to the US Global Strategy Council Forum,* Wednesday, 27 September 1989, p.53 (from the verbatim account by Neal R. Gross).

Nayyer, Vice Admiral (ret'd), *Evidence to the United States Global Strategy Council Forum,* Washington DC, 9 October 1989.

Nehru, Jawaharlal, *India's Foreign Policy: Selected Speeches September 1946-April 1961,* Publications Division, Ministry of Information and Broadcasting, Government of India, New Delhi, 1961, p.58.

'New Science and Technology Role Focuses Research Efforts on Key Areas', *Current News Supplement,* US Department of Defense, 1 May 1992, p.B28.

'Nuclear Power and the Nuclear Fuel Cycle' (quarterly review of overseas events), Australian Nuclear Science and Technology Organisation, December 1993.

Peck, Robert A., written testimony before the US Congress, *Subcommittee on Asian and Pacific Affairs, Committee on Foreign Affairs,* House of Representatives, 18 February 1988.

'Pentagon dumps "critical technologies" plan', *Current News Supplement,* US Department of Defense, Thursday, April 23 1992, p.B30.

Starred question in the *Rajya Sabha* No. 24, 1990, Parliament of India, to be answered on 27 March 1990 by Dr Raja Ramanna, supplementary question of Suresh Kalmadi.

Schaffer, Howard, Deputy Assistant Secretary of State, statement, US Congress, *Subcommittee on Asian and Pacific Affairs, Committee on Foreign Affairs,* House of Representatives, 8 March 1989.

Science Advisory Council to the Prime Minister, *Perspectives in Science and Technology,* Vol.1, Vikhas, New Delhi, 1990.

Steel Authority of India, *19th Annual Report 1990-1991.*

Sundrum, R.M., 'Growth and Income Distribution in India: Policy and Performance Since Independence', in Debesh Bhattacharya, 'Growth and Distribution in India During the Last Four Decades', paper provided for the *Standing Committee on Foreign Affairs, Defence and Trade of the Australian Senate's Inquiry into Australia-India Relations*, 11 July 1989.

U.S. Arms Control and Disarmament Agency, *World Military Expenditures and Arms Transfers 1989*, US Government Printing Office, Washington DC, 1990.

US Congress, Office of Technology Assessment, *Global Arms Trade*, US Government Printing Office, Washington DC, 1991.

US Department of Defense, *Current News Supplement*, September 3 1992, p.B-16.

US Government, Department of Commerce, *Emerging Technologies: A Survey of Technical and Economic Opportunities*, Washington DC, Spring 1990.

US Government, Department of Defence, *Soviet Military Power: Prospects for Change 1989*, US Government Printing Office, Washington DC, 1989.

US Government, Department of Defense, *The Department of Defense Critical Technologies Plan for the Committee on Armed Services*, United States Congress, Washington DC, 15 March 1989, Revised 5 May 1989.

US National Science Foundation, *Indian Scientific Strengths: Selected Opportunities for Indo-US Cooperation*, Washington DC., 1987.

US Office of the Press Secretary, The White House, *Fact Sheet on Non-Proliferation and Export Control Policy*, Washington, 27 September 1993.

Verrier, E., *A New Deal for Tribal India*, Ministry of Home Affairs, New Delhi, 1963.

Index